Self, Social Structure, and Beliefs

Self, Social Structure, and Beliefs

Explorations in Sociology

EDITED BY

Jeffrey C. Alexander, Gary T. Marx,
and Christine L. Williams

UNIVERSITY OF CALIFORNIA PRESS
Berkeley   Los Angeles   London

University of California Press
Berkeley and Los Angeles, California

University of California Press, Ltd.
London, England

Library of Congress Cataloging-in-Publication Data

Self, social structure, and beliefs : explorations in sociology /
edited by Jeffrey C. Alexander, Gary T. Marx, and Christine L.
Williams
    p.   cm.
Includes bibliographical references and index.
ISBN 0-520-24136-3 (hc : acid-free)—ISBN 0-520-24137-1 (pb : acid-
free)
    1. Social structure.   2. Sociology.   3. Sociology—Philosophy.
I. Alexander, Jeffrey C.   II. Marx, Gary T.   III. Williams, Christine L.,
1959–
HM706.S445   2004
301—dc22   2003017202

Manufactured in the United States of America

13   12   11   10   09   08   07   06   05   04
10   9   8   7   6   5   4   3   2   1

The paper used in this publication is both acid-free and totally
chlorine-free (TCF). It meets the minimum requirements of ANSI/
NISO Z39.48–1992 (R 1997) *(Permanence of Paper)*. ∞

CONTENTS

Chapter 1

Mastering Ambivalence

Neil Smelser as a Sociologist of Synthesis

Jeffrey C. Alexander, Gary T. Marx, and Christine L. Williams

Future historians will write about Neil Smelser as an iconic figure in twentieth-century sociology's second half. Smelser has had an extraordinarily active career not only as a scholar but also as a teacher and organizational leader. Every participant in this volume has proudly been a "Smelser student" in one form or another. The distinction of these contributions speaks directly to Smelser's power as a teacher. His immensely impressive and varied performances as organizational leader are perhaps less well known, but they speak equally clearly of scholarly power exercised in a more political manner. His roles have included being advisor to a string of University of California chancellors and presidents; referee of the nation's most significant scientific training and funding programs, from the National Science Foundation to the departments of leading universities; organizer of the *Handbook of Sociology* and the new *International Encyclopedia of the Social and Behavioral Sciences;* and, most recently, director of the Center for Advanced Study in the Behavioral Sciences.

In many respects, both Neil Smelser and the social sciences matured together in the second half of the last century. Smelser expanded his areas of research to include sociology, psychology, economics, and history at the same time that newly synthetic cross-disciplinary programs, area studies, and applied programs appeared. Through his work with commissions and foundations and as a spokesperson for the social sciences, he sought a greater public role for sociology and helped to foster the gradual infiltration of their findings and methods into other disciplines, practical settings, and popular culture. Smelser's early interest in comparative international studies anticipated their expansion, an increase in international collaboration, and greater awareness of globalization issues. His move from optimism about positivist approaches and functionalism in the 1950s to a more guarded optimism and plurivocality today has paralleled broader doubts within the academy and greater tolerance for other ways of knowing.

There is one fundamental respect, however, in which Smelser has broken with dominant trends. The last thirty years have been marked by increasing fragmentation and seemingly endless specialization. It has been an age of centrifugal conceptual forces and centripetal methodological rigor. These post-1960s scientific developments have unfolded against a background of ideological jeremiads, the continuous reference to social crisis, and alternations between elegies and eulogies to revolutionary social change. Through all this Smelser has continued to uphold generality and synthesis as worthy scientific goals. He has maintained his intellectual commitment to uniting divergent disciplinary perspectives, and even expanded significantly his own disciplinary reach. He has become ever more dedicated to bridging various conceptual and methodological divides. He has also maintained a quiet and impressive serenity about the continuing possibility for progressive social reform and democratic political change. He has kept his eye on the ball as well as on the ballpark, on what is enduring as well as what is new.

This book honors Smelser primarily as a man of ideas. It does so by exploring the sociological pathways that he has inspired others to take. In this brief introduction, we first make some general points about Smelser's intellectual career, highlighting what we take to be his most significant contributions. We conclude by returning to Smelser as a man and a teacher. It has been these human qualities, not only his intellectual ideas, that have inspired his students to move forward on our diverse paths of intellectual life.

SMELSER THE SCHOLAR

Because he started so early and so fast, lasted so long, and matured so well, Neil Smelser has had an active life as theorist and researcher spanning almost fifty years at the time of this writing, and it shows no signs of slowing down. In 1962, at the age of thirty-two, he became editor of the *American Sociological Review*, the most influential editorial position in the discipline. Almost thirty-five years later, in 1996, he was elected president of the American Sociological Association, in recognition not only of his lifetime achievement but also of the influence, both scientific and organizational, that he had wielded over those decades.

Neil Smelser began his public life as a wunderkind. Having barely settled into Oxford as a Rhodes scholar in 1952, he was tapped by Talcott Parsons, his Harvard mentor, to advise him about preparing for the Marshall Lectures at Cambridge. Parsons wanted to demonstrate that his newly developed AGIL theory could handle economics.[1] However, he had stopped reading in that discipline before John Maynard Keynes's *General Theory*. Smelser was au courant with the Keynesian revolution and AGIL besides.

During their collaboration, it was actually Smelser, not Parsons, who suggested the scheme of double interchanges that allowed AGIL to be applied to social systems. This brilliant conceptual innovation formed the core of their jointly written book, *Economy and Society* (1956), which accomplished what its subtitle promised: an integration of economic and social theory. Along with Smelser's later work, especially *The Sociology of Economic Life* (1963), *Economy and Society* laid the foundations for the new field of economic sociology that has become central to the discipline today. It was only three years later that Smelser published the extraordinarily innovative and deeply researched book *Social Change in the Industrial Revolution: An Application of Theory to the British Cotton Industry* (1959); and only three years after that, he brought out the equally pathbreaking *Theory of Collective Behavior* (1962).

While Smelser gained great distinction for this rush of early work, he also aroused great controversy. It was high noon for the functionalist paradigm. Smelser was its crown prince and its clear leader-in-waiting. His work was not only systematic, original, and erudite but also intellectually provocative and aggressive. It brimmed with great ambition and utter self-confidence, and it seemed to suggest that, with the emergence of action theory, the solution to sociology's struggles had arrived. Revealingly, the second chapter of *Social Change in the Industrial Revolution* was titled "Some Empty Boxes," and the chapter that followed was titled "Filling the Boxes." In *Theory of Collective Behavior,* Smelser began with the pronouncement that, "even though many thinkers in this field attempt to be objective," they had not succeeded. Because of their failure, "the language of the field . . . shrouds its very subject in indeterminacy." The aim of his study, he proclaimed, would be to "reduce this residue of indeterminacy" by "assembling a number of categories" so that "a kind of 'map' or 'flow chart'" could be constructed of the "paths along which social action moves." While he was strongly assertive, his goal appropriately was to *reduce,* not eliminate, the residue of indeterminacy.

The youthful Neil Smelser did, in fact, succeed in filling his boxes, forever broadening our view of the industrial revolution as a multidimensional social process—political, economic, familial, cultural, and scientific, and very much contingent, all at the same time. He also managed to create an utterly new and fascinating conceptual social map, one that simultaneously separated and intertwined the different dimensions of collective behavior, social structure, and social movements in a value-added manner never before achieved. What he could not do, however, was assure the continuing sovereignty of functionalist theory. In the history of social science, much more than conceptual precision and explanatory power is involved. Every powerful approach tends to overreach and is partial and, to a degree, situationally conditioned.

Thirty years after his unabashed and triumphal entrance on the sociological scene, Neil Smelser penned a "concluding note" to his penetrating essay "The Psychoanalytic Mode of Inquiry." He warned his readers to be careful of their imperialist urge. Was he not looking back with rueful reflection on the grand ambitions and urgent polemics of those early years?

> Whenever a truly novel and revolutionary method of generating new knowledge about the human condition is generated—and the psychoanalytic method was one of those—there emerges, as a concomitant tendency, something of an imperialist urge: to turn this method to the understanding of everything in the world—its institutions, its peoples, its history, and its cultures. This happened to the Marxian approach (there is a Marxist explanation of everything), to the sociological approach generally (there is a sociology of everything), and to the psychoanalytic approach (there is a psychoanalytic interpretation of everything). (Smelser 1998c: 246)

In the halcyon days of the Parsonian revolution, there had always been a functionalist approach to everything—though few approaches, if any, could rival the power and insight generated by those developed by Smelser himself.

By the late 1960s, the functionalist approach had stalled. Attacked as ideologically conservative, accused of every imaginable scientific inadequacy, functionalism eventually lost its position of dominance. Yet Smelser's postfunctionalist career has also been an extraordinary one. He did not blame the enemies of functionalism for his tradition's weakening. Instead, he targeted the nature of Parsonian thinking itself. He engaged in implicit self-criticism. This required courage and maturity.

Smelser accused foundational functionalism of hubris, of overreaching conceptually and underreaching empirically. He dressed it down for being one-sided and polemical. After making those observations on the imperialism of every "truly novel and revolutionary method" that we noted above, Smelser continued with the suggestion that "it is always legitimate to ask about the relative *explanatory* power of the method in settings and circumstances in which it was not invented." Only on the basis of such further reflection is it possible to be objective about "what are the emergent strengths *and weaknesses* of the method" (Smelser 1998c: 246, italics added).

It was just such a commitment to the task of explanation, over and above the allegiance to any particular theory, that allowed Smelser not only to stay afloat but also to flourish after the functionalist ship sank. When Parsons published his first collection of articles, in 1949, he called them *Essays in Sociological Theory*. When, two decades later, Smelser published his own, he called them *Essays in Sociological Explanation* (1968). His ambitions were tied to the scientific goals of discipline, not to any particular approach.

In 1997, in his presidential address to the American Sociological Association, Smelser developed what has already become the most influential essay of his later career. In "The Rational and the Ambivalent in the Social Sciences," he developed an argument that exposed one-sided intellectual polemics as a simplistic defense against the ambivalence that marks human life. "Because ambivalence is such a *powerful, persistent, unresolvable, volatile, generalizable,* and *anxiety-provoking* feature of the human condition," Smelser suggested, "people defend against experiencing it in many ways." For intellectual life, the "most pernicious" of these defenses is splitting, which involves "transferring the positive side of the ambivalence into an unqualified love of one person or object, and the negative side into an unqualified hatred of another" (1998d: 176–77, original italics). Smelser went on to directly apply this critical observation to sociology itself. Admonishing his colleagues that, "in our search for application of the idea of ambivalence, we would do well to look in our own sociological backyard," he observed, "There is almost no facet of our existence as sociologists about which we do not show ambivalence and its derivative, dividing into groups or quasi-groups of advocacy and counteradvocacy" (1998d: 184).

In his third major historical-cum-theoretical monograph, *Social Paralysis and Social Change: British Working-Class Education in the Nineteenth Century* (1991), Smelser demonstrated how this advice generalized from the path that he had now chosen for himself. Rather than declaring all preceding theoretical boxes empty and announcing that he would now proceed to fill them in, his new approach made carefully circumscribed criticisms. It proposed a theoretical model based on reconciliation and synthesis. After reviewing Whiggish, functionalist, Marxist, and status-group approaches to the history of British working-class education, Smelser suggests that each must be "criticized as incomplete, limited, incapable of answering certain problems, and perhaps even incompatible with the others." The alternative, he writes, is "to develop a perspective that is synthetic," that "incorporates insights from approaches known to have usefulness" (1991: 16–18).

From his first, vivid entry into the field of intellectual combat, Neil Smelser exhibited one of the most lucid and coherent minds that ever set sociological pen to paper. As his career continued to develop, he revealed another distinctive capacity: he became one of the most incorporative and inclusive of thinkers as well. In fact, it has been Smelser's penchant for combining opposites—the acceptance of sociological ambivalence without fear or favor—that has perhaps most distinctively marked his intellectual career. Here are some of the most important binaries that Smelser has successfully combined:

- He is one of the most abstract of theorists, yet he became an acknowledged "area specialist" in British history.
- He is a grand theorist, but he employed grand theory exclusively to develop explanations at the middle range.
- He is a functionalist, but he devoted his theoretical and empirical attention almost entirely to conflict.

- He is a liberal advocate of institutional flexibility, but he has written primarily about social paralysis and the blockages to social change (cf. Smelser 1974).
- He is a psychoanalyst who has highlighted the role of affect, but his major contributions have attacked psychologistic theorizing and explained how to fold the emotional into more sociological levels of explanation (e.g., Smelser 1998b, 2004; Smelser and Wallerstein 1998).
- He is a trained economist, but he has strenuously avoided economism, and he is a persistent student of economic life who has demonstrated how it is thoroughly imbedded in noneconomic institutions (Smelser 1968a).
- He is a systems theorist who devoted his most recent historical monograph to exploring the unbending primordiality of class.
- He is a close student of social values (e.g., Smelser 1998a) who rejects any possibility of purely cultural explanations.
- He is a theorist of social structure who eschews any form of structural determinism (Smelser 1968c, 1997: 28–48).
- He was a protégé of Talcott Parsons whom Parsons's sworn enemy, George Homans, publicly singled out for distinct praise.[2]

By avoiding the defense against ambivalence, Smelser demonstrated a remarkable ability to take the sword from the hands of those who would destroy him. He showed how Karl Marx and Friedrich Engels could be viewed as conflict-oriented functionalist theorists (1973). He made the gendered division of family labor an independent variable in social change (1959, 1968b) decades before many feminist theorists made arguments along these same lines. He borrowed from Alexis de Tocqueville the idea of intransigent "estates" to explain that functional positions in the educational division of labor could be understood as status groups seeking the protection of their own power (1974). He used the idea of "truce situations," an idea that John Rex (1961) had introduced as the antithesis to functionalist consensus theory, to explain why the social differentiation, at the heart of functionalist change theory, developed in a back-and-forth, stuttering motion rather than a smooth and unfolding way. He explained how the differentiation between instrumental and expressive activities actually had been continued, not overturned, by the feminist revolution, and how this often corrosive process of social and cultural rationalization could explain the emergence of the new kinds of child-caring institutions and the increasingly difficult and negotiated character of socialization from childhood to adulthood (1998e).

Behind these specific and intellectual innovations, two overarching metathemes have animated Neil Smelser's contributions to sociology. First, there is the insistence that social reality must be parsed into relatively autonomous analytic levels that, in empirical terms, are concretely interconnected. As he wrote in his intriguing and continuously instructive Berlin lectures, *Problematics of Sociology*, "even though the micro, meso, macro, and global levels can be identified, it must be remembered that in any kind of social organization we can observe an interpenetration of these analytic levels" (1997: 29). There is every "reason to believe," he insisted, that all "levels of reality are analytically as important" as every other. Smelser's empirical and theoretical work consistently displays the deepest agnosticism about assigning causal apriority. His plurivocality is epistemological and insistent. He absolutely refuses to be absolute. He does not privilege any particular sector or level. Here lies the source of Smelser's famous theft from economic price theory—the notion that causality must be conceived as a "value-added" process (1962: 18–20). This apparently simple yet, in reality, quite subtle idea represents a seminal contribution to sociological thought. Social structure, beliefs, and emotions are all important, as is every level inside them. It seems fitting to incorporate this idea into the title for this honorary book.

Second, there is a deep sense that social structure can never, under any circumstances, be separated from the analysis of social process, from the study of social movement, from the flux and flummox of social change. Every book that Smelser has written, every article on social structure, every study of beliefs, and every discussion of emotions has been a study in the constructive and destructive crystallization of structures.

This double preoccupation with plurality and process, in the context of accepting ambivalence and ambiguity, led Smelser in his most recent historical monograph to a wonderfully sociological rendering of the British notion of "muddling through":

> Like all such stereotypes, this one demands skepticism and a nonliteral reading. Nevertheless, it can be argued that if any sequence of social change manifested the principle of muddling through, the one I have studied in this volume is a good candidate.... Almost every proposal, whether ultimately successful or not, was accompanied by a series of disclaimers. These were that past good work in the area would not be dishonored; ongoing efforts would not be disturbed; what was being added would be no more than a helpful supplement to cover certain gaps; and the claims, rights, and sensibilities of interested parties would not be offended.... The aim was to squeeze limited increments of social change by and through them without disturbing them. *[But] the results were often much more than proponents claimed in their modesty. And in the long run, the policy ... revolutionized the educational system.* The road to that end was marked, however, by a great deal of muddling through. (1991: 370, italics added)

Smelser writes here about the ultimate effects of what initially were intended to be modest proposals for reform. He might, in addition, be speaking about the cumulative effects of the flow of theoretical proposals he has generated in the latter part of his long scientific career. They, too, were accompanied by disclaimers and by the concern not to dishonor past good work. They, too, were launched in a manner designed to not overly disturb ongoing sociological efforts of other kinds, and were presented as helpful supplements rather than as unfriendly displacements. Indeed, Smelser did succeed in his effort not to offend the rights and sensibilities of other sociological parties. All the same, he challenged their claims, and in the long run his work has had, if not revolutionary, then certainly fundamental intellectual effects. Over the course of fifty years in the sociological trenches, he has muddled through in a remarkable and inspirational way.

SMELSER THE TEACHER AND MENTOR

Few twentieth-century sociologists touched so many lives in so many positive ways as Neil Smelser. These include the lives of not only his immediate students and those who have learned from his voluminous writing but also those who have indirectly benefited from his role as a leading advocate for the social sciences and higher education.

These chapters by a small fraction of his students and colleagues are testament to his profound impact. Ernest Hemingway advised authors to show rather than to tell. This volume goes far in showing some of the intellectual and stylistic strengths that Neil passed on to his students. His intellectual legacy lies partly in his substantive contributions to diverse fields, such as British history, social change, collective behavior, higher education, the economy, and psychoanalysis, and partly in his exceptional leadership and service roles as a social science statesperson and representative.

His legacy also lies in the many lives he has touched through his teaching and cooperative scholarly endeavors. To many of us he demonstrated that the division between teaching and research was too sharply drawn. For the inspired instructor, teaching was a major vehicle for exploring ideas and exercising intellectual curiosity. It could be a kind of testing ground where ideas that would later appear in print were first put forth. Teaching was a means of coming to better terms with the contradictions in the world and within the social thought that sought to comprehend that world.

Teaching was also a way to communicate the love of ideas and appreciation of the rich intellectual heritage we were bequeathed. In his Social Theory 218 class, taken by most Berkeley graduate students over the more than three decades between 1958 and 1994, Neil communicated, as he continues to communicate, a sense of reverence for those giants of social and psychological thought who sought to understand the vast changes in culture, social organization, and personality associated with the development of the modern world. He showed us that we are not alone—that the social and ethical questions which assume such great importance today were wrestled with by the nineteenth- and early-twentieth-century pioneers of the field. Yet his respect was tempered with critical analysis and the insight that every way of seeing is also a way of not seeing. He honored our intellectual past without being stifled by it. Clearly there was lots of work left to be done, given new social conditions and the fallibility of any single approach considered against the richness of social reality.

Academic researchers are nourished by a rich network of inherited ideas initially obtained from those with whom we study. Under the best of conditions, our teachers go beyond offering substantive knowledge and methodological guidance to offering models for how to be in the world. We learn from our mentors directly, through the transmission of ideas, as well as indirectly, through observation. Those of us privileged to have been Neil's students and colleagues have been doubly blessed in this regard. We have benefited from his knowledge and intellect as expressed in his writings and lectures, from his incisive, but diplomatic and supportive, criticism of our work, and from his mentoring and guidance in how to be in the academic world.

In a world where many self-impressed academic egos could make Narcissus appear to have an inferiority complex and dwarf the sense of entitlement felt by the Pharaohs, Neil stands out by his support for and interest in others, his humility, and his low-key, friendly, western American manner. Perhaps the self-confidence that flows from unmatched career success and from good psychoanalysis partly accounts for this. But it also speaks to something more basic: he is simply a nice guy. And one who is also judicious, tolerant, conscientious, balanced, and fair. He sees that the big picture can be known only by looking at the many small pictures that make it up, and that our understanding of the latter is limited unless considered in light of broader, often interdependent factors.

The chapters in this volume are inspired by the authors' contact with the ideas and persona of Neil Smelser. Beyond their rich content, the work reflects some basic themes that Neil demonstrates and has passed on as a scholar and a human being. Like Neil, these chapters are intellectually diverse, crossing disciplines, methods, cultures, and time periods. They share Neil's emphasis on documenting the empirical and unique, not as ends in themselves, as with most journalists and historians, but as building blocks in the quest for more general and enduring (if not necessarily universal) statements about societies. Like Neil with his broad intellectual palette, the authors use a variety of methods (historical case studies, surveys, interviews, and simply thinking). Yet the starting point is always the question rather than the method. Unlike the strand of social inquiry that begins by asking which questions a preferred method can answer, the focus here is on which methods are *needed* to answer the question. Answers do not stand alone, and, as in

Neil's work, in many of the chapters in this volume there is an effort to integrate diverse materials and methods.

Following Neil's model, most of the chapters deal with topics not easily quantified, such as historical change and subjectivity, yet they do so in a logical and systematic fashion. The authors draw upon the empirical to limit, justify, and extend the conceptual, while the conceptual brings some definition and order to the formless flow of the empirical. In some chapters there is attention to comparative international aspects, and in almost all of them the logic of comparative analysis can be found, even when the comparisons are between social forms rather than countries or cultures.

The chapters use theory as a compass more than as a fixed road map. While informed by the values and pressing issues of the day (e.g., change, equality, democracy, freedom, civil liberties, individuality, and citizenship), the chapters are balanced and scholarly. They put the pursuit of truth before the passion for change, without in any way denying the ubiquity and necessity of change in many areas. Indeed, as Neil's extensive efforts to advance national and international understanding of, and resources for, the social sciences make clear, purposive change not grounded in empirical fact and conceptual understanding is likely to fail, particularly in the long run.[3] The basic commitment is to advancing knowledge about important social questions. If there is a dominant method, it is one called *thought*—to be judged by its scholarship, imagination, logical rigor, and empirical support.

Finally, while not lacking in argument or point of view, the articles, like Neil, are nondoctrinaire. They acknowledge complexity and the appropriateness of multiperspicacity. Many seek to go beyond being cross-disciplinary to being interdisciplinary and integrative.

Beyond sharing the abstract characteristic noted above, these articles are diverse in subject matter, method, and degree and kind of explicit theoretical argument. The coherence exists at a general level. This contrasts with many such volumes in which acolytes honor their mentor by exploring themes narrowly within the mentor's orbit. This again speaks to Neil's style, encouragement, and openness. He did not seek to build a school. His own independence and awareness of the variety of approaches appropriate to understanding a complex and changing world prevented this. There seems to be little of the often latent oedipal conflict found in many teacher-student situations. Rather, he was broadly supportive and encouraged us to follow our muse, guided by a quest for excellence and a willingness to work hard. Budding scholars worthy of the name (and the scholarly enterprise) are indeed well served when offered resources, support, and guidance to pursue their own interests, rather than being expected to add another plank to the building of their mentors.

Gary Marx, one of Neil's first Berkeley students, discussed the idea for a book such as this with Christine Williams, one of Neil's last students. Later, in planning for this volume, they learned that Jeff Alexander, a student at Berkeley during the middle years of Neil's career, was also planning such a volume, and we joined forces.

Neil's career has covered almost five decades, various locales (Cambridge, London, Berkeley, Palo Alto), and diverse academic, editorial, special-assignment, and service roles. In the language of football, Neil is a triple (or more) threat. These chapters are intended to reflect the research side. An appreciation of his contributions to teaching and his various public service roles is also in order.

Even restricting our emphasis to research alone, we have had to be more selective than we wished. Neil has taught numerous students, chaired more than fifty Ph.D. committees, and served as an outside member on many more. In editing this volume, we sought to make it broadly representative of the major areas Neil has worked in and of students across his career by including a sampling of his students who have themselves gone on to make significant contributions to knowledge. A few authors here are colleagues with whom he has worked particularly closely—they are his students in a less formal sense. Given the scope and scale of Neil's career, there are many other colleagues who could have contributed to this volume. We are sorry that resource constraints prevented our casting an even wider net.

NOTES

1. AGIL refers to the four "pattern variables" in Parsons's theory of social action. In particular, these are *adaptation, goal attainment, integration,* and *pattern maintenance,* later changed to *latency.*

2. From Homans (1964: 815):

> My next contention is that even confessed functionalists, when they seriously try to explain certain kinds of social phenomena, in fact use non-functional explanations. . . . A particularly good example of this new development in functionalism is Neil Smelser's book, *Social Change in the Industrial Revolution: An Application of Theory to the British Cotton Industry, 1770–1840.* The book is not just good for my purposes: it is good, very good, in itself. It provides an enormous amount of well organized information, and it goes far to explain the changes that occurred. The amusing thing about it is that the explanation Smelser actually uses, good scientist that he is, to account for the changes is not the functionalist theory he starts out with, which is as usual a non-theory, but a different kind of theory and a better one.

3. For examples, see Adams, Smelser, and Treiman 1982; Smelser and Gerstein 1986; Gerstein, Luce, Smelser, and Sperlich 1988; and Luce, Smelser, and Gerstein 1989.

REFERENCES

Adams, Robert, Neil Smelser, and Donald Treiman. 1982. *Behavioral and Social Science Research: A National Resource.* Washington, D.C.: National Academy Press.

Gerstein, Dean, R. Duncan Luce, Neil Smelser, and Sonja Sperlich, eds. 1988. *The Behavioral and Social Sciences: Achievements and Opportunities.* Washington, D.C.: National Academy Press.

Homans, George C. 1964. "Bringing Men Back In." *American Sociological Review* 29 (6): 809–18.

Luce, R. Duncan, Neil Smelser, and Dean Gerstein, eds. 1989. *Leading Edges in Social and Behavioral Science.* New York: Russell Sage Foundation.

Parsons, Talcott, and Neil J. Smelser. 1956. *Economy and Society: A Study of the Integration of Economic and Social Theory.* New York: Free Press.

Rex, John. 1961. *Key Problems of Sociological Theory.* London: Routledge and Kegan Paul.

Smelser, Neil J. 1959. *Social Change in the Industrial Revolution: An Application of Theory to the British Cotton Industry.* Chicago: University of Chicago Press.

———. 1962. *Theory of Collective Behavior.* New York: Free Press.

———. 1963. *The Sociology of Economic Life.* Englewood Cliffs, N.J.: Prentice-Hall.

———. 1968a. "The Methodology of Comparative Analysis of Economic Activity." In Smelser, *Essays in Sociological Explanation,* pp. 62–75. Englewood Cliffs, N.J.: Prentice-Hall.

———. 1968b. "Sociological History: The Industrial Revolution and the Working Class Family." In Smelser, *Essays in Sociological Explanation,* pp. 76–91. Englewood Cliffs, N.J.: Prentice-Hall.

———. 1968c. "Towards a General Theory of Social Change." In Smelser, *Essays in Sociological Explanation,* pp. 192–280. Englewood Cliffs, N.J.: Prentice-Hall.

———. 1973. "Introduction." In Smelser, ed., *Karl Marx on Society and Social Change,* pp. vii–xxxix. Chicago: University of Chicago Press.

———. 1974. "Growth, Structural Change, and Conflict in California Public Higher Education, 1950–1970." In Smelser and Gabriel Almond, eds., *Public Higher Education in California,* pp. 9–142. Berkeley and Los Angeles: University of California Press.

———. 1991. *Social Paralysis and Social Change: British Working-Class Education in the Nineteenth Century.* Berkeley and Los Angeles: University of California Press.

———. 1997. *Problematics of Sociology: The Georg Simmel Lectures, 1995.* Berkeley and Los Angeles: University of California Press.

———. 1998a. "Collective Myths and Fantasies: The Myth of the Good Life in California." In Smelser, *The Social Edges of Psychoanalysis,* pp. 111–24. Berkeley and Los Angeles: University of California Press.

———. 1998b. "Depth Psychology and the Social Order." In Smelser, *The Social Edges of Psychoanalysis,* pp. 197–217. Berkeley and Los Angeles: University of California Press.

———. 1998c. "The Psychoanalytic Mode of Inquiry in the Context of the Social and Behavioral Sciences." In Smelser, *The Social Edges of Psychoanalysis,* pp. 197–216. Berkeley and Los Angeles: University of California Press.

———. 1998d. "The Rational and the Ambivalent in the Social Sciences." In Smelser, *The Social Edges of Psychoanalysis,* pp. 168–96. Berkeley and Los Angeles: University of California Press.

———. 1998e. "Vicissitudes of Work and Love in Anglo-American Society." In Smelser, *The Social Edges of Psychoanalysis,* pp. 93–110. Berkeley and Los Angeles: University of California Press.

————. 2004. "Psychological Trauma and Cultural Trauma." In Jeffrey C. Alexander, Ron Eyerman, Bernhard Giesen, Neil J. Smelser, and Piotr Sztompka, *Cultural Trauma*. Berkeley and Los Angeles: University of California Press.

Smelser, Neil, and Dean Gerstein, eds. 1986. *Behavioral and Social Science: Fifty Years of Discovery*. Washington, D.C.: National Academy Press.

Smelser, Neil, and Robert S. Wallerstein. 1998. "Psychoanalysis and Sociology: Articulations and Applications." In Smelser, *The Social Edges of Psychoanalysis*, pp. 3–35. Berkeley and Los Angeles: University of California Press.

PART I

Self

Introduction

Christine L. Williams

Neil Smelser is a professionally trained psychoanalyst who maintained a clinical practice for several years while managing his more visible career as academic sociologist and statesman. This fact is not well known to the many who know him principally through his published work. But his interests in the unconscious, the irrational, and the ambivalent are apparent to anyone who knows him personally and to everyone who was his student. Some of his students were directly influenced by him to seek psychoanalytic training themselves. To others Smelser imparted a respect for and inquisitiveness about personality and selfhood, and the conviction that no social problem can be adequately understood without grasping the complex and hidden motives of individuals involved in social life. In scattered essays only recently collected, but mainly through personal advising, Smelser taught us that understanding any social fact requires that we pay attention to the needs and desires of individuals.

Ambivalence is a key theme in the three chapters we have organized into this section. Smelser argued that extreme feelings of love and hate are likely to arise in any social situation of high dependency. The quintessential expression of ambivalence is the child's relationship to the parent, but any social arrangement that an individual is not entirely free to leave is likely to elicit this emotional response. Ambivalence is experienced in highly idiosyncratic ways, but it tends to elicit predictable responses, such as defense mechanisms. In other words, no two people experience dependency in identical ways, but psychoanalysis can help us to identify recurrent patterns in their responses. By arguing for the importance of the self, then, Smelser never gave up the quest to discern patterns, structures, and organization.

Although Smelser convinced many of us of the enriching possibilities of a psychoanalytically informed sociology, he stopped short of endorsing the method as the ultimate solution to any problem. The psychological does not replace the sociological or the cultural, he insists; it is but another dimension of the human experience that sociologists ignore to their detriment and impoverishment. A single academic discipline cannot fully comprehend the rich complexity of social life.

Paradoxically, Smelser rarely got specific about how to combine psychoanalysis and sociology. Although he convinced many of his students of the importance of personality, his own empirical work rarely commented on individual motives. Clearly this reflected some ambivalence on his part, but it meant that his students were left on their own to put into practice what he preached. In doing so they inevitably refined those lessons, pushed them in new directions, and broke new theoretical ground.

For example, the contributors to this section emphasize the creative efforts of individuals to forge meaning and purpose in their lives. Smelser never ventured into this type of analysis, but he set the stage for it by teaching us that it is a fallacy to assume that an identical underlying motive drives everyone involved in a social activity. (This is one of the problems with rational choice theory or any other monocausal model of human behavior.) But he left it up to others to discover just what those myriad motives might be in any given social setting.

Nancy Chodorow draws out some of the implications of this thesis in her chapter in this volume. Chodorow followed Smelser's example and became a psychoanalyst after establishing her career in sociology. Smelser was one of the few sociologists who encouraged her move in this direction, as he shared with her an impatience with a sociological establishment that refused to recognize individuality. Chodorow speculates on the possible unconscious fears of sociologists that lead them to eschew the rich variety and boundless creativity of individuals. Overcoming these fears is clearly helped by having mentors like Smelser who recognize the constraining artificiality of disciplinary boundaries and encourage students to carve their own paths.

Chodorow's chapter illustrates the vast richness of individual meaning-making through an examination of the myriad ways that World War II is experienced by members of her generation, the college graduates of the class of 1965. World War II was an event of such mammoth and world-changing importance that a psychological response was required of all who lived through it. However, she shows that the particular response of any person is individually created, contingent on the biographical details, internal conflicts, and creativity of each person affected. Thus, like Smelser, Chodorow pushes the disciplinary boundaries of sociology to include a depth psychology. But unlike Smelser, she examines intrapsychic dynamics through individual case studies, demonstrating empirically the rich variety of human responses to social events.

The present-day struggle of the autonomous individual to find meaning is also the central theme in the chapters by Arlie Russell Hochschild and Yiannis Gabriel. But instead of turning inward, they look outward at the social, cultural, and historical constraints on individuals intent on realizing their ambivalent longings. Both find consumer capitalism to be one of the primary forces organizing the individual's quest for meaning.

There seems to be no limit to capitalism's drive to commodify social life. At least that is the impression given by a job advertisement for a personal assistant that is analyzed by Arlie Russell Hochschild and her class of undergraduate Berkeley students. Hochschild finds that the contradictory human needs for connection and intimacy on the one hand, and freedom and control on the other, come together in the search for the perfect commodity. Advertisements today promise to end our ambivalence: the myth of capitalism is that through buying something we can become perfect selves with perfect relationships.

A rich man advertising for a paid wife-companion is an extreme case of commodification, but Hochschild sees it as an outcome of a historical process of differentiation. Like Smelser, she argues that the moral value of this arrangement does not reside in the facts themselves; it has to be understood in context. The gradual weakening of the family is perhaps most critical in this regard: as individuals become less secure about the reliability of care provided to them by their families, she argues, they seek out substitutes, which capitalists are only too eager to provide.

That social life is multileveled and full of internal contradiction is a view shared by all three of these students of Smelser. Yiannis Gabriel shows us what happens when sociologists ignore this insight: we end up with one-dimensional accounts. Gabriel illustrates this problem through a discussion of two contemporary critics of consumer capitalism: Richard Sennett and George Ritzer. While Sennett sees our current economic and social order as promoting opportunism, insecurity, and disenchantment among workers, Ritzer sees consumerism as a pleasurable source of individual choice, playfulness, and fantasy. Using Smelser's analysis of ambivalence, Gabriel shows us how both "sides" are correct: Sennett's insecure, fragmented workers may be the same people as Ritzer's fantasizing and demanding consumers. Discontent in one sphere of life may lead us to pursue pleasure in another.

The specific forms of our ambivalence have a history and a social organization. In the past, Gabriel argues, the metaphor of the iron cage captured the constraints on our ability to provide for our contradictory needs for freedom and community. Today, a more apt metaphor is the glass cage, which captures the titillating allure of the shopping mall experience as well as the constant surveillance, insecurity, and fragility that characterize our current economic arrangements. Finding personal meaning and a purpose in life is difficult under these circumstances—as it probably was in previous times—

but the task is not hopeless, as is shown by recent empirical studies of individuals who manage to find a "voice" despite the constraints.

These three chapters demonstrate that accepting ambivalence as an indelible part of the human condition is key to achieving a deeper and richer understanding of social life. And because social life is multidimensional, no one theory, discipline, or perspective is adequate to this task. Without mythologizing him, we have Smelser to thank for all that.

Chapter 2

The Sociological Eye and the Psychoanalytic Ear

Nancy J. Chodorow

Traditionally, in the academy, when we think about a person's work and its influence, we mean what he or she has written. In the case of most academics, this is probably sufficient. In the field of psychoanalysis, by contrast, although influence certainly comes through writing, there is an assumption that the most influential writers are influential because they are among the best practitioners. Influence in the field is in the first instance personal: the transmission of clinical capacities and personal self-understanding from one's own training analyst, oral presentations that do not usually lead to publication, personal supervision of one's work while in training, and continuous consultation with colleagues when one is in the midst of a treatment stalemate or clinical conundrum. Unlike the academy, then, psychoanalysis has, in addition to its nationally and internationally recognized theorists and writers, its locally, nationally, and internationally recognized master clinicians and personally powerful mentors (on recognition in psychoanalysis, see Chodorow 1986, 1991).

Neil Smelser has, indisputably, made his mark as an eminent scholar, and it is his scholarly work that we celebrate in this volume. But he has also used his eminence, and his commitment to the values of the academy, to be a public spokesman, a policy maker, a bridge to government and university governance, and a practitioner and theorist of educational reform and innovation. He is also a psychoanalyst, and, like the psychoanalytic colleagues with whom he early formed a private and, in recent years, a public identification (Smelser 1998), he has been an academic most personally, generously, and continuously devoted to students. Thus, though my contribution here elaborates and addresses substantive and theoretical themes on the social edges of psychoanalysis, it is necessary, as we evaluate the character of this work, to address what I see—in the psychoanalytic tradition—as the personal effect that Smelser has had on my scholarly work.

The question of ambivalence takes central place in *The Social Edges of Psychoanalysis*. Smelser sees ambivalence as "a fundamental existential dilemma in the human condition," which draws us, he argues, away from unidimensional accounts of human motivation and self-understanding like rational choice theory or the conscious intentionality of phenomenology (1998: 189). Neil was himself, we can infer, ambivalent about his interest in psychoanalysis. He undertook training—hardly an easy endeavor, requiring, as it does, seven to ten years of classes, supervision of clinical work, and personal analysis. But, as he also notes, from 1965 to the 1990s, he published allusions to this abiding interest only in occasional essays—essays written for invited occasions—and these in widely scattered journals and volumes (1998: xviii). This indirect acknowledgement of identity and interest was transformed when he published "Depth Psychology and the Social Order" in 1987 in a mainstream sociology collection, and especially in his 1997 presidential address to the American Sociological Association, "The Rational and the Ambivalent in the Social Sciences" (Smelser 1998), in which he must have been (I am guessing here) the first ASA president to address Freud extensively and in a positive light.

But, even as Smelser regarded his psychoanalytic interests perhaps with some ambivalence, in terms of his sociological identity his support for younger sociologists with similar interests was completely unambivalent. I was a second-year graduate student whom Neil had never met, living at the other end of the country from Berkeley, at Brandeis—a sociology department probably known as maverick, radical, and not top rank. But when Neil's student (also only in his second year) Jeff Alexander asked Neil if he would read a paper I had written on Parsons's theory of socialization and the psyche, he immediately said yes. A few years later, when I had written a completely idiosyncratic dissertation, coating feminism and psychoanalysis with a thin and rather brittle Parsonian and Western Marxist sociological veneer, Smelser enthusiastically recommended its publication. Supported by Smelser and, like him, following our mentors and admired elders in the Harvard Social Relations Department, I also undertook psychoanalytic training.

In short, I probably could not have done otherwise than persist in what I have characterized as my enduring preoccupation with "the relations between inner and outer, individual and social, psyche and culture, that place where the psychological meets the cultural or the self meets the world" (1999: 6). And I could not have forgone what I have called, even more radically for a social scientist, "fall[ing] intellectually in love": my "passionate attachment" to psychoanalysis (1989: 8). Neil Smelser was personally encouraging for twenty crucial years, as I went from graduate student to full professor in sociology and became a psychoanalyst as well. And he was professionally instrumental in my attaining each of these steps. His message, from the moment I knew him, and the message that I know he has given to many,

many students who wished to chart their own course of intellectual endeavor, was purely psychoanalytic: if you are fortunate enough to have found your identity and your passion, these are much more important on a human existential scale than the social and cultural constraints of a profession.

I spend this time in personal autobiography to emphasize two elements in Smelser's contribution. (To become psychoanalytic again, this personal autobiography is both intrapsychic—about my unconscious and its expression—and intersubjective, acknowledging that we shape the particular expression and development of our unconscious fantasies in and through our relationships.) One element is the theoretical and professional commitment we share to psychoanalytic modes of thought in themselves. The other is his professional behavior that also ties him to psychoanalysis— behavior I do not claim even to have begun to achieve in the ways that Neil has: his fostering in others of personal identity and meaning from within against the external constraints and restraints of professional marketability or the cost-benefit evaluations of rational choice.

For my own contribution here, I address and extend lacunae I find in sociology, specifically, the great sociological ambivalence, suspicion, and even antipathy to personal individuality. In my experience, sociologists are by and large extremely critical of psychological thinking and view a focus on the individual as a move away from the important forces of culture and social structure. Since I find the study of individuals in all their unique complexity the most interesting topic of the human sciences, this is a particularly striking phenomenon for me. The study of individuals is almost entirely missing in the current social sciences, with the exception of some anthropology and, occasionally, qualitative sociology. One of the best theories and methods for studying individuals as internal, complex, experiencing selves is psychoanalysis, and the relevance of this theory and clinical practice to the social sciences and our understanding of human life and its meaning is the subject of my most recent book, *The Power of Feelings* (1999).

Neil Smelser shares my concerns, but as he notes, and as is apparent from the overall thrust of his professional work, he is ambivalent. He cautions us in "Social and Psychological Dimensions of Collective Behavior" against assuming that social conditions have the same impact on all individuals. Sociological explanations of collective behavior rest, as they must,

on the unspoken assumption that the various social factors exert their influence on the individual human mind. . . . [But] how can it be imagined, for example, that the social condition of being unemployed (strain) has the same impact on all individuals it affects? . . . If we ignore this diversity of psychological meanings of the same event for different individuals, we are guilty of presenting an unwarranted psychological generalization about human reactions to economic deprivation. (1998: 44–45)

He points in "The Politics of Ambivalence" to activists' fears that understanding the psychological dimensions of their participation on different
sides of issues would " 'psychologize the issues away' as expressions of individual problems and, therefore, not matters for political concern." He continues: "To explore the psychological dimensions of a social problem is not
to ignore the problem, but, instead, to probe into ever-present aspects of any
process of change in institutional and group life" (1998: 133). In a hypothetical example in "Some Determinants of Destructive Behavior," he claims
that both collective action and the individual action of each person within
the collective are contingently and historically determined, dependent on
multiple factors: "None of the determinants alone is sufficient to produce
the episode, but when all combine, it is very likely to occur" (1998: 91, a clear
acknowledgement of the influence of Erikson on Smelser's thinking; see
Erikson 1950: 37–38).

In "The Presence of the Self," Susan Krieger says, "The expression of an
individual perspective in social science is a difficult accomplishment in part
because individuality is theoretically unpopular. . . . Because the social sciences are generalizing sciences, there is a natural tendency to de-emphasize
the particular and internal nature of the self and to see the self in intellectual terms" (1991: 43). Krieger goes on to describe approaches to the self in
different fields: the sociological hollow core that reflects external forces; the
self of experimental psychology described in terms of measurable external
behaviors or cognitive processes; the economist's self that expresses preference functions; the political scientist's self that is symbolized in rights, powers, and acts of political participation; the anthropologist's self that takes
different forms in different cultures, and the historian's self that reflects historical circumstances and changes over time according to prevailing definitions. The exceptions are usually insurgent: recent feminist epistemology
and methodology that emphasizes life history, biography and autobiography, psychoanalytic anthropology and sociology, the sociology of emotions,
and reflexive ethnography.

To take an example specifically from sociology, sociologists usually interest themselves in structures, practices, processes, and social relations that
characterize groups, organizations, and other supra-individual entities. They
tend to think that individual experience is created, shaped, or structured
through these social dynamics and structures and to see sociological actors
in terms of a single dimension of action—for example, rational choice,
impression management, measured and scaled attitudes, and political or
economic actor. When sociology theorizes individuals, it is by social categories, according to their race, class, gender, ethnicity, and so forth. Sociology envisions both individual and collective agency through the lens of these
social categories and socially oriented action, so that both individual and collective behavior are portrayed in terms of their relations to institutions and

social processes rather than in terms of individually idiosyncratic goals or beliefs. Similarly, agency and resistance are evaluated not in terms of personal goals or interpretations, but in relation to structures of inequality or domination, and intersectionality theory leads us to conceive not of unique individuals who internally experience and help to shape their lives but of individuals only as joint products of race, gender, and class forces. Practice theory describes culturally and situationally embedded, goal-oriented enactment.

Sociologists are trapped by a legacy that separated individual experience, subjectivity, and action from structures and institutions and that construed the former as determined by the latter. This legacy began with structural-functionalism but continued with most Marxisms. Postmodernism-post-structuralism argues against cultural holism and for the complexity, contingency, and historicity of cultures, as well as for the multiple contradictions, rather than functional interrelations, among cultural elements. But at the same time, these theories agree with traditional structuralism about the autonomy of the cultural. Poststructuralism may have made central to its critique of structuralism the absence of a subject, but it argues that subjectivity is constructed discursively and politically from without. The "structure-agency" problem is itself an artifact of this construction of theoretical reality: if traditions like symbolic interactionism or pragmatism had been more hegemonic, if Georg Simmel and Sigmund Freud had been as canonical as Karl Marx, Max Weber, and Emile Durkheim, social scientists would not need to look for a connection between structure and individual or collective action.

Like sociology, although with more apparent tension, anthropology has also minimized individual selfhood. This tension develops because, while the ethnographic encounter makes the individuality of informants palpable, such that from its earliest moments anthropology has described individuals, the goal of most ethnography has been to make generalized claims about particular cultures, even if these claims are based on information observed and gathered in particularized interactional moments. Like most accounts in qualitative sociology, contemporary anthropological accounts that portray a person in relation to culture may or may not have a complex view of culture, but they often have an unelaborated concept of the person—of an internally differentiated self, an inner world, and complex unconscious mental processes. By looking only at elements of meaning that are culturally shared and not those that are individually particular, anthropologists and qualitative sociologists extract a part from the whole, away from how meaning is personally experienced, skimming off one part of experience, so that experience becomes less rich than it actually is. They lose understanding of how individual psychologies enact or express cultural forms and give these forms emotional force, depth, and complexity.

As I argue in *The Power of Feelings,* the core of individuality is in the realm of personal meaning. As with social determinism, thinkers from a variety of fields have tended to assume that cultural meanings have determinative priority in shaping experience and the self. Even those who think in a more constructionist vein claim that actors create meaning by drawing upon available tangles or webs of cultural meaning. Meanings still come entirely from a cultural corpus or stock. People create and experience social processes and cultural meanings psychodynamically—in unconscious, affect-laden, nonlinguistic, immediately felt images and fantasies that everyone creates from birth, about self, self and other, body, and the world—as well as linguistically, discursively, or in terms of a cultural lexicon. Social processes are given, and they may lead to some patterns of experiencing in common, but this experiencing will be as much affective and nonlinguistic as cognitive. All social and cultural experiences are filtered, shaped, and transformed through a transferential lens. In order fully to understand human social life, we must theorize and investigate personal meaning.

People, then, are historically and biographically changing individuals who create psychodynamically their own multilayered sense of meaning and self—consciousness determines life just as much as life determines consciousness. Individuals are interesting and complex in themselves and worthy of study for this reason alone. All the people we study have inner lives and selves that affect and shape how they act and feel. They may not always be aware of this inner life, which is experienced unconsciously as well as consciously, but you cannot understand or interpret what they are telling you if you think they always say what they mean. (Thus, I teach my students to see themselves not as recorders of interviews but as listeners and interpreters of meanings communicated through affect and transference as much as through language.) Also, we as researchers have complex inner lives. As Krieger puts it, "If we do not talk about ourselves, and if we acknowledge only the general forces that affect who we are and what we know, we ignore the full reality that informs our work" (1991: 45). As one of my students in a course on feminist methodology put it, as she reflected upon a field experience in which she had tried to study shop-floor labor process according to the precepts of Marxist ethnography, "The difficulty was that I had beliefs and a personality."

In addition to its being interesting in its own right, studying individual subjectivities gives us an enriched and fuller understanding of society and culture. All social scientists whose theories and findings make assumptions about human nature and human motivation must address individual experience and agency, and one major component of that experience and agency is psychodynamic. Approaches to agency and practice that assume only conscious, rational, strategic goals and maneuvers do not comprehend the action they purport to explain. Personal meaning is a central organizing experience for each individual, and society or culture do not precede or determine these lives. Rather, there are complex relations between personal meaning and cultural meaning, and between individual lives and society. In any individual life, many different social and cultural elements interact. Also, each person herself or himself puts together these elements and elements of self and identity in idiosyncratic, conflictual, contradictory, changing, personalized ways. (It is a revelation to sociology students to try and account for a single life in all its social, historical, and familial context and personal uniqueness.) Individuality is important in any social science context that involves interaction with others or observation of them.

Even those few social scientists who do study the emotions, conceptions of self, and unconscious life seem suspicious of and do not tend to pay attention theoretically and ethnographically to psychological individuality. These scholars tend to turn emotions and self into something else. Anthropologists of self and feeling claim that emotions are pragmatic, linguistic and discursive, and employed for cultural communication and practice. Their investigations ask how the web of cultural emotion- and self-meanings interrelates with, contributes to, and is enriched by other cultural webs of meaning or meaning-imbued practices, but not how these cultural meanings interrelate with, and gain meaning from, webs of personal meaning. Sociologists of emotion focus on the feelings rules that are imposed by the culture and that people react to. But if you read the sociologists of emotion and the anthropologists of self and feeling, the striking palpable anxiety, pain, and confusion of people engaged in cultural emotions and feelings is not theorized— the "me" whose emotional life is being shaped and reshaped according to cultural patterns is explained, but the "I" of the experiencer is left untheorized.

Finally, being a psychoanalyst as well as a sociologist, I suggest that the psyche itself plays a part here. In many cases, thinking in terms of individual action and fantasy is, simply, terrifying. If we keep things impersonal, call something "racism" or "nationalism" or "misogyny" or "homophobia," we need not keep in the front of our minds that individuals, with conscious and unconscious intentions, with, indeed, conscious reasons and rationalizations that make such behaviors all right, engage, in specific instances, in lynching, mass murder or genocide, rape (or, in the case of the intersection of nationalism and misogyny, mass rape of women and girls), or the murder of homosexuals (for some attempt to look at individual motivation in these kinds of cases, see Chodorow 1998, 2000a).

Moreover, I speculate that people attracted to the social sciences have a pretheoretical, emotional predilection to feel and believe that things come *from society* or *from culture*. This unquestioned belief is reinforced through studying the social sciences, but the social sciences resonate in turn with an already present inner sense of truth. For people who naturally look at the world like this, it is very difficult and anxiety-provoking to fully consider that we also create our psychological life and consciousness—rather than believe that this life and consciousness is determined by external conditions—or to consider that our consciousness, psyches, modes of being, and social and cultural conditions may be mutually shaping. As I once put it, "By character, perhaps, those who become social scientists tend intuitively to be paranoid externalizers who projectively see troubles and opportunities as coming from without; those who become analysts tend intuitively to be omnipotent (or depressive) narcissists who see the world as created from within" (1999: 221).

To concretize my argument that understanding personal affective meaning is central to our understanding of historical and social processes and forces, I draw from a project in which I was privileged to participate. As I noted earlier, as an undergraduate I cut my social scientific teeth, as Neil did, in the interdisciplinary Harvard Social Relations Department. Thirty-five years later, Maria Tymoczko and Nancy Blackmun, writing *Born into a World at War* (2000), collected narrative accounts from members of my undergraduate class, and I wrote an epilogue, "Individuals in History and History through Individuals" (Chodorow 2000b, adapted and expanded in Chodorow 2002). Although any psychoanalytic project is implicitly and explicitly Freudian, it is specifically to Erik Erikson that those of us who wish to understand the intertwining of psyche and society in individuals owe a special debt (see Smelser 1998). I used the narratives to illustrate Erikson's claim that history, social models, cultural prototypes, and images of good and evil "assume decisive concreteness in every individual's ego development" and "appear in specific transferences and resistances" (1959: 18, 29). Erikson is not being a historical or social determinist here. He is describing individualized usages of historical and cultural contributions to identity that are deeply implicated in selfhood, personalized through identifications with parents, and related in complex ways to life goals and goals that are shunned. These identities are tied up with affects like shame, guilt, and fear and defenses like denial and projection.

Following Erikson, I looked at the intertwining of individual and cultural-historical experience, how history, society, and culture—which we see through a sociological eye—become involved in the experience of self and enliven those fantasies and conflicts that we hear with a psychoanalytic ear. I listened to the narratives as, perhaps, a psychodynamic ethnographer, for affect, fantasy, and unspoken as well as spoken words and beliefs. What I heard showed that people bring personal interpretations to both unconsciously and consciously transmitted cultural and historical circumstances and to parental fantasies and identity. When we listen with a psychoanalytic ear, our conception of the effect of war is broadened and our sense of the effects of being born during the war is decentered.

Members of the class of 1965 form part of a classic generation. As Karl

Mannheim puts it, people of the same age are a generation insofar as they participate in characteristic social and intellectual currents of a period, and experience the interaction of forces that make up a new situation (1928: 304). They lived, as Mannheim would put it, in the same "historico-social space" or "historical life community," and they are from a remarkably fine-tuned birth cohort, nearly all of whom were born in 1943 and 1944. But their individuality is equally prominent: these writers from the class of 1965, born during the same years, form part of a generation and became a group who found themselves at the same college in the same period of history, but they have no common cultural or historical origins whatsoever. We find among them those who most stand for the great destruction and genocide wrought by the Nazis—the children of German Jewish and eastern European Jewish survivors—but other accounts remind us that there were also survivors of the great brutality experienced by those from countries invaded by the Japanese. One narrative calls our attention to the American internment of U.S. citizens and immigrants of Japanese origin—a Sansei son who lived in an internment camp while his Nisei father was in the U.S. Army in a strategic role. Life stories from both European- and American-born writers document how closely the experiences of the generation born during World War II tie into the cold war that followed so soon afterward. The son of a German war widow gives us insight into the consequences of Germany's policies for some ordinary German citizens, and a Japanese-born woman illuminates what it was like to make do as a child in Japan (we do not, for political reasons and in cultural practice, call German and Japanese children born into a world at war survivors, but they most certainly were). One writer filters a childhood in war not through the lens of an American child, but of an English child in a bombed-out city with food shortages. Many others experienced the effect of war because they and their families had to move—as a result of evacuation, expulsion, internment, army family stationing, war work demands on the father—or because of the absence or loss of fathers. Thus, members of this "generation" were born in Europe and the United States to Jewish Holocaust survivors, refugees, or those in hiding; they were born to German mothers who became war widows and in countries invaded by the Japanese like Indonesia or China. They were born in England, Japan, and Slovenia. They were born throughout the United States—perhaps while fathers were in the army—where mothers worked in Rosie the Riveter jobs or took their children home to their own parents because fathers, like mine, did scientific war work.

As one would predict in people from such widely varied backgrounds and experience, the manifest content of each narrative preserves individuality in all its contextual and internal richness and variation. At the same time, listening for affect, conflict, and transference, and using my own experience, enabled me to find commonalities, specifically, a pervasive sense of loss and depressive affect, the themes of silence and explosions, occasional defensive mania, preoccupation with father-absence, and mothers taken for granted. I also could see the very different ways that history and culture are experienced—filtered through parents, culture and media, reconstructions, conscious stories, and unconscious transmissions. World War II thus assumes decisive concreteness in the life of anyone born into it, but it is a different war for each person. You can elucidate various psychic and narrative themes that characterize many people's experiences, but it turns out that you can never predict the exact effect or outcome of an experience, even when it comes to how a family will react to losing members in concentration camps. The "same" event or experience—Kristallnacht, being the child of Holocaust survivors, being a survivor oneself—can be experienced and handled in many different ways. Among the children of survivors, there is everything from ebullient optimism and a claim that all is right with the world to simple relief at having survived to emotional frozenness and painful depression. In some families, there is silence and occlusion of a loss too painful to acknowledge. Other families, by contrast, celebrate survival and make cheerful, positive thinking a goal rather than mourn their losses. One writer whose uncle was killed in Auschwitz and whose parents endured ten years of separation calls these the "happiest ten years" in his parents' lives, and claims that they led a "charmed existence" (Stolper 2000).

How did I avoid stressing "causal association among aggregated social facts," or "the objectively determinable opportunities and constraints of the social structure for individuals and groups," and stress instead "clinical inference about uniquely convergent *patterns* of forces in the individual's psyche . . . the internal representation . . . of that reality" (Smelser 1998: 198–99)? How was my psychodynamic method meant to elucidate "ideographic patterns about individuals [rather than] the aggregative mode of inference" (1998: 225)? Basically, I listened for affect—that is, the emotional tonalities of the various contributions as well as the consciously described feelings— and for transference templates—the unconscious pictures of self and other that seemed to affect contributors' views of the world. I listened for conflict and resistances, for when I thought a contributor was avoiding something or covering it up, so that what I picked up did not quite hang together. And I kept in mind the use of the self, or my own countertransferences—the fact that it was I, and not just anyone, listening to these stories, and that they evoked affects and memories for me as well. I explored society and history through my own individual senses.

I started from what we might call my own countertransference. I was born in January 1944, so I was six months old on D-day and a year and a half on V-E day. During a trip to France in the early 1990s, I visited Omaha and Utah Beaches. From a childhood visit, I remembered vividly the concrete bunkers and gun emplacements left by the Germans, so bizarre to find on a beach. But on this visit, I also noticed various monuments with inscriptions like "In

Memory of the 248th Engineering Division of the U.S. Army, died June 1944," or "In Honor of the Men of the 126th Division of the United States Marines, landed June 6, 1944," listing all the men who had died during that invasion. I began to cry and could not stop weeping. Since before memory I have been mesmerized by footage of the D-day landings, those men with weapons and vehicles rising out of the waters onto the beach. This is perhaps my fantasy image of this landing: to this day, I am not sure if this is how the real footage goes, I was obviously too young to have seen such footage in contemporary newsreels, and my father did not go away to war.

I also recalled a dream that had been important during the analysis I undertook as part of my psychoanalytic training. I am standing up in my crib, and my mother and my analyst's mother (my analyst's mother in my fantasy, of course), both dressed in unmistakably 1940s suits and hats, are going off to Times Square to celebrate V-E day. The dream portrays loss and being left as well as the exciting images of those V-E day celebrations, neither of which was part of my actual experience of the war (although, after she read my paper, my mother did tell me how she had picked me up on V-J day and told me that this was a very great day in history).

Events and cultural images of World War II have thus entered my fantasy life, in dreams and day images, and they even place me at the right age—as in my dream—within historical events. A final set of memories is relevant: because of the postwar mobility of scientists that sent my family to rural Stanford in 1947, I was a Jewish New Yorker who grew up in California from the age of three, who at age four wanted to be a cowgirl (maybe a cowboy?), and who yelled with her friends, while playing "king of the mountain," "Bombs over Tokyo!," having no idea what it meant. I also puzzled over why most of my friends thought World War II took place in the Pacific and was against Japan, not about Hitler and the Jews.

I introduce these memories to concretize both individuality and personal meaning. First, they document the individuality of my historical and social experience while also documenting the inevitable consequences of belonging to a particular generation or age cohort. As I have put it in other work (Chodorow 1999), there are common experiences that demand psychological processing and response, but the particular psychological processing and response are individually created. Second, I use myself to suggest that historical and social processes, when they matter, always matter emotionally and unconsciously to individuals, as well as register in their consciousness and cognition.

However, there are also prevalent patterns in people's affective and fantasy creation of their experience. To begin with cultural-affective identity, one contributor says, "We are not baby boomers" (Field 2000): these accounts do not display the buoyant optimism of baby boomers and their sense of limitless possibility. Members of this generation and cohort seem self-aware about our historical location (we are not postmodern). Some of us participated in "never trust anyone over thirty" politics, but these accounts, perhaps especially those from the children of immigrants, document a sense of orientation to parents, of trying to support parents and do what they want. People describe being born not during postwar prosperity to united families with optimistic parents, but, in all cases, to families in which parents were directly or indirectly affected by war. In the most tragic cases, families were torn apart and destroyed, leaving few survivors. In other families, fathers were often far away when a child was born or for some time afterward, and mothers—often far from home themselves—were worried and overwhelmed. When our families moved, it was not always part of a general pattern of American mobility or a function of economically determined job transfers in a growing economy, but often because of dislocation and war. There was a general cultural atmosphere of anxiety and fear about the present and future, such that, before we could speak, this anxiety, along with love and concern, was communicated by parents.

Psychoanalytic listening requires that we attend to childhood, an admonition that we, as social scientists, take particularly from Erikson. While calling upon psychoanalysts to theorize how history assumes decisive concreteness in the individual psyche, Erikson makes a complementary demand upon historians and social scientists: "Students of history continue to ignore the simple fact that all individuals are born by mothers; that everybody was once a child; that people and peoples begin in their nurseries; and that society consists of individuals in the process of developing from children into parents" (1959: 18). The 1943–1944 birth cohort are people whose direct experience of the war occurred while they were mainly preverbal babies and toddlers. Childhood does not determine the rest of life, but in childhood we are forming our selves, and the personal filtering of history, through our parents especially, is least cognized. The stories attest to the psychic weight of early childhood, the deep affective resonances of experience that cannot at the time—and can only sometimes after—be named. One contributor, an American-born Gentile who was obsessed with the Holocaust, remembers in midadulthood her own personal, two-year-old holocaust of losing her mother and father at the same time, when her mother left for several months to be with her sick mother in another state and her father retreated into work. She remembers World War II news and music playing on the radio as she lay on the floor desolate. One of our country's eminent psychologists describes with great candor how he manages early feelings of terror and loss: he cannot sit through violence in movies, skips sections on violence in books, and has shied away from or avoided entirely the study of affects in his professional work.

When we begin from and refer to childhood, we are very much in the modality of all the senses, not just in the mode of intellectual reflection. An English man, slightly older than the other contributors, remembers the basic elements of daily life, those that matter to children. He remembers the physical surround of rubble in the street and rooms open to the sky. For him, "war's end was associated with food": you could get oranges and bananas (Graham-White 2000). He ties current life experience to this childhood time, wondering whether he is a light sleeper because of a childhood spent in one of the most bombed cities in England, and he contrasts "the" war with *his* war, which was food shortages, two uncles missing in action, and German prisoners of war marched up the streets. A Japanese and a German contributor also remember basics like food and hunger.

Psychoanalytic listening helps us to see how society and history assume decisive concreteness in the individual in the form of specific transferences and resistances. It also allows us to trace significant affective and familial themes—salient patterns of subjectivity that in no case characterize all the contributions but often characterize several. To begin, there is a pervasive emotional tonality. Members of this generation experience the world through what we might consider, loosely, a depressive lens. Not everyone is sad, and no one is sad all the time, but this tonality pervades the volume. Sadness and a depressive tone, and even in some cases a sense of emptiness and hopelessness, can come from loss and mourning. This is especially clear in the accounts of children of survivors—not just of Jewish Holocaust survivors but also those who fled Asian countries or countries being taken over by the Soviet advance. These were children born to parents trying to survive during the war under terrible conditions, parents who, after the war's end, would then, during their children's early years, have learned more about their own familial losses as well as about the scale of the war's devastation. People also describe puzzlement; especially for those who were very young children at the time, not knowing why things happen can lead to a sense of futility. A generalized sense of loss also results from displacement. This is visible even in my own reactions, though I had no trauma beyond a postwar cross-country move with a mother then separated from her family of origin, as well as in the reactions of those who, like their parents, lost native language, homeland, and familiar culture. In addition to themes of loss that I infer have been filtered through parents, there is the direct experience of loss and separation reported especially by the children of soldiers—American soldiers, German and English soldiers, Slovenian soldiers. Contributing, finally, to this depressive tonality is the general anxiety and fear that, I believe, simply hung over the world during the infancy of this group.

Another, more specific theme, though not found in as many narratives, is a sense of horror: at holocausts in the generic sense as well as the specific Holocaust. Crashing, explosions, and massacres reappear in stories and associations. The shattered glass of Kristallnacht, along with the murder of relatives, is evoked in several accounts. A Chinese American woman describes learning about the rage-filled devastation and torture of the Rape of Nanking, and a Malaysian the brutal Japanese invasion of Malaysia. One woman's father worked on the Manhattan Project: somehow, she did not quite know how, he was involved in the largest explosion of all time, which her mother captured in poetry.

At the end of the spectrum opposite from explosions and shattering glass, silences are described, including a contribution from a professional musician who titles her contribution "Silence" (Oppens 2000). There turns out to be wide variation in how Holocaust-surviving parents talked or did not talk about their experience or about what happened to family members. Contributors felt these silences and figured out the truth in adulthood through books. Or they learned about the successes and survivals, but not about those who died. One says, "We never talked about the people who had disappeared, or sorrow or loss or thwarted ambitions or bitterness"; another says, "The most important family events could not be discussed"; and a third describes his parents' "route of silence" (Tanz 2000; Oppens 2000; Gardner 2000). This not talking, I imagine, was not only a conscious choice to spare children but also a way of surviving psychically.

Parents are not only filtered through emotional tone but also are found directly in mind. Here, fathers and mothers appear differently. Fathers loom large. Sons idealize soldier-fathers and their brave exploits; other sons and daughters of soldier-fathers describe father-absence. (It is no accident that father-absence was such a preoccupation in psychology in the 1940s and 1950s. It was, of course, one of the roots of my own early interest in the parental division of labor that resulted in *The Reproduction of Mothering* [1978].) Several describe the inability to connect emotionally with fathers until late in life, or they tell of wistfully watching fathers who were able to form closer attachments to siblings born after the war or who had formed solid attachments with those born before. One contribution is titled "Wartime Separation, or Why It Took My Father Fifty Years to Get Used to Me" (Hayler 2000). Another says, "My sister, my mother, my grandparents, a dog—all inhabit my earliest memories, but my father is not there" (Lewis 2000). One man describes the wrenching experience of his father simply disappearing for five years after getting on a plane in Warsaw and not debarking in Prague—it was only five years later that his family was able to find out that the father had been abducted and imprisoned. In another early-cold-war narrative, a Slovenian father disappeared for several months in 1944–1945. A German draftee father sent his last letter in January 1945 and was presumably killed shortly thereafter. His son says, "Being 'lost' is worse than dead" (Katzlberger 2000).

Mothers, in contrast to fathers, appear in more varied guises but are never a central focus. Survivor children tend to subsume them into the parental couple. If mothers were depressed, distracted, or finding it difficult to cope—as many of the mothers were while raising children on their own with husbands away at war, or while under conditions of siege, or while hiding—their children's longing for their presence is less articulate than for fathers.

Mothers are not objects of curiosity and wonder, but rather are described in passing. Contributors say, "My mother and I went . . . did . . . found . . ." One woman describes the working-class jobs held by her mother and female relatives. Only one or two mothers are described as energetic and feisty.

It may be the occupational hazard of psychoanalytic listening that one hears silences, shatterings, explosions, sadness, absence, and loss, just as it may be the occupational hazard of sociological looking that ones sees inequality, exploitation, power, and rents in the social fabric. In working on the social edges of psychoanalysis, or the psychoanalytic edges of sociology, it is always tempting (and always to be avoided) to cut through the social totality to elaborate psychological themes in common, or to cut through that which constitutes the psychic complexity of any individual to pick out certain patterns or elements in common, as I have just done. So, before concluding, I remind readers—as I describe these psychic difficulties—that I am writing about a very successful cohort who made it, from all parts of the world and all manner of experience, to one of the best universities in the country and who have drawn from their educations and early childhoods to create rich and fulfilling lives.

Scholars and writers today wonder about how to represent the Holocaust—the major cataclysmic and tragic event of the twentieth century—or if it can be represented at all. I in no way claim to be holding in mind this event in all its horrific and sweeping wholeness, or to be, in looking at narratives of a few people born into a world at war, providing a new explanation for the war or even documentation about it. Rather, I use this example to suggest that individual lives, and the patterns of affect and fantasy that these express, can give us a window into social and historical processes. We do not, in paying attention to internal worlds of fantasy and affect, "reduce" the social to a set of individual experiences or psychologize it away. Rather, listening with a psychoanalytic ear gives depth and richness to what we see with a sociological eye.

NOTE

Portions of this chapter appeared in Chodorow 2000b and 2002 (Nancy J. Chodorow, "Born into a World at War: Listening for Affect and Personal Meaning." *American Imago* 59 [3] [2002]: 297–315. © The Johns Hopkins University Press. Reprinted with permission of The Johns Hopkins University Press). For my title, I am indebted in part to Everett Hughes (1971).

REFERENCES

Chodorow, Nancy J. 1986. "Varieties of Leadership among Early Women Psychoanalysts." In L. Dickstein and C. Nadelson, eds., *Women Physicians in Leadership Roles*, pp. 45–54. Washington, D.C.: American Psychiatric Press.

————. 1989. *Feminism and Psychoanalytic Theory.* New Haven: Yale University Press; and Cambridge, U.K.: Polity.

————. 1991. "Where Have All the Eminent Women Psychoanalysts Gone? Like the Bubbles in Champagne, They Rose to the Top and Disappeared." In Judith N. Blau and Norman Goodman, eds., *Social Roles and Social Institutions,* pp. 167–94. Boulder: Westview Press.

————. 1998. "The Enemy Outside: Thoughts on the Psychodynamics of Extreme Violence with Special Attention to Men and Masculinity." *JPCS: Journal for the Psychoanalysis of Culture and Society* 3 (1): 25–38.

————. 1999. *The Power of Feelings: Personal Meaning in Psychoanalysis, Gender, and Culture.* New Haven: Yale University Press.

————. 2000a. Contribution to "Homophobia: Analysis of a 'Permissible' Prejudice. A Public Forum of the American Psychoanalytic Association and the American Psychoanalytic Foundation." *Journal of Gay and Lesbian Psychotherapy* 4: 21–27.

————. 2000b. "Individuals in History and History through Individuals." In Maria Tymoczko and Nancy Blackmun, eds., *Born into a World at War,* pp. 299–312. Manchester, U.K.: St. Jerome's Publishing.

————. 2002. "Born into a World at War: Listening for Affect and Personal Meaning." *American Imago* 59 (3): 297–315.

Erikson, Erik H. 1950. *Childhood and Society.* New York: W. W. Norton.

————. 1959. "Ego Development and Historical Change." In *Identity and the Life Cycle: Selected Papers,* pp. 18–49. New York: International Universities Press.

Field, Hugh. 2000. "Trolling along at the Bottom." In Maria Tymoczko and Nancy Blackmun, eds., *Born into a World at War,* pp. 181–87. Manchester, U.K.: St. Jerome's Publishing.

Gardner, Howard. 2000. "Dissolving Repression: A Half-Century Report." In Maria Tymoczko and Nancy Blackmun, eds., *Born into a World at War,* pp. 201–6. Manchester, U.K.: St. Jerome's Publishing.

Graham-White, Anthony. 2000. "Bombs and Brambles." In Maria Tymoczko and Nancy Blackmun, eds., *Born into a World at War,* pp. 107–9. Manchester, U.K.: St. Jerome's Publishing.

Hayler, Laurel Strange. 2000. "Wartime Separation, or Why It Took My Father Fifty-Five Years to Get Used to Me." In Maria Tymoczko and Nancy Blackmun, eds., *Born into a World at War,* pp. 261–64. Manchester, U.K.: St. Jerome's Publishing.

Hughes, Everett C. 1971. *The Sociological Eye.* Chicago: Aldine.

Katzlberger, Klaus Peter. 2000. "Life Goes On." In Maria Tymoczko and Nancy Blackmun, eds., *Born into a World at War,* pp. 111–21. Manchester, U.K.: St. Jerome's Publishing.

Krieger, Susan. 1991. "The Presence of the Self." In *Social Science and the Self,* pp. 43–48. New Brunswick: Rutgers University Press.

Lewis, Kevin. 2000. "Innocence and Experience." In Maria Tymoczko and Nancy Blackmun, eds., *Born into a World at War,* pp. 285–94. Manchester, U.K.: St. Jerome's Publishing.

Mannheim, Karl. 1928. "The Problem of Generations." In *Essays on the Sociology of Knowledge,* ed. P. Kecskemeti, pp. 276–322. 1952. New York: Oxford University Press.

Oppens, Ursula. 2000. "Silence." In Maria Tymoczko and Nancy Blackmun, eds., *Born into a World at War*, pp. 123–25. Manchester, U.K.: St. Jerome's Publishing.

Smelser, Neil J. 1998. *The Social Edges of Psychoanalysis*. Berkeley and Los Angeles: University of California Press.

Stolper, Matthew W. 2000. "Their Happiest Ten Years." In Maria Tymoczko and Nancy Blackmun, eds., *Born into a World at War*, pp. 77–85. Manchester, U.K.: St. Jerome's Publishing.

Tanz, Christine. 2000. "Hiding in the Open." In Maria Tymoczko and Nancy Blackmun, eds., *Born into a World at War*, pp. 127–51. Manchester, U.K.: St. Jerome's Publishing.

Tymoczko, Maria, and Nancy Blackmun. 2000. *Born into a World at War*. Manchester, U.K.: St. Jerome's Publishing.

Chapter 3

The Commodity Frontier

Arlie Russell Hochschild

An advertisement appearing on the Internet on March 6, 2001, read as follows:

(p/t) Beautiful, smart hostess, good masseuse—$400/week.

Hi there. This is a strange job opening, and I feel silly posting it, but this is San Francisco, and I do have the need! This will be a very confidential search process. I'm a mild-mannered millionaire businessman, intelligent, traveled, but shy, who is new to the area, and extremely inundated with invitations to parties, gatherings and social events. I'm looking to find a "personal assistant," of sorts. The job description would include, but not be limited to:

1. Being hostess to parties at my home ($40/hour)

2. Providing me with a soothing and sensual massage ($140/hour)

3. Coming to certain social events with me ($40/hour)

4. Traveling with me ($300 per day + all travel expenses)

5. Managing some of my home affairs (utilities, bill paying, etc.) ($30/hour)

You must be between 22 and 32, in-shape, good-looking, articulate, sensual, attentive, bright and able to keep confidences. I don't expect more than 3 to 4 events a month, and up to 10 hours a week on massage, chores and other miscellaneous items, at the most. You must be unmarried, unattached, or have a very understanding partner! I'm a bright, intelligent 30-year-old man, and I'm happy to discuss the reasons for my placing this ad with you on response of your email application. If you can, please include a picture of yourself, or a description of your likes, interests, and your ability to do the job. No professional escorts please! No sex involved! Thank you.[1]

What activities seem to us too personal to pay for or do for hire? What is it about a social context and culture that persuades us to feel as we do about it? This ad reveals a certain cultural edge beyond which the idea of paying for a service becomes, to many people, unnerving.[2]

To be sure, a transaction that seems perfectly acceptable to some people in one context often seems disturbing to others in another. Notions of agreeableness or credibility also change over time. Indeed, I wonder if American culture is not in the midst of such a change now. A half century ago, we might have imagined a wealthy man buying a fancy home, car, and pleasant vacation for himself and his family. Now, we are asked to imagine the man buying the pleasant family or, at least, the services associated with the fantasy of a family-like experience.

In this chapter, I explore some reactions to this ad, selecting from the treasure trove of Neil Smelser's extraordinary corpus of creative work, especially his work on the relationship between family and economy and the psychological function of myth. Together, these ideas help us develop another of his key insights—that "economic man" is a culturally and emotionally complex being.

I use the ad above as a cultural Rorschach test. What, I have asked upper-division students at the University of California, Berkeley, is your response to this ad? Their response was largely negative—ranging from anxious refusal ("He can't buy a wife") to condemnation ("He shouldn't try to buy a wife") to considerations of the emotional and moral flaws that might have led him to write the ad. The students were not surprised by the ad, but they were disturbed by it.

So how did the ad disturb the students, and why? After all, family history is replete with examples of family arrangements that share some characteristics with the commercial relationship proposed in this ad. To answer this question, I propose that students, like many others in American society today, face a contradiction between two social forces. On one hand, they face a commodity frontier. As the market creates ever more niches in the "mommy industry," the family is outsourcing more functions to be handled by it. Through this trend, the family is moving, top class first, from an artisanal family to a postproduction family. And with this shift, personal tasks—especially those performed by women—become monetized and impersonalized.[3]

On the other hand, the family—and especially the wife-mother within it—has, as a result, become a more powerful, condensed symbol for treasured qualities such as empathy, recognition, love—qualities that are quintessentially personal. The resulting strains between these two trends have led to a crisis of enchantment. Are we to hold onto the enchantment of the wife-mother in the familial sphere, or can purchases become enchanted too? Each "faith"—in family or marketplace—brings with it different implications for emotion management. Each is also undergirded by the mistaken assumption that family and market are separate cultural spheres.

RESPONSES TO THE AD:
CULTURAL SENSITIVITIES TO THE COMMODITY FRONTIER

I distributed copies of the ad posted by the shy millionaire to seventy students in my class on the sociology of the family at the University of California, Berkeley, in the spring of 2001 and asked them to comment. I also followed up the survey with conversations with some half dozen students about why they had answered the way they did. While many came from Asian immigrant families and believed in the importance of strong family ties, quite a few were also heading for workaholic careers in Silicon Valley, where outsourcing domestic life is fast becoming a fashionable, if controversial, way of life. So, while hardly typical of the views of educated American youth in general, the views of these students hint at a contradiction between economic trends that press for the outsourcing of family functions and a cultural fetishization of in-sourced functions.

Most students expressed a combination of sympathy ("He's afraid to go out and get a girlfriend" or "He's pathologically shy") and criticism or contempt ("He's selfish," "He's a loser," "He's a creep," "He's too socially conscious"). Others expressed fear ("This ad is scary"), anger ("What a jerk"), suspicion ("He's a shady character"), and disbelief ("This is unreal").[4]

Perhaps the most eloquent response came from a young woman, a child of divorce who still "believes in love." As she put it:

> It is a very sad commentary on the state of relationships today. Even family life is being directly sought in commodity trade. Forget the messy emotions. Just give me the underlying services and benefits money can buy. And what's the point of trying, when all it brings are pain, strife and divorce? Then the act of sexual interaction is relativized and commodified, but *not* as prostitution. Clearly the intrinsic value [of the sensual massage] to the buyer is much higher [$140 an hour], so we're not talking a shoulder rub. But even the beautiful intertwinement of loving, caring, spiritually connected partners in lovemaking is reduced to mechanized, emotionless labor for hire. Is it any wonder there's so much smoldering rage in such a graceless age?

Another commented, "This takes the depersonalization of relationships to new heights." At the same time, most of the respondents said the ad was thinkable. It was plausible. It was not surprising. As one student put it, referring to the San Francisco Bay Area and Silicon Valley, it could happen "at least around here." Referring to another Website he had seen, one young man said, "Given the website www.2kforawife.com [a website advertising for a wife, no longer up as of July 2001], I'm not that surprised." A minority of the students condoned the ad: "If he has the money to burn, by all means." Or they anticipated that, given the high salary, *others* would respond to it, if not quite condone it. Indeed, a number of the students spoke of living in a culture in which market-home crossovers were unsurprising. As one put it,

"My reaction is one of 'Sure, this is normal.' My own reaction surprises me because I know years ago . . . I would have been shocked and angry. But now I am desensitized and accept that relationships don't always happen in the nice, neat boxes I once thought they came in." Only four out of seventy thought the ad was a hoax.

HOW WAS THE AD DISTURBING?

For most of these young, educated Californians, the ad seemed to strike a raw nerve, and the first question to ask is: how did it do this? First of all, it disturbed many students that a familial role was shown to be divisible into slivers, a whole separated into parts, as the student above referred to the "beautiful intertwinement of loving, caring, spiritually connected partners in lovemaking." Second, it bothered the students that this taken-apart wife-mother role was now associated with varying amounts of money. Traveling together was to be worth three hundred dollars a day. Managing home affairs, thirty dollars an hour. Thus, the divisibility and commercialization were offensive. But perhaps they were doubly so because the separate tasks were then implicitly associated with more diffuse, personal characteristics apparently unrelated to the tasks. As one person noted, "It seems like he's looking for a personal assistant [to do these tasks]. . . . Yet he is specific about the *kind of woman* he wants—he mentions the word *sensual* more than once. She needs to be attractive, young, in shape, sensual, bright. (All marriageable qualities). If he just wanted these tasks done, why couldn't an old, fat man do them?" Another observed that the millionaire wanted someone ready to hear confidences, someone available to travel, and who thus could orient her schedule to his, which, even more than looks and age, implies a diffuse "intertwined" relationship.

The students were also disturbed, perhaps, by what often comes with monetization—a cultural principle of giving that characterizes market deals—short-term tit-for-tat exchanges. Commercial exchanges often provide a shortcut around other principles of giving—long-term tit-for-tat exchanges or altruism. One person remarked, "The man wants a wife, but he doesn't want to be a husband." He wants to receive, but not to give—except in cash. In other words, by offering money as the totality of his side of the bargain, the man absolves himself of any moral responsibility to try to give emotionally in the future. As one put it, "For him, money took care of his side of the deal." The students did not congratulate the man on his monetary generosity, though they understood the sums he offered to be high. Indeed, one woman commented, "He is taking the easy way out. He doesn't want to have to deal with what a partner may need from him emotionally and physically. So he is just looking for the benefits without the work." Another said, "He's advertising for a sexless, no-needs wife. While I do not object to this on principle, I do think it sad that he would have no need to *give* in a relationship. It seems lonely and false" (emphasis mine). A few others also pointed out that the man stood to lose, not gain, through his financial offer. As one person put it, "The man's losing the chance to give. He's cheating himself."

Students were also disturbed by a closely related issue—the absence of emotional engagement. Here, they focus directly on his emotional capacity and need. One complained that the man was emotionally empty, detached, invulnerable: "He has a strong desire to be in total control." Another young woman remarked, "He must feel very unloved and unable to give love." They thought he *should feel* something for the woman who does what he has in mind. The man who posted the ad said he had a "need," another observed. But what is his "need" for these services? "I find it amusing," the student said, "that [the man] calls this a need." In later conversation, he explained, "The man mentions luxury items he doesn't really need, but what he does need, emotionally, he's not asking for or setting it up to get." Another commented, apparently not in jest, "It is so fascinating to me the things men will do to avoid emotional attachment."

Not only was emotion missing but so was the commitment to emotion work—to work on feelings in order to improve the relationship. As one put it, "He wants to hire someone to fulfill his needs but without the hassle [of a relationship]." Another complained, "I was disgusted [that the man is buying] the grunt labor of a relationship." In a sense, the students were observing the absence of an implied inclination to pay any allegiance to familial feeling rules or to try to manage emotions in a way mindful of them. He was buying himself out of all this.

Finally, for some, it was not the splintering of the wife-mother role or the commodification of each part that posed a problem as much as it was the fact that—partly because of these processes—the emotional experience of being together, which was supposed to be *enchanted,* was *disenchanted.* For a couple to feel their relationship is enchanted, they must feel moved to imbue the world around them with a sense of magic that has, paradoxically, power over them, the magic now coming from "outside." In an enchanted relationship, not only the relationship but also the whole world feels magical. And it does so through no apparent will of one's own. The individual externalizes his or her locus of control. This sense of enchantment is similar to Sigmund Freud's notion of "oceanic oneness," which some associate with religion, and which all, Emile Durkheim argues, associate with the sacred.

This dimension of experience is here curtained off, not as it impacts the worst part of a close relationship, but as it impacts the best. As one student observed, "It almost seems like the man wants to pay a woman to do the fun things that couples do together." He was disenchanting fun.

In sum, the man's money buys him freedom. It buys him the right to depersonalize a relation. The man wants to pay the woman instead of owing anything else to her in any other way. He does not want to have to feel anything toward her. He exempts himself from family-feeling rules. He wants not to *have to* have fun. He wants to feel free to have to a relationship—impersonal or personal—as he wishes and on the terms he wishes. Money *liberates* him, as Georg Simmel observes. But as the respondents noted repeatedly, he is also using money to narrow the relational possibilities. In the end, they felt that the options he was free to choose between were themselves stripped of meaning by (1) the separation between exclusive sex expression, intimacy, and affection, (2) the attachment of money to each part of what is imagined to be whole, (3) a noncommittal stance toward the emotion work and feeling rules that often apply in intimate engagement, and (4) the implicit disenchantment with the whole complex they associate with adult sexual-emotional love. In a sense he seemed to them as to he would to Simmel, as if he were trapped by what many would call "liberation." And as Smelser would observe, the man was creating for himself a context in which he would be called upon to employ a mechanism of ego defense—depersonalization.[5]

WHY WAS THE AD DISTURBING?

All of this says *how* the ad was disturbing but not *why*. Why, we can ask, did the students sound this alarm? The answer is not, after all, self-evident. History is replete with examples of family patterns that illustrate each of the various ways in which this ad offended these students. For example, in traditional China and many parts of Africa and the Moslem world, polygamy challenges the idea of the unity of love with sexual exclusivity. In Europe, the tradition of maintaining a bourgeois marriage and a mistress—sometimes paid for by allowances or gifts, though not through salary—also disrupts the expectation that marriage, intimacy, affection, sexual exclusivity, and often procreation will form parts of one whole. A more covert pattern combines a conventional marriage and children with an intense homosexual relationship, again separating parts of this whole.

In the realm of parenting, too, history provides many examples of differentiation. In upper-class households, people do not hold their breath at the slicing and dicing of "a mother's role" into discrete paid positions such as those of nanny, cook, chauffeur, therapist, tutor, and camp counselor, to mention a few. In the antebellum South, slave women cared for and nursed children and sometimes served the head of household as concubines. In all these times and places, people felt no commitment to the feeling rules and forms of emotion work that uphold the ideal of the romantic love ethic and the enchantment created by it. So the question becomes why, given all this, did this ad hit a certain contemporary cultural nerve?

The answer, I suggest, is that the ad strikes at a flash point between an advancing commodity frontier, on one hand, and the hypersymbolized but structurally weakened core of the modern American family.

THE COMMODITY FRONTIER

The commodity frontier, Janus-faced, looks in one direction to the marketplace and in another to the family. On the market side, it is a frontier for *companies* as they expand the number of market niches for goods and services covering activities that, in yesteryear, formed part of unpaid "family life." On the other side, it is a frontier for *families* that feel the need or desire to consume such goods and services.

On the company side, a growing supply of services is meeting a growing demand for "family" jobs. In a recent article in *Business Week,* Rochelle Sharpe notes, "Entrepreneurs are eager to respond to the time crunch, creating businesses unimaginable just a few years ago." These include "breast feeding consultants, baby-proofing agencies, emergency babysitting services, companies specializing in paying nanny taxes[,] and others that install hidden cameras to spy on babysitters' behavior. People can hire bill payers, birthday party planners, kiddy taxi services, personal assistants, personal chefs, and, of course, household managers to oversee all the personnel."[6] One ad posted on the Internet includes in the list of available services "pet care, DMV registration, holiday decorating, personal gift selection, party planning, night life recommendations, personal/professional correspondence, and credit card charge disputes." The services of others are implied in the names of the agencies that offer them—Mary Poppins, Wives for Hire (in Hollywood), and Husbands for Rent (in Maine).[7] One agency, Jill of All Trades, organizes closets and packs up houses. Clients trust the assistant to sort through their belongings and throw the junk out. As the assistant commented, "People don't have time to look at their stuff. I know what's important."[8] Another Internet job description read, "Administrative assistant with corporate experience and a Martha Stewart edge to manage a family household. . . . A domestic interest is required and the ability to travel is necessary. Must enjoy kids! This is a unique position requiring both a warmhearted and business-oriented individual."[9]

Not only do the qualities called for in the assistant cross the line between market and home, the result can cross a more human line as well. As Rochelle Sharpe describes it, "Lynn Corsiglia, a human resources executive in California, remembers the disappointment in her daughter's eyes when the girl discovered that someone had been hired to help organize her birthday party. 'I realized that I blew the boundary,' she says."[10] Lynn Corsiglia felt she had moved, one might say, to the cultural edge of the commodity frontier as her daughter defined that edge.

This expansion of market services applies mainly to executives and professionals—both single men and women, and "professional households with-out wives," as Saskia Sassen has called them.[11] Often faced with long hours at work, many employees see the solution not in sharing or neglecting wifely chores, but in hiring people to do them. With the increasing gap between the top 20 percent and bottom 20 percent of the income scale, more rich can afford such services, and poorer and marginally middle-class people are eager to provide them. As their income rises, wealthy people—especially those in high-pressure careers—take advantage of the goods and services on this frontier, and many poor people aspire to do so.

The commodity frontier has impinged on Western domestic life for many centuries. It is doubtful that Queen Victoria clipped her toenails or breast-fed her children. Indeed, in early modern Europe, it was common for urban upper-class parents to give their babies over to rural wet nurses to raise dur-ing the first years of life.[12] So the commodity frontier has a history as well as a future trajectory, and both are lodged in a local sense of what belongs where in order for life to seem right.

Still, we can perhaps say that, within American and European culture, modernization has recently altered the character of the commodity frontier. We can speak crudely of newer and older expressions of it. Relative to ours today, eighteenth- and nineteenth-century commodification of domestic life involved a greater merger between service and server. An eighteenth-cen-tury white Southern aristocrat who bought a slave bought the person, not the service—the ultimate commodification.[13] And the indentured servant dif-fered from the slave only in degree.

The millionaire's ad for a "beautiful, smart hostess, good masseuse," by contrast, strikes us as modern. It is purely the services, classified and priced, that are up for purchase, at least apparently. The ad seems to tease apart many aspects of what was once one role. Structural differentiation between family and economy, a process Smelser traces in English history, becomes here a cultural idea in a commercial context, which lends itself to an almost jazzlike improvisation. As in jazz, the ad plays with the idea of dividing and recombining, suggesting different versions of various combinations.[14]

Especially in its more recent incarnation, the commercial substitutes for family activities often turn out to be better than the "real" thing. Just as the French bakery may make bread better than Mother ever did, and the clean-ing service may clean the house more thoroughly, so therapists may recog-nize feelings more accurately. Even child care workers, while no ultimate substitute, may prove more warm and even-tempered than parents some-times are. Thus, in a sense, capitalism is not competing with itself, one com-pany against another. Capitalism is competing with the family, and particu-larly with the role of the wife and mother.

A cycle is set in motion. As the family becomes more minimal, it turns to the market to add what it needs and, by doing so, becomes yet more minimal. This logic also applies to the two functions Talcott Parsons thought would be left to the family when all the structural differentiation was said and done—socialization of children and adult personality stabilization.

There is a countertrend as well. The cult of Martha Stewart appeals to the desire to resist the loss of family functions to the marketplace. The "do-it-yourself" movement of course creates a market niche of its own for the implements and lessons needed to "do it yourself."

Still, the prevailing tending is toward relinquishing family functions to the market realm. And various trends exacerbate this tendency. Most important is the movement of women moving into paid work. In 1950, less than a fifth of mothers with children under six worked in the labor force, while a half century later, two-thirds of such mothers do. Their salary is also now vital to the family budget. Older female relatives who might in an earlier period have stayed home to care for their grandchildren, nephews, and nieces are now likely to be at work too.

In addition, the workday has recently been taking up more hours of the year. According to an International Labor Organization report, Americans now work two weeks longer each year than their counterparts in Japan, the vaunted long-work-hour capital of the world. And many of these long-hour workers are also trying to maintain a family life. Between 1989 and 1996 for example, middle-class married couples increased their annual work hours outside the home, from 3,550 to 3,685, or more than three extra 40-hour weeks of work a year.[15]

Over the last half century, the American divorce rate has also increased to 50 percent, and a fifth of households with children are now headed by single mothers, most of whom get little financial help from their former husbands and most of whom work full-time outside the home.[16] Like the rising proportion of women who work outside the home, divorce also, in effect, reduces the number of helping hands at home—creating a need or desire for supplemental forms of care.

If there are fewer helping hands at home, the state has done nothing to ease the burden at home. Indeed, the 1996 welfare reforms reduced state aid to parents with dependent children, causing responsibility to devolve to the states, which have in turn reduced aid, even for food stamps. Many states have also implemented cutbacks in public recreation and parks and library programs designed to help families care for children.

In addition to the depletion of both private and public resources for care, there is an increasing uncertainty associated with cultural ideas about the "proper" source of it. The traditional wife-mother role has given way to a variety of different arrangements—wives who are not mothers, mothers who are not wives, second wives and stepmothers, and lesbian mothers. And while these changes in the source of care are certainly not to be confused with a depletion of care, the changing culture itself gives rise to uncertainties about it: Will my father still be living with me and taking care of me fifteen years from now, or will he be taking care of a new family he has with a new wife? Will the lesbian partner of my mother be part of my life when I am older? In addition to a real depletion in resources available for familial care, then, the shifting cultural landscape of care may account for some sense of anxiety about it.

Thus, as the market advances, as the family moves from a production to a consumption unit, as it faces a care deficit, and as the cultural landscape of care shifts, individuals increasingly keep an anxious eye on what seems like the primary remaining symbol of abiding care—the mother.

THE HEIGHTENED SYMBOLISM OF MOTHER

The more the commodity frontier erodes the territory surrounding the emotional care furnished by the wife-mother, the more hypersymbolized the remaining sources of care seem to become and the more the wife-mother functions as a symbolic cultural anchor to stay the ship against a powerful tide.[17] The symbolic weight of "the family" is condensed and consolidated into the wife-mother, and increasingly now into the mother. In *A World of Their Own Making* (1996), the historian John Gillis argues that the cultural meanings associated with security, support, and empathy—meanings that once adhered to an entire community—were in the course of industrialization, gradually transferred to the family.[18] Now we can add that, within the family, these symbolic meanings have increasingly associated with the figure of the wife-mother.

The hypersymbolization of the mother is itself partly a response to the destabilization of the cultural as well as economic ground on which the family rests. As a highly dynamic system, capitalism destabilizes both the economy and the family.[19] The shakier things outside the family seem, the more we seem to need to believe in an unshakable family or, failing that, an unshakable figure, the wife-mother.

In addition, in the West, capitalism is usually paired with an ideology of secular individualism. As an understanding of life, secular individualism leads people to take personal credit for the highs of economic life and to take personal blame for the lows. It leads us to "personalize" social events. It provides an intrapunitive ideology to go with an "extrapunitive" economic system.

The effect of the impact of destabilizing capitalism on one hand and inward-looking individualist ideology on the other is to *create a need* for a refuge, a haven in a heartless world where, as Christopher Lasch has argued, we imagine ourselves to be safe, comforted, healed. The harsher the environment outside the home, the more we yearn for a haven inside the home. Many Americans turn for comfort and safety to the church. But the great geographic mobility of Americans often erodes ties to any particular church as it does bonds to local neighborhoods and communities.[20] In addition, divorce not only creates a greater need for supportive community, it also tends to reduce the size of that personal community, as the research on networks by Barry Wellman suggests.[21]

Like other symbols, the symbol of mother is "efficient." That is, the family farm, local community, or even whole extended family—which one can not transport from place to place—does not do the symbolic work. Rather, all the meanings associated with these larger social entities are condensed into the symbol of one person, the mother, and secondarily, the immediate family. As Smelser observes, Americans entertain a "romance" of family vacations, family homes, and family "rural bliss," and, along with the hypersymbolization of the mother, these have probably grown in tandem with the forces to which they are a response.

In sum, the students may have seen in the millionaire's ad, and in the commodity frontier itself, an "attack" on a symbol that had become a psychological "holding ground." Trends in the family may seem to them to deplete domestic care and to reduce a sense of certainty about the nature and source of it.

The attack on this symbol, as it is seen, may create a crisis of enchantment. To "believe in" the wife-mother figure, one must submit to a sense of enchantment, magic, and even a sense of being in love as a source of meaning in and of itself. At the same time, through the enormous growth in advertisement, documented by Juliet Schor in *The Overspent American* (1998), the commodity frontier seems to chip away at just this enchantment too. Is it the wife-mother complex that is enchanted, the student may be led to wonder, or the services that pick up where she leaves off? And through advertising, is the commodity frontier gradually "borrowing" or "stealing" the enchantment of what seems like an ever more necessary remaining anchor against a market tide?

COMMODITIES AND THE MYTH OF THE AMERICAN FRONTIER

As Smelser has observed in his important analysis of the myth of California, every myth has an element of reality. At the same time, it has an emotional element—located somewhere in our mental life between daydream and ideology.[22]

We have a "myth" of the American frontier, and, of course, there really was a western frontier, which, over the course of three hundred years, many Americans moved to extend. The very possibility that a young man on a New England farm could set out for a more fertile and extensive plot of land out west led his parents to be more lenient, the historian Philip Greven (1972) shows, in hopes of motivating him to stay.

Attached to this real geographic frontier is a larger set of meanings, perhaps including the idea that one can always leave something bad for something better. One need not stay and live with frustration and ambivalence: one can strike out to seek one's fortune on the emotional frontier. American heroes from Daniel Boone and Paul Bunyan to the "restless cowboy" analyzed by Erik Erikson start somewhere and end somewhere else. At the end of Samuel Clemens's *Huckleberry Finn,* Huck says, "I reckon I got to light out for the Territory ahead of the rest, because Aunt Sally she's going to adopt me and sivilize *[sic]* me and I can't stand it."[23] This is the myth of the individual's quest for liberty.

Myths grow and change, and as part of change, myths can extend themselves to other areas of life. And perhaps we have seen a symbolic transfer of the fantasy of liberation from a geographic frontier to a commodity frontier. For the geographic frontier, the point of focus is a person's location on land. For the commodity frontier, the point of focus is a location in a world of goods and services.

Instead of "going somewhere," the individual "buys something," which becomes a way of going somewhere. If, on the geographic frontier, the individual seeks to discover a land of milk and honey, so on the commodity frontier he or she hopes to purchase and control the emotional equivalent of this. In either case, the frontier represents freedom and opportunity.

In the past, on the commodity frontier the fantasy of a perfect purchase might more often center on some feature of external reality. One might dream of buying a perfect house, on a perfect lot of land, signifying one's rise in social station. But today, as more elements of intimate and domestic life become objects of sale, the commodity frontier has taken on a more subjective cast. So the modern purchase is more likely to be sold to us by implying access to a "perfect" private self in a "perfect" private relationship. For example, a recent ad in the *New Yorker* magazine for the "Titan Club, an Exclusive Dating Service" illustrates this:

> Who says you can't have it all? Titan Club is the first exclusive dating club for men of your stature. You already have power, prestige, status and success. But, if "at the end of the day" you realize "someone" is missing, let Titan Club help you find her. Titan Club women are intelligent, diverse, sexy and beautiful. With a 95% success rate, we are confident that you will find exactly what you are looking for in a relationship.[24]

The fantasy of the perfect relationship is linked to the fantasy of the perfect personality with whom one has this relationship. Consider an ad for KinderCare Learning Centers, a for-profit childcare chain: "You want your child to be active, tolerant, smart, loved, emotionally stable, self-aware, artistic, and get a two-hour nap. Anything else?"[25]

The service will produce, it implies, the perfect child with whom a busy parent has a perfect relationship. This ad promises a great deal about ambivalence. It promises to get rid of it. If Titan delivers "exactly what you are looking for in a relationship" and if KinderCare delivers exactly the personality you want in your own child, they also deliver a state of unambivalence. And this is the hidden appeal in the marketing associated with much modern commodification. Thus, the prevailing myth of the frontier, commodification, and the subjective realm have fused into one—a commodity frontier that is moving into the world of our private desires. And to do so it borrows or steals—only time will tell—from the sense of enchantment earlier reserved for the home.

One further word about the relation between the commodity frontier and ambivalence—a topic central to Smelser's thinking. One way we "go west," I've suggested, is to buy goods and services that promise a family-like experience. But in doing so, we also pursue the fantasy of a life free from ambivalence. The very act of fleeing ambivalence also expresses it. Commercial substitutes for family life do not eliminate ambivalence. They express and legitimize it. To return to our example of the shy millionaire, we might say he is trying to act on two impulses. On one hand, he seeks the perfect woman to be by his side for many different purposes. This is one side of the ambivalence. On the other hand, he seems to avoid entanglement with her. That's the other side of the ambivalence. Indeed, the man may be curtailing his conception of what it is he "needs" to fit into the narrow window of what he can purchase. One might say, then, that one latent function of an ad like this is to stake out a moral territory that allows for intimacy at a distance.

THE RICOCHET OF THE COMMODITY IMAGES

The Frankfurt school of sociology and more recent scholars such as Schor and Kuttner have criticized consumerism without focusing on the family, and family scholars such as William Goode, Steven Mintz, and Susan Kellogg have focused on the family without attending much to consumerism. Indeed, with the exception of Viviana Zelizer, Christopher Lasch, Jan Dizard, and Howard Gadlin, few scholars have focused on the relationship between these two realms. Perhaps this is because the two realms, once structurally differentiated, are assumed to be culturally free of one another as well. And perhaps this is why we tend to dissociate our ideas about the family from our ideas about the commodity frontier.

But these two realms are not separate. Culturally speaking, they ricochet off one another continually. As a cultural idea, commodification bounces from marketplace to home and back again. We buy something at the store. We bring it home. We compare what we have at home with what we bought. That comparison leads us to reappraise what we have at home. We make something at home. We go to the store. We compare what we think of buying with what we make at home. The reappraisal works the other way. In this way, events on the "frontier" are continually having their effect back home.

We like to think of home as a haven in a heartless world, a safe, benign sphere separate from the dangerous and hostile world outside, or—a related formulation—we see the family as a place of emotional expressivity separate from the emotionless, depersonalized world of the marketplace. (Home takes one side of the pattern variables; the marketplace takes the other.) As Zelizer has so beautifully shown, we have clearly different images of each. At home we act out of love. We are not cold and impersonal like people in the marketplace. And contrariwise, in the market, we say, we judge people on professional grounds. We do not let personal loyalties interfere. Each image is used as a foil, as the negative, as the "not" of the other—as, in the ego defense, splitting. In my research on a Fortune 500 company, reported in *The Time Bind* (1997), I discovered a number of managers who said they brought home management tips that helped them run their homes "smoothly." And sometimes people described themselves using work imagery. One man humorously spoke of having a "total quality" marriage, and another seriously spoke of a good family as being like a "high productivity team." One man even explained that he improved his marriage by realizing that his wife was his primary "customer."[26]

The roles and relationships of the marketplace often become benchmarks for the appraisal of roles and relationships at home. For example, one married mother of three (whom I interviewed about patterns of care in her life) described the following:

> I had my husband's parents and aunt and uncle for a week at our summer cabin. It's rather small, and it rained most of the week except for Saturday and Sunday. And my mother-in-law offered to help me make the meals and helped me clear the dishes. But you know, the real work is in figuring out what to eat and shopping. And the nearest store was at some distance. And I began to resent their visit so much I could hardly stand it. You know, *I don't run a bed-and-breakfast!*

This woman chose a market role—an entrepreneur managing a bed-and-breakfast—as a measuring rod to appraise the demands made on her as a daughter-in-law and relative. She measured what she did as an *unpaid relative* against another picture of life as a *paid employee*. On the family side of the commodification frontier, she felt she was doing too much and felt a right to resent it. On the market side, she imagined she would have been fairly compensated. In this way, she was tacitly measuring the opportunity costs of not working. Her life in the market world was with her in her imagination, as part of a potential self even when she was far outside that world.[27]

Other women whom I have interviewed for a forthcoming book felt overburdened at home. Some have said to their husbands, "I'm not your maid."

One very well-to-do grandmother said about spending "too much" time with her own grandchildren, "I'm not their babysitter, you know."[28]

Twenty-five years from now, it may be that remarks passed at home will refer to new hybrid roles—"I'm not your paid hostess/masseuse"—as if that role were as normal and ordinary as any other. Or even "I'm not your half-wife," as if it had attained the moral weight of "wife" on one hand or "secretary" on the other. The market changes our benchmarks. Though no one intends it to, the market influences the norms that guide our lives at home.

Through this borrowing from one side by the other of the commodity frontier, society itself expresses ambivalence about the family. Indeed, commodification provides a way in which people individually manage to want and not want certain elements of family life. The existence of such market substitutes becomes a form of societal legitimation for this ambivalence.

Finally, we can wonder what might cross through the heads of those who replied to the shy millionaire's ad. Five of the sixty students from my class said they were tempted to reply to the ad. One confided, "Since this [questionnaire] is anonymous, I feel like I'd like to respond to this ad. It's a good deal, I think [crossed out, and over it written 'maybe']." Another said, "I am almost tempted to apply [sic] to this ad, except I don't meet the qualifications." Yet another replied, "If it's real, I'd do it." A number of people disparaged the ad but predicted that others in the class would probably happily answer it. "The worst part," said one, "is that someone who needed the money probably took him up on his offer." In his essay on ambivalence, Smelser points out that sometimes we are ambivalent about our inner fantasies and impulses, and sometimes we are ambivalent about the real world outside ourselves. The commodity frontier is real, and maybe it is a good sign if we feel ambivalent about it.

NOTES

This chapter appeared earlier in different form in Arlie Hochschild, *The Commercialization of Intimate Life: Notes from Home and Work*, © 2003 by Arlie Hochschild (University of California Press).

1. Ad found on the Internet, courtesy of Bonnie Kwan.

2. On the topic of the meaning of money and purchasing, see the foundational work of Viviana Zelizer (1994, 1996, 2000). In "Payments and Social Ties" (1996), she makes a persuasive case that money and the market realm (e.g., shopping, buying) can be assigned any number of meanings. Our job, she argues, is to study them, not prejudge them. This is what I attempt here.

On the point of discerning the "edge," please see Eviatar Zerubavel's *The Fine Line* (1991).

3. While many theorists would not question this ad or the "wife and mother industry," a good number see it as problematic but on very different grounds. In *The Minimal Family* (1990), Jan Dizard and Howard Gadlin argue that the commodification

of former family activities takes the familism out of families. In *The Overspent American* (1998), Juliet Schor critiques American overconsumption of natural resources as a troubling model to be emulated by the rest of the world. In *Everything for Sale* (1997), Robert Kuttner critiques the retreat from government protection of the "public good." Thorstein Veblen, Schor, and Barbara Ehrenreich critique it from the vantage point of status seeking.

4. One person argued that the man tried to make this proposition "sound" like a normal transaction. But he wondered how the man could explain his hireling's role "in his life to his business partners." One suspicious student remarked, "This is a crazy man who wants a sex slave. Why else would he say 'no sex' while also stipulating that the woman has to be beautiful and unattached?" Another noted, "You don't know what's behind the screen." While a number were suspicious of the man's *motives,* very few suspected the veracity of the *ad* itself. I myself believe the ad is real. Even if it were a hoax, the ad is so close to reality that virtually all the students took it as real, and so it might as well have been real.

5. In "Depth Psychology and the Social Order" (1998), Smelser distinguishes between four categories of ego defense, each with its corresponding relevant affect and object. At one time or another, people doubtless resort to all of these types of defenses in the course of confronting the threat of commodification and the cultural incongruities it introduces. But one ego defense stands out—depersonalization.

6. Sharpe 2000: 108–10. The president of a Massachusetts-based agency, Parents in a Pinch, reported that, rather than grandparents themselves helping working parents, she found that frequently grandparents bought the service for a busy working daughter as a gift. Presumably many of them were themselves also working and too busy to help out.

7. A radio announcement made on commercial radio in southern Maine, July 2000.

8. Sharpe 2000: 110.

9. Internet notice found on www.craigslist.org, "Part Time Personal Assistant Available."

10. Sharpe 2000: 110.

11. Sassen 2001. Sassen argues that globalization is currently creating new social class patterns. The professional class in rich countries now draws more exclusively on female immigrant labor, which, she argues, is itself a product of economic dislocations that stem from globalization.

12. Mintz and Kellogg 1988.

13. It is not that the "old" commodification does not occur today. In *Disposable People* (1999), Kevin Bales shows how globalization is giving rise to a "new" slavery every bit as serious as the "old" one. But slavery in the modern era is different from slavery in the past, for it strikes the modern Western mind as not only immoral but also old.

14. See Neil Smelser 1959. Dividing up the wife-mother role as implied in the ad is "structural" in the sense that a person in a given role (a paid hostess-masseuse outside the family) carries out a function a wife might be expected to perform inside the family. But it is also psychological and cultural, for this role is the focus of strongly felt beliefs. And these in turn are strongly related to the gemeinschaft side of the Parsonian pattern variables—affectivity, diffuseness, ascription, particularism.

15. Doohan 1999. A *New York Times* (September 1, 2001) report suggests that Americans added a full week to their work year during the 1990s, climbing to 1,979 hours on average last year, up 36 hours from 1990. Greenhouse 2001.

16. McLanahan and Sandefur 1994.

17. See Hays 1996.

18. In *A World of Their Own Making,* Gillis points out very different assumptions about the public/private divide, and about the degree to which the private was thought to need protection from the public. We can also distinguish between different "bandwidths" of commodification: commodities that are chipped off from family life versus commodities chipped off from nature, etc.

19. Certainly, American life before the advent of industrial capitalism was unstable, and there are some ways in which industrial capitalism has, through the creation of a middle class, removed many people from the hardships of poverty and, in so doing, stabilized family life. See Mintz and Kellogg 1988. At the same time, the dynamism of capitalism, coupled with a state that—by European standards—does little to protect workers from market fluctuations and changing economic demands, and that offers few provisions for aid in family care, makes America a somewhat harsher, if freer, society in which to live.

20. See Putnam 2001. As Claude Fischer has pointed out, geographic mobility itself is not new to Americans. While rates of long-distance mobility have remained relatively constant since the mid–nineteenth century, mobility within local areas has actually decreased. Professor Claude Fischer, lecture, Center for Working Families, University of California, Berkeley, April 2001.

21. Wellman et al. 1997; Wellman 1999.

22. In Smelser's insightful essay "Collective Myths and Fantasies: The Myth of the Good Life in California," he notes that a myth is a "psychodynamic blending of fiction and fact to complete the inevitable logic of ambivalence in myth. . . . There is no happy myth without its unhappy side." So, too, with the myth of infinite commodification, there is the bright side—the fantasy of the perfect "wifelike employee"—and also the dark side—the fear of estrangement and existential aloneness. See Smelser 1998a: 111–24.

23. Clemens 1962: 226. See also Erikson 1950.

24. Dating services and mail-order bride services commodify *the finding* of wives, of course, though not the wives themselves (*New Yorker* [June 18, 25, 2001]: 149).

25. The center accepts children six weeks to twelve years of age and provides a number to call for the center nearest you. Hochschild 1997: 231.

26. Heard on Maine Public Radio, October 14, 2001.

27. For a discussion of the "potential self," see Hochschild 1997: 235.

28. Thanks to Allison Pugh (Department of Sociology, University of California, Berkeley) for this example.

REFERENCES

Bales, Kevin. 1999. *Disposable People: New Slavery in the Global Economy.* Berkeley and Los Angeles: University of California Press.

Bellah, Robert. 1994. "Understanding Caring in Contemporary America." In Susan

S. Phillips and Patricia Benner, eds., *The Crisis of Care: Affirming and Restoring Caring Practices in the Helping Professions,* pp. 21–35. Washington, D.C.: Georgetown University Press.

Clemens, Samuel Langhorne. 1962. *Adventures of Huckleberry Finn.* Norton Critical Editions. New York: W. W. Norton and Company.

Dizard, Jan, and Howard Gadlin. 1990. *The Minimal Family.* Amherst: University of Massachusetts Press.

Doohan, John. 1999. "Working Long, Working Better?" *World of Work, the Magazine of the International Labour Organization,* no. 31 (September–October).

Ehrenreich, Barbara. 2001. *Nickel and Dimed.* New York: Metropolitan Books.

Erickson, Erik. 1950. *Childhood and Society.* New York: Norton.

Gillis, John. 1996. *A World of Their Own Making: Myth, Ritual, and the Quest for Family Values.* New York: Basic Books.

Greenhouse, Steve. "Americans' International Lead in Hours Worked Grew in the 90's Report Shows." *New York Times,* September 1, 2001.

Greven, Philip. 1972. *Four Generations.* Ithaca, N.Y.: Cornell University Press.

Hays, Sharon. 1996. *The Cultural Contradictions of Motherhood.* New Haven, Conn.: Yale University Press.

Hochschild, Arlie Russell. 1983. *The Managed Heart.* Berkeley and Los Angeles: University of California Press.

———. 1997. *The Time Bind.* New York: Metropolitan Books.

Kuttner, Robert. 1997. *Everything for Sale: The Virtues and Limits of Markets.* New York: Alfred A. Knopf.

McLanahan, Sara, and Gary Sandefur. 1994. *Growing Up with a Single Parent.* Cambridge: Harvard University Press.

Mintz, Steven, and Susan Kellogg. 1988. *Domestic Revolutions: A Social History of American Family Life.* New York: Free Press.

Putnam, Robert. 2001. *Bowling Alone.* Cambridge: Harvard University Press.

Sassen, Saskia. 2003. "Global Cities and Circuits of Survival." In Barbara Ehrenreich and Arlie Russell Hochschild, eds., *Global Woman.* New York: Metropolitan Books.

Schor, Juliet. 1998. *The Overspent American: Upscaling, Downshifting, and the New Consumer.* New York: Basic Books.

Sharpe, Rochelle. 2000. "Nannies on Speed Dial." *Business Week* (September 18): 108–10.

Shore, Bradd. 1996. *Culture in Mind: Cognition, Culture, and the Problem of Meaning.* New York: Oxford University Press.

Smelser, Neil. 1959. *Social Change in the Industrial Revolution: An Application of Theory to the British Cotton Industry.* Chicago: University of Chicago Press.

———. 1963. *The Sociology of Economic Life.* Englewood Cliffs, N.J.: Prentice-Hall.

———. 1998a. "Depth Psychology and the Social Order." In Smelser, *The Social Edges of Psychoanalysis,* pp. 197–217. Berkeley and Los Angeles: University of California Press.

———. 1998b. *The Social Edges of Psychoanalysis.* Berkeley and Los Angeles: University of California Press.

Swidler, Ann. 2001. *Talk of Love: How Culture Matters.* Chicago: University of Chicago Press.

Veblen, Thorstein. 1979. *The Theory of the Leisure Class.* New York: Penguin.

Zelizer, Viviana A. 1994. *The Social Meaning of Money.* New York: Basic Books.

———. 1996. "Payments and Social Ties." *Sociological Forum* 11 (3): 481–95.

———. 2000. "The Purchase of Intimacy." *Law and Social Inquiry* (fall).

Zerubavel, Eviatar. 1991. *The Fine Line: Making Distinctions in Everyday Life.* New York: Free Press.

Chapter 4

The Glass Cage

Flexible Work, Fragmented Consumption, Fragile Selves

Yiannis Gabriel

Even when individuals and groups try to break out of what Weber called the "iron cage" of rationality, they find themselves still caged, because they are again constricted by the narrowness of the alternatives they envision.
NEIL SMELSER, *"Vicissitudes of Work and Love in Anglo-American Society,"* 1998

It was said in ancient times that all roads led to Rome. Significantly, current sociological discussions of our times, whether labeled late modernity or post-modernity, lead back to Max Weber. While many different social thinkers appear to epitomize modernity—as critics, apologists, analysts, or exemplars—Weber marks the point of numerous radical departures that aim to theorize the transition from what was the high noon of modernity to whatever comes after.

In this chapter I engage with two such radical departures from the work of Weber, each of which seeks to capture something of the essence of contemporary society in juxtaposition to that high noon. In particular, I examine the discourse that starts with a critique of Weber's Protestant ethic and concludes that such an ethic is no longer hegemonic (even if we assume that at some point it was). Work, in contemporary society, is not regulated by a set of religious ideas and attitudes aimed at placing humans at the center of a moral universe; it is not even a means of attaining identity and selfhood. Second, I examine the proposition that, contrary to the disenchantment of the world brought about by modernity, we are currently part of a reenchantment of the world, at least in the West, signaled by an ever closer association between the management of organizations and the orchestration of collective fantasies and the venting of collective emotions, after the model of Disneyland. Fantasy and emotion, far from being exiled from contemporary culture by ever more rational processes, become the vital ingredients of a consumer-driven capitalism traveling across continents with the speed of electrons on the Internet. Indeed, fantasy and emotion have become driving forces in and out of organizations as individuals strive to attain precarious selfhoods in a society saturated with images, signs, and information.

These two discourses are interrelated, and numerous authors have developed diverse, interwoven lines of argument. All the same, I focus especially on two writers who have made important and complementary contributions to these discourses, Richard Sennett and George Ritzer. I argue that both offer sharp analyses of contemporary societies, but that both underestimate certain tendencies which run counter to their core theses. They both end up with highly individualistic accounts, arguing that for different reasons new capitalism increases freedom at the price of insecurity, meaninglessness, and isolation. I then use some of Smelser's arguments as a corrective to show that even a society like ours is characterized by a fundamental ambivalence between freedom and community, dependence and independence. This view permits a less one-dimensional prognostication of the future than those afforded by Sennett's and Ritzer's analyses. The core thesis here is that the abatement of Weber's iron law of rationality has exposed us neither to the freedom of a garden of earthly delights nor to the desolation of an anomic law of the jungle. Instead, I propose, the iron cage is being replaced by new forms of entrapment, for which I offer the metaphor of a glass cage.

Is there a massive and irreversible discontinuity that separates our time from the time to which we now refer as modernity? And if such a discontinuity exists, is it a material discontinuity, marked by radically different technologies, economic relations, international institutions, forms of production and consumption, and political formations and organizations? Or is it, equally importantly, a discursive discontinuity, entailing radically different ways of talking about things, experiencing things, and theorizing about them? Is the preoccupation with discontinuity itself evidence of change or evidence of deeper continuity (le plus ça change . . .)? In addressing such questions, numerous authors have turned to the apparent contrast between the solidity of things modern and the apparent flux of things current. While modernity featured solid buildings, solid organizations, solid relations, solid selves, and solid signifiers, our times are characterized by flux, mutation, reinvention, and flexibility. To be sure, modernity, as all its great theorists emphasized, featured unprecedented changes—the emergence of cities, the erection of factories, the rise of the state, and the domination of scientific thinking and bureaucracy. But within modernity, the solidity of factories, organizations, selves, and concepts was a realistic project, and one frequently attained and celebrated. Not so in our times, when solidity is revealed as a mirage, an illusion that becomes unsustainable. Our thoughts, emotions, and experiences, as well as those furtive realities we encounter, are in constant flux, a flux that recalls the views of Cratylus, teacher of Plato and disciple of Heraclitus, who went one up on his teacher. Not only is everything in flux, he argued, but even the meaning of words is in flux, so there is little point in seeking to make sense of anything or to communicate with others. He is reported as having stopped talking, as simply moving his little finger when someone addressed him, maybe to indicate that he had heard a sound.

Flexibility, along with flux, fluidity, and flow, is one of the much vaunted qualities of our times. It applies to individuals, organizations, and even entire societies, suggesting an ability and a willingness not merely to adapt and change but to radically redefine themselves, to metamorphose into new entities. Flexibility is the opposite of rigidity, which, not accidentally, marks the chief quality of bureaucracy, Weber's enduring conceptual masterpiece and dominant organizational form of modernity. The flexible organization (variously referred to as a network, postmodern, post-Fordist, postbureaucratic, shamrock, etc.) has emerged as the antidote to Weberian bureaucracy, a concept of organization that does away with rigid hierarchies, procedures, products, and boundaries in favor of constant and continuous reinvention, redefinition, and mobility. Success, for such organizations, is not a terminus, a state of perfect stable equilibrium, but a process of irregularity, innovation, and disorder, in which temporary triumphs occur at the edge of the abyss and can never be regularized into blissful routine.

The flexible organization is currently hailed as an ideal organization type for today, as Weberian bureaucracy was held to be fifty years ago. Its characteristics are well described by Stewart Clegg:

> Where the modernist organization was rigid, postmodern organization is flexible. Where modernist consumption was premised on mass forms, postmodernist consumption is premised on niches. Where modernist organization was premised on technological determinism, postmodernist organization is premised on technological choices made possible through "de-dedicated" micro-electronic equipment. Where modernist organization and jobs were highly differentiated, demarcated and de-skilled, postmodernist organization and jobs are highly de-differentiated, de-demarcated and multiskilled. Employment relations as a fundamental relation of organization upon which has been constructed a whole discourse of the determinism of size as a contingency variable increasingly give way to more complex and fragmentary relational forms, such as subcontracting and networking. (1990: 181)

Many theorists have taken up the implications of flexible organizations for individuals at work. One of the most acute analyses has been offered by Richard Sennett in his book *The Corrosion of Character: The Personal Consequences of Work in the New Capitalism* (1998). Sennett argues that new flexible work arrangements promote a short-term, opportunistic outlook among employees, one that destroys trust and loyalty. Insecurity and fear of being on the edge of losing control are endemic. Careers become spasmodic and fragmented, their different steps failing to generate cohesive or integrated life stories. Exposed to intrusive monitoring of performance, employees feel constantly on trial, yet they are never sure of the goals at which they are aiming. There are no objective measures of what it means to do a good job, and those celebrated for their achievements one day easily find themselves on the receiving end of redundancy packages the next. The chameleon-like qualities of the new economy—constant job moves, no commitments, no sacrifices—are in opposition with traditional family values of duty, commitment, constancy, and caring. A generational gulf grows between parents and their children who find little to admire or respect in them. The result is a corrosion of moral character. In times past, moral character provided a sense of both continuity and constancy to the individual as well as anchoring him or her to a set of reciprocal relations of caring, obligation, and interdependence. Dependence comes to be seen as shameful, as evidence of personal failure, in a society where individuals need no one and are needed by no one.

Sennett illustrates his arguments with a few well-chosen case studies. In one of those lightning strikes of serendipity in an airport lounge, Sennett met Rico, the son of one of the characters of his earlier book *The Hidden Injuries of Class* (Sennett and Cobb 1973), a janitor who had worked throughout his life in pursuit of the American Dream. Rico, a seemingly successful consultant after four job changes in a few years, is deeply disenchanted. Unlike his father, whom Sennett had presented as a self divided between an institutional superstructure and an authentic inner person, Rico suffers from a decentered self, a self without a core. Money has not made him happy, and in his self-image he comes close to being what nineteenth-century Russians obsessed about, the man whom no one needs. His rage is hardly articulated as he finds himself unable to offer himself as a role model to his children or even to relate with them at any level. Rico is truly a man with stories, but unlike his oppressed and humiliated father, a man without *a story*. The narrative of his life is just not storylike; it does not hold together.

Other case studies presented by Sennett involve the employees of a Boston bakery he had visited thirty years earlier. The hardworking Greeks, toiling in atrocious conditions, have been replaced by a transient mosaic of nationalities pointing mice on Windows screens, never coming into physical contact with flour or bread. Elsewhere, Sennett encounters the delegates of the Davos World Economic Forum, true Olympians oiling the wheels of global markets, and laid-off IBM employees, as they go through the usual process of shock, mourning, scapegoating, and final reconciliation with their predicament. Wherever he focuses, Sennett observes different elements of the same picture—flexibility, dictated by global markets and ever changing technologies, promotes opportunism, short-termism, and insecurity while destroying values, trust, community, and caring. A deep anxiety and insecurity permeate workplaces. This, by itself is not new. Earlier generations of employees worried: they worried because of the vagaries of the labor markets, social injustice, and lack of control over their fate. Today's employees, however, perceive themselves as having choices that can make the difference between success and failure. "I make my own choices; I take full responsibility for moving around so much," says Rico, who seems to abhor dependency above all else (Sennett 1998: 29).

Sennett offers a perceptive account of Weber's views on the Protestant work ethic, capturing the tragic predicament of its archetypal character—the "driven man" engaged in a ceaseless, yet ultimately futile, struggle of proving his moral worth through hard work against the immutable rigor of predestination. Against this, he sets the superficiality of present-day workplaces, with teams of employees engaged in furtive pursuits of value through the power of images, signs, and symbols. The old-fashioned work ethic, with its self-denial and future orientation, its claustrophobic organizations and hierarchic authority, is displaced by a work ethic in which only the present matters, one in which the organization becomes an arena for continuously mutating games in which individuals find themselves pitched against each other, individually or in teams. Hard work has not, of course, been transcended; on the contrary, individuals in offices, factories, and other workplaces work frenetically and hard for long hours, not in pursuit of an individual or organizational goal, but more as a desperate attempt to stay ahead in the game or, as Sennett fails to acknowledge, as an ostentatious attempt to display commitment for an organization for which they feel neither respect nor loyalty (Schwartz 1987; Epstein, Seron, et al. 1999; Gabriel and Schwartz 1999).

Frenetic activity becomes a defense against the prospect of failure, today's major taboo, which brings unalloyed shame on the loser. Hate of dependency, absence of compassion and caring, scorn for loyalty, and the elevation of choice into a supreme value are key features of this work ethic, sustained by psychological structures that are insecure, decentered, and continuously changing. Conspicuously absent from these structures are the supports of community, family, and legitimate authority. Trade unions, community bonds, religious groups, and even family ties have little to offer by way of compensation to the corroded character of the chameleon-individual, the flexible individual whose essential virtue is to respond to the corporate call for flexibility by denying himself or herself an inner core.

Sennett's deeply pessimistic book does not offer any prescriptions for the future, nor does it identify any dynamic for change; it concludes, against hope, that "a regime which provides human beings no deep reasons to care about one another cannot long preserve its legitimacy" (1998: 148). Yet the discontents that he describes, and in particular the chronic inability to form coherent identity narratives, are so profound that one wonders how societies, and especially North American society, have survived thus far without collapsing. George Ritzer's latest thesis offers a clear answer to this question.

Ritzer, well known for his McDonaldization thesis, is, in *Enchanting a Disenchanted World* (1999), as single-mindedly focused on consumption as Sennett is on work. Consumption, argues Ritzer, plays an ever increasing role in the lives of individuals, as a source of meaning, pleasure, and identity. It takes place in settings that "allow, encourage, and even compel us to consume so many of those goods and services" (2). These settings, which include theme parks, cruise ships, casinos, tourist resorts, sports venues, theaters, hotels, restaurants, and above all shopping malls, are referred to as means of consumption, or "cathedrals of consumption" to indicate their quasi-religious, enchanted qualities. They are part of a process that parallels McDonaldization (called by some "Disneyization"), which, thanks to TV and Internet shopping, now extends to the home, which is converted from an arena of interpersonal relations into a highly privatized consumption outpost.

Ritzer's central thesis is that today's management sets its eyes firmly, not on the toiling worker, but on the fantasizing consumer. What management does is furnish, in a highly rationalized manner, an endless stream of consumable fantasies inviting consumers to pick and choose, thus creating the possibility of reenchanting a disenchanted world through mass festivals in the new cathedrals of consumption. Ritzer offers prodigious illustrations of the ways in which consumption is constantly promoted, enhanced, and controlled in these new settings not so much through direct advertising as through indirect means such as spatial arrangements, uses of language, images, signs, festivals, simulations, and extravaganzas, as well as the cross-fertilization ("implosion") of products and images. Above all, consumption gradually colonizes every public and private domain of social life, which become saturated with fantasizing, spending, and discarding opportunities. Thus, schools, universities, and hospitals are converted from sober, utilitarian institutions into main terrains of consumption, treating their constituents as customers, offering them a profusion of merchandise and indulging their fantasies and caprices. Hyperconsumption is a state of affairs where every social experience is mediated by market mechanisms.

Ritzer is far too alert to the cruel, exploitative, pervasive, and invasive qualities of contemporary consumption to join the current choruses of postmodern celebrants. Nevertheless, his account is considerably more upbeat than some of his earlier work. Along with Zygmunt Bauman (1993), he argues that postmodernity creates the possibilities of a real "reenchantment" of the world after modernity's struggle to rationalize it. Human emotion, spontaneity, and irrationality regain their legitimacy. Mystery, magic, and sentimentality become vital cultural ingredients sustained in a highly rational manner by consumerism. Ritzer's conclusions amount to an assertion of the inevitability of the ever-escalating hegemony of consumerism:

The alternatives to consumption all seem retrogressions into a past that is not likely to be resuscitated. As far as the economy may plunge in the midst of the deepest of recessions or depressions, it will recover and the consumer, as well as the means of consumption needed to help generate and satisfy the needs of the consumer, are likely to enjoy a rebirth that will make them even more than they are today. Those who worry about consumer society, consumerism, the cathedrals of consumption, and the increasingly dizzying array of commodities have genuine concerns and many battles to fight, but the most immediate issue is how to live a more meaningful life within a society increasingly defined by consumption. (1999: 217)

In a strange way Ritzer, in this particular work, appears as oblivious to the discontents of the workplace as does Sennett to the apparent consolations of consumption. But ultimately the pictures generated by each author could be said to complement each other. It is because of the discontents of contemporary flexible workplaces that individuals turn to consumption for meaning, identity, and fulfillment. And it is because of the corrosion of character that a culture of narcissism dominated by image, fantasy, and superficiality is on the ascendant. At every level, one book stops at precisely the point where the other takes off. Consider, for instance, the reconfiguration of emotion in our time. Sennett observes, analyses, and critiques the de-emotionalization of family and work lives, only for Ritzer to point out the new territories of emotion, the cathedrals of consumption. Or consider Sennett's observation that contemporary individuals need no one and are needed by no one. Ritzer's corollary is that needs and desires are increasingly met not in the sphere of human contacts and community but through the bond-free mechanisms of the markets. The important thing is that both authors are talking about the same individuals—Sennett's insecure, fragmented, deracinated, chameleon-like employees are Ritzer's fantasizing, demanding, deciding, and spending consumers. Viewers of the award-winning film *American Beauty* will have no difficulty recognizing both sides of the argument in the symbolically impoverished, image-dominated lives of its suburban characters. The film vividly portrays the precarious work identities of its adult protagonists, the generational gulf between parents and children that is transcended only through sexual fantasy, and the universal obsessions with house interiors, video images, and the physical body.

Where both approaches stop short is in recognizing forces that run counter to their main theses. Work flexibility (for which read insecurity and impoverishment) and hyperconsumption march on, uncontested, feeding off each other. The accounts of both employees and consumers that are presented are slightly monochromatic, and the reader begins to long for a discussion of ambivalence, conflict, and resistance. Identity and character may be fashioned not only through submission to the dominant forces of the workplace or the shopping mall, well described in these two books, but also in opposition to such forces. Today's employees, like today's consumers, may be managed, prodded, seduced, controlled. Yet, their response cannot be taken for granted. Consumers can and do, in everyday practices, dodge, subvert, or evade the controlling strategies of manufacturers, planners, and advertisers. Employees, for their part, display a bewildering range of responses to managerial calls for flexibility: at times they comply willingly or ritualistically, and at other times fear and insecurity dominate their responses, but frequently they show ingenuity in supplanting and contesting management discourses, turning them into objects of amusement, cynicism, or confrontation.

As we saw, both approaches mark radical departures from core Weberian themes. Sennett offers a sophisticated reading of the Protestant ethic to highlight its degeneration into meaningless, frenetic workaholic activity, which fails to feed identity narratives. Ritzer's core thesis is that postmodernity has created a counterpoint to modernity: reenchantment, albeit at a cost, in lieu of rational disenchantment. Both authors agree that for different reasons new capitalism increases freedom at the price of insecurity, meaninglessness, and isolation. Another eminent Weberian commentator, Smelser, has taken a more nuanced view, arguing that all societies, including ours, are characterized by a fundamental ambivalence between independence and dependence. This view permits a less monochrome analysis than those afforded by Sennett's and Ritzer's discussions.

Smelser's work in many ways prefigures the arguments put forward by Sennett and Ritzer. He captures the nervous, transient qualities of what he calls "the age of temporariness, the age of intermittency, or perhaps the age of sequential bonding" (1998b: 180). Unlike Sennett, however, he views short-term bonds, like more traditional bonds, as generating ambivalence, a set of "powerful, persistent, unresolvable, volatile, generalizable, anxiety-provoking" emotions that are a feature of the human condition (177). The value in Smelser's approach lies in his ability to demonstrate that ambivalence was a feature of both Weber's "driven man" and his contemporary successor, the result of a core existential dilemma between freedom and community, dependence and independence. Loyalty, according to this view, is not an all or nothing affair, but there are possibilities of limited exit or opting out that do not supplant social bonds. Even temporary employees find themselves socially bound with their employers. Using Albert O. Hirschman's 1970 concept of *voice*, Smelser argues that individuals acknowledge the shortcomings and frustrations of such bonds, working out their ambivalence in public and incorporating themselves into institutional arrangements.

This approach is entirely consistent with the view of employees using a wide repertoire of tactics—symbolic, political, and practical—to resist the controlling strategies of their employers, a view that Sennett himself had promoted in his earlier work (Sennett and Cobb 1973). To Sennett's view that today's workplace denies employees a voice, that it simply mutes their hopes and their discontents, depriving them of the possibility of arriving at a narrative constituted as life story, Smelser's approach suggests that, in spite of the formidable forces intent on silencing them, individuals and groups in today's organizations strive but eventually discover voices of their own: "Voice . . . is intermediate; some degree of loyalty is presupposed, and some degree of alienation and opposition—a wish to exit, as it were—is acknowledged. Some arena is established for 'working out' public ambivalence and conflict—with varying effectiveness—and 'working it into' institutional arrangements. . . . Voice is manifested in democratic institutions" (1998b: 188). Voice, then, is not a consequence of dependence (as Sennett's analysis might lead us to believe), but a means for expressing and working through ambivalence: "Most democratic institutions appear as 'voices'— available mechanisms to work these ambivalences through, continuously if never completely satisfactorily" (189). This may not be a confident voice narrating a simple tale of achievement, success, survival, and sacrifice, but it is a voice that allows different constructions of identity to be experimented with, developed, modified, rejected, and reconstructed. These mutations are not external to the project of identity, but define this project.

To be sure, today's capitalism deploys subtler, more pervasive, and more invasive strategies of control, including cultural and ideological controls (emphasizing the importance of customer service, quality, and image; affirming the business enterprise as an arena for heroic or spiritual accomplishments, etc.), structural controls (continuous measurements and benchmarking, flatter organizational hierarchies, etc.), technological controls (electronic surveillance of unimaginable sophistication), spatial controls (open-plan offices, controlled accesses), and so forth than it did a generation ago. Those influenced by the work of Foucault have developed the idea of discursive controls that operate through language, labeling, classification, and so forth, which are invisible but unyielding (Townley 1993; Grey 1994; Knights and Vurdubakis 1994; Marx 1995, 1999; Wilkinson, Morris, et al. 1995).

In spite of such formidable disciplinary mechanisms, today's workplace creates, if anything, even greater possibility of voice (and here I am moving beyond Smelser's conceptualization), with employees displaying a bewildering range of responses that qualify, subvert, disregard, or resist managerial calls for flexibility. At times they comply willingly, grudgingly, or ritualistically, at other times fear and insecurity dominate their responses, but frequently they show ingenuity in supplanting and contesting management discourses, turning them into objects of amusement, cynicism, or confrontation (Jermier, Nord, and Knights 1994; Sturdy 1998; Gabriel 1999a). Thus within formal organizations, there are spaces that are unmanaged and unmanageable; in these spaces, individuals can fashion identities that amount neither to conformity nor to rebellion, but that are infinitely more complex and rich than those deriving from official organizational practices (Gabriel 1995).

What we have here is a picture where traditional rational or bureaucratic controls are being replaced by an array of controls that operate through language, emotion, space, and exposure. The demise of the iron cage of rationality can be seen as leading to a different form of entrapment, an entrapment not as rigid as that effected by traditional bureaucracy but one that affords greater ambiguity and irony, a *glass cage* perhaps, an enclosure characterized by total exposure to the eye of the customer, the fellow employee, the manager. The very visibility of the glass cage to the unforgiving gaze places severe limits on the overt control that managers are able to exercise, with employees frequently finding themselves in the position of children capable of embarrassing their parents in the presence of strangers. Why a glass cage? Undoubtedly, the glass cage suggests the chief quality of Foucault's Panopticon, that curious combination of Catholic obsession with the omnipotent eye of God and Protestant preoccupation with clean efficiency. Like the Panopticon, the glass cage acts as a metaphor for the formidable machinery of contemporary surveillance, one machine that deploys all kinds of technologies, electronic, spatial, psychological, and cultural. Appearances are paramount; image is what people are constantly judged by. But unlike the Panopticon, the glass cage also suggests that the modern employee is part of a cast exposed to the critical gaze of the customer, with all the kicks, excitements, and frustrations that this implies. It evokes an element of exhibitionism and display, the employee becoming part of the organizational brand on show, a brand easily tarnished or contaminated by the activities of a few whistleblowers or disenchanted employees, but a brand that ennobles and uplifts all who are part of it. It also evokes the fundamental ambivalence in the nature of much contemporary work—an ambivalence between the anxiety of continuous exposure and the narcissistic self-satisfaction of being part of a winning team or formula.

While formal rationality is the chief force behind Weber's iron cage, the glass cage emphasizes the importance of emotional displays and appearances. In particular, it highlights the emotional labor (the "smile," the "look") that has become part of the work of ever-increasing segments of the workforce (Hochschild 1983), an emotional labor that is not merely external (i.e., discovering emotional displays suitable for the requirements of different social situations) but also *internal.* That is, this effort is spent in coping with conflicts, contradictions, and ambivalences and in keeping some sense of order in potentially chaotic emotional states, such as those highlighted by Smelser. The glass cage suggests both the rhetorical "transparency" and "openness" of the contemporary workplace, but also the discretion and fragility of contemporary control systems. Unlike an iron cage, which frustrates all attempts at escape with its brutish and inflexible force, a glass cage is discreet, unobtrusive, at times even invisible—it seeks to hide the reality of entrapment rather than display it, always inviting the idea or the fantasy that it may be breached, even if at the price of serious potential injury. The image of such a cage suggests that it may not be a cage at all but a wrapping box, a glass palace, or the Louvre pyramid, a container aimed at highlighting the uniqueness of what it contains rather than constraining or oppressing it.

Smelser's work also prefigures several of Ritzer's arguments. Reading his classic essay "Collective Myths and Fantasies: The Myth of the Good Life in California" (1998a), one swiftly realizes that the myth of California has mutated into a generic fantasy of consumer society. California, as Smelser argues, represents a land to which people "escape"; it stands for what is new, for gold, for plenty, and the good life; like all myths, the myth of California is a collective fantasy, and a key feature of this fantasy—in contrast to the rigors of the old country, the Protestant ethic, and the reality principle in its different guises—is that it is a place where *success comes easy:* "Perhaps the most dramatic elaboration [of the California myth] was that of the Hollywood myth, which added the element of instant exhibitionism to that of instant narcissism—the magical rise to stardom with the world at one's feet. The magic includes also the notion of being 'discovered' and plucked from obscurity by a powerful director" (1998a: 117). Note how astutely Smelser identifies the shifting meaning of success, from the product of hard work, achievement, and heroism to the magic of "being discovered," which involves nothing more than luck, self-presentation, and finding oneself at the right place at the right time. This recalls the "chameleon qualities" highlighted by Sennett, only in reverse—whereas the chameleon blends with its environment, the star, like gold in the eye of the prospector, shines persistently. This difficulty of displaying chameleon-like flexibility—willingness to play any part, to do any job, to work any patch—while also boasting unique star qualities seems to define the predicament of the individual under the sway of the Hollywood myth. The psychoanalytic configuration of the myth is a liberation of the pleasure principle at the expense of the reality principle (this is the fantasy of "being discovered") and an unleashing of narcissism (rather than heroic individualism—the trademark of modernity) combined with boundless exhibitionism, the ego that wishes to be admired for who he or she is rather than for what he or she has achieved. (See Gabriel 1999b.)

This brings us exactly to Ritzer's cathedrals of consumption, those glass palaces of fantasy, fun, and display; California may have been their spiritual birthplace, but they are now ubiquitous globally. The cages of consumption, like the workplace cages, are made of glass. Glass is a hard and fragile medium, providing an invisible barrier, allowing the insider to see outside and the outsider to see inside. It is also a distorting medium in which light is reflected and refracted, creating illusions and false images. Finally, glass is a framing medium—its mere presence defines that which lies behind it as something worthy of attention, protection, and display. The glass cage of consumption entails deliberate display; it is a place where the gaze of the prospector meets the look of the prospect. In this glass cage, new fashion trends can be spotted, new badges can be identified, new lifestyles can be explored, and new identities can be experimented with. Viewing the spaces of consumption as glass cages in their own right highlights the subtle forms of coercion, enticement, and control exercised over the consumer under the illusion of choice and freedom. Like the docile queues of Disneyland, once enticed into the cathedrals of consumption, consumers are captive. They have no choice but to observe, to look, to desire, to choose, and to buy. As Ritzer argues, "People are lured to the cathedrals of consumption by the fantasies they promise to fulfill and then kept there by a variety of rewards and constraints" (1999: 28). Of course, glass cages look quite different to those outside; they look shining, glamorous, and full of enticing objects. Those denied access, through their lack of resources, mobility, looks, or whatever, feel truly excommunicated. To them, being inside the cage represents real freedom. As Bauman (1988) has forcibly argued, the new poor are those "failed consumers" who end up outside the world of consumption, having the welfare state make choices on their behalf. For those inside the cage, on the other hand, the hungry faces of those outside is a constant reminder that there are far worse places in which to be. Inside the cage, too, consumers are frequently separated from objects they cherish by invisible barriers created by the limits of their buying powers—these are cages within cages.

One of the most important and innovative facets of Smelser's treatment of the California myth is his gradual unmasking of the myth's shadow—the downside of easy success, narcissism, image, and fantasy. This entails cautionary tales from the past, such as the demise of the Donner party and the San Francisco earthquake and the endless examples of California dreams turned into nightmares (overdosing film stars, vast social inequalities, health epidemics, racial conflicts, etc.), as well as enduring fears of retribution in the future. Glass structures, palaces, and cages may seem immune to wear and tear but are notoriously susceptible to fracture and collapse. Cathedrals of consumption are nowhere near as enduring as those Gothic cathedrals of the past; nor do the rewards that they afford offer a permanent salvation to the human spirit. We are once again looking at ambivalence, which characterizes our experience of even the most attractive and glamorous myth. And the ambivalence regarding the myth of California stems from the enduring psychological grip of those older myths of hard work, self-control, sacrifice, and altruism that characterize the Protestant ethic. The myth of easy life and success then turns into a hubris, inviting its nemesis. Smelser observes that neither the myth of California nor the countermyths of puritanism are fresh any longer:

> There is something stale about all of them, and I think that staleness stems from our own realization of inappropriateness; new solutions do not seem to be forthcoming or even suggested by that family of myths. We keep running around the same sets of mythological tracks. It would be foolish to envision a radical break with the dualism of a mythical past that has been part of our psychic structure for so many centuries. But given its apparently increasing irrelevance, I would, personally, hope that we might expand our horizons for some more appropriate mythical alternatives in the decades to come. (1998a: 123)

If such myths have lost their ability to grip our imaginations, it is probably because they have, like so many others, been appropriated, normalized, globalized, and routinized. The myth of California has become commodified, a managed fantasy, like those that Ritzer has highlighted in his work. But the hegemony of such fantasies is not unopposed. Once again, Smelser's use of the concept of voice suggests a way of looking at the dynamics of the glass cages of consumption in a richer light. Today's consumers, like today's employees, may be managed, prodded, seduced, controlled. Yet, their response cannot be taken for granted. Consumers can and do, in everyday practices, dodge, subvert, or evade the controlling strategies of manufacturers, planners, and advertisers. The cathedrals of consumption are frequently defaced, modified, redefined, or ignored, just as workplaces are (de Certeau 1984; Fiske 1989; Gabriel and Lang 1995). Consumers, if anything, are becoming increasingly unmanageable, eccentric, and paradoxical. Casualization of work and career reinforces casualization of consumption. Consumers increasingly lead precarious and uneven existences, one day enjoying unexpected boons and the next sinking to bare subsistence. Consumption itself becomes fragmented, spasmodic, and episodic—consumers may, at one moment, be seduced by images and slavishly seek to emulate them, while at the next they may rebel against them, distort them, and subvert them. They may crave difference one moment, and the next yearn for similarity and sameness. They may display loyalty and then disloyalty to the same brands. They may act purely in self-interest and then show great concern for the environment, Third World exploitation, and social inequalities. They may be driven by uninhibited materialism and then suddenly turn to spiritual quests. Identities themselves become less centered on consistent tastes, values, and images. Fads, fashions, and tastes become ever arbitrary, the connections between signs and signifiers fleeting.

The argument, then, is that, like today's producers, today's consumers do not find it easy to discover their voice; and when they discover it, it is often a voice that talks in paradoxes, ambiguities, and contradictions. Their life stories are not fixed—that is, not a constant pilgrimage to the cathedrals of consumption—nor are they as simple as the California myth would have it. As Bauman has argued, the model of the pilgrim ill suits the contemporary consumer, who is more of a tourist organizing his or her life around particular episodes, games, or experiences:

> In the life-game of the postmodern consumers the rules of the game keep changing in the course of playing. The sensible strategy is therefore to keep each game short—so that a sensibly played game of life calls for the splitting of one big all-embracing game with huge stakes into a series of brief and narrow games with small ones. . . . To keep the game short means to beware long-term commitments. To refuse to be "fixed" one way or the other. Not to get tied to the place. Not to wed one's life to one vocation only. Not to swear consistency and loyalty to anything and anybody. Not to *control* the future, but to *refuse to mortgage* it: to take care that the consequences of the game do not outlive the past to bear on the present. (1996: 24, emphasis in the original)

This, then, seems to parallel the life-game of postmodern producers, whose strategies are summed up as entailing flexibility, reinvention, and movement, in short as amounting to tactics. Tactics are not planned in advance, nor do they serve an overall design, but they unravel as life does, with its accidents, misfortunes, and serendipities. It is out of such episodes that all of us construct and reconstruct our fragile selves, moving from glass cage to glass cage, at times feeling anxiously trapped by it, at others feeling energized and appreciated, and at others depressed and despondent.

Let us summarize the argument. I started by presenting two theories that engage with long-standing Weberian themes. Sennett argues that the Protestant work ethic has dissolved under the regime of the flexible workplace with its demands for adaptable, quiescent employees, its replacement of visible, tangible work with manipulation of images and signs, and its supplanting of the traditional values of loyalty, sacrifice, and long-term commitment. The result is a corrosion of character, with an attendant inability to construct meaningful life narratives and identities. Ritzer, for his part, highlights the continuous shift from work to consumption as a source of meaning and identity, identifying the cathedrals of consumption as spaces where consumers are lured and enticed with a profusion of well-orchestrated and minutely managed fantasies. He argues that this represents a reenchantment of the world, thus undoing the disenchantment brought about by rationalizing modernity. This reenchantment encourages individuals to express themselves by embracing lifestyles, icons, and signs. It is itself the product of rationalization, albeit one in which rational calculation and planning are applied to spectacle, image, and experience. I argued that both of these approaches, compelling as they are, tend to present too monochromatic an account of contemporary culture. Using ideas from Smelser, notably the enduring ambivalence of individuals when presented with the existential dilemma of community versus freedom, and dependence versus independence, I argued that both flexible workplaces and cathedrals of consumption represent more fragile, contestable, and multivalent terrains than anticipated. Using the metaphor of the glass cage, I suggested that both pose certain unique constraints (quite distinct from those we encounter at the high noon of modernity), generate certain distinct discontents, and afford certain unique consolations. Shared features of the glass cage of work and the glass cage of consumption include an emphasis on display, an invisibility of constraints, a powerful illusion of choice, a glamorization of image, and an ironic question mark as to whether freedom lies inside or outside the cage. Above all, there is an ambiguity as to whether the glass is a medium of entrapment or a beautifying frame. It is tempting to argue that the two glass cages are after all the same.

The typical McDonald's restaurant offers an example of where the two are brought remarkably close together—a glass cage for employees and customers alike. Employees develop their own survival mechanisms within them, testing the rules, evading the managerial gaze, and engaging in diverse attempts of turning work into a game (Leidner 1993). Customers, for their part, may seek to use the spaces in ways consistent with their traditions and needs, different from those for which they were designed. Thus, describing McDonald's customers in Korea, Sangmee Bak observes that "these consumers are creatively transforming the [McDonald's] restaurants into local institutions" (1997: 160). Moreover, many customers of these restaurants are employees in their leisure time, whose experience of the glass cage is one of both work and consumption.

It may be objected that, unlike McDonald's, numerous workplaces resist the glass cage metaphor by staying out of the public eye, quietly exploiting their employees' physical labor with no need for display and emotional labor. It may indeed be premature to argue that all of modernity's iron cages have been dismantled and displaced by postmodern glass substitutes. Yet, a video camera surreptitiously smuggled into a sweatshop can shatter a company's image and undo the work of millions of dollars worth of advertising, a leaked internal memo can virtually demolish a corporate colossus, and a small band of environmental activists acting tactically in front of television cameras can bring a multinational to its knees. When the goings-on in the Oval Office of the White House can be rehearsed in minuscule detail in front of the entire nation, it may well be that the era of the iron cage has finally given way to the era of the glass cage.

Chameleons cannot have exciting stories to narrate. Their lives are devoid of both great heroism and great suffering; one suspects that the most exciting things they may be able to narrate are incidents of close escapes. They may also suffer from a certain degree of identity confusion or crisis, unless they can accept the fact that theirs is a skin of changing colors. Not surprisingly, then, Sennett argues that today's human chameleons have trouble constructing coherent and attractive life narratives. They may dream that one day they will be spotted by some roving director from Hollywood or Silicon Valley, but in truth theirs are lives of episodes, in the original sense, inserts into the action that do not alter the central plot. Boons and reverses succeed each other for no particular reason and with no end in sight. There are regular visits to cathedrals of consumption but no lasting solace. However, if we listen to Smelser, we begin to get a richer, more complex, and more ambivalent picture. People across the ages have struggled with certain core dilemmas. Even those of earlier generations may have lacked the coherent life narratives that we now so comfortably attribute to them. They too led lives of ambivalence, confusion, and anxiety, dreamed of freedom even as they craved for community, and made choices little knowing their long-term implications. Their constraints were different from those of our age; their discontents too may have been different, as indeed were their consolations. But in the last resort, the fragility of human experience is not the result of the flexible workplaces and fragmented consumptions of our age, but rather the product of its confrontation with different cages across historical eras.

REFERENCES

Bak, S. 1997. "McDonald's in Seoul: Food Choices, Identity, and Nationalism." In J. L. Watson, ed., *Golden Arches East: McDonald's in East Asia*, pp. 136–60. Stanford, Calif.: Stanford University Press.

Bauman, Z. 1988. *Freedom*. Milton Keynes, U.K.: Open University Press.

———. 1993. *Postmodern Ethics*. Oxford: Basil Blackwell.

———. 1996. "From Pilgrim to Tourist—or a Short History of Identity." In S. Hall and P. Du Gay, eds., *Questions of Cultural Identity*, pp. 18–36. London: Sage.

Clegg, S. 1990. *Modern Organizations: Organization Studies in the Postmodern World*. London: Sage.

de Certeau, M. 1984. *The Practice of Everyday Life*. Berkeley and Los Angeles: University of California Press.

Epstein, C. F., C. Seron, et al. 1999. *The Part-Time Paradox: Time Norms, Professional Life, Family, and Gender*. New York: Routledge.

Fiske, J. 1989. *Understanding Popular Culture*. London: Unwin Hyman.

Gabriel, Y. 1995. "The Unmanaged Organization: Stories, Fantasies, and Subjectivity." *Organization Studies* 16 (3): 477–501.

———. 1999a. "Beyond Happy Families: A Critical Re-Evaluation of the Control-Resistance-Identity Triangle." *Human Relations* 52 (2): 179–203.

———. 1999b. *Organizations in Depth: The Psychoanalysis of Organizations*. London: Sage.

Gabriel, Y., and T. Lang. 1995. *The Unmanageable Consumer: Contemporary Consumption and Its Fragmentation*. London: Sage.

Gabriel, Y., and H. S. Schwartz. 1999. "Organizations, from Concepts to Constructs:

Psychoanalytic Theories of Character and the Meaning of Organization." *Administrative Theory and Praxis* 21 (2): 176–91.

Grey, C. 1994. "Career as a Project of the Self and Labour Process Discipline." *Sociology* 28 (2): 479–97.

Hirschman, A. O. 1970. *Exit, Voice, and Loyalty: Responses to Decline in Firms, Organizations, and States.* Cambridge: Harvard University Press.

Hochschild, A. R. 1983. *The Managed Heart: Commercialization of Human Feeling.* Berkeley and Los Angeles: University of California Press.

Jermier, J. M., W. Nord, and D. Knights. 1994. *Resistance and Power in Organizations.* London: Routledge.

Knights, D., and T. Vurdubakis. 1994. "Foucault, Power, Resistance, and All That." In J. M. Jermier, W. Nord, and D. Knights, eds., *Resistance and Power in Organizations,* pp. 167–98. London: Routledge.

Leidner, R. 1993. *Fast Food, Fast Talk: Service Work and the Routinization of Everyday Life.* Berkeley and Los Angeles: University of California Press.

Marx, G. T. 1995. "The Engineering of Social Control: The Search for the Silver Bullet." In J. Hagan and R. Peterson, eds., *Crime and Inequality,* pp. 235–46. Stanford, Calif.: Stanford University Press.

———. 1999. "Measuring Everything That Moves: The New Surveillance at Work." In I. Simpson and R. Simpson, eds., *The Workplace and Deviance,* pp. 165–89. Greenwich, Conn.: JAI Press.

Ritzer, G. 1999. *Enchanting a Disenchanted World: Revolutionizing the Means of Consumption.* Thousand Oaks, Calif.: Pine Forge Press.

Schwartz, H. S. 1987. "Anti-Social Actions of Committed Organizational Participants: An Existential Psychoanalytic Perspective." *Organization Studies* 8 (4): 327–40.

Sennett, R. 1998. *The Corrosion of Character: The Personal Consequences of Work in the New Capitalism.* New York: Norton.

Sennett, R., and J. Cobb. 1973. *The Hidden Injuries of Class.* New York: Random House.

Smelser, N. J. 1998a. "Collective Myths and Fantasies: The Myth of the Good Life in California." In N. J. Smelser, *The Social Edges of Psychoanalysis,* pp. 111–24. Berkeley and Los Angeles: University of California Press.

———. 1998b. "The Rational and the Ambivalent in the Social Sciences." In N. J. Smelser, *The Social Edges of Psychoanalysis,* pp. 168–96. Berkeley and Los Angeles: University of California Press.

———. 1998c. "Vicissitudes of Work and Love in Anglo-American Society." In N. J. Smelser, *The Social Edges of Psychoanalysis,* pp. 93–110. Berkeley and Los Angeles: University of California Press.

Sturdy, A. 1998. "Customer Care in a Consumer Society: Smiling and Sometimes Meaning It?" *Organization* 5 (1): 27–53.

Townley, B. 1993. "Foucault, Power/Knowledge, and Its Relevance for Human Resource Management." *Academy of Management Review* 18 (3): 518–45.

Wilkinson, B., J. Morris, et al. 1995. "The Iron Fist in the Velvet Glove: Management and Organization in Japanese Manufacturing Transplants in Wales." *Journal of Management Studies* 32 (6): 819–30.

PART II

Social Structure

Introduction

Gary T. Marx

The five chapters in this section treat highly varied topics—the limits of rational choice, types of exchange, religion, trust, and higher education. Yet to varying degrees they all directly reflect six lessons learned from Neil Smelser as a teacher and scholar.

These lessons are (1) that social analysis must avoid reductionism as well as "parallel trackism," in which analytic borders are impenetrable; (2) that we must attend to different levels of social analysis; (3) that, where possible, we must identify reciprocal influences and integrate levels, paradigms, and specialized theories; (4) that we must generate abstract analytic categories, whether treated as single dimensions or combined to form typologies and ideal types; (5) that we must apply middle-range approaches rather than a general theory to the richness of an ever-changing empirical world; and (6) that we must consider both social structure and social process and recognize that, while behavior (whether of individuals, groups, or institutions) is contingent on prior (highly variable but not unlimited) social circumstances, it is also fluid and dynamic, reflecting unique local circumstances and individual agency. A related idea is that the very social and cultural structures that give legitimacy and stability to behavior are subject to inherent tensions and contradictions, resulting in specific forms of deviance, conflict, change, and varied interpretations of objectively similar behavior.

In contrast to the academic stables overflowing with one-trick ponies, whether of explanation, level of analysis, method, or a preferred focus on social order or social change, Neil Smelser has encouraged pluralism and, where possible, the integration of diverse intellectual perspectives. His tent is substantively inclusive but not indiscriminately so. Its supports rest on standards of excellence, theoretical imagination, and the search for connections. When we unreflectively restrict our focus, our careers may be advanced, but we risk missing interconnections and do not see how barely visible cultural assumptions and limitations of time and place may limit our understanding.

The need for tolerance and the need to avoid reducing explanation to one perspective—whether involving rational choice, power, psychoanalysis, culture, or social structure—require no justification within the better sectors of sociology. Yet intellectual breadth and pluralism, at their best, need not imply the spineless relativism characteristic of contemporary approaches imported from the humanities, or the isolation from each other and failure to seek interaction effects and integration that currently characterize many specialized approaches.

There is a wonderful scene in the film *Chinatown* in which Jack Nicholson tries to determine how Faye Dunaway is related to a young woman in her family. At first Dunaway responds, "She's my sister," then "She's my daughter," and under Nicholson's grilling she continues to say, "She's my sister," then "She's my daughter." Finally, in response to Nicholson's demanding which it is, she replies, "Both," indicating an atypical relationship with her father. The nonbinary nature of that encounter illustrates a central theme of Neil's career: careful and systematic thought and empirical inquiry may suggest that seemingly rival approaches to social reality can each be helpful and advance our understanding through integration. Where you stand depends on where you sit, and it is important to move around.

The first three chapters in part II deal with rational choice, a theme that has been central to much of Neil Smelser's work, from his first book, *Economy and Society* (1956), with Talcott Parsons, to his 1997 presidential address on ambivalence.

Alberto Martinelli critiques rational choice in both its traditional economic and contemporary sociological forms. Rational choice is limited to a particular subset of questions. Among the limitations of the traditional rational choice approach are favoring the actions of individuals over social structures; ignoring the role of cultural factors in structuring markets and even rationality itself; the failure to attend to the source of preferences; and the exclusion of expressive, nonrational, and irrational forms of social action and symbolic meanings.

Martinelli also notes limitations in the more sociological approaches, such as that of James Coleman. Among these limitations is this one: models of free choice do not apply to situations where free choice does not exist, as in the case of slavery. There are no "natural persons"; rather, there are persons responding to historically specific cultural values and institutions, and even rational action relies on nonrational assumptions. Rational choice also has difficulties with the problem of social order, with accounting for social change and innovation and for macro-level questions involving collectivities and institutions. As Smelser argued, rational choice is most useful under those social conditions that institutionalize its basic characteristics and conditions, such as market commodities.

Consistent with the explicit and implicit messages of Neil's work in this area over almost five decades, Martinelli notes that the subject matter of sociology requires a variety of middle-range conceptual approaches, rather than a single unified general theory. From the plethora of available perspectives, the sociologist should choose those most appropriate to the question and level of analysis.

The next chapter, by Stephen Warner, also draws on the theoretical power of ambivalence in accounting for aspects of religious attitudes and behavior. Contrary to the claims of theorists looking at (and often from) Europe, Warner notes that religion, particularly in the United States, has not withered away in the face of the cultural pluralism and scientific rationality that were supposed to threaten its viability. Warner's statement of a "new paradigm" for the understanding of U.S. religion points to a key difference in social organization between Europe and the United States—the constitutive disestablishment of religion in the latter—that helps account for the variation in religious vitality. In effect, there has been an "open market" for religion in the this country for two centuries that allows churches to flourish by reflecting and engaging the culture of their local and subcultural constituents.

In the spirit of Smelser's ecumenical approach and analysis, Warner does not reject the power of rational choice perspectives. He points out that designating the U.S. religious system as an "open market" makes use of rational choice theory but does not represent an exclusive commitment to it. An adequate understanding of religion requires attention to both rational choice and ambivalence and the specification of the conditions under which one, rather than the other, may be more appropriate. Thus a rational choice "supply side" strategy is helpful to understand the activities of religious organizations (including contemporary "seeker churches"), but the premise of ambivalent motivation recommends itself for understanding the "demand side" of individual motivations behind religious behavior and attitudes. Especially when religion is a vestige of childhood dependence, analysts should expect that ambivalent motivations will deeply color its expression.

Viviana Zelizer expands on a phenomenon noted in Smelser's analysis of social change in the industrial revolution: the development of differentiated ties that cross household boundaries and involve household members in distinct forms of exchange. New forms of integration and differentiation involving what Zelizer calls "circuits of commerce" appear. These involve four elements: boundaries around transactions, ties among participants, a distinctive set of transfers or claims occurring within the ties, and distinctive transfer media.

Within the broad concept of circuits of commerce, Zelizer identifies three types of differentiated tie: corporate circuits, local currencies, and intimate circuits. In each of these we can see examples of the personal mixed with regularized media and transfers and ties that vary in intensity, scope, and durability.

Her analytic categories help us to see how individuals bridge the seemingly unbridgeable gap between social solidarity and monetized transactions and call attention to the complex interplay of monetary transfers and social ties—whether impersonal or intimate. Zelizer rejects the incompatibility usually declared to exist between the world of intimacy and that of impersonal rationality. She also rejects the reductionist view that this presumed separation is simply a special case of some more general principle, whether rationality, culture, or politics. Such approaches fail to deal with the degree of interconnection between various ties.

A precondition for many kinds of exchange is trust, since individuals often lack adequate information to make informed decisions. Robert Wuthnow offers a theoretical framework for situating trust in relation to the broad conception of social structure characterizing Neil Smelser's work. In this conception, norms and values are prominent. Wuthnow suggests a number of warrants for trust that reflect the norms of different social structures (e.g., sincerity, affinity, effectiveness, competence, and fairness). He also considers secondary warrants for explaining what goes wrong when trust is violated.

Wuthnow offers survey research data suggestive of some of the broader social norms with which trust is associated. He shows how the institutionalization of trust varies across contexts of professional-client relationships, local communities, and religion and seeks to account for this. In calling attention to trust as an aspect of the normative system, Wuthnow rejects the reductionist view that trust is only a matter of individual psychology or rational calculation.

Yet while drawing on the central Weberian idea that legitimations give stability to social structure over time, he also notes that the inherent tensions and contradictions of social structure are a source of change. Justifications for trust may vary between settled and unsettled times, as well as across institutional settings. Wuthnow equally rejects a rigid sociological determinism. While he emphasizes how social structures, which exist prior to the individual, pattern expectations, he is hardly a sociological determinist. Rather, he notes that behavior is partly a function of individual interpretation, calculation, and negotiation, as interacting individuals draw from a variety of cultural perspectives in strategically pursuing their ends.

Burton Clark focuses on social change in international higher education through an analysis of the organizational foundations of system and institutional capability. As his work, and that of some of Neil's other students, suggests, social change is ubiquitous and rooted in social structure. Social structure and social change cannot be understood apart from each other. Pressures for change are inherent in social organization, and the form of social organization conditions how people respond to change. Clark notes the usefulness of specifying levels of analysis. The university is uniquely bottom-heavy as an organizational type. Certainly macrostructures constrain and enable, but microstructures serve as the organizational basis for the work of universities. The proliferation and specialization of local departments and programs drive change under appropriate conditions.

Clark expands on Neil Smelser's concept of academic differentiation and joins it to Joseph Ben-David's idea of competition in higher education. This integrated and interactive approach yields stronger insights than would a focus on either one in isolation or as a single cause. Clark helps us to better understand why some universities succeed and others fail, and why some national systems of higher education do better at handling contradictory values and responding to change than others do. Extensively differentiated and competitive national systems are more successful than their opposites. Competition is possible in differentiated environments and serves to further differentiation. The lack of differentiation constrains because a single type of institution or discipline cannot offer the multiple competencies required of varied and changing environments. The lack of competition is likely to mean that institutions conform to traditional patterns and engrained mythologies. Competition can turn passivity into autonomy and the search for distinctive niches that give a comparative advantage.

Chapter 5

Rational Choice and Sociology

Alberto Martinelli

The question of rationality has been a major concern of Neil Smelser's theoretical investigation, evident in works ranging from *Economy and Society* (1956) to his presidential address to the American Sociological Association in 1997. In *Economy and Society,* Talcott Parsons and Smelser argue that economic rationality is the core of the value system of the economic subsystem. It is an empirical feature of the system, not a postulate as in standard economic theory. In social system theory, the idea of the rational applies at two levels: at the general societal level, it is a value among others and is ranked differently in different cultures. At the economic subsystem level, it refers to the effective implementation of the basic goal of this subsystem, that is, economic production. In its double meaning, economic rationality has both a universal aspect, related to one of the functional imperatives of the social system, and a culturally dependent aspect, since economic rationality is greater the more differentiated is the economy from other subsystems and the stronger is the force of economic values with regard to other values. Thus, in contemporary American society, the influence of economic rationality is greater than elsewhere. In my introduction to the Italian edition of *Economy and Society* (1970), I criticized the ambiguous characterization of rationality both as an empirical feature of different societies and as an analytical ingredient of any social system, since it conveys the idea that an historically specific economic organization, and its core values of efficiency and productivity, become functional requisites of any society, and that contemporary American society represents the most advanced stage of an evolutionary process.

Forty years later, in his presidential address, "The Rational and the Ambivalent in the Social Sciences" (1998), Smelser implicitly takes into account this kind of critique. In discussing the two major contemporary meanings of the rational in contemporary social sciences—that is, rational choice and rationality as an organizational or institutional strategy—he focuses on the circumscribed, although relevant, role of rationality in explaining social phenomena. He suggests "a way of resuscitating the role of nonrational forces in individual, group and institutional behavior, employing the idea of ambivalence" (171). In this chapter, I examine rational choice as one of the main paradigms in contemporary social sciences.

Rational choice, a paradigm that derives from the British utilitarian tradition, is today dominant in economics, where it has been developed in neoclassical economic theory and modified and elaborated through methodological refinements such as game theory. But it is also increasingly important in political science, and it is spreading in law, anthropology, organization theory, and management science. And it is gaining ground in sociology as well. It may be a paradox, as Milan Zafirovski (1999) argues, that modern rational choice theory is exported to other social sciences dealing with noneconomic phenomena at the time when a growing number of economists are questioning its adequacy as an explanation of economic phenomena. But it is a reality, and we have to understand why.

The attitude of sociology toward rational choice has been ambivalent. On the one hand, the critique of rational utilitarianism is an inherent part of the sociological tradition; on the other, despite this long-standing hostility, a greater number of rational choice assumptions are present in standard sociological theory than most sociologists are prepared to admit. It is recognized that rational choice can describe, analyze, and predict individual behavior in a wide array of different situations and contexts of action. This is no surprise, since the postulates of this theory are drawn from the core values of modern Western civilization—that is, individualism, rationalism, utilitarianism—which now characterize global market capitalism, foster extended rationalization of world organizations and markets, and orient a significant portion of actual behavior in contemporary societies. Yet rational choice is criticized as too unilateral and incapable of accounting for the basic sociological questions of social order and social change. It is judged hardly useful when collectivities instead of individuals, and macro-level structures and institutions instead of micro-level action, are to be analyzed.

This ambivalence is partly related to the fact that several different versions of rational choice exist. According to a simplified version of Jon Elster's 1979 classification, three formulations of the theory can be identified. First is the classical maximization approach assuming utility and profit optimization (with transitivity, independence, and completeness), perfect competition and information, accurate calculation, and the like. Second is the theory of bounded rationality that rejects the premise of optimization in terms of "satisficing," but retains utility and profits as objective functions and ends. And third is the stochastic, game theory model, where rationality is strategic rather than parametric and information and transaction costs play a key role.

In general, "hard," "thick," "first-order," "perfect rationality" models can be distinguished from "soft," "thin," "second-order," "quasi-rationality" models of rational action. A basic criterion to distinguish between the two types is that the former tend to specify actors' motivations or purposes *ex ante,* while the latter tend to say nothing about these motivations.

In this chapter, I start with the original "opposition" between sociological theory and rational utilitarianism. Second, I briefly review the key concepts of rational choice and their main sociological critiques, with a few references to the contributions of James Coleman, George Homans, and Raymond Boudon, which adopt a rational choice approach, although one adapted and transformed. Third, I critically assess Coleman's theory, the main attempt to build a general sociological theory based on rational choice. I then discuss Smelser's attempt at developing a supplement to rational choice through its analysis of ambivalence. I conclude with some reflections on the multiplicity of paradigms and the difficulties of general theory building in sociology, and I state my preference for a "tool kit version" of rational choice rather than a general theory perspective.

THE CLASSICAL CRITIQUES OF RATIONAL UTILITARIANISM

The critique of rational utilitarianism is an inherent part of the sociological tradition. I argued elsewhere (Martinelli 1986) that the very genesis of sociology as a modern social science can be seen as a critique of classical economics' fundamental postulate of the *homo economicus* and of its conception of market equilibrium as the spontaneous outcome of a multitude of rational individual actions. Economic rationality—including its maximands (utility and profit) and preferences—is relative, endogenous, and immanent, not absolute, endogenous, and transcendent to society. The sociological critique points out that rational economic action is embedded in a social context and presupposes the binding power of social institutions such as legal contracts. Free market transactions and self-interested motivations are not enough to make cooperation possible in a utilitarian, individualistic society and must be superseded and counterbalanced by other institutions and values fostering social cohesion.

Karl Marx, Emile Durkheim, and Vilfredo Pareto, in spite of their basic differences, share the notion of an original "opposition" between sociological theory and the basic postulates of intentional rational action. Marx dismissed purposive action by stressing the role of structural variables, first of all the necessary relations of production, as stated clearly in the "Preface to the *Critique of Political Economy*": "In the social production of their existence, men enter into necessary, determinate relations, independent from their will, which correspond to a given degree of development of productive forces" (1913: 47).

Durkheim strongly rejected methodological individualism as the proper perspective for sociology, stressed the notion of independent social facts, and contested the spontaneous order of the market in favor of normative elements that are necessary to make even economic exchanges possible.

Pareto highly valued rational action, but only in explaining the economic aspect of social life. Rationality becomes for him the criterion to distinguish the domains of different social sciences. In the *Trattato di sociologia generale*, after criticizing "the very common error which lies in denying the truth of a theory because it cannot explain every part of a concrete fact," he argued that different theories explain different aspects of an empirical phenomenon (1964: 19–20). Rational action is not the domain of sociology and political science, since social and political action do not pass the test of scientific means-ends maximization.

Max Weber had a different view. In his essay "Ueber einige Kategorien der verstehenden Soziologie" (1922), he defined the task of sociology to bring the forms of social action back to the meaningful action of the participant individuals. Individualism, intentional purposive action and rationality are key elements in his theoretical framework, and he states that the behavior that can be interpreted as rational behavior is often the most proper ideal-type in sociological analysis. By distinguishing between the rationality of ends and the rationality of values, Weber tried to break the linkage between rationality and utilitarianism and to avoid the reduction of all types of rationality to economic rationality, as various proponents of rational choice still do.

Finally, Parsons, while condemning utilitarianism in his effort to separate sociology and economics, and emphasizing the priority of culture, also assumed purposive action as a key element of his theory.

Contemporary sociological contributions have echoed and developed the classical approaches in order either to criticize and reject rational choice theory or to transform and adapt one or more core elements of it to the requirements of sociological analysis.

KEY CONCEPTS OF RATIONAL CHOICE THEORY

Before I outline the basic ingredients of rational choice theory through an adapted version of Gary Becker's definition (1981), it is useful to first define purposive action and individualism as the methodological preconditions, and then discuss its basic components: rational maximizing behavior, market equilibrium, and stable preferences.

First, there is the teleological principle of individual purposive action as methodological precondition. As Coleman puts it, rational choice rejects the concept of social action as expressive, nonrational or irrational, or as caused by external factors with no teleological intermediation of intention or purpose (1990: 5–9). The latter part of Coleman's statement, the teleological intermediation of intention or purpose, is widely accepted by sociologists. Following the successful battle against positivist sociology, in fact, most sociological research views behavior as purposive and then deriving from a process of choice. The means-ends scheme and the relevance of values, goals, and preferences as motivating factors of behavior are widely accepted. On the other hand, the exclusion of expressive and nonrational or irrational forms of social action (a complete reversal of Pareto's position) is by no means shared by most sociologists.

Second, there is the concept of methodological individualism, which can be traced to the works of Joseph Schumpeter and Ludwig von Mises, according to which societal-level phenomena can be adequately explained only in terms of actions of individuals. Rational choice theory assumes the analytical priority of individuals over social structures, an assumption that is still the object of heated debate among sociologists.

Third, there is the concept of (utilitarian-economic) rationality as optimization of the means-ends relation through consistent cost-benefits calculations. Rationality is the maximization or optimization of well-defined objective functions or ends, such as utility, profit, wealth, and other maximands or, alternatively, such as the minimization of costs, including transaction costs, and other disutilities. It requires that actors possess complete information about their tastes, their resources, prices, and other market conditions. The general idea is that those actions are chosen that will have the best consequences in terms of the actor's own aims. Given the restrictions on an actor's available resources, such as income, time, market prices, availability of goods, and so on, the set of action alternatives is reduced to a smaller subset of actions possible in a particular situation. This set of opportunities is then evaluated in light of an actor's aims, in the sense that the actor forms preferences among alternatives that fulfill some consistency requirements. Sociological critiques tend to concentrate on the image of men as rational egoists and as "perfect statisticians," as Kenneth Arrow ironically put it. In order to respond to these critiques, economists have progressively relaxed some of these highly simplified typifications; for instance, when the costs of information and transaction become too high, economic actors turn to trust (in contracts) and to authority (in organizations) to minimize those costs. But nonrational and irrational elements that are present in all behavior including economic behavior—such as active distortion of information on the part of actors—the process of symbolization of commodities and work (which endows systems of meanings above and beyond their reference to assumed utility preferences), and the role played by affect in all interaction including economic interaction are important instances of omitted relaxations of the assumptions of rational choice and means-ends optimization (Smelser 1998).

Fourth, there is the concept of stable preferences. The actor's preferences (related to his or her interests, values, and tastes) and the restrictions to choice are the basic explanatory variables of rational action. Actors are assumed to optimize their utility and to form basic preferences that are invariant over time. Preferences are also assumed to be characterized by consistency, transitivity, completeness, and independence. They are treated as stable, exogenous, and given. They are the starting point, not the object of analysis, because any behavior could be "explained ex post" by the assumption that the actor had a preference for that particular action (Harsanyi 1969: 513–38). In order to avoid this kind of tautological explanation, George Stigler and Gary Becker elaborated the heuristic principle that behavioral changes should be explained by changes in the restrictions of behavior and not by changing preferences related to utility (1974). These tastes and preferences are then assumed to be stable. They need not neglect the actor's history. In fact, they can be contingent on past choices. And they do not require that the actor knows for sure the outcome in advance. In fact, in situations of risk and uncertainty where the actor does not know for certain what the consequences of his actions will be, he will choose the action that will yield the highest expected utility. Many sociologists question the stability of preferences through time and space.

Fifth, there is the concept of market equilibrium, according to which the market is the most efficient mechanism for exchange and resource allocation in conditions of scarcity. Basic elements are the law of supply and demand and the concept of marginal utility. The greater the amount that an individual has of a certain good, the less interested she is in getting more of it and the smaller the utility she derives from it. If the price of a good relative to the price of another alternative increases, the amount of the good that will be chosen decreases, and vice versa, through the interplay of supply and demand. The interaction between buyer and seller produces an equilibrium point at which exchange occurs. The equilibrium point marks a convergence of supply and demand, utility and cost. The market is the product of goal-directed actions by numerous people who do not necessarily intend to generate a spontaneous order. Many sociologists disagree with the core image of the market as a spontaneous order—running from Adam Smith's "invisible hand" to standard contemporary economics—although they can accept the idea that social institutions are the result of human action but not necessarily the result of human design.

SOCIOLOGICAL ADAPTATIONS OF RATIONAL CHOICE

In order to overcome some of the basic objections to these assumptions, such as the portrait of individuals as rational egoists, the large number of situations where individuals do not act rationally, the stability of preferences through time and space, the spontaneous order of the market, and the like, sociologists advocating rational choice have tried to ease some of the basic assumptions and to embrace a loose version of the theory.

Thus, for methodological individualism, Coleman argues that rational choice theory constitutes the micro-level foundation for explaining the functioning of macrostructures or social systems (1989). But he argues that macro-level events should be explained through a combination of three types of propositions: macro-to-micro propositions that express the effects of societal level factors upon individuals; micro-to-micro propositions that describe micro-level processes; and micro-to-macro propositions that show how the individual level aggregates to produce societal changes. Even more important, he pays great attention to the role of corporate actors, such as firms and the state, and to their growing importance at the expense of individual actors. Coleman's position, then, comes close to what Steven Lukes (1968) labeled "truistic social atomism" (society consists of individuals, and institutions consist of people plus rules and roles), an attitude shared by almost all sociologists.

As far as economic rationality is concerned, rational choice advocates have tried to redefine the concept to answer critiques of their conception of individuals as rational egoists. In Homans's reformulation of rational choice theory, for instance, the concepts of economic theory are adapted to sociological needs (1974). He argues that, faced with alternatives, a rational individual will choose the one in which, according to his perception, the value of the result multiplied for the probability it occurs is higher. He points out that, whereas economists measure value by the common measure of money, sociologists emphasize values that have a greater subjective character, although one can assume that social recognition, prestige, power, and survival have universal meaning as well. And he redefines the concept of marginal utility in terms of deprivation and satisfaction. Rational individuals will do something only if its value exceeds what they leave in order to do it, both in terms of direct costs and forecast opportunities.

In order to come to terms with expressive, nonrational, or irrational action—which he excludes from the object of sociological inquiry—Coleman argues that "much of what is ordinarily described as nonrational or irrational is merely so because the observers have not discovered the point of view of the actor, from which the action is rational" (1990: 18). In a similar vein, Boudon argues that rationality is always related to local contexts and to the immediate experience of actors ("positional rationality"), and to the roles to which actors have been socialized ("dispositional rationality"). For Boudon a behavior is rational insofar as an actor can offer good reasons in accounting for his or her conduct (1987).

As far as stable preferences are concerned, as I said earlier, thick versions of rational choice theory tend to specify actors' motivations or purposes *ex ante* and to consider preferences as given, while soft versions tend to say nothing about motivations and preferences, or to "explain" behavior *ex post*, as in the case of Boudon's good reasons in accounting for one's behavior.

The problem with these corrections and adaptations of rational choice is that they create new problems. The problem of rational choice applications outside economics is that, wherever the assumptions of rational choice are accepted in their strong version, the theory is logically more consistent but is inadequate to interpret and explain social relations that are much more complex than economic life. And wherever a weak version is adopted, assumptions become more reasonable but the rational choice perspective tends to lose its specific character. Many recent versions of rational choice incorporate notions of unstable preferences, risk and uncertainty situations, incomplete information, power differentials among actors, satisficing, rather than maximizing, "bounded rationality" models. But in so doing they stretch the idea of the rational to the point of theoretical degeneration, where "rational" becomes more or less synonymous with "adaptive."

If we abandon, as in the soft sociological versions of rational choice theory, Pareto's and Parsons' definition of rationality as the coincidence of subjective and objective (verifiable) relations between means and ends, and utilities and rationalities of individuals become idiosyncratic matters, they are useless for theory building. If they cannot be homogenized, how can one make a statement about aggregate functions? As Mark Granovetter and Richard Swedberg (1992) have objected, thick rationality models commit teleological misspecification by reducing human purposes to the utilitarian or economic, while their thin counterparts are unnecessarily agnostic and/or ultimately tautological.

The discussion of these questions can be further developed by looking at Coleman's work, which represents the most important attempt to employ the rational choice paradigm to lay the foundations of a general sociological theory.

JAMES COLEMAN'S *FOUNDATIONS OF SOCIAL THEORY* AND HIS CRITICS

Coleman starts coherently from the level of the "individual person" (or "natural person," "concrete person," or "personal actor") as the natural unit of observation; the individual person acts purposively, rationally, and "unconstrained by norms," pursuing self-interest and seeking pleasure. Then Coleman turns, first, to the analysis of "elementary actions and relations"—that is, the interactions among rational actors interested in resources and control over them, in light of such concepts as authority and trust. And, second, he turns to the study of "structures of action," involving market exchange, authority systems, and trust systems, with most examples drawn from fiduciary and political leadership. In other words, Coleman analyzes the social preconditions of exchange; alternative goods to money such as social approval, social support, power, and social capital (defined as networks of social relations); the different institutional settings that influence the behavior of actors; and the resulting allocation (with arguments resembling those of Oliver Williamson's about markets and hierarchies).

Coleman's task becomes increasingly difficult as he moves from micro- to macrolevels of analysis, since the latter are more difficult to interpret in a rational choice perspective. Thus, elementary forms of collective behavior such as panic and hostile crowds are seen as instances of individuals transferring control to another person (a leader). Normative systems are seen as purposively generated and enforced out of self-interest. Political coalitions are explained as the outcome of aggregated individual decisions. And corporate actors are analyzed—in a particularly long section—in terms of individual rights, social choice, and the granting and revoking of authority.

The final substantive part (before the formalized representation of his theory), is a study of systems of corporate actors, of intergenerational relations, and of the general conditions of modern society, which echoes the classical studies by Ferdinand Toennies and Emile Durkheim on the transition from gemeinschaft to gesellschaft and from the *solidarité mechanique* to the *solidarité organique,* as well as the functionalist theory of modernization.

Coleman's main thesis is that purposively constructed social organizations—such as firms, trade unions, professional organizations, single-purpose voluntary organizations, and government—have replaced the primordial institutions, such as family, clan, ethnic groups, and community, eroding the social capital on which societal functioning depended. The new rational choice social science should therefore contribute to understanding how power is distributed in society and how individuals can satisfy their interests in a society dominated by corporate actors, thus filling the voids created by the erosion of social capital, first of all in the realm of family and education.

Some critiques of Coleman's theory, as of other versions of rational choice, are just misconceptions about this type of analysis, such as the erroneous beliefs that rational choice views people as ruthlessly self-seeking, assumes they possess complete information about alternatives, or necessarily assumes conservative politics. They do not deserve much attention. But others are to be taken seriously.

A first critique focuses on the ambition to develop a general theory of social action. Coleman tries to build it on the assumption of the "natural person." In so doing he makes the "errore comunissimo" stigmatized by Pareto (1964: 19): he tries to push his theory so far as to cover all empirical cases. Coleman argues, for instance, that even in the case of slavery it is rational to accept it, since slavery is preferable to death (1990: 88). In other examples he defines trust and power in terms of a prudential calculus, and tries to explain social phenomena such as good manners, musical fads, and fashion as mere rational transfer to others of the control over our actions. Would it not be better to acknowledge that theories based on free choice do not apply to situations in which free choice does not exist, or where, on the contrary, alternatives are not limited? And would it not be wiser, as I argue later, to aim at what Arthur Stinchcombe (1992: 200) defines as "a toolkit version of rational choice theory" and to adopt Elster's notion of generalizations as mechanisms rather than theories (where, by *mechanisms,* Elster means small and medium-size descriptions of ways in which things happen; 1979)?

The second critique, related to the first, concerns Coleman's double neglect of both historical differences and social differences. The rational choice approach does not apply indifferently to all historical societies and to all individuals, but it applies to a varying degree to different actors playing different roles according to the social organization and the cultural values of their own society. As Smelser points out, "What is forgotten is that the free economic agent and the free citizen are themselves the products of a specific complex of cultural values and institutions. They are certainly not 'natural persons.' They behave according to norms that endorse and reward such behavior" (Smelser 1990: 781). There are no "natural persons," but historically specific cultural values and institutions. The historical actors and classes that invented classical utilitarian and democratic philosophies were themselves struggling for institutions (democratic representation and market capitalism) that were less oppressive than the absolute monarchy, the guild system, and mercantilism, and that permitted and rewarded conditions of liberty and the right to choose. In the process they developed theories about choice, calculation, and rationality. Besides, the rational choice approach applies to a different degree to different actors according to their sociological characteristics—that is, status, role, social background, constraints and opportunities of their social milieu, and so on.

Third, Coleman can be criticized for embracing a view of modernity that stresses too much the role of purposive social organizations and underplays the continuing role of primordial institutions. The contemporary debate on multiple modernities—that is, of multiple paths toward and through modernity—and the rich evidence in empirical studies of modernization and development for the persistence of traditionalism in modern societies (Martinelli 1998) show the limits of Coleman's functionalist perspective on social change.

Fourth, it can be objected that, even when the action is rational-utilitarian, it must rely on nonrational assumptions. As Alessandro Pizzorno points out, the value of a good is based not only on the perceived utility for the individual but also on a kind of intersubjective recognition. The actor must refer to others to verify that the value he grants to a given good is not an illusion. Utilitarian evaluations are then expressed also on the basis of collective identities that guarantee the validity and stability of preferences (1983, 1986).

The fifth critique concerns the role of norms. According to Dennis

Wrong's critique of Coleman, the fundamental flaw of all rational choice theories is that they ignore socialization and draw an artificial distinction between self-interests and both the interests of others and normative standards (1994). Socialization precedes self-interested (or any other type of action) and therefore rational choice fails to constitute a self-sufficient theoretical standpoint for the understanding of human nature in society (Wrong 1994). In a similar vein, Peter Blau remarks that the central task of sociology is not explaining individual behavior but explaining how the structural context of the social environment influences people's life chances (1997). And Jeffrey Alexander reproaches Coleman for limiting himself to discrete, separated, and independent individuals, and thus ignoring the normative dimension (1992: 209). Coleman tries to answer this type of criticism, stating that it is true that he deals with individuals, but that "this is the starting point," and that well-functioning social systems contain "persons whose self-interests have been broadened to include the interests of others, as persons with internalized sanctions, both of which lead to actions ordinarily termed altruistic. And it contains also the external incentives and sanctions found in institutions that can be effective even for discrete, separated, independent, narrowly self-interested individuals" (1992: 271–72). To take the end point, that is, the concrete social system and the socialized persons within it, as the elements for social theory, continues Coleman, is to take for granted what is to be explained, falling into Parsons' error of considering individuals as norm followers. I tend to agree with the notion of a circular relation between action and socialization. But it is difficult to accept the idea that social norms are but one of the many social productions that result from the unintended consequences of individual rational action, as some rational action sociologists affirm (Heckhathom 1997).

Sixth, and closely related to the previous point, critics attack Coleman's *Foundations* for not successfully coping with the problem of social order. According to this line of criticism, one can argue that, as Mancur Olson's "free rider" argument proves, it is sometimes more rational to violate norms than to conform to them. It can also be argued that, since society cannot rest only on coercion, its members must also act according to some kind of solidarity and perceive their common interests beyond their self-interests. It is an updated version of the old Durkheimian argument that utilitarian principles will never be sufficient to fully explain the emergence of the social order, and that contracts are enforced by the institution of contract law and internalized feelings of a moral obligation to deal fairly with one's partners.

Seventh, I think that rational choice models are limited in their ability to explain social change and innovation. Rational choice can, in fact, explain action in a routinized context in the presence of a limited set of well-known alternatives, but it is in trouble when confronted with any change that does not take place in an institutionalized context and does not allow a precise assessment of costs and benefits. The theoretical foundations of this type of critique can be found in Weber's and Schumpeter's analyses of processes and actors of change. In fact, both in Weber's notion of charisma and in Schumpeter's notion of entrepreneur there are basic nonrational components. The former is defined in terms of a relation between the leader and the followers that is radically different from the rationality of democratic political institutions. The latter transcends the elements of economic rationality to include the typical capabilities of leadership and such motivating forces as the dream to create a private kingdom, the will to conquest, and the impulse to fight.

Some rational choice models have tried to explain changes in terms of the unintended consequences of social action—that is, personal and collective effects that result from the juxtaposition of individual behaviors, although they are not included in the actors' explicit objectives (as in Boudon's case study of the choice of different types of high school education in France, 1977). The unintended consequences are often unpredictable and undesirable for the actor involved, as shown by the well-known metaphor of the prisoner's dilemma. This is a promising line of inquiry. While unintended consequences are a major source of change, they are just one source.

SMELSER'S CONTRIBUTION: THE LOGIC OF AMBIVALENCE

Smelser has discussed rational choice theory on several occasions: besides his critique of Coleman mentioned above in the Georg Simmel Lectures, in the essay "Economic Rationality as a Religious System," and in his 1997 presidential address at the American Sociological Association (1995, 1998). I consider his analysis of the relations between the rational and the ambivalent to be his most interesting contribution to the subject.

Smelser (1998) starts by stating his intention in developing a supplement to the rational choice approach, then identifies the key ingredients, and then adds some critical comments. He remarks that "rational" is a relative, not an absolute, notion in two major ways. First, it varies according to the time perspective and the level of analysis. The same item of behavior (smoking) may be rational in the short run (it gratifies) and not in the long run (it increases the probability of death). The same item of behavior (dumping toxic waste in the river) may be rational for the individual firm (it minimizes costs) and not rational for the community (it creates environmental pollution). But rational choice behavior is relative also in a second sense, insofar as a number of conditions must be present in order to make it possible. These conditions refer both to interpersonal relations and to institutional contexts. Mutual trust and predictability between exchanging partners are necessary social-psychological conditions. A stable medium (money), stable institutional settings (markets), and stable legal orders (guaranteeing contract and property rights and punishing deviant behavior) are basic institutional conditions. As Granovetter points out, the focus on these two important limits of rational economic theory—that is, interpersonal relations (both horizontal and vertical, such as trust and cooperation and power and obedience) and contextual constraints and opportunities (such as information flows)—is the distinctive character of the specific branch of economic sociology (2001).

Smelser remarks further that "neither reason nor choice is necessary for what passes as rational choice analysis," because behavior is in fact determined by a given set of preferences and by a number of objective factors such as price and quantity. "Regarded correctly, rational choice is an intervening psychological constant typically invoked when assigning meaning to and explaining links between market and other conditions and rates of behavior" (1998: 173). Moreover, in spite of its relation to utilitarianism—the chief principle of which is seeking pleasure and avoiding pain—rational choice analysis leaves little place for affect and emotions.

Smelser's final comment—that rational choice theory relies almost exclusively on univalent orientations—is the most interesting one, since it opens the way to the logic of ambivalence. Rational choice does not consider the fundamental reality of human ambivalence: that is, the fact that actors can love and hate at the same time, that they can be attracted and repulsed by the same object simultaneously, and that these contrasting emotions can make a rationally optimal choice impossible. Smelser suggests the notion of ambivalence as a second major psychological postulate, not opposed to, but different from and complementary to the postulate of rational choice. The postulate of ambivalence differs from the latter one in the double sense that preferences are not univalent (either positive or negative) but rather imply opposing affective orientations, and that they are essentially unstable. He says, "The notion of ambivalence leads us to understand and explain a range of behaviors and situations beyond the scope of rational choice explanations, however far the latter may be stretched" (1998: 175).

The social situations that foster ambivalence are those in which actors are dependent on one another. Whatever the form of dependence—emotional as in love, political as in power relationships, ideological as in collective movements—the common distinctive element is that freedom to leave is costly, and therefore choice is limited. As a result, models of behavior based on the postulate of ambivalence are best applicable to relations of dependence. Smelser reviews major areas of interactions where ambivalence grows.

The area of social relationships where ambivalence is most evident is the family, first of all in the relations between parents and children. Sigmund Freud is the great theorist of ambivalence who made the principle of ambivalence a cornerstone of psychoanalytic thought (1953, 1955). But Freud's prototypical setting for the development of ambivalence is the situation of the young child, dependent on his or her parents for survival, protection, and love and dependent on their authority. According to Smelser, "The child's objects of ambivalence are those by whom he or she is entrapped" (1998: 181). Adolescence is the protracted experience of partial escape, a period in which the negative side of ambivalence toward parents and siblings is repeatedly "acted out," sometimes in extreme ways. Once independence is more or less reached, the positive side of ambivalence comes back. Love relations in general are the most common ground on which ambivalence develops. Relations of "voluntary emotional dependence," as Smelser calls them (182), arise from the half-voluntary, half-involuntary actions of falling in love and becoming friends. These relations often imply other forms of dependence, as in the differential power of husband and wife in many cultures or the differential status among friends, but they are always based on emotional dependence.

However, the most interesting areas are those that do not pertain to the private realm of life or to special contexts such as total institutions, but to economic and political behavior—that is, two areas where rational choice has scored its greater success. In consumer markets, for instance, we often observe ambivalent attitudes toward luxury goods that are symbols of the status systems in community and society and that draw mixed reactions. Another interesting area of ambivalent choices, and of institutional mechanisms aiming at converting them into absolute preferences, is democratic politics. The electoral process is a way of converting individual ambivalence into absolute preference. But the growing rate of nonvoting in mature democracies—higher in two-party systems where the range of alternatives is more limited—is a symptom that public ambivalence toward political leaders and party programs is more or less permanent and never resolved. Public opinion surveys, which ask a sample of citizens how strongly they approve or disapprove of a political candidate or some issue of public concern, constitute another political institution that contributes to reducing ambivalent feelings and to delegitimizing ambiguity. A third relevant setting for ambivalence is those collective movements that demand commitment, faithfulness, and adherence from their members, such as contemporary identity movements that challenge the authority of the nation-state. In spite of their ingroup solidarity and out-group hostility, these movements show ambivalent feelings toward both their own leaders and the authorities at whom their protest is directed. Building on Albert O. Hirschman's notions of exit, voice, and loyalty (1970), Smelser suggests that these movements can often choose voice whenever the exit option is too costly and the loyalty option is barred by the strong feeling of separate identity, another instance of ambivalent behavior.

The logic of ambivalence is an alternative methodology for the study of social interaction that proves particularly fruitful in situations where choice is not institutionalized and therefore rational choice is hardly applicable.

RATIONAL CHOICE AND THE MULTIPARADIGMATIC CHARACTER OF SOCIOLOGY

Rational choice is a good antidote in the social sciences against the weaknesses of both structuralist and normative theories. Structuralist approaches seem unable to explain why the same structural constraints result in very different forms of collective action. And normative theories tend to take for granted that individuals act according to institutionalized norms. In this respect, rational choice theory has contributed to "bring[ing] men back in," but, since "social life is never wholly utilitarian[,] . . . people do not in fact maximize their utilities through consistent and precise cost-benefit calculations" (Homans 1990: 77, 81). Besides, there is some truth in William Goode's remark that rational choice remains a form of analysis in which "almost everyone engages" (1997, 24). Moreover, rational choice, contrary to many alternative paradigms, like the culturalist ones, specifies the assumptions clearly and can therefore be tested empirically. Besides, rational choice has a parsimonious set of explanatory variables and develops logically consistent models.

On the other hand, it requires an extreme reduction of the explanatory elements of social action. Rational choice theory seems to work well for those relations and structures in which voluntary exchange is an institutional principle, such as free markets, contractual authority systems, and trust relations in banking and finance, and when the actor has a free choice and is confronted with a limited set of alternatives. In other words, as Smelser puts it, "such a model is most useful under those social conditions that institutionalize its characteristics and conditions," such as a typical market for commodities (1990: 780). Difficulties arise when those values are not a matter of consent and the ensuing institutions are not present.

The applicability of rational choice in sociological analysis is much more limited than in economics. It does not seem to provide the best way to deal with the basic sociological questions of social order and social change, and it is judged hardly useful when collectivities instead of individuals, and macro-level structures and institutions instead of micro-level action, are to be analyzed.

Coleman's attempt has been an ambitious one. In spite of its limitations, he has employed rational choice to try to bridge the gap between action and system—a fundamental problem in sociological theory—that a few others, from Parsons to Anthony Giddens, have tried to cope with, with controversial results at best. But, Coleman's effort also has limitations.

The scope of application of rational choice to sociological research can actually be much more limited. Rational choice theory should be seen as just one of the theoretical frameworks that can be employed in the interpretation and explanation of concrete social phenomena, alongside others such as a variety of institutionalist, culturalist, and structuralist approaches. Sociological theorizing should proceed according to a "tool kit view" rather than a "general theory" perspective. The previous discussion of Smelser's analysis of ambivalence and trust provides examples of how rational choice can be superseded by other approaches.

The multiplicity of paradigms and theoretical approaches clearly appears to be a basic distinctive character of contemporary sociology. For most sociologists this is perceived as an advantage. Giddens's remarks that "the fact that there is no single theoretical approach which dominates the whole of sociology" demonstrates that "the jostling of rival theoretical approaches and theories is an expression of the vitality of the sociological enterprise" (1989: 715). And Boudon argues that "sociology is in crisis when it pretends to have reached the conditions of a 'normal science' and to be led by a unique paradigm" (1987: 188). Not all sociologists are indeed convinced of this advantage, given the fact that some of them prefer to turn to the rational action paradigm of economics; but most seem persuaded that the subject matter of sociology requires a plurality of conceptual perspectives and methods of investigation, and that alternative theoretical approaches can be tested with regard to the analysis of specific phenomena.

The advantages and disadvantages of having a core paradigm for a discipline tend to balance each other. The case of economics is illuminating in this respect. In economics, alternative approaches do exist, but they do not challenge the core paradigm, which is based on the combined assumptions of rational maximizing behavior, market equilibrium, and stable preferences. This "creative simplification" of human action has brought undeniable theoretical achievements, which are exemplified in Leon Walras's general equilibrium model as a response to the question of the efficient functioning of a market economy made of millions of individual decisions. But it has also fostered limitations in the number and type of hypotheses that can be derived from the paradigm, as well as logical contradictions and difficulties in the empirical validation of the theoretical hypotheses; and it has constrained the "imagination" of scholars in providing interpretations of emerging economic processes.

The reverse seems true for sociology: the freedom from paradigmatic "dogma" has been bought for the price of more precarious accumulation of knowledge, greater ambivalence, and bitter paradigmatic fights that often amount to a waste of intellectual energies. The absence of a central paradigm has prevented widely accepted solutions to central theoretical questions. A question similar to that of the economists' relation between rational individual actors and general market equilibrium is at the heart of the sociological inquiry: what is the relationship between structure and agency? The question of this relationship is related to the problem of the micro-macro links (Alexander et al. 1987) and to the debate between the supporters of causal model building and the supporters of *Verstehen* (understanding) in social science. But there is no theoretical answer to these questions that could parallel Walras's general equilibrium model. The preference that most sociologists seem to share for multiple paradigms could, then, be as well a forced preference, since major attempts to provide a unifying paradigm, from Talcott Parsons to James Coleman to Anthony Giddens, have not lasted or have not been accepted by the majority of scholars. Failures may be due to the fact that the features of *homo sociologicus* are different from those of *homo economicus* and do not allow the creative simplification of the hyper-rationalist assumption, or to the fact that core theoretical questions have to be rephrased or that more adequate responses must be worked out.

In this situation, however, most sociologists working in specialized fields have not been paralyzed by the absence of a unified grand theory, but have proceeded along the most viable paths of Robert Merton's middle range theories, Arthur Stinchcombe's tool kit of analytical instruments, and Jon Elster's concept of mechanisms. As the latter author argues, "There should be a shift in emphasis in social sciences from theories to mechanisms"—that is, "small and medium-sized descriptions of ways in which things happen. A mechanism is a little causal story, recognizable from one context to another. A theory has greater pretensions: it is supposed to tell you which mechanisms operate in which situation. . . . Generalizations should take the form of mechanisms, not theories" (Swedberg 1990: 72). This approach, which is close to Weber's and Simmel's attitude toward sociology, seems particularly valid for sociological research in specialized areas. In fact, in these situations, the analyst-interpreter will extract from the tool kit those tools, models, and mechanisms she considers relevant, adapt them to the concrete research questions, and verify the correspondence on the basis of the available data and methods.

According to this approach, the best way to assess the value of a theory is to assess the validity of competing paradigms in the interpretation, explanation, and prediction of social phenomena. In so doing we can avoid seeing the case of rational choice as just another instance of the war of paradigms between supporters and antagonists of a given paradigm, one of those familiar cycles of enunciation and denunciation, attack and counterattack over the "imperialism" of economics in social sciences, which consume intellectual energies without having perceptible effects on the development of either economics or sociology and political science.

In this respect, both rational choice supporters (rational individualists) and their antagonists (culturalists or institutionalists) have tried to wage war in their rival's territory. Thus, on the one hand, some institutional and cultural sociologists have criticized rational choice in its very core empirical domain,—that is, economic activities and behavior, stressing the importance of culture, institutions, nonrational motives, and so on in the analysis of economic phenomena such as entrepreneurship, economic development, and markets as social constructions. On the other hand, rational choice theorists have applied their paradigm to the analysis of phenomena such as family and religion, where types of action other than goal-oriented rationality, such as affective, traditional, value-rational types of action, seem stronger, as in the studies of the family and religion.

Becker's work deals with the behavior of family members in a market-oriented framework and is based on three basic assumptions: the concept of human capital, exemplified by such activities as childbearing, a theory of time allocation in conditions of scarcity of this basic resource, and the concept of households as organized groups whose members try to maximize a common objective of production. In this perspective, marriage is interpreted as a goal-oriented behavior where actors make decisions by evaluating the basic commodities that can be provided by the prospective partners, basic commodities such as "children, prestige and esteem, health, altruism, envy, through cost-benefit calculations and pleasure of the senses" (Becker 1981: 8); divorce is explained in terms of expectations of the advantages and disadvantages of the partnership in the future and as a consequence of imperfect information in the marriage market (South and Lloyd 1995); the decision to have children is seen as a result of specific investments by their parents; and the division of labor and gender roles within the family are explained in terms of comparative advantages and market opportunities for each marriage partner. Although rich empirical evidence has been cited to support it, this approach is severely limited by its inability to explain conflict, exploitation by one partner, breakdown in cooperation, and conversely, by its failure to account for such aspects of marriage as trust, altruism, and unselfishness. Even less convincing is the attempt to explain religious preferences as the result of individual choice in a religious market (Durkin and Greely 1991; Iannaccone 1995).

Better results stemming from more convincing studies have been achieved in other fields of sociological research, such as deviance (Carroll and Weaver 1986; Clarke and Felson 1993) and political collective action (Oberschall 1994; Opp 1994). In the former area, the situational approach that tries to explain deviant behavior in terms of costs and opportunities for illegal actions, and that focuses on the degree and probability of criminal punishment, has effectively challenged the predominant approach in the sociology of deviance, that of the labeling theory. In the latter, Olson's analysis of the logic of collective action has obliged students of political collective action to review interpretations focusing only on the quest for identity and solidaristic incentives (1965). Rational choice is just one approach to the study of human action; its scope of applicability varies greatly from one type of empirical phenomena to the other. A major reason for this different applicability can be traced, as Smelser argues, to a fundamental existential dilemma in the human condition—that is, freedom versus constraint, or autonomy versus dependence, where neither pole can be realized in full or exclusive form. In the scientific division of labor among social sciences, economics and part of political science (democratic theory) have stressed the freedom side, whereas parts of sociology, anthropology, and social psychology, which focus on interpersonal relations and contexts of action, have gone toward the other.

NOTE

A first, shorter, version of this chapter was presented as a paper at the International Political Science Association (IPSA) Fiftieth Anniversary Conference, Naples, October 1999, Roundtable on Rational Choice (with Ted Lowi, John Ferejohn, and Alessandro Pizzorno).

REFERENCES

Alexander, J. 1992. "Shaky Foundations: The Presuppositions and Internal Contradictions of James Coleman's *Foundations of Social Theory.*" *Theory and Society* 21 (2): 203–17.

Alexander, J. C., B. Giesen, R. Munch, and N. J. Smelser. 1987. *The Micro-Macro Link.* Berkeley: University of California Press.

Arrow, K. J. 1984. *The Collected Papers of Kenneth Arrow.* Vol. 1. Oxford: Basil Blackwell.

Becker, G. S. 1981. *A Treatise on the Family.* Cambridge: Harvard University Press.

Becker, G. S., and G. J. Stigler. 1974. "Law Enforcement, Malfeasance, and Compensation of Enforcers." *Journal of Legal Studies* 3: 1–18.

Boudon, R. 1977. *Effets pervers et ordre social.* Paris: Presses Universitaires de France.

———. 1987. "Razionalità e teoria dell'azione." *Rassegna italiana di sociologia* 2: 175–203.

Carroll, J., and F. Weaver. 1986. "Shoplifters' Perceptions of Crime Opportunities: A Process-Tracing Study." In D. B. Cornish and R. V. Clarke, eds., *The Reasoning Criminal: Rational Choice Perspectives on Offending,* pp. 19–38. New York: Springer.

Clarke, R. V., and M. Felson. 1993. *Routine Activity and Rational Choice.* London: Transactions Publishers.

Coleman, J. 1990. *Foundations of Social Theory.* Cambridge: Harvard University Press, Belknap Press.

———. 1992. "The Problematics of Social Theory: Four Reviews of *Foundations of Social Theory.*" *Theory and Society* 21 (2): 263–83.

Durkin, J. T., Jr., and A. Greely. 1991. "A Model of Religious Choice under Uncertainty." *Rationality and Society* 3: 178–96.

Elster, J. 1979. *Ulysses and the Sirens: Studies in Rationality and Irrationality.* Cambridge: Cambridge University Press.

Freud, S. 1953. "Three Essays on Sexuality." In James Strachey, ed., *The Standard Edition of the Complete Psychological Works of Sigmund Freud.* 7: 125–243. 1905. London: Hogarth Press.

———. 1955. "Notes upon a Case of Obsessional Neurosis." In James Strachey, ed., *The Standard Edition of the Complete Psychological Works of Sigmund Freud.* 10: 153–249. 1909. London: Hogarth Press.

Giddens, A. 1989. *Sociology.* Oxford: Polity Press.

Goode, W. 1997. "Rational Choice Theory." *American Sociologist* 28 (2): 22–41.

Granovetter, M. 2001. "A Theoretical Agenda for Economic Sociology." In M. F. Guillen, R. Collins, P. England, and M. Meyer, eds., *Economic Sociology at the Millennium.* New York: Russell Sage.

Granovetter, M., and R. Swedberg. 1992. *The Sociology of Economic Life.* Boulder, Colo.: Westview Press.

Harsanyi, J. C. 1969. "Rational Choice Models for Political Behavior versus Functionalist and Conformist Theories." *World Politics* 21: 513–38.

Heckhathom, D. D. 1997. "The Paradoxical Relationship between Sociology and Rational Choice." *American Sociologist* 28 (2): 6–15.

Hirschman, A. O. 1970. *Exit, Voice, and Loyalty: Responses to the Decline in Firms, Organizations, and States.* Cambridge: Harvard University Press.

Homans, G. C. 1974. *Social Behavior: Its Elementary Forms.* New York: Harcourt, Brace, Jovanovich.

———. 1990. "The Rational Choice Theory and Behavioral Psychology." In C. Calhoun, M. Meyer, and R. Scott, eds., *Structures of Power and Constraint: Papers in Honor of Peter M. Blau,* pp. 77–90. Cambridge: Cambridge University Press.

Iannaccone, L. R. 1995. "Voodoo Economics? Reviewing the Rational Choice Approach to Religion." *Journal for the Scientific Study of Religion* 34 (1): 76–89.

Lukes, S. 1968. "Methodological Individualism Reconsidered." *British Journal of Sociology* 19 (2): 119–29.

Martinelli, A. 1970. Introduction to the Italian edition of T. Parsons and N. J. Smelser, *Economy and Society,* pp. 9–58. Milan: Angeli.

———. 1998. *La modernizzazione.* Bari: Laterza.

Martinelli, A., and N. J. Smelser. 1990. "Economic Sociology: Historical Threads and Analytic Issues." *Current Sociology* 38 (2–3): 1–49.

Marx, K. 1913. Preface to the *Critique of Political Economy.* 1859. Chicago: Kerr.

Merton, R. K. 1949. *Social Theory and Social Structure.* Glencoe, Ill.: Free Press.

Merton, R. K., with E. Barber. 1976. *Sociological Ambivalence and Other Essays.* Glencoe, Ill.: Free Press.

Oberschall, A. R. 1994. "Rational Choice in Collective Protest." *Rationality and Society* 6: 79–100.

Olson, M. 1965. *The Logic of Collective Action.* Cambridge: Harvard University Press.

Opp, K. D. 1994. "Repression and Revolutionary Action: East Germany in 1989." *Rationality and Society* 6 (1): 101–38.

———. 1998. "Can and Should Rational Choice Theory Be Tested by Survey Research?" In H. P. Blossfeld and G. Prein, eds., *Rational Choice Theory and Large-Scale Data Analysis,* pp. 204–30. Boulder, Colo.: Westview Press.

Pareto, V. 1964. *Trattato di sociologia generale.* 1916. Milan: Comunità.

Pizzorno, A. 1983. "Sulla razionalità della scelta democratica." *Stato e mercato* 7: 3–46.

———. 1986. "Sul confronto intertemporale delle utilità." *Stato e mercato* 16: 3–25.

Smelser, N. J. 1990. "Can Individualism Yield a Sociology?" *Contemporary Sociology* 19 (6): 778–83.

———. 1995. "Economic Rationality as a Religious System." In R. Wuthnow, ed., *Rethinking Materialism: Perspectives on the Spiritual Dimension of Economic Behavior,* pp. 73–92. Grand Rapids, Mich.: W. E. Eerdmans Publishing.

———. 1997. *Problematics of Sociology: The Georg Simmel Lectures, 1995.* Berkeley and Los Angeles: University of California Press.

———. 1998. "The Rational and the Ambivalent in the Social Sciences." In N. J. Smelser, *The Social Edges of Psychoanalysis,* pp. 168–94. Berkeley and Los Angeles: University of California Press.

South, S. J., and K. M. Lloyd. 1995. "Spousal Alternatives and Marital Dissolution." *American Journal of Sociology* 60: 21–35.

Stinchcombe, A. 1992. "Simmel Systematized: James S. Coleman and the Social Forms of Purposive Action in His *Foundations of Social Theory.*" *Theory and Society* 21 (2): 103–202.

Swedberg, R. 1990. *Economics and Sociology: Redefining Their Boundaries: Conversations with Economists and Sociologists.* Princeton: Princeton University Press.

Von Mises, L. 1949. *Human Action: A Treatise on Economics.* New Haven: Yale University Press.

Voss, T., and M. Abraham. 2001. "Rational Choice Theory in Sociology: A Survey." In S. R. Quah and A. Sales, eds., *The International Handbook of Sociology.* London: Sage.

Weber, Max. 1922. "Ueber einige Kategorien der verstehenden Soziologie." In *Gesammelte Aufsatze zur Wissenschaftslehre.* Tubingen: Mohr.

Wrong, D. 1994. *The Problem of Order: What Unites and Divides Society?* New York: Free Press.

Zafirovski, M. 1999. "What Is Really Rational Choice?" *Current Sociology* 47 (1): 47–132.

Chapter 6

Enlisting Smelser's Theory of Ambivalence to Maintain Progress in Sociology of Religion's New Paradigm

R. Stephen Warner

Sociology of religion is in the midst of a theoretical shift that I identified (and tried to accelerate) in a widely cited article now over a decade old (Warner 1993). Exactly what the new approach—variously called "the new paradigm," the "religious markets" perspective, and "the economic approach to religion"—entails, whether it is properly called a "paradigm" or "theory" shift, and how far its scope extends are issues I return to below. Yet there can be no doubt that a fundamental divide exists between the new sociological understanding of religious vitality, especially in the United States, and the older wisdom that expected European-style secularization to be the fate of religion across the modern world. This divide pits the new view—broadly shared by Rodney Stark, Roger Finke, Laurence Iannaccone, and me, among others, who, to my mind, include Nancy Ammerman and Mary Jo Neitz—against such "old paradigm" figures as Steve Bruce, Karel Dobbelaere, Frank Lechner, and Bryan Wilson.[1] My primary disciplinary goal in this chapter is to encourage fence-sitters to line up with the new paradigm by recognizing that it does not entail the rational choice postulates articulated within it by Finke, Iannaccone, and Stark but is open to other social-psychological perspectives.

Neil Smelser, whom I first encountered as my theory professor when I was a Berkeley undergraduate in 1962, figures in this chapter as my mentor over the long term of my career. Especially since his 1997 American Sociological Association presidential address (1998), he has been my chief stimulus in thinking through why the "new paradigm," as I have defined it, does not rest on a rational choice theory of human motivation and can be strengthened by recognizing the applicability of ambivalence.

This chapter has four parts. First, I briefly trace the development of the new paradigm in the sociology of religion. Second, I cite what would be anomalies in the new paradigm if its foundation were to be taken as rational choice theory. Third, I draw on Smelser's work on ambivalence to help explain those anomalies without abandoning the fundamental insight of the new paradigm. Finally, I briefly outline some theoretical implications.

BACKGROUND TO THE "NEW PARADIGM"

About the time that the flurry of interest in 1960s-era "new religious movements" was about to fade, the resurgence of fundamentalism and other forms of conservative religion in the 1970s and 1980s led to renewed interest in religion among sociologists and to a growing awareness that conventional theoretical expectations were not working. Having been led to expect that religion would survive in modern society only in otherworldly forms among the underprivileged in society's backwaters or in harmless mysticism among the idle elite, sociological researchers, often dissertation students, kept coming back from the field with challenges to the reigning perspective. These researchers encountered thriving, not merely surviving, religious movements that they found among educated and affluent people, not the disinherited, at society's crossroads instead of its margins. Many of these movements were making a difference, whatever we might think of it, in their communities, challenging school boards and boycotting places of entertainment. And instead of being solitary practitioners, the people in these movements came together to celebrate their faith, not only expressing preexisting solidarities but often creating new ones.

The religious movement I first studied, in 1976, was that of an evangelical revival in the Presbyterian church of Mendocino, California. Many of my informants were newcomers both to their religion, being what they called "new Christians," and to their small-town place of residence, being what I called "elective parochials" (1988: ch. 3). My study originally had been intended to address issues in political sociology: I wanted to understand how a respectable old institution, which happened to be one of the oldest Protestant churches in California, could flourish after having been taken over by a radical movement of young people of dubious reputation, who happened to be late-1960s-style "hippie Christians." The political sociology frame failed (because the conflicts in the church did not occur at the places the theory expected between the straight and the hip). But having invested heavily in the ethnographic fieldwork, I was not about to give up. I realized that the study could make a major contribution to sociology of religion, but that was a field in which, despite having done my graduate work at Berkeley, one of its major centers, I had no training. My theory training at Berkeley, much of it with Smelser (cf. Smelser and Warner 1976), was the grounds not only of my employability (teaching sociological theory has been my bread and butter for over thirty years) but also of my confidence that I could teach myself a new field to salvage my project.

So, using techniques honed under Smelser's tutelage—he always insisted that you could not claim to understand a theory until you had paid attention not only to its concepts and propositions but also to the way these ideas were connected to the empirical phenomena they were supposed to explain—I read the literature bearing proximately and remotely on evangelicalism and religious institutions. I focused both on what was asserted explicitly and on what was assumed implicitly. At length, I found much that was of value, but probably in ways that the authors of the various books and articles I read did not intend (1979). Teaching sociology of religion by then at the University of Illinois at Chicago (UIC), I also began to explore Chicago-area religious institutions with the students in my classes, going with them to their churches, synagogues, mosques, and temples, some of which seemed to be languishing while others flourished. The general realization dawned on me that churches and other religious institutions flourish when they reflect, as well as engage, the cultures of the people who are their local constituents. Such religio-cultural localism is possible, in turn, because religion in the United States is disestablished, or, as I put it in the conclusion to the book that came out of the Mendocino study, "for Americans, religion and community autonomy go hand in hand." The local congregation is where "the laity have historically had their way" (Warner 1988: 290–91). But as I read the extant sociology of religion—a field founded in the 1900s by Europeans for whom the demise of a once-powerful established church loomed large in the background, and presided over in the 1960s by Americans who saw in the imminent collapse of the self-appointed WASP establishment the long-expected end of the road for conventional religion in the United States—I found that field ill prepared to recognize the local and popular roots of American religious vitality. The surprisingly novel idea that *the disestablishment of U.S. religion was the key to its robust appeal,* and thereby to its vitality, was the germ of my next project, which eventuated in the formulation of what I came to call the new paradigm.

I worked on the disestablishment-vitality idea during a year's fellowship at the Institute for Advanced Study at Princeton made possible by the reception of the book on the evangelicals of Mendocino. It was then that I realized that others were coming to conclusions about American religion similar to mine, including Mary Jo Neitz (1987) and Nancy Ammerman (1987), who had discovered instances of vital but not modernized religion in the midst of the modern world, Roger Finke and Rodney Stark (1988, 1989; see now also Finke and Stark 1992), sociologists who spoke of "religious economies," and the economist Laurence Iannaccone (1991), who spoke of "religious market structures." I saw that still others, especially historians (Littel 1962; Mead

1963), had long recognized that the genius of American religion lay in its disestablishment, and they also used economic imagery to understand it (Bilhartz 1986; Butler 1989; Hatch 1989; Stout 1991; Carpenter 1997). This view was diametrically opposed to the one according to which disestablishment eroded the "taken-for-granted" quality of religion that shored up its "plausibility," a view central to the sociology of religion inspired by the European founders of the discipline and the (European) religious history they took for granted (Berger 1969).

My sociological colleagues and the American religious historians we consulted agreed that the secret of American religious vitality is what some of us called the "open market" for religion in the United States, a condition that has prevailed for two hundred years, since the early Republican period. Under disestablishment, there is no state subsidy for religion, but there is also no state licensing of religion. When religion is disestablished, it is not just the property or the prerogative of the privileged. Disestablishment serves to stimulate the energies of entrepreneurs, because anyone can hang out a shingle and set up a church. Because that is so, it often makes good sense for ordinary people to embrace their religions, and religion is therefore more often an arena of agency than a setting of victimization. Accordingly, I proposed that corollaries to the disestablishment of (or open market for) American religion are that orthodoxy, whether in doctrine or structure, is not privileged, that religion is a space available for subcultures, and that religion can be an area of empowerment for minorities (1993). I gathered materials on such nonhegemonic religious institutions and movements as the black church, immigrant churches, gay churches, women's involvement in American religion, and twelve-step groups. Such was the outline of what by 1991 I was calling a new paradigm for the study of American religion. Much progress has been made on the new paradigm in the past decade (Warner 2002).

As much as I felt (and still feel) that Stark, Finke, and Iannaccone, who explicitly embraced rational choice theory, were saying things broadly similar to what I was saying, I had several reasons for not thinking of the new paradigm as a general application of economic or rational choice theory. First and most important, some of those who regarded America's religious disestablishment as a deviant state or degenerate condition for religion (and thereby adhered to what I called the Eurocentric old paradigm) themselves employed economic models to analyze what they saw as the system's tenuousness and shallowness (Berger 1969: ch. 9; Moore 1994; cf. Warner 1993: 1053). If economic theory was central to the construction of their old paradigm, it could not be what defined the new paradigm. Second, the idea of economists that I (as well as historians Terry Bilhartz [1986] and Nathan Hatch [1989]) found most congenial for understanding American religion was "supply side" imagery, the openness of the system to the efforts of would-be religious entrepreneurs. I passed this image on to Finke (1997), but I was less taken by "demand side" imagery, the idea that people's orientation to the religions offered them is analytically identical to their orientation to goods on the consumer market, an approach taken by Stark, Iannaccone, and their colleagues (Stark and Bainbridge 1987; Stark and Finke 2000; Iannaccone 1990; cf. Warner 1993: 1057). Third, I was most confident of what we knew about religion in the United States, which is, after all, the site of the populations and institutions on which most contemporary sociology of religion has been done, as well as the field of expertise of the historians from whom many of us have learned so much. Thus the new paradigm as I understood and clearly labeled it was a model specifically for "the sociological study of religion in the United States," an institutionally distinct system where religion was constitutively disestablished (Warner 1993: 1046, 1055, 1080), not a theory of religion in general. Because I was not proposing a new theory of religion but a new, or better yet, newly asserted, vision of the fundamental properties of American religion, as distinct from the European religion that had originally inspired the founders of sociology of religion, I properly called my construction a "paradigm," not a "theory" (Warner 1993: 1044; 1997a, 1997b).

As one steeped in the tradition of sociological theory, I had more general reasons to be leery of rational choice as a general theory. First, as Talcott Parsons argues, sociology entailed the foundational idea that social action is structured; accordingly it had to reject the economists' competing idea that wants are exogenous (or, as Parsons said, "random" [1949: 59–60]). As I perceive this particular case, religion enjoys diffuse support in the American value system; the needs met by religion in the United States may be met through other institutional channels in other societies (e.g., political movements in much of modern Europe). Second, sociologists of the economy are suspicious of the idea that a market can be "unregulated," a formulation that Stark and Finke seem drawn to (2000; Finke and Stark 1992). As I said in a 1994 conference devoted to internal discussion, "What we new paradigm scholars had hit upon was not so much an economic theory of an unregulated religious market as the institutional secret of American religion as an open religious market, where barriers to entry were low but religion was a respected, popular, and, to a great extent, protected, idiom" (Warner 1997a: 95). Third, at the Institute for Advanced Study in 1988, Susan Harding helped me see that rational choice formulations are usually oblivious to power, assuming the availability of choice to all; as a result of her prodding, I saw in particular that women's chances of finding empowerment in religion depended on there being a differentiation between family and religious institutions (Warner 1993: 1072). Religious disestablishment does not empower women or youth under a system of household monopolies (Collins 1975: ch. 5); minorities generally are not empowered when the religious system is one of *cuius regio, eius religio* (Chaves and Gorski 2001). If it is the case that religion in the United States empowers minorities, as it is, part of the reason has to do with the particularities of social structures in the United States—for example, the fact that the black church is not simply the church of plantation owners that black people attend, and women's place in the church is not simply a function of their status as particular men's wives (cf. Heyrman 1998).

Nonetheless, just because I did not conceive the new paradigm to be a general theory of religion, I would not have felt compelled to theorize my uneasiness about rational choice were it not for three additional stimuli. First is the fact that, despite my intention, my 1993 article is often glossed in the literature (most recently by Christiano, Swatos, and Kivisto 2002: 42) as one of the "seminal" contributions to "the rational choice theory" of religion. I want to set the record straight. Second is the research that I am currently directing in the Youth and Religion Project at UIC, where, in interviews and focus groups with college students and depth studies of their religious institutions and those in which they were raised, we keep encountering cases of enthusiastic embrace and equally vehement rejection of religious identity that are hard to account for in terms of rationality. Third, I now teach Smelser's presidential address to the American Sociological Association, "The Rational and the Ambivalent in the Social Sciences" (1998), in my contemporary theory course to show the continuity in functionalism's response to rational choice theory (cf. Parsons 1954), and I have found it to be a fount of wisdom for my studies of religion in general. Smelser has helped me see my way around the limitations of rational choice theory as applied to religion (Warner, Martel, and Dugan 2001).

(WHAT WOULD BE) ANOMALIES IN AMERICAN RELIGION (IF WE WERE TO ADOPT A RATIONAL CHOICE THEORY)

It would be a mistake to reject out of hand the application of rational choice theory to religious phenomena, especially in the hands of such insightful scholars as Stark, Iannaccone, and their associates. Their applications are not crude. In particular, the implication that many American church leaders seem both drawn to and repelled by—that churches flourish when they pander to popular taste—is almost directly opposite the implication drawn by these theorists themselves (Warner 2002). They say instead that churches flourish when they are "strict" and impose "gratuitous costs" on their members (Iannaccone 1994). Moreover, rational choice assumptions do not yield unambiguous predictions, which, if it were true, might render the perspective a straitjacket, a theoretical iron cage that left no room for theoretical creativity or individual agency. To the contrary, one who uses a rational choice theory of religion can enrich our understanding, as does Stark in his explanation of the rise of Christianity (1996). Anti-rational-choice crusading is uncalled for.

In conceptualizing rational choice, I follow the formulations of Iannaccone (1997) and Stark and Finke (2000). Rational choice theory explains choice of action as a means of maximizing utilities given the constraints imposed by circumstances, where (1) the utilities actors care about tend not to vary across actors and situations; (2) as a consequence, the *explanans,* or independent variable, is the set of circumstances facing actors, including both expected benefits and costs of contemplated actions and the religious alternatives offered; and (3) the benefits and costs of religious participation are in large measure a function of the ideas about the supernatural taught by the particular religious alternative chosen. Accordingly, the rational choice perspective views actors as generic, not idiosyncratic; indeed, for theoretical purposes, actors are interchangeable. The outlook of such generic actors is not clouded by ignorance, and they can fairly well judge what is in their enlightened self-interest. Although this perspective may appear to diminish individuality, it rests at bottom on the same humane instinct as the admonition that we should not judge one of our fellows until we have walked a mile in her or his shoes.

I find rational choice theory most helpful to understand the "supply side" of choices made by religious organizations and entrepreneurs, but less so when what we are trying to understand is the "demand side" of people's motivations for being religious or irreligious (cf. Pizzorno 1986). What I see in American religion suggests that we must take into account much besides circumstances, or objective realities, including inclinations that vary from group to group, from person to person, and, most critically, within persons. Consider:

Of the one-third or so of Americans who are not affiliated with a religious institution (the "unchurched"), most are believers in religious ideas. In other words, defection from or refusal to participate in religion is *not* accounted for primarily by unbelief (Smith et al. 1998: 154–73; Stark and Finke 2000: 76–77). With the literally hundreds of denominations and other religious communities available to Americans and our system of open communications, one would think that people could find a church to accord with their beliefs. Something else must be keeping them away.

Many who are affiliated with a religious institution (the "churched") do not personally subscribe to the doctrines their religious communities teach (Ammerman 1997). Something else must be keeping them there.

Some of the unchurched believers are those people who say they are "spiritual, but not religious." The meaning of religious affiliation seems to differ from person to person.

When Protestants have differences with their churches, they tend to switch to denominations where they fit in. When Catholics part company with their churches, they tend to stay away altogether (Sherkat 2001). The meaning of religious affiliation seems to differ from group to group.

Evangelism—or proselytization—often makes nonevangelicals angry; it does not merely leave them indifferent, as product advertising would. Having one's religious affiliation questioned is different from being invited to buy a new car. Correlatively, leaving one's religion is a cause of great pain for people who seem to have many reasons to get out (Warner 1993: 1079; Warner, Martel, and Dugan 2001). Religious affiliation is not affectively neutral.

Protestant fundamentalists rail against the Godless secular society, but frequently, as in the energy they put into educating their offspring, they aspire to achieve the prestige conferred by the standards of that society. They seem to have mixed motives (Carpenter 1997).

Instrumental motivation, *do ut des,* does not work well in religious affairs. Such is the wisdom of social science (Warner 1993: 1070–71; cf. Smilde 2003), as well as of religion itself. ("Those who want to save their life will lose it, and those who lose their life for my sake will find it" is one of the rare sayings attributed to Jesus in all four gospels.) Many of the purported benefits of religion, including the well-being of individuals and the realization of their communities' aspirations, come only as a by-product of religious commitment and do not serve as its goal. So although religion does good things for people individually and collectively, it cannot be explained by motivation to seek those good things. This stricture seems particularly salient for the understanding of the black church. It is difficult to see where in the motivational structure of the hypothesized economic actor might reside the wellspring of the passion, and especially the courage, that religion has historically engendered among African Americans (Chappell 2002).

In the Youth and Religion Project particularly, we have come across orientations to religion that are puzzling if one assumes that religious involvement is simply rational. For example, in a focus group of Latina college students, mainly Mexican American women of Catholic heritage, most of the participants expressed anger with the church of their upbringing and said they had abandoned its practice; yet two of them had recently baptized their children in the Catholic church and only one had taken the step of actually leaving the church for the Protestant alternative. In a focus group of college men defined as "Christian," those who were the children of immigrants (they were Asian Americans) insisted that they had much to learn from their (also Christian) parents religiously, whereas several of those who were European Americans dismissed the idea that they had anything to learn from their parents—this despite the distinct probability that the Asian American immigrant youth could correct their parents' English, while the latter had learned their English, as well as their religion, from their parents. On the other hand, Muslim women in another focus group, most of them children of immigrants from India and Pakistan, spoke of the enthusiasm with which, as students new to college, they had adopted the religiously mandated *hijab*, or head covering, that their mothers had shunned. Some of them reported with pride (there is no other word for it) that their sisters and even their mothers were following suit. The Youth and Religion Project learned that the most active, popular religious group on the UIC campus (where Catholics, mainline Protestants, and Jews can gather in buildings they own under the tutelage of religious professionals of their own persuasion) is the student-run Muslim Student Association, which meets for weekly prayer in whatever room of the student union is available on Friday afternoon. Off campus, we have studied the successful youth program of a "seeker church" that goes to great lengths to remove any "religious" trappings from their services in order to attract hundreds of twenty-something singles (Kovacs 2000). Analyzing these services, where one seldom sees a cross and never a hymnal, we nonetheless could not believe that those who flock to them are uninterested in religious things (God, sin, and salvation). Meanwhile, for years my sociology of religion class has regularly enrolled students who claim to be spiritual but not religious and those (sometimes the same people) who were raised in a church (usually Catholic) and claim not to have been back since they moved out of their parents' home. These students are bewildered to find that the church today, with women serving as "lectors," "commentators," and "Eucharistic ministers," is not the same as the one they left.

HOW SMELSER HELPS

The focus group component of the Youth and Religion Project was intended to help us begin to understand what college students, most of them newly emancipated from their parents' homes, felt about their religion—what they found positive in it and what negative (Warner, Martel, and Dugan 2001). They told us plenty, and, from earlier acquaintance with UIC students, we were not surprised to hear that the Mexican American women had almost nothing good to say about the Catholic church, and that the second-generation Indo-Pakistani women had nothing bad to say about Islam and the Prophet Mohammed. All complaints that we might have expected these high-achieving, Americanized Muslim women to lodge against their religion were lodged instead against the *cultures* of the countries from which their parents had immigrated. In fact, the extemporaneous conversations we elicited from these eighteen- to twenty-two-year-old women neatly replicated discourse we had read in ethnographic accounts of their religio-ethnic communities.

What we were not prepared for was the admission on the part of two of the Mexican American women, late in the discussion, that for all their differences with the church, they had been married there and had their sons baptized there. One said:

For me it's kind of funny, when I started questioning the Catholic church. When I got married, where was I going to get married? My husband was Catholic. And how was I going to raise my child? . . . I can't really get married in the Catholic church, because I'd be a hypocrite because I disagree with most of the things. I haven't gone to church in, like, years. Only once in a big while. Finally, I ended up getting married in the Catholic church because that's what I grew up with. I baptized my son into the Catholic church, although I don't agree completely with the Catholic church, but that's all I know.

She actually did know of an alternative—the Protestant missions that line the side streets in Chicago's Mexican neighborhoods and that had converted one of the other focus group participants—but to judge from the rest of the discussion, she likely shared the disdain for Protestant proselytizers expressed by Spanish-language front-door stickers made available to Mexican families by the Catholic archdiocese. The stickers say that the family that dwells herein is Catholic, thank you.

The other young mother in the focus group explained that her warmly embraced Mexican culture was inextricable from her reluctant Catholicism: "It's, like, synonymous with Catholicism. A lot of the traditions are viewed as Catholic. . . . So I want my child to grow up with those traditions. They're synonymous with the Catholic religion. . . . I don't agree with the ideology, but I agree with the tradition. I want to instill in him those morals, those values, those traditions."[2] The Youth and Religion Project had intended the focus groups to elicit from students the good and bad news about religion. We did not really expect to hear people say both that they did and did not want to be part of the Catholic church.[3] We had not expected that their feelings would be so mixed, so ambivalent.

Rational choice theory presupposes rationality, which is another way of saying that people know what they value and can weigh the things they value against one another. One objection many scholars of religion raise against such a presupposition stems from their conviction that people value religion differently from other things, such that worship services and, say, secular entertainment are incommensurable for many of the people who participate in both. Yet pastors as much as rational choice theorists know that at least some members of their congregations experience trade-offs between church and the Super Bowl. Ambivalence is something else, something that defies the very foundation of rationality, because it means that people both want and do not want the same thing, or, more typically, both hate and love the same object. Having encountered such an explicit instance of ambivalence, we decided to consider what might be the general place of ambivalence in religious social psychology. For that purpose we turned to "The Rational and the Ambivalent in the Social Sciences" (1998), Neil Smelser's presidential address to the American Sociological Association.[4]

Smelser argues that intrapsychic ambivalence—"the simultaneous existence of attraction and repulsion, of love and hate" toward the same object (5)—is an emotional state the existence of which can be expected under certain circumstances, and that in such circumstances it vitiates the assumption of actors' rationality. To that extent and in such circumstances, theorists must entertain the postulate of ambivalence as an alternative to that of rational choice. Following Freud, Smelser thinks that the circumstances that generate ambivalence are especially found in relationships that are inescapable, those on which the actor is dependent, those from which she is not free to leave. Smelser's "general proposition is that dependent situations breed ambivalence, and correspondingly, models of behavior based on the postulate of ambivalence are the most applicable" in situations of dependence (8). Parent-child relationships are relationships of dependence and the locus classicus of ambivalence. Another prime setting for ambivalence is found in "those groups, organizations, and social movements that demand commitment, adherence and faithfulness from their members." This category includes "churches, ethnic and racial identity groups" (6, 9). Following this reasoning, the Youth and Religion Project, focused as it is on the intersection of these two settings, should have expected to encounter expressions of ambivalence all along and should from the outset have entertained the postulate of ambivalence as a presupposition in designing the research.

As much as sociology of religion rightly regards U.S. religion ever since disestablishment as a key element of the U.S. "voluntary sector" and an aspect of civil society standing between the state and the economy, religion is ordinarily not experienced by children—at least not those who grow up in religiously affiliated families—as a realm of their own free choice. Many of the Youth and Religion Project's youthful informants, indeed, recall that they were "forced" to go to Sunday school. Those students who are disappointed to learn that the church they left as soon as they could has moved in the direction of values they profess (e.g., inclusion of women) seem almost to embrace ambivalence, as if the church they love to hate has no right to change. Whatever the attitude of grownups toward their religion, dependent minors for the most part do not experience it as something they are free to take or leave.

Dependence is itself a variable. Thinking back on the difference between the Asian American and European American college men on how much they felt they had to learn from their parents, we supposed that the former might be objectively less dependent on their parents than the latter.[5] To be sure, the Asian students' expression of respect for their parents may testify to the cultural power of Confucian filial piety (and their white counterparts' disdain for their parents' knowledge may similarly stem from the culturally approved American discourse of generational rebellion). Yet it seems equally likely that the Asian students were *in fact* less dependent on their immigrant parents and more likely to have learned their own way in American society, while the white students *in fact* learned the rudiments of their culture from their parents and might well expect to make their first down payments on the security of their parents' highly appreciated bungalows.

If dependent relationships breed ambivalence, those relationships from which individuals are free to withdraw, or those in which they know that they will live only temporarily, are settings wherein individuals can indulge impulses toward emotional involvement with psychological impunity. Referring to such relationships as "odyssey" situations, Smelser includes ocean voyages, summer camps, the college years, and scholars' temporary residence at his own Center for Advanced Study in the Behavioral Sciences (9). "People, sometimes strangers, are thrown together in physical proximity, but they know this close contact will end in time." Such situations are "typically lived and remembered with unalloyed sentimentality and nostalgia." In such settings, we should expect to find less ambivalence generated; indeed, about them we should expect to find an exhilarating experience of freedom expressed. More generally, as Smelser quotes Edward Lawler, "positive emotion generated by choice processes strengthens affective ties to groups credited with making choice opportunities available" (9, citing Lawler 1997).

Here, we thought Smelser had unlocked a secret of the collective enthusiasm of Muslims on the UIC campus, given a strategic particularity of their religious practice. Whereas the obligatory day of Christian worship is Sunday, the corresponding day for Muslims is Friday. Since most UIC students commute to school from home, many Christian students are no doubt pressured to accompany their parents to church, whereas Muslims' communal prayer occurs at school on a school day. Insofar as the primary religious venues for our Muslim women are on campus rather than the mosques they may have attended with their parents as children, religious involvement for the UIC Muslims may partake of the "odyssey" experience, something associated with the college years, not with their families of origin. By contrast, the Mexican American women, living at home and no doubt subject to Sunday-morning nagging, experience their religion not as a campus-based activity—they seem unaware of the Newman Center—but in the context of their parents' and grandparents' parishes. Thus for many UIC Mexican American students, religion is something imposed on them, whereas for their Muslim peers, religious activity is freed from parentally imposed obligations and associated instead with the new friends they have made in the university. Evangelical Christianity, the second most visible student religious community on the UIC campus—and the religiosity of the most popular off-campus college-age groups we studied—defines itself by a ritual, being "born again," in which individuals publically take charge of their religious lives by "turning around" from the past and declaring themselves to be new persons.

To speak of variations in ambivalence brings up another contribution of Smelser's paper. Having essayed an explanation of the *generation* of ambivalence in relationships of dependence, he also, although less systematically, considers the various *expressions* of ambivalence, the ways it is manifested, taking a lead once again from Freud. Being a *"powerful, persistent, unresolvable, volatile, generalizable,* and *anxiety-provoking* feature of the human condition" (6, emphasis in the original), ambivalence is something we try to avoid experiencing, seldom successfully. "Ambivalence tends to be unstable, expressing itself in different and sometimes contradictory ways as actors attempt to cope with it" (5). Originating in one relationship, ambivalence may find expression in another, as mixed feelings about one's father are projected onto one's analyst or one's God. Ambivalence may be repressed, reversed (where the negative emotion is given a positive expression, as in "love thine enemy"), displaced (appearing in seemingly unrelated thoughts and actions), projected, or split.

An example of "splitting ambivalence" is where the positive side of the ambivalence is transferred into "an unqualified love of one person or object and the negative side into an unqualified hatred of another" (6). With less extreme expressions, what the UIC Muslim women say about religion and culture is an excellent example of such splitting: everything admirable and conducive to their aspirations is attributed to Islam (Williams and Vashi 2001), everything suspect and deleterious is attributed to Indian, Pakistani, or Palestinian culture (Warner, Martel, and Dugan 2001). Convinced that the Mexican culture they feel to be central to their own identities is inextricable from the Catholicism they disdain, our Mexican American women did not have such a luxury.

Another common example of splitting that Smelser cites is the expression of in-group solidarity and out-group hostility, where the actually complex world of social relations is viewed "dichotomously—as friends or enemies, believers or non-believers, good or evil" (10). Mexican Americans who do, despite the risk of disinheritance, convert to Protestantism dichotomize their religious trajectory—although once again, their way of expressing themselves is less extreme than Smelser puts it.[6] Such converts speak, both in our focus groups and in my sociology of religion class, of their preconversion affiliation in highly pejorative terms: "I used to be Catholic, but now I'm Christian." Of such either/or thinking, Smelser comments, "We do not understand the full significance of this categorization, but one of its apparent functions is to diminish the internal ambivalence bred by commitment by splitting it between inside and outside. I know of no mechanism that better protects the fragile solidarity of these intense groups" (10). Being a Protestant does not come easily to Chicago Mexican Americans; it is not a simple rational choice.

We think it reasonable to hypothesize that the legions of baby boomers and GenXers who report that they are "spiritual but not religious" (Roof 1993: 76–79; Beaudoin 1998: 23–26) find in that expression a way of splitting the ambivalence they feel about religious institutions, especially those whose Sunday schools and masses they felt forced to attend. Interest in religious things—prayer, relationship with God, ultimate meaning, and help in times of distress—remains high with members of these cohorts even as many have dropped out of church (or never went in the first place); it is not helpful to regard them as simple unbelievers. God is good; church is bad. Some prefer to go it alone in their spiritual quest (Bellah et al. 1985). But many wish to reach out to others, like those who flock to "seeker churches" that radically minimize any churchlike appearance, meeting in "auditoriums" instead of sanctuaries and offering "teachings" instead of "sermons" in rooms furnished with folding chairs and overhead projectors instead of pews and hymnals. The designers of such churches, like the one studied by the Youth and Religion Project that attracts so many college- and post-college-age singles, evidently think of young people's attitude toward religion in terms similar to those suggested by Smelser's ambivalence theory. If it reminds them of church, out it goes. If it appears to be something you'd never see in church, give it a try.

One youth program we studied—we call it "Soul Station"—applies this principle, as it were, in reverse. Sponsored by a highly modernized church in the Reformed tradition, which itself traditionally scorns "religious" things like statues and stained glass in favor of Bible stories and transparent preaching, Soul Station's Saturday-night college-age worship features candles, icons, low lighting, and long periods of silent meditation (Cravens and Warner 2001). Previous generations already threw out the mystical religious trappings; as members of what has been called the "Millennial Generation," Soul Station youth may reintroduce them (Howe and Strauss 2000: 234–37).

SOME IMPLICATIONS

I have argued that the attribution of rationality, in its technical sense, to the relationship of individuals to their religion, or irreligion, is misleading insofar as such relationships may symbolize relationships of dependence, particularly the universal, though variably intense, dependence of minors on their caretakers. Dependence generates ambivalence, and, at a minimum, ambivalence compromises rationality. Ambivalent persons may irrationally reject what they really want and may irrationally embrace things that are not good for them.

I have not argued that religion is a particular arena for the free play of the irrational. Maturity means emancipation from juvenile dependence. For purposes of sociological theory, we assume that adults are free to make informed choices, subject, of course, to their own conceptions of right and wrong as well as a myriad of objective constraints (Rubinstein 2001). In particular, the argument of this chapter should not be confused with a competing theory that attributes irrationality to religious commitment itself, so-called plausibility theory (Berger 1969). According to this theory, religious beliefs are maintained to the extent that believers are shielded from awareness of potentially disconfirming alternatives, especially competing religions and modern science. Theorists of European secularization have adduced this theory to explain what they see as the fatal consequences for religion of "modernity," particularly the Enlightenment and the encounter with cultures outside of Christendom. According to this theory, religion, especially conservative religion, persists in the modern world only when its objective implausibility is shored up by "plausibility structures," devices whereby the community of believers isolates itself from engagement with the outside world.

It will be clear that plausibility theory, the theoretical heart of the old paradigm, is precisely what I set out to overturn in formulating the new paradigm. Beyond the sociological commonplace that people like to surround themselves with like-minded others, there is no evidence for the claims of plausibility theory (Stark and Finke 2000), whose advocates may fairly be accused of projecting their own cognitive insecurity onto the rest of society. Conservative religion is not especially vulnerable in contemporary America (Smith et al. 1998), and scientific rationality is not popularly hegemonic. In contrast to European religion, which secularization theorists perceive to have reached its apogee five hundred years ago under conditions of establishment, American religion developed in the crucible of modernity and disestablishment (Warner 1991), enlisting a vast population during a century of rapid urbanization and cultural diversification.

Thus we need not return analytically to the dependent minor's view of U.S. religion—in the past or the present—as anything less than voluntary.[7] A decade ago, I wrote that the old paradigm view of U.S. religion, which contrasts an imagined past where religion was a given with a present where religion is optional, "narrates the psychological experience of intellectuals who emerge from religiously conservative families to the religiously indifferent world of the academy." Thus it appeals to those who "have undergone psychologically" the process "that the old paradigm attributes sociologically to Western society as a whole" (Warner 1993: 1054).[8]

There is another respect in which this chapter, along with its theoretical catalyst, does not reject rationality as a working assumption. Like Smelser, I have as my goal not to supplant rationality but to supplement it. The attentive reader will have recognized that the logic I attribute to seeker churches, which lower perceived "religious" barriers to participation in actually religious communities, is a rational one: they do what is in their power to meet their goals, which, most grandly, are to save souls and most immediately to fill seats. Although both rational choice and ambivalence can be usefully employed as *postulates*, or presuppositions of theorizing (which we do when we *assume* that children who inherit their religion from their parents will be ambivalent about it and when we *assume* that religious leaders will respond to what they see as the needs of their constituents and organizations), neither is, or ought to be, an ideology that demands consistency. Moreover, we have also treated ambivalence, and could treat rationality, as an *explanandum,* a dependent variable, specifically a sentiment whose variable intensity can be explained. This chapter is in part a recommendation to sociologists of religion that they consider the applicability of the logic of ambivalence to the understanding of religious activity and religious feelings.

NOTES

1. Peter Berger, whom I identified in 1993 as the leading champion of "the old paradigm," seems to have switched sides. He now acknowledges that the proposition underlying his early work—that modernity inevitably leads to secularization—was mistaken when applied to the United States, and that the European experience, which served as the model for his early work, is itself exceptional, not a promising base on which to generalize (1969, 2001).

2. "In classical Catholicism, exit was virtually impossible" (Smelser 1998: 12).

3. One of our focus group participants expressed the hope that she "can still consider myself Catholic and kind of not."

4. References to this article hereafter are by page number only.

5. "More than other family systems, the American makes the child highly dependent emotionally on its parents, particularly the mother." For boys especially, this situation is highly conducive to the development of a "deep ambivalence toward moral values" (Parsons 1954: 344–45).

6. The Youth and Religion Project's focus-group participants and sociology of religion students of Mexican background report that their families warn that their becoming Protestant would mean renouncing their cultural heritage; some families threaten to throw them out of the house.

7. The past since about 1800. Before then, religion was indeed established in some of the American colonies and, to varying degrees, obligatory.

8. In the interest of full disclosure, I should acknowledge that I myself did not grow up in a religious family and was in fact baptized (in the Presbyterian Church, U.S.A.) at my own initiative at age fifteen.

REFERENCES

Ammerman, Nancy. 1987. *Bible Believers: Fundamentalists in the Modern World.* New Brunswick, N.J.: Rutgers University Press.

———. 1997. "Golden Rule Christianity: Lived Religion in the American Mainstream." In David Hall, ed., *Lived Religion in America,* pp. 196–216. Princeton, N.J.: Princeton University Press.

Beaudoin, Tom. 1998. *Virtual Faith: The Irreverent Spiritual Quest of Generation X.* San Francisco: Jossey-Bass.

Bellah, Robert N., Richard Madsen, William M. Sullivan, Ann Swidler, and Steven M. Tipton. 1985. *Habits of the Heart: Individualism and Commitment in American Life.* Berkeley and Los Angeles: University of California Press.

Berger, Peter L. 1969. *The Sacred Canopy: Elements of a Sociological Theory of Religion.* Garden City, N.Y.: Anchor.

———. 2001. "Reflections on the Sociology of Religion Today." *Sociology of Religion* 62 (winter): 443–54.

Bilhartz, Terry D. 1986. *Urban Religion and the Second Great Awakening: Church and Society in Early National Baltimore.* Rutherford, N.J.: Fairleigh Dickinson University Press.

Butler, Jon. 1989. *Awash in a Sea of Faith: The Christianization of the American People, 1550–1865.* Cambridge: Harvard University Press.

Carpenter, Joel A. 1997. *Revive Us Again: The Reawakening of American Fundamentalism.* New York: Oxford University Press.

Chappell, David L. 2002. "Religious Revivalism in the Civil Rights Movement." *African American Review* 36 (winter): 581–95.

Chaves, Mark, and Philip S. Gorski. 2001. "Religious Pluralism and Religious Participation." *Annual Review of Sociology* 27: 261–81.

Christiano, Kevin J., William H. Swatos Jr., and Peter Kivisto. 2002. *Sociology of Religion: Contemporary Developments.* Walnut Creek, Calif.: Alta Mira.

Collins, Randall. 1975. *Conflict Sociology: Toward an Explanatory Science.* New York: Academic Press.

Cravens, Mary Jean, and R. Stephen Warner. 2001. "The High Intensity Youth Ministry at Soul Station: An Exception to the Pied Piper Model." Paper presented at the annual meetings of the Midwest Sociological Society, St. Louis, April 4.

Finke, Roger. 1997. "The Consequences of Religious Competition: Supply-Side Explanations for Religious Change." In Lawrence A. Young, ed., *Rational Choice Theory and Religion: Summary and Assessment,* pp. 46–65. New York: Routledge.

Finke, Roger, and Rodney Stark. 1988. "Religious Economies and Sacred Canopies: Religious Mobilization in American Cities." *American Sociological Review* 53 (February): 41–49.

———. 1989. "How the Upstart Sects Won America: 1776–1850." *Journal for the Scientific Study of Religion* 28 (March): 27–44.

———. 1992. *The Churching of America, 1776–1990: Winners and Losers in Our Religious Economy.* New Brunswick, N.J.: Rutgers University Press.

Hatch, Nathan O. 1989. *The Democratization of American Christianity.* New Haven: Yale University Press.

Heyrman, Christine Leigh. 1998. *Southern Cross: The Beginnings of the Bible Belt.* Chapel Hill: University of North Carolina Press.

Howe, Neil, and William Strauss. 2000. *Millennials Rising: The Next Great Generation.* New York: Vintage.

Iannaccone, Laurence R. 1990. "Religious Practice: A Human Capital Approach." *Journal for the Scientific Study of Religion* 29 (September): 297–314.

———. 1991. "The Consequences of Religious Market Structure." *Rationality and Society* 3 (April): 156–77.

———. 1994. "Why Strict Churches Are Strong." *American Journal of Sociology* 99 (March): 1180–211.

————. 1997. "Rational Choice: Framework for the Scientific Study of Religion." In Lawrence A. Young, ed., *Rational Choice Theory and Religion: Summary and Assessment,* pp. 25–45. New York: Routledge.

Kovacs, Daniel. 2000. "Social Class and Youth Ministries." Senior honors thesis, University of Illinois at Chicago, Department of Sociology.

Lawler, Edward J. 1997. "Affective Attachments to Nested Groups: The Role of Rational Choice Processes." In J. Skvoretz, J. Szmatka, and J. Berger, eds., *Status, Networks, and Structures: Theory Development in Group Processes,* pp. 387–403. Stanford, Calif.: Stanford University Press.

Lechner, Frank J. 1991. "The Case against Secularization: A Rebuttal." *Social Forces* 69 (June): 1103–19.

Littel, Franklin Hamlin. 1962. *From State Church to Pluralism.* Chicago: Aldine.

Mead, Sidney E. 1963. *The Lively Experiment.* New York: Harper and Row.

Moore, R. Laurence. 1994. *Selling God: American Religion in the Marketplace of Culture.* New York: Oxford University Press.

Neitz, Mary Jo. 1987. *Charisma and Community: A Study of Religious Commitment within the Charismatic Renewal.* New Brunswick, N.J.: Transaction Books.

Parsons, Talcott. 1949. *The Structure of Social Action: A Study in Social Theory with Special Reference to a Group of Recent European Writers.* Glencoe, Ill.: Free Press.

————. 1954. "Psychoanalysis and the Social Structure." In *Essays in Sociological Theory,* pp. 336–47. Rev. ed. Glencoe, Ill.: Free Press.

Pizzorno, Alessandro. 1986. "Some Other Kinds of Otherness: A Critique of 'Rational Choice' Theories." In A. Foxley et al., eds., *Development, Democracy, and the Art of Trespassing: Essays in Honor of Albert O. Hirschman,* pp. 355–73. Notre Dame, Ind.: Notre Dame University Press.

Roof, Wade Clark. 1993. *A Generation of Seekers: The Spiritual Journeys of the Baby Boom Generation.* San Francisco: HarperSanFrancisco.

Rubinstein, David M. 2001. *Culture, Structure, and Agency: Toward a Truly Multidimensional Sociology.* Thousand Oaks, Calif.: Sage.

Sherkat, Darren E. 2001. "Tracking the Restructuring of American Religion: Religious Affiliation and Patterns of Religious Mobility, 1973–1998." *Social Forces* 79 (June): 1459–93.

Smelser, Neil J. 1998. "The Rational and the Ambivalent in the Social Sciences." *American Sociological Review* 63 (February): 1–15.

Smelser, Neil J., and R. Stephen Warner. 1976. *Sociological Theory: Historical and Formal.* Morristown, N.J.: General Learning Press.

Smilde, David. 2003. "Skirting the Instrumental Paradox: Intentional Belief through Narrative in Latin American Pentecostalism." *Qualitative Sociology* 26 (fall): 313–29.

Smith, Christian, with Michael Emerson, Sally Gallagher, Paul Kennedy, and David Sikkink. 1998. *American Evangelicalism: Embattled and Thriving.* Chicago: University of Chicago Press.

Stark, Rodney. 1996. *The Rise of Christianity: How the Obscure, Marginal Jesus Movement Became the Dominant Religious Force in the Western World in a Few Centuries.* Princeton, N.J.: Princeton University Press.

————. 1997. "Bringing Theory Back In." In Lawrence A. Young, ed., *Rational Choice Theory and Religion: Summary and Assessment,* pp. 3–24. New York: Routledge.

Stark, Rodney, and William Sims Bainbridge. 1987. *A Theory of Religion*. New York and Bern: Peter Lang.

Stark, Rodney, and Roger Finke. 2000. *Acts of Faith: Explaining the Human Side of Religion*. Berkeley and Los Angeles: University of California Press.

Stout, Harry S. 1991. *The Divine Dramatist: George Whitefield and the Rise of Modern Evangelicalism*. Grand Rapids, Mich.: Eerdmans.

Warner, R. Stephen. 1979. "Theoretical Barriers to the Understanding of Evangelical Christianity." *Sociological Analysis* 40 (spring): 1–9.

—————. 1988. *New Wine in Old Wineskins: Evangelicals and Liberals in a Small-Town Church*. Berkeley and Los Angeles: University of California Press.

—————. 1991. "Starting Over: Reflections on American Religion." *Christian Century* 108 (September 4–11): 811–13.

—————. 1993. "Work in Progress toward a New Paradigm for the Sociological Study of Religion in the United States." *American Journal of Sociology* 98 (March): 1044–93.

—————. 1997a. "Convergence toward the New Paradigm: A Case of Induction." In Lawrence A. Young, ed., *Rational Choice Theory and Religion: Summary and Assessment*, pp. 87–101. New York: Routledge.

—————. 1997b. "A Paradigm Is Not a Theory: Reply to Lechner." *American Journal of Sociology* 103 (July): 192–98.

—————. 2002. "More Progress on the New Paradigm." In Ted G. Jelen, ed., *Sacred Markets, Sacred Canopies: Essays on Religious Markets and Religious Pluralism*, pp. 1–29. Lanham, Md.: Rowman and Littlefield.

Warner, R. Stephen, Elise Martel, and Rhonda E. Dugan. 2001. "Catholicism Is to Islam as Velcro Is to Teflon: Ambivalence about Religion and Ethnic Culture among Second Generation Latina and Muslim Women College Students." Paper presented at the annual meetings of the Society for the Scientific Study of Religion, Columbus, Ohio, October 19.

Williams, Rhys H., and Gira Vashi. 2001. "Hijab and American Muslim Women: Creating the Space for Autonomous Selves." Paper presented at the annual meetings of the Midwest Sociological Society, St. Louis, April 4.

Chapter 7

Circuits of Commerce

Viviana A. Zelizer

One of the several important analytic stories in Neil Smelser's classic *Social Change in the Industrial Revolution* (1959) concerns English cotton workers' provisions for savings and security. In the heyday of cottage textile production, according to Smelser, the relatively undifferentiated "friendly society" sustained the equally undifferentiated working-class household by managing savings and security while providing—at least for men—settings for drinking, sociability, and confirmation of workers' standing within their craft community. With the increasing industrial differentiation that accompanied mechanization of spinning and then of weaving, runs the argument, arrived differentiation of both family structure and extrafamilial arrangements for savings and security. The Poor Law, savings banks, pawnshops, building societies, cooperatives, and newly streamlined friendly societies took over segments of the social work once performed in undifferentiated fashion by earlier friendly societies. The new specialization, Smelser tells us, implemented the rise of independence as a value applying to individual workers, households, and social life in general. It also complemented withdrawal of households from the sphere of production for more thorough specialization in consumption.

In the case of the cooperative movement, Smelser sums up his argument in these terms:

> Beginning with a period of disturbance, the co-operative movement began to concern itself with several institutional problems which had resulted from the gradual differentiation of the family unit from industrial production and marketing. The resulting gulf between the family and economic processes required social units to stabilize the family's position in the market. Having been pushed into disequilibrium through a process of differentiation in the industrial revolution, therefore, the working classes in turn initiated several sequences of dif-

ferentiation which produced new social units to protect the family in its new industrial environment. (1959: 383)

Thus new, specialized institutions for savings and security arose in response to the accentuated problem of fortifying families in the face of a turbulent, impersonal market.

We need not accept the whole theoretical apparatus at work in Smelser's analysis to recognize either the depth of the transformation he identified or the subtlety with which he differentiated what other historians have often lumped together as insignificant, inefficient, and overlapping social institutions. My aim here is not to mount a full-scale review of Smelser's forty-year-old analysis. That effort, would, among other things, lead to considering the place of women and children of working-class households in the light of more recent work on consumption, bargaining, and household utility schedules. Instead I want to expand on one suggestion of Smelser's description that has been little recognized and whose implications later analysts have regularly misconstrued.

Despite the movement of textile production to shops and factories, Smelser's account does not show us households retreating from economic activity. Instead it shows us two other changes: increased specialization of households in unpaid work, and multiplication of ties between households and nonhousehold institutions. Smelser's account emphasizes economic institutions such as banks, pawnshops, and building societies. But organizations outside the household also included governmental institutions such as courts, magistrates, parish councils, and Poor Law authorities. Observers have often read this set of changes as setting up impermeable barriers between family and economy. In fact, it involves rather the opposite transformation: formation of multiple, differentiated relations between family members or activities, on one side, and extrafamilial institutions, on the other.

Scholars have had trouble recognizing this proliferation of differentiated, crosscutting ties because they have commonly assumed incompatibility between two worlds: the world of intimacy and the world of impersonal rationality. They have seen market relations, specialized firms, organized work, rationality, and impersonality on one side of the barrier between the two worlds. They have seen domestic solidarity, mutual aid, sentiment, and intimacy on the other. Worries about the incompatibility, incommensurability, or contradiction between intimate and impersonal relations follow a long-standing tradition. Since the nineteenth century, social analysts have repeatedly assumed that the social world organizes around competing, incompatible principles: gemeinschaft and gesellschaft, ascription and achievement, sentiment and rationality, solidarity and self-interest. Their mixing, goes the theory, contaminates both: invasion of the sentimental world by instrumental rationality desiccates that world, while introduction of sentiment into rational transactions produces inefficiency, favoritism, cronyism, and other forms of corruption.

Explicitly or implicitly, most analysts of intimate social relations join ordinary people in assuming that the entry of instrumental means such as monetization and cost accounting into the worlds of caring, friendship, sexuality, parent-child relations, and personal information depletes them of their richness, hence that zones of intimacy thrive only if people erect effective barriers around them. Thus emerges a view of *Hostile Worlds:* of properly segregated domains whose sanitary management requires well-maintained boundaries.

Uncomfortable with such dualisms and eager to forward single-principle accounts of social life, opponents of Hostile Worlds views have now and then countered with reductionist *Nothing But* arguments: the ostensibly separate world of intimate social relations, they argue, is nothing but a special case of some general principle. Advocates of Nothing But views divide among three principles: nothing but economic rationality, nothing but culture, and nothing but politics. Thus for economic reductionists, caring, friendship, sexuality, and parent-child relations become special cases of advantage-seeking individual choice under conditions of constraint—in short, of economic rationality. For cultural reductionists, such phenomena become expressions of distinct beliefs. Others insist on the political, coercive, and exploitative bases of the same phenomena.

Neither Hostile Worlds formulations nor Nothing But reductionisms deal adequately with the intersection of intimate social ties and ordering institutions such as money, markets, bureaucracies, and specialized associations. Careful observers of such institutions always report the presence, and often the wild profusion, of intimate ties in their midst.

In order to describe and explain what actually goes on in these regards, we must move beyond Hostile Worlds and Nothing But ideas. Let me propose an alternative third way: the analysis of *differentiated ties*. More specifically, let me insist that in all sorts of social settings, from intimate to impersonal, people differentiate strongly among different kinds of interpersonal relations, marking them with distinctive names, symbols, practices, and media of exchange. Ties themselves do vary from intimate to impersonal and from durable to fleeting. But almost all social settings contain mixtures of ties that differ in these regards. Those ties typically connect people within the setting to different arrays of others both within and outside the setting. Such differentiated ties often ramify into what Randall Collins (2000) calls "Zelizer circuits." Each distinctive social circuit incorporates somewhat different understandings, practices, information, obligations, rights, symbols, and media of exchange. I call these *circuits of commerce* in an old sense of the word, where commerce meant conversation, interchange, intercourse, and mutual shaping. They range from the most intimate to quite impersonal social transactions.[1]

By definition, every circuit involves a network, a bounded set of relations among social sites. "Circuit," however, is not simply a fancy new name for "network." Two features distinguish circuits from networks as usually conceived. First, they consist of dynamic, meaningful, incessantly negotiated interactions among the sites—be those sites individuals, households, organizations, or other social entities. Second, in addition to dynamic relations, they include distinctive media (for example, legal tender or localized tokens) and an array of organized, differentiated transfers (for example, gifts or compensation) between sites. More specifically, any commercial circuit includes four elements:

1. It has a well-defined boundary with some control over transactions crossing the boundary.
2. A distinctive set of transfers of goods, services, or claims upon them occurs within the ties.
3. Those transfers employ distinctive media.
4. Ties among participants have some shared meaning.

In combination, these four elements imply the presence of an institutional structure that reinforces credit, trust, and reciprocity.

Without using the term *circuits*, anthropologists have frequently noticed the phenomenon. Over forty years ago, Paul Bohannan (1955, 1959) discerned what he called spheres of exchange among the Tiv. Each sphere, according to Bohannan, specialized in a restricted set of commodities that people could not exchange across spheres. In this analysis, modern money supplanted such spheres by making a medium of universal exchange available. Subsequent anthropologists followed Bohannan's error in supposing that restricted spheres of exchange disappeared with the onset of modern society or the integration of nonliterate people into the metropolitan world. Frederick Pryor (1977) formalized the idea, identifying "exchange spheres" as social arrangements in which valuables of one delimited set cannot be exchanged for valuables of another such set without the breaking of a prohibition or without one of the parties' losing prestige if the transaction becomes widely known. For Pryor an "exchange circuit" is the special case of an exchange sphere in which goods within the set cannot be traded symmetrically—for example one can get B for A, C for B, and A for C, but not A for B, B for C, or C for A. Pryor actually recognizes that money in complex societies shares some characteristics of exchange spheres and circuits, by excluding certain goods and services, but he fails to pursue that insight into the contemporary world.

Recent ethnography has moved one step beyond Pryor, noting how the integration of previously distinct economies has refuted the widespread expectation that state-backed currencies would obliterate those economies' differentiated monetary spheres. Concerning Melanesia, Joel Robbins and David Akin remark:

> Widespread social scientific expectations that global capitalist expansion would quickly overwhelm traditional Melanesian economies have been confounded by the latter's dynamism and resilience. Indeed, many local systems of exchange appear to have flourished rather than withered from linkage with the world economy, and state currencies and imported goods mingle within formal exchange systems fundamental to social reproduction. Far from the advent of money having consigned indigenous currencies to irrelevance, the two instruments of exchange are clearly in dialogue throughout Melanesia. (Akin and Robbins 1999: 1; see also Crump 1981; Parry and Bloch 1989; Guyer 1995)

Thus, anthropologists have recognized most elements of commercial circuits in nonliterate as well as in developing social settings and even occasionally advanced capitalist countries (see Bloch 1994). They have not, however, assembled those elements into a working model or traced their variations within contemporary capitalist economies. Similarly, economists are increasingly paying attention to the phenomenon that Jérôme Blanc calls "parallel monies." Pointing to the vibrant presence of multiple monies in contemporary economies—ranging among foreign currencies circulating alongside national legal tender, merchandise coupons, school vouchers, local currencies, and commodities such as cigarettes used as media of exchange—Blanc contends that such parallel currencies "are not a residual and archaic phenomenon, which would imply their disappearance with the increasing rationalization of money in westernizing societies; it concerns as well, and especially so, developed and financially stable economies. As witnessed by the emergence of a vast number of parallel monies in the last quarter of the 20th century, we cannot conclude that social modernity will destroy these instruments" (2000: 321). Still, neither anthropologists nor economists have specified the social processes through which people create, sustain, and change distinctive configurations of media, transfers, and social relations.

We can gain theoretically and empirically by picking up where the anthropologists and economists have left off. Many apparently disparate social phenomena incorporate circuits of commerce. Sensitized by the concept, we can detect interesting parallels among the segregated world of professional boxers, favor-trading networks maintained by Russian households, French amateur gardeners, Australian hotel managers, rotating credit associations, direct sales organizations, and migrants' use of remittances (see, e.g., Wacquant 1998, 2000; Ledeneva 1998; Weber 1998; Ingram and Roberts 2000; Biggart 1989, 2001; Durand, Parrado, and Massey 1996).

To illustrate the concept and the range, let us focus on just three cases. The cases run from ostensibly impersonal to very personal: corporate circuits, local currencies, and intimate transactions.

CORPORATE CIRCUITS

For most economic observers, modern organizations represent the fortress of rationality. Circuits also emerge, however, within corporate structures. Firms themselves create social circuits by organizing differentiated systems of payments and mobility; sociologists have often called attention to these systems as internal labor markets. But those systems in their turn generate sets of social relations—circuits, in my use of the word.

Corporations usually mark such internal circuits formally by means of distinctive media, transfers, and interpersonal ties. At the grossest level, modes of payment themselves differentiate circuits: hourly, weekly, monthly, or annual wages; payment in cash, kind, or check; presence or absence of distinctive perquisites (see, e.g., Dalton 1959). On the issue of perquisites, Calvin Morrill's 1995 study of thirteen substantial corporations identifies regular markers of boundaries between middle managers and top managers. For top managers, reports Morrill, corporations regularly paid for the following "goodies," as some executives called them:

first-class transportation (e.g., private planes, helicopters, and limos);

child care for children at exclusive day-care centers;

vacation homes;

special office furniture and equipment (computers, health equipment, kitchens, saunas, and Jacuzzis);

entertainment (e.g., personal season tickets to professional sporting events, theater, symphony, and other artistic events and series);

miscellaneous items and functionaries (boats, luggage, private chefs, masseuses, private athletic trainers, dog groomers, private security personnel, and "sitters" to keep pets, children, parents, spouses, and relational partners occupied during business trips or when accompanying executives on business trips). (1995: 38)

In fact, comments Morrill, top executives frequently measured their success in terms of access to such perquisites rather than sheer income alone. Some members of higher ranking, more powerful circuits typically take home less money than the highest-earning members of other less prestigious and powerful circuits.

Differences between distinctive payment systems commonly set strong boundaries to occupational mobility, information flow, and sociability; movement within the boundaries in these regards remains much more intensive than movement across boundaries (Tilly 1998: 103–16). As a consequence, formally established circuits generate distinctive idioms, practices, understandings, and qualities of social relations. Without emphasizing them, Rosabeth Kanter identifies, for example, remarkable differences in relations among women on the "exempt" and the "nonexempt" sides of the major formal circuit boundary within the large corporation she calls Indsco. Her female managers (the exempt) live relatively isolated lives with little mutual aid and social contact among the women. In contrast, the secretarial and clerical workers (nonexempt) engage in constant conversation, mutual assistance, and job trading (Kanter 1977: especially 147–51). The same division marks off distinctly different payment systems, with annual salaries and associated perquisites on one side, and weekly wages on the other. Where categorical boundaries, such as those of gender, race, ethnicity, and education, cut across formal boundaries established by the organization, they often promote the formation of further circuits, unauthorized but powerful in their effects.

Morrill identifies another variant of circuit formation within corporations: the building of social structure and distinctive culture into cliques. Take the striking demonstration of this phenomenon in Morrill's 1995 ethnography of executives employed by a company he called Playco, a large American corporation. Responding to structural transformations within the firm that accompanied a rash of hostile takeovers, these executives generated a new public style of competition and conflict resolution. The new system by no means simply matched material rewards to task performance. Instead the system demanded adherence to a symbolically charged code of honor. Honorable executives, or "white hats," who followed the rules were rewarded not only with reputation and esteem but also, Morrill found, with expanded power and greater access to resources than their dishonorable "black hat" colleagues enjoyed.

Although Morrill emphasizes cultural differentiation, he clearly documents a corresponding differentiation of interpersonal ties. For example, Playco's chief executive officer described one product team, called the "wild bunch," in these telling terms: "That team has been successful with our home computer lines, but they're a bunch of outlaws. . . . In what way? They don't understand how we do business at [Playco]. There are appropriate ways and inappropriate ways of fighting. The members of [the wild bunch] never learned that. Their days are numbered here" (1995: 193). Anyone who has worked in large organizations recognizes the Playco case as only one instance of a general phenomenon. High executives often create their own circuits across ranks and divisions as they collect information, pursue programs of change, and organize younger people's chances of promotion. Circuits of distinctive media, transfers, and social ties organize a significant part of day-to-day social processes within corporations.

LOCAL CURRENCIES

A less obvious, but no less intriguing, instance of circuit building comes from a recent proliferating movement in Europe and the Americas: the local money movement. Here the variation in media is even more evident than in most corporate circuits. In a partial reconstitution of the multiple monetary circuits that existed before governments imposed national legal tenders, many communities around the world have over the past two decades been creating their own distinctive currencies. During the nineteenth century, American stores, businesses, and other organizations often produced their own currency, mostly as a way to counter the scarcity of small change. Even company towns, labor exchanges, churches, and brothels sometimes issued their own monies. Similarly, during the United States' Great Depression of the 1930s, many schemes of barter and scrip grew up in economically hard-pressed areas (for a more general review of labor exchanges dating from the depression, see Diehl 1937).

Creating a medium to mark a circuit, then, is not a new strategy. Plenty of current practices include one version or another of specialized media. Discount coupons in grocery chains, frequent flier miles on airlines, and credit purchasing within local communities involve formation of distinctive circuits. Food stamps likewise establish their own configurations of media, transfers, and interpersonal ties. Or consider the case of affinity credit cards, issued by a given community or organization and having proceeds earmarked for that group. Local currencies, however, are uniquely situated within distinct spatial territories. The recent deliberate creation of local monies simply dramatizes the significant place of interpersonal circuits in the organization of ostensibly impersonal economic life. Unlike their predecessors, however, many of the new local currencies come out of a broader movement seeking to escape what participants commonly regard as the corrupting effects of national and global economies.

From the Australian "Green Dollars" and the French "Grain de Sel" to the Italian "Misthòs," the German "Talent," the Mexican "Tlaloc," the Argentine "creditos," and the "Self-Sufficient Economic Development," or "SEEDS," of Mendocino, California, local currencies mark geographically circumscribed circuits of commerce (see Helleiner 1999, 2000; Rizzo 1999; Servet 1999). These currencies belong to well-organized local groups that go by names such as local exchange and trading schemes (LETS), *systèmes d'échange local* (SEL), Banca del Tempo (BdT), Sistema di Reciprocità Indiretta (SRI), Club de Trueque, Tauschring, and HOURS.

In the year 2000, an obviously incomplete listing by the Schumacher Society, specialists in promoting local currencies, included thirty-three such groups in the United States alone.[2] Observers of Germany, France, and Italy report some three hundred such circuits in each country, including such currencies as Grain de Sel (Ariège), Piaf (Paris), Cocagne (Toulouse), and Talent (Germany) (see, e.g., Laacher 1999; Pierret 1999). In the United States, along with the Mendocino SEEDS, we find such fetching currency names as Kansas City's Barter Bucks, New Orleans' Mo Money, Berkeley's BREAD, and High Desert Dollars in Prescott, Arizona. Although some enthusiasts for these local arrangements imagine they are doing away with money entirely, in fact they are creating new forms of money devoted to distinctive circuits.

Discussions of local money often mention, and sometimes confuse, four rather different phenomena: pegged currencies, time exchanges, commodity-based systems, and barter. *Pegged currencies* establish a distinct local medium whose value corresponds to that of legal tender. *Time exchanges* take their value from hours of effort contributed by their members. *Commodity-based systems* involve coupons, vouchers, and credits that are ultimately redeemable only in certain earmarked goods or services. *Barter* includes direct exchange of goods and services for each other without intervention of a currency. Although combinations of all four systems appear here and there, the overwhelming majority of deliberately organized local monetary systems fall in the range of the first two, from pegged currencies to time exchanges.

To see the actual working of local currency circuits, we can focus on one example each of those two types; first, pegged systems, and then, time exchanges. In neither case is the local currency convertible into national legal tender. In local exchange and trading schemes (LETS), members transfer goods and services using a locally circumscribed medium, usually pegged to a national currency. At least two major variants of LETS exist. Some create tokens to represent their currency, while others rely on telephone-linked or computer-based central accounts without physical tokens. How do LETS work? Participants generally pay an entrance fee and subscribe to a service listing available goods and services provided by members of a circuit. Buyers and sellers contact each other and negotiate a price; their transaction is then recorded by the local LETS office.

These local monetary systems range from half a dozen members to several thousand. Observers report a total of some 20,000 LETS members in England, and 30,000 in France, a figure suggesting an average of about 100 members per circuit (see Williams 1996; Laacher 1999). In his excellent survey of local currencies, Jérôme Blanc estimates 250,000 members of LETS across the world at the beginning of the year 2000 (2000: 243). The systems vary with respect to each of the elements of circuits identified earlier:

1. a well-defined boundary with some control over transactions crossing the boundary;
2. a distinctive set of transfer of goods, services, or claims upon them occurring within the ties;

3. those transfers employing distinctive media;
4. ties among participants having some shared meaning.

For example, the hundreds of French SEL vary in the networks on which they build: local memberships are held by engineers, ecological enthusiasts, city people who have fled to the country, and low-income populations. In the French town of Pont-de-Montvert, of the local SEL's 130 members, 15 are children who exchange toys, books, and musical instruments (Servet 1999: 45).

Although no one has looked comparatively at the composition of local monetary systems in detail, available descriptions leave the impression that they tend to be socially homogeneous and, on balance, relatively high in status. All restrict participation in some regards. In Germany some Tauschring circuits restrict their membership to the elderly, the handicapped, foreigners, or women. Others expand their circuit to include whole communities or firms (Pierret 1999). Even those, however, remain radically delimited as compared to the scope of legal tender.

Accordingly, local trading systems also specialize in different arrays of goods and services. In France, for example, exchanges in urban SEL concentrate on transportation, administrative service, education, bodily care, and counseling (Laacher 1999). In rural areas, on the other hand, participants are more likely to trade in food products, clothing, construction, and machine repair. As a French commentator observes, "Courses in analytic philosophy offered in Ariège are less likely to find takers than food or transportation. In Paris, a laying hen or farm tools would most likely be less in demand than administrative services computing" (Laacher 1998: 251). Significantly, many SEL circuits ban transfers of certain goods and services as morally, ecologically, or politically off-limits. Banned commodities include firearms, animals, goods manufactured by third-world exploitation, and in one case, a member's book on "how to get rich quick" (Bayon 1999: 73–74). Denis Bayon, an investigator at the University of Lyon, reports, "One of the SEL made an interesting specification concerning 'massages.' An internal document distinguishes erotic massages (growing out of members' personal relations), therapeutic massages (that require the intervention of qualified professionals, eligible for social security reimbursement and exchanges in national currency) and massages designed for general well-being and relaxation" (1999: 73–74). The first two kinds of massage, according to Bayon, are forbidden, the third acceptable. More generally, this circuit favors treatment by means of alternative medicines.

At first, the list of exchanges at the BdT of Ferrara, Italy, seems enormous: it ranges across *lavori e servizi vari* (for example, animal sitting, assistance with school papers, making ice cream, proofreading, company for the elderly, reading aloud), *consulenze* (for example, assistance with computers, social activities, organizing a library), and *lezioni* (for example, lessons in martial arts, dance, German, tai chi, photography).[3] Nevertheless the list concentrates heavily on small and personal services, excluding a wide range of consumer goods and commercially available services.

When it comes to pricing the goods and services they exchange, local trading systems commonly reject existing market prices for their own negotiated tariffs. Often the local price reflects the circuit's greater evaluation of services that, in the members' estimation, the national market undervalues. What is more, apparently equivalent goods and services fetch different prices depending on the parties' evaluation of the relationship. In a report from the Centre Walras, Etienne Perrot notes, "The personality of the provider and the affective dimension of SEL relationships lead the 'client' to pay a *prix d'ami* [friend's price] independent from strict economic calculation" (1999: 386). Similarly, Bayon observes:

> We do not set against each other the hours of baby-sitting, or the hours of reading stories to children. . . . It's Jean-Paul my neighbor who watched my child yesterday, it's Hélène who came to read "scary stories" to my young children, etc. At the core of SELs . . . we find chains of exchange and solidarity mixing and interweaving with each other as invisible threads designing the common good. It's Jacques who tells Françoise he needs someone to help him with housework, or precisely Françoise knows Pierre who was helped by Luc, etc. It's people who join in to share chores. (1999: 80–81)

As a result, Bayon continues, "The structure of 'prices' in SEL currency would make an ordinary economist scream. The 'same' (but precisely it is not the same) hour of ironing gives us here 50 grains, there, 60 grains, here 40 grains, etc. An oversized new pair of shoes bought by mistake will be given here for 100 grains, there 150 grains" (81). By the same token, SEL members, according to Bayon, reject prices that seem morally excessive to them, regardless of the amount that the good or service would bring in national currency outside the circuit.

Even the best managed SEL, however, eventually discover that they cannot insulate their circuit entirely from the rest of the world. In 1998, a landmark lawsuit in France, for instance, finds external labor unions trying to control exchanges of goods and services that they themselves have an exclusive right to produce (Laacher 1999).[4] It also shows courts retranslating SEL's own unit of currency into its national equivalent and interpreting it in terms of market value. Thus, a SEL circuit's boundary becomes something each SEL must not simply draw but defend.

Time exchanges attempt to reinforce that boundary by insulating themselves more firmly from national currencies. While pegged systems have become much more common in Europe and Canada, time-based systems prevail in the United States. HOURS, the community currency pioneer in

Ithaca, New York, is the best known of the more than thirty American local monetary circuits. Each prints its own, fully legal, local currency. The United States government, however, regulates the physical dimension of notes—smaller than dollar bills—and requires their issue in denominations valued at a minimum of $1.

Since the currency's creation in 1991, over seven thousand Ithaca HOURS have been issued. Each of the HOURS, which must be spent in local transactions, is valued at ten dollars. The organization estimates that, through the multiplier effect, the equivalent seventy thousand dollars has added several million dollars to the local economy. HOURS have gained strong local legitimacy: grants of Ithaca HOURS have been awarded to thirty-five community organizations, political candidates solicit HOURS, the town's Chamber of Commerce accepts them, the Department of Social Services distributes HOURS to its clients, and the local credit union offers HOUR-denominated accounts.[5] During the summer of 2000, in what it hailed as "the world's largest local currency loan," the Ithaca HOUR system issued three thousand HOURS (thirty thousand dollars) to the Alternatives Federal Credit Union; the loan covered 5 percent of contract work involved in building the credit union's new headquarters (*HOUR Town*, summer 2000). Like their European counterparts, American authorities take Ithaca HOURS seriously enough to impose income and sales tax on transactions taking place within the system.[6]

To join Ithaca HOURS, participants pay a small fee in exchange for their first two HOURS; the goods or services they offer as well as those they request are then printed in the bimonthly *HOUR Town* newspaper.[7] Three categories of HOURS members participate in the Ithaca circuit: individuals with listings in the group directory, employees of participating businesses who collect part of their wages in HOURS, and other HOURS supporters. In Ithaca and elsewhere, HOURS exchanges range across auto repair, carpentry, counseling, errand running, editing, grant writing, Internet training, notarizing, trucking, weddings, and yoga. Generally, price-setting reflects hours of work but is still subject to bargaining over the relative value of different kinds of labor.

Concretely, this system produces whole rounds of life for some participants: as Elson, a retired Ithaca craftsman who earns HOURS doing heating and air conditioning consulting, reports, "My wife and I spend HOURS at the Farmer's Market, where we browse and chat with old friends. We dine at restaurants, buy apples for mother's homemade apple pie and applesauce. I had my hearing aid repaired and get periodic massages for my failing back. Also I was very pleased last winter to hire two girls with HOURS to shovel heavy snow. They used the HOURS for rent" (Glover, n.d.). Other HOURS circuits place greater restrictions on relations and transfers. Kansas City's Barter Bucks, for instance, are earned by city volunteers as payment for one day's work on a farm and are then spent back in the city to buy produce from the farmer at the Farmer's Market. In Toronto, Dollars are awarded as grants to community organizations; the group's "Spirit at Work" project fosters caring services by offering honoraria or Toronto Dollars gift certificates to needy volunteers.

Zealots among local currency advocates commonly reject compromises built in by systems like Ithaca HOURS or LETS that permit variable valuation of members' time. Purists insist on strong insulation from anything that resembles the commercial market and on strict equivalents of hourly inputs. They often justify this strictness with an appeal to moral values of equality and community. Consider the notable case of Time Dollars, a system of chits use to regulate exchange of services such as elderly care, tutoring, phone companionship, house cleaning, and reading to the blind. A central coordinator keeps a record of time spent and received: exchange rates are fixed. Unlike the negotiated HOURS pricing system, here all hours of service have identical value.[8] And, in contrast to the expansiveness of Ithaca HOURS, Time Dollars organizers deliberately restrict the range of services and the participants within their circuit.

Notice one of Time Dollars' earliest and most successful projects, Brooklyn's Member to Member Elderplan, a social health management organization that allows seniors to pay 25 percent of their premiums in Time Dollars, earned by providing social support for other seniors. For each hour they serve, members get a credit, which they "bank" in Elderplan's computer, to be spent when they need help. Services exchanged include shopping, transportation, bereavement counseling, and telephone visiting among housebound members (Binker 2000; Rowe n.d.). Meanwhile, in Suffolk County, Long Island, welfare mothers can earn enough Time Dollars to make a down payment toward a computer by bringing their children to the public library for computer lessons, and in Washington, D.C., teenagers earn Time Dollars by serving on youth juries sentencing first-time juvenile offenders (Cahn 2001). These systems have a remarkable feature: instead of simply facilitating short-term exchanges, they allow people to accumulate credits over a long period, against a day of need. As a result, beyond their immediate payoff, Time Dollars systems require greater guarantees of continuity in availability of services than other sorts of local monies. Authorities recognize the difference of Time Dollars transactions by refraining from taxing them.

Indeed, one subset of currency systems concentrates on the transfers of caring personal services among people with strong commitments to each other. Time Dollars and some of the LETS circuits have already shown these principles in operation: they often restrict the range of services that members may exchange, setting an ethical standard for those services. What is more, they commonly assure this restriction by limiting membership as well. Advocates of Time Dollars, in fact, often call them the "currency of caring."

A distinctive time exchange variant appears in New York City's Woman-share, a women-only group restricted to one hundred members exchanging their skills; members receive "credits" from the Womanshare "bank" to be spent on other members' services. It is designed to "honor what is tradi-tionally called 'women's work'—work that has been denigrated in our cul-ture,"[9] and participants, as the *New York Times* describes it, "have planted one another's gardens, cooked for the weddings of one another's daughters, seen one another through illnesses and grief, vacationed together, counseled one another on changing careers or wardrobes" (Kaufman 1993).

In both systems—pegged currencies and time exchanges—the very cre-ation and coordination of local monies establishes distinctive circuits of inter-personal relations. To manage their currencies, for instance, participants regularly create standards, institutions, and practices, such as local meetings to decide the issue of new notes, newsletters, Websites, catalogues of available goods and services, monthly potluck dinners, and trading fairs. In Ithaca, the organizers of Ithaca HOURS have created a formal organization that elects officers and holds regular public meetings. An instructional *Hometown Money* Starter Kit and Video, produced by the Ithaca HOURS inventor, Paul Glover, has sold briskly to over six hundred communities, offering other local money organizers step-by-step advice on how to create currencies.

Participants often reinforce their community by incorporating locally meaningful symbols into their monetary tokens. Ithaca HOURS, for example, feature native flowers, waterfalls, crafts, and farms, while LETS networks, which do not rely on physically distinct monies, use symbolically charged names. In Britain, for instance, Greenwich uses "anchors," Can-terbury "tales," and Totnes "acorns" (Helleiner 2000: 46–47). Here, as else-where, the choice of a medium actually involves commitment to a particu-lar network of social relations, a localized symbol system, and set of transfers.

What *meanings* do organizers of local currencies attribute to ties among members? In fact, competing positions have arisen within the local currency movement. Time Dollars' creator Edgar Cahn claims moral and political superiority for the strict hour system, as compared to others, in these terms:

> LETS is expressly a currency designed to create an *alternative* economy, one that seeks to offer much that the global market economy offers but on a more decent, human, sustainable basis. . . . Time Dollars . . . are designed to rebuild a fundamentally different economy, the economy of home, family, neighbor-hood and community. . . . Home, family, and neighborhood are *not* an alter-native economy. They are the CORE Economy. (2001, 2)

With Cahn's position at one ideological extreme, local monetary circuits also vary greatly in the meaning that they attribute to relations within them. While some of their advocates mean them to protect local commercial interests, others insist that local monies build community ties, forging social along with monetary bonds. Local currencies often serve as potent ideological symbols of what Nigel Thrift and Andrew Leyshon (1999) see as alternative moral economies countering global financial markets. At times, organizers' ideologies dip into the wells of communitarian cooperativism and even anarchist thinking.

In the latter vein, savor the tone of a French pronouncement:

> The resurgence of parallel or alternative experiences goes beyond its microscopic dimensions representing the health of civil society. . . . Social cleavage is the chasm into which the state, having forsaken its duties as guardian of the public interest, will now collapse. By rejecting its role as an actor, the state reveals its failure and its self-contradiction. Civil society had made the state responsible, but its ethical treason and its political withdrawal are now on the way to forcing it to give up its function, without glory or honor. (Latour 1999: 83)

As this pronouncement suggests, communitarian advocates of local currencies easily slip over into radical libertarianism, a program for the dismantling of governmental controls on behalf of individual freedom.[10]

Others take on a missionary tone. For example, from Argentina's Club de Trueque we get the following pronouncement: "Our system has extended to Spain (the Basque Country), Uruguay, Brazil, Bolivia and now Ecuador and Colombia. The web page has also allowed us to advise faraway countries, such as Russia and Finland. . . . We are not building barriers to protect our domestic economies, but the foundations and walls for the great cathedral our millennium demands" (Primavera 1999; see also DeMeulenaere 2000; Guerriero 1996). Such ideological and moral resolutions result in a paradox: while local money practices directly challenge Hostile Worlds ideas, their ideologies often reinforce those very same ideas by postulating a frontier between the impure external world of legal tender and the purity of local money. Indeed, the effort of Manchester LETS organizers to integrate their exchanges extensively into the national economy outrages other British LETS organizers. Critics of the Manchester plan, Keith Hart reports, prefer "sealing off a more wholesome kind of circuit from the contamination of capitalism" (1999: 283).

Although most enthusiasts of local currencies are practical activists rather than high-flying social critics and theorists, the movement has attracted attention from critics and theorists (e.g., Williams 1996; Lee 1996; Thorne 1996; Neary and Taylor 1998; Hart 1999; Thrift and Leyshon 1999; Boyle 2000; Helleiner 2000). In their *Beyond Employment*, for example, Claus Offe and Rolf Heinze lay out a program of reform clearly influenced by the local money movement. Their Cooperation Circle program has the following components:

1. It centers on exchange of services among households.
2. It employs a principle of equivalence represented by media deliberately insulated from legal tender.
3. The accounting system depends on time expended, with the implication that every member's time is equivalent.
4. The currency and the membership network form as a function of potential service exchanges.
5. They exclude services that are widely available in markets mediated by legal tender.
6. They are designed to operate in milieux—especially urban milieux— where participants do not all know each other, and where trust-maintaining institutions must be built into the design.

They depend on "supportive, promotional initiatives by provincial or municipal authorities or other sponsors" (Offe and Heinze 1992: 52–55). In short, Offe and Heinze are specifying a boundary, transfers, media, and ties among participants.

As local currency systems create their particular forms of commercial circuits, we can expect more social thinkers to treat them as promising alternatives to the prevailing organization of work and exchange. That worries practitioners such as Paul Glover, founder of Ithaca HOURS. The academic, he predicts, "is going to dissect this like a living cadaver. . . . Part of my aggravation with the academics is that they pile on this as a phenomenon, a novelty, something they can study, write papers about, pass the papers back and forth to each other, getting comfortable salaries. And I'm out here up to my neck in it day to day, translating what I learn into actual programmes" (quoted in Boyle 2000: 114; see also Savdié and Cohen-Mitchell 1997). Glover is certainly right to think that local monies are attracting widespread attention among scholars. But scholars and activists can benefit each other: activists gain by knowing where their particular practices fit into the range of possible practices, while scholars gain from drawing on the practical experience of activists.

As we might reasonably expect, it turns out that local currencies overlap with our third sort of circuit: the circuit of intimacy.

INTIMATE CIRCUITS

What about intimate circuits of commerce? Monetized intimate ties loom as the ultimate nightmare for Hostile Worlds analysts and the strongest challenge for Nothing But reductionists. Many observers assume that when money enters relations between spouses, parents, and children, or caregivers and care recipients, intimacy inevitably vanishes. Nothing But opponents, on the other hand, typically argue that monetized intimate relations reduce to another indistinguishable market exchange, exercise in coercion, or expression of general cultural values. Thus they deny effectively any special features of intimacy as such.

Let us think of relations as intimate to the extent that transactions within them depend on particularized knowledge and attention deployed by at least one person, knowledge and attention not widely available to third parties. Many analysts are tempted to define intimacy by the emotions it typically evokes, such as intense, warm feelings. This is a mistake. As students of emotions such as Arlie Hochschild have shown, intimate relations, from gynecology-patient to husband-wife, vary systematically in how they express or inhibit emotions. The definition of intimacy proposed here follows that lead.[11]

Intimacy thus defined connects not only family members but also friends, sexual partners, healer-patient pairs, and many servant-employer pairs as well. Although Hostile Worlds doctrines lead to the expectation that commercial transactions will corrupt such relations and eventually transform them into impersonal mutual exploitation, close studies of such relations invariably yield a contrary conclusion: across a wide range of intimate relations, people manage to integrate monetary transfers into larger webs of mutual obligations without destroying the social ties involved. As Carol Heimer puts it: "Universalistic norms generate responsibilities to particular others as named nodes in a functioning network" (1992: 145; see also Zelizer 2000a, 2001). People do so precisely by constructing differentiated circuits of commerce.

Consider the debate over paid care, which has emerged as a crucial issue on the national agenda. With the aging of the baby-boom generation, and as most mothers in the United States participate in paid work, the care of children, the elderly, and the sick is being seriously reconsidered. Would the generalization of payment for such care destroy caring itself? Would its subjection to calculation in terms of legal tender rationalize away its essential intimacy?

Increasingly impatient with standard Hostile Worlds or Nothing But answers, feminist analysts—sociologists, economists, philosophers, and legal scholars—are rethinking the economics of intimacy generally and of care in particular. Some argue that care should acquire full market value, while others defend new conceptions of rewards for caring, and still others carry out empirical studies that document what actually takes place in paid systems of care (e.g., England and Folbre 1999; Nelson 1999; Williams 2000; Folbre 2001; for a highly accessible synthesis, see Crittenden 2001). In the process, we are discovering how interpersonal circuits of intimacy shape monetary media.

Take for instance Deborah Stone's 1999 study of home care workers in New England, which documents two points of great importance for my argument:

1. A highly bureaucratized monetary payment system for intimate personal care does not by any means produce a cold dehumanized relationship between caregiver and recipient.
2. Caregivers actually manipulate the payment system to make sure they can provide care appropriate to the relationship. Although they do not usually create new currencies, they redefine the media of payment.

Deeply concerned with the effects of turning care into a profit-making business, Stone investigated how changes in Medicare and managed care financing restructured caring practices. Interviewing home care workers, she discovered a payment system that compensated caregivers exclusively for patients' bodily care, not for conversation or other forms of personal attention or assistance. She also discovered, however, that home care workers did not transform themselves into unfeeling bureaucratic agents. They remained, Stone reports, "keenly aware that home health care is very intimate and very personal" (1999: 64).

The care providers she interviewed included nurses, physical therapists, occupational therapists, and home care aids. Almost without exception, they reported visiting clients on their days off, often bringing some groceries or helping out in other ways. The agency's warnings against becoming emotionally attached to their clients, aides and nurses told Stone, were unrealistic: "If you're human" or "if you have any human compassion, you just do" (1999: 66). To circumvent an inadequate payment system, home care workers define their additional assistance as friendship or neighborliness. Or they simply manipulate the rules, for instance by treating other than the officially approved problems and sometimes even attending to a patient's spouse's health. To be sure, as Stone remarks, inadequate payment structures exploit paid caregivers' concerns for patients. Her interviews conclusively demonstrate, however, that monetary payment systems do not obliterate caring relations.

In short, Stone is observing the creation of interpersonal caregiving circuits with their own representations of values, symbols, and practices. Caregiving circuits are not unique. Similar circuits involving their own monetary practices arise in networks of kinship, friendship, and neighborhood, not to mention within households.

CONCLUSIONS

To be sure, this chapter has met only one of the challenges raised by Smelser's classic analysis of social change in the industrial revolution. It has elaborated on a phenomenon that Smelser noticed in passing but did not emphasize: the formation of differentiated ties crossing household boundaries and involving household members in distinct circuits of commerce. The chapter has not provided a coherent, comprehensive answer to the larger question posed by Smelser: how do new forms of differentiation and integration, such as commercial circuits, arise and change? As Smelser himself hinted, the analysis suggests that culturally embedded, problem-solving people devise solutions to pressing new social challenges by inventing novel commercial circuits.

Corporate circuits, local monies, and intimate circuits obviously differ in their settings and contents. We should resist, however, the ever present temptation to array them along a standard continuum from genuine, general, impersonal markets, at one end, to nonmarket intimacy, at the other. To do so would reconstruct the very gesellschaft/gemeinschaft dichotomies that a clear recognition of circuits helps us escape. In all three types of circuits, we find intense interpersonal ties commingling with regularized media and transfers. In all three, for that matter, we find ties that vary greatly in their intensity, scope, and durability. Differences among the three types of circuits depend not on overall extent of rationalization or solidarity but on variable configurations of media, transfers, interpersonal ties, and shared meanings attached to their intersection.

How then should we generalize these three cases? Here is a rapid summary.

- Neither Hostile Worlds nor Nothing But accounts adequately describe, much less explain, the interplay of monetary transfers and social ties, whether relatively impersonal or very intimate.
- Both intimate and impersonal transactions work through Differentiated Ties, which participants mark off from each other through well-established practices, understandings, and representations.
- Such differentiated ties often compound into distinctive circuits, each incorporating somewhat different understandings, practices, information, obligations, rights, symbols, idioms, and media of exchange.
- Far from determining the nature of interpersonal relationships, media of exchange (including legal tenders) incorporated into such circuits take on particular connections with the understandings, practices, information, obligations, rights, symbols, and idioms embedded in those circuits.
- Indeed, participants in such circuits characteristically reshape exchange media to mark distinctions among different kinds of social relations.

These are the means by which people bridge the apparently unbridgeable gap between social solidarity and monetized transactions.

NOTES

I have adapted a few passages from Zelizer 2000a, 2000b, 2001. I thank Nina Bandelj, Bernard Barber, Jérôme Blanc, Randall Collins, Eric Helleiner, Alexandra Kalev,

Andrew Leyshon, Gary T. Marx, Alex Preda, Arthur Stinchcombe, and Charles Tilly for their advice, suggestions, and assistance.

1. For a clear statement of the assertion that such circuits emerge from small-scale social interactions, see Collins 2000. In fact, as we shall see, they can also form through borrowing of organizational models across social settings.

2. Www.schumachersociety.org/cur_grps.html. The E. F. Schumacher Society. June 2001. Local Currency Groups. Accessed on 25 June 2001.

3. Www.comune.fe.it/bancadeltempo/listaispir.htm. Banca Del Tempo di Ferrara. February 1999. La Lista di Ispirazione. Accessed on 25 June 2001.

4. The appeals court finally decided to support the exemption, recognizing that the SEL members involved in the dispute were not guilty of "clandestine labor"; see Laacher 1999.

5. Www.schumachersociety.org/cur_grps.html. Accessed on 25 June 2001.

6. On the legal aspects of local currencies, see Solomon 1996.

7. Www.ithacahours.org. Ithaca HOURS Local Currency. June 2001. Ithaca HOURS Local Currency Home Page. Accessed on 25 June 2001. In 2001, to manage the growing volume of participants and transactions, organizers began issuing an annual *HOUR Directory*.

8. For a contrasting way of negotiating time's monetary value, see Yakura 2001.

9. Www.angelfire.com/ar2/womanshare/principl.html. Womanshare: A Cooperative Skill Bank. 1999. Statement of Principles. Accessed on 25 June 2001.

10. For an illuminating discussion of local currencies as a political movement challenging neoliberal ideologies by changing consumption patterns, see Helleiner 2000.

11. For an extended discussion of intimate transactions, see Zelizer 2000a, 2001.

REFERENCES

Akin, David, and Joel Robbins, eds. 1999. *Money and Modernity: State and Local Currencies in Melanesia*. Pittsburgh: University of Pittsburgh Press.
Bayon, Denis. 1999. *Les S.E.L., "Systèmes d'échanges locaux": Pour un vrai débat*. Levallois-Perret: Yves Michel.
Biggart, Nicole Woolsey. 1989. *Charismatic Capitalism: Direct Selling Organizations in America*. Chicago: University of Chicago Press.
———. 2001. "Banking on Each Other: The Situational Logic of Rotating Savings and Credit Associations." *Advances in Qualitative Organization Research* 3: 129–53.
Binker, MaryJo. 2000. "Volunteers Use Time Dollars to Help Others." Www.timedollar.org/Articles/Articles2000/Points_of_light.htm. Timedollar Institute. January 2001. Accessed on 25 June 2001.
Blanc, Jérôme. 2000. *Les monnaies parallèles*. Paris: L'Harmattan.
Bloch, Maurice. 1994. "Les usages de l'argent." *Terrain* 23: 5–10.
Bohannan, Paul. 1955. "Some Principles of Exchange and Investment among the Tiv." *American Anthropologist* 57: 60–70.
———. 1959. "The Impact of Money on an African Subsistence Economy." *Journal of Economic History* 19: 491–503.
Boyle, David. 2000. *Funny Money: In Search of Alternative Cash*. 1999. London: Flamingo.

Cahn, Edgar S. 2001. "On LETS and Time Dollars." *International Journal of Community Currency Research* 5; www.geog.le.ac.uk/ijccr/5no2.html. Accessed on 25 June 2001.

Collins, Randall. 2000. "Situational Stratification: A Micro-Macro Theory of Inequality." *Sociological Theory* 18: 17–43.

Crittenden, Ann. 2001. *The Price of Motherhood.* New York: Metropolitan Books.

Crump, Thomas. 1981. *The Phenomenon of Money.* London: Routledge and Kegan Paul.

Dalton, Melville. 1959. *Men Who Manage.* New York: Wiley.

DeMeulenaere, Stephen. 2000. "Reinventing the Market: Alternative Currencies and Community Development in Argentina." *International Journal of Community Currency Research* 4; www.geog.le.ac.uk/ijccr/4no3.html. Accessed on 25 June 2001.

Diehl, Karl. 1937. "Labor Exchange Banks." In Edwin R. A. Seligman, ed., *Encyclopaedia of the Social Sciences,* 7: 637–44. 1930–35. New York: Macmillan.

Durand, Jorge, Emilio A. Parrado, and Douglas S. Massey. 1996. "Migradollars and Development: A Reconsideration of the Mexican Case." *International Migration Review* 30: 423–44.

England, Paula, and Nancy Folbre. 1999. "The Cost of Caring." In Ronnie J. Steinberg and Deborah M. Figart, eds., "Emotional Labor in the Service Economy." Special issue of *Annals of the American Academy of Political and Social Science* 561: 39–51.

Folbre, Nancy. 2001. *The Invisible Heart: Economics and Family Values.* New York: New Press.

Glover, Paul. n.d. *Hometown Money: How to Enrich Your Community with Local Currency.* Ithaca, N.Y.: Ithaca Money.

Guerriero, Leila. 1996. "Siglo XXI: La Vuelta al Trueque." *Revista La Nación* (November 3): 44–49.

Guyer, J. I., ed. 1995. *Money Matters.* Portsmouth, N.H.: Heinemann.

Hart, Keith. 1999. *The Memory Bank: Money in an Unequal World.* London: Profile Books.

Heimer, Carol A. 1992. "Doing Your Job and Helping Your Friends: Universalistic Norms about Obligations to Particular Others in Networks." In Nitin Hohria and Robert G. Eccles, eds., *Networks and Organizations: Structure, Form, and Action,* pp. 143–64. Boston: Harvard Business School Press.

Helleiner, Eric. 1999. "Conclusions—the Future of National Currencies?" In Emily Gilbert and Eric Helleiner, eds., *Nation-States and Money: The Past, Present, and Future of National Currencies,* pp. 215–29. London: Routledge.

———. 2000. "Think Globally, Transact Locally: Green Political Economy and the Local Currency Movement." *Global Society* 14: 35–51.

Ingram, Paul, and Peter W. Roberts. 2000. "Friendships among Competitors in the Sydney Hotel Industry." *American Journal of Sociology* 106: 387–423.

Kanter, Rosabeth Moss. 1977. *Men and Women of the Corporation.* New York: Basic Books.

Kaufman, Michael T. 1993. "Trading Therapy for Art to Forge a Community." *New York Times,* May 19.

Laacher, Smaïn. 1998. "Economie informelle officielle et monnaie franche: L'exemple des systèmes d'échange locaux." *Ethnologie française* 28: 247–56.

———. 1999. "Nouvelles formes de sociabilités ou les limites d'une utopie politique: L'exemple des systèmes d'échange locale (SEL)." *International Journal of Commu-*

nity Currency Research 3; www.geog.le.ac.uk/ijccr/3n02.html. Accessed on 25 June 2001.

Latour, Germain. 1999. "Crépuscule de l'État ou l'économie au péril de la république." In Jean-Michel Servet, ed., *Exclusion et liens financiers,* pp. 380–83. Paris: Economica.

Ledeneva, Alena V. 1998. *Russia's Economy of Favours: Blat, Networking, and Informal Exchange.* New York: Cambridge University Press.

Lee, R. 1996. "Moral Money? LETS and the Social Construction of Local Economic Geographies in Southern England." *Environment and Planning* A 28: 1377–94.

Morrill, Calvin. 1995. *The Executive Way.* Chicago: University of Chicago Press.

Neary, Michael, and Graham Taylor. 1998. *Money and the Human Condition.* New York: St. Martin's Press.

Nelson, Julie A. 1999. "Of Markets and Martyrs: Is It OK to Pay Well for Care?" *Feminist Economics* 5: 43–59.

Offe, Claus, and Rolf G. Heinze. 1992. *Beyond Employment: Time, Work, and the Informal Economy.* Cambridge, U.K.: Polity Press.

Parry, Jonathan, and Maurice Bloch, eds. 1989. *Money and the Morality of Exchange.* New York: Cambridge University Press.

Perrot, Etienne. 1999. "La compensation des dettes de SEL." In Jean-Michel Servet, ed., *Exclusion et liens financiers,* pp. 384–91. Paris: Economica.

Pierret, Dorothee. 1999. "Cercles d'échanges, cercles vertueux de la solidarité. Le Cas de l'Allemagne." *International Journal of Community Currency Research* 3; www.geog.le.ac.uk/ijccr/3n02.html. Accessed on 25 June 2001.

Primavera, Heloisa. 1999. "Como formar un primer Club de Trueque pensando en la economia global." Www3.plala.or.jp/mig/howto-es.html. Accessed on 25 June 2001.

Pryor, Frederick L. 1977. *The Origins of the Economy: Comparative Study of Distribution in Primitive and Peasant Economies.* New York: Academic Press.

Rizzo, Pantaleo. 1999. "Réciprocité indirecte et symétrie: L'émergence d'une nouvelle forme de solidarité." In Jean-Michel Servet, ed., *Exclusion et liens financiers,* pp. 401–8. Paris: Economica.

Robbins, Joel, and David Akin. 1999. "An Introduction to Melanesian Currencies: Agency Identity and Social Reproduction." In David Akin and Joel Robbins, eds., *Money and Modernity: State and Local Currencies in Melanesia,* pp. 1–40. Pittsburgh: University of Pittsburgh Press.

Rowe, Jonathan. n.d. "Life-Enhancing Social Networks for the Elderly." Www .timedollar.org/Applications/Elderly_article.htm. Timedollar Institute. Accessed on 25 June 2001.

Savdié, Tony, and Tim Cohen-Mitchell. 1997. *Local Currencies in Community Development.* Amherst, Mass.: Center for International Education.

Servet, Jean-Michel, ed. 1999. *Une économie sans argent: Les systèmes d'échange local.* Paris: Seuil.

Smelser, Neil J. 1959. *Social Change in the Industrial Revolution: An Application of Theory to the British Cotton Industry.* Chicago: University of Chicago Press.

Solomon, Lewis D. 1996. *Rethinking Our Centralized Monetary System: The Case for a System of Local Currencies.* Westport, Conn.: Praeger.

Stone, Deborah. 1999. "Care and Trembling." *American Prospect* 43: 61–67.

Thorne, L. 1996. "Local Exchange Trading Systems in the United Kingdom: A Case of Re-Embedding?" *Environment and Planning* A 28: 1361–76.

Thrift, Nigel, and Andrew Leyshon. 1999. "Moral Geographies of Money." In Emily Gilbert and Eric Helleiner, eds., *Nation-States and Money: The Past, Present, and Future of National Currencies,* pp. 159–81. London: Routledge.

Tilly, Charles. 1998. *Durable Inequality.* Berkeley and Los Angeles: University of California Press.

Wacquant, Loïc. 1998. "A Fleshpeddler at Work: Power, Pain, and Profit in the Prize Fighting Economy." *Theory and Society* 27: 1–42.

———. 2000. *Corps et âme.* Marseilles: Agone.

Weber, Florence. 1998. *L'Honneur des jardiniers.* Paris: Belin.

Williams, Colin C. 1996. "The New Barter Economy: An Appraisal of Local Exchange and Trading Systems (LETS)." *Journal of Public Policy* 16: 85–101.

Williams, Joan. 2000. *Unbending Gender: Why Family and Work Conflict and What to Do about It.* New York: Oxford University Press.

Yakura, Elaine K. 2001. "Billables: The Valorization of Time in Consulting." *American Behavioral Scientist* 44: 1076–95.

Zelizer, Viviana. 2000a. "The Purchase of Intimacy." *Law and Social Inquiry* 25: 817–48.

———. 2000b. "How and Why Do We Care about Circuits?" *Accounts: A Newsletter of Economic Sociology* (Economic Sociology Section of the American Sociological Association) 1: 3–5.

———. 2001. "Transactions intimes." *Genèses* 42 (March 2001): 121–44.

Znoj, Heinzpeter. 1998. "Hot Money and War Debts: Transactional Regimes in Southwestern Sumatra." *Comparative Studies in Society and History* 40: 193–222.

Chapter 8

Trust as an Aspect of Social Structure

Robert Wuthnow

Whom can you trust these days? Many doctors seem more intent on earning high incomes than on truly caring for their patients. Some public officials will say almost anything to get elected. Neighbors seldom see one another often enough to know if they can depend on one another for help. Marriage partners make vows they do not expect to keep. Students cheat on exams. Are things getting worse, or have people always been untrustworthy? What is trust, anyway, and how should we think about it?

Although discussions of trust can be found in literary, philosophical, and religious sources dating back thousands of years, sociologists have paid relatively little attention to studying trust until recently. Within the past few years, questions about trust have been raised by sociologists interested in such wide-ranging topics as social network analysis, game theory, voter turnout, deviance and social control, and comparative economic systems. Yet the place of trust in more general sociological conceptions of human behavior remains unclear.

My aim in this chapter is to situate the idea of trust in relation to one strand of sociological theory that has played a central role in the discipline's intellectual development and that emphasizes social structure. This strand emanates mainly from Max Weber's ideas about meaningful social action and Emile Durkheim's ideas about the moral basis of society—ideas that came together in the work of Talcott Parsons, Robert Merton, Reinhard Bendix, Wilbert Moore, Lewis Coser, Philip Selznick, Clifford Geertz, Peter Berger, and others to form a conception of social structure in which norms and values play a prominent role.

For present purposes, I take the work of Neil Smelser as the primary representation of this normative perspective on social structure. Smelser's work was fundamentally influenced by his early collaboration with Talcott Parsons and by his reading of Weber and Durkheim, as well as by an extensive engagement with virtually all of the scholars who contributed to this normative understanding of social structure (Smelser 1988). By *normative,* I refer to the emphasis found in this tradition of sociology on the rules and expectations that govern social life. Norms range from "formal, explicit regulations found . . . in legal systems to informal, sometimes unconscious understandings found, for instance, in neighborhood cliques" (Smelser 1962: 27). According to this perspective, social structure consists largely of the regularity or patterned behavior that results from people conforming to the rules and expectations embedded in the social contexts in which their action takes place. Throughout his career, Smelser was particularly interested in the dynamic relationships among the norms around which roles and institutions form, the higher-order values that legitimate social practices, and the tensions that cause change in patterns of behavior. His theoretical work was also increasingly critical of economistic perspectives (such as rational choice theory) that in his view did not fully take social structure into account (Smelser 1992, 1995; Smelser and Swedberg 1994).

This understanding of social structure seems a likely place to begin in seeking to integrate the concept of trust into a more general understanding of human behavior. At one level, trust can be regarded as an expectation that relevant others will behave according to certain norms that make their behavior dependable, predictable, or, as we say, trustworthy. Any investigation of trust must, therefore, pay attention not only to the behavior of individual actors but also to the norms and expectations embedded in the social settings in which these actors behave. The link between individual behavior and these embedded norms and expectations suggests that trust must be conceived of as an element of social structure.

To associate trust with social structure in this way implies that trust can usefully be examined in the same terms that have been used to understand other forms of normative behavior, such as etiquette, conformity (or deviance), dating, and job performance. In all of these cases, relevant questions include the extent to which norms are shared and communicated to newcomers through agents of socialization, the reward structures and systems of enforcement that undergird normative conformity, and the ways in which normative behavior is influenced by differential access to material resources.

I argue that trust must also be understood in relation to the active ways in which people negotiate with the normative structure in which their behavior takes place. To say that someone is trustworthy in a particular situation implies that it seems valid—or warranted—to regard someone this way. Trustworthy behavior is thus warranted in terms of scripts or arguments that make sense in relation to norms governing certain kinds of behavior. Recent efforts to extend earlier ideas of social structure by bringing notions of cultural scripts into the picture are helpful in this regard.

To show how trust can be understood as an element of social structure, I consider some specific ways in which it functions in three settings: professional-client relations, local communities, and religious behavior. For each of the three, I present some examples of the ways in which people consider their reasons for trusting or not trusting others. These reasons provide some support for the idea that trust is closely linked with the prevailing norms of particular social situations.

I conclude this introductory section by observing that what follows is not meant as an effort to present a general theory of trust but rather as an attempt to bring discussions of trust into closer conversation with long-standing ideas about social norms. In doing so, I suggest neither that trust offers special insights about issues that have been overlooked in the social sciences, nor that it needs to be replaced with other concepts; instead, trust is a concept that occurs routinely enough in ordinary speech that we must take it into account but also subject it to the kind of scrutiny that goes beyond merely taking it at face value.

RECENT DISCUSSIONS OF TRUST

A brief review of the literature that has emerged over the past decade or so gives a preliminary sense of how trust has been conceptualized and why it is currently regarded as an important idea that deserves greater theoretical and empirical attention than it has thus far received. Not all of this literature has been the work of sociologists; indeed, political scientists have shown at least as much interest in trust as sociologists have. Yet both in sociology and in political science, the diversity of ways in which trust has been conceptualized has meant that scholars sometimes seem to be writing about different things, or at least could benefit by an effort to bring their various perspectives closer together.

One of the most ambitious attempts to present a theoretical perspective on trust was included in James Coleman's 1990 formulation of a rational-choice approach to the entire field of sociology. Coleman situates his discussion of trust as a problem faced by a rational actor who is trying to decide whether to engage in a transaction with another person. Because the reward an actor hopes to gain from his or her investment often does not occur immediately, the actor must factor some assessment of risk into his or her calculations. There are two kinds of risk: those not under the control of the person with whom the actor is about to engage in a relationship (for example, bad weather or a stock market crash), and those under this person's control (for example, his or her willingness to stick to a bargain). Coleman says trust pertains to the second kind of risk. Trust is thus part of a rational actor's effort to calculate the costs and benefits of entering into a specified relationship with another person. It often depends largely on the amount of information that can be obtained about the other person and whether this information indicates that the person is dependable. Trust is a fundamental aspect of social exchange, Coleman suggests, because it encourages people to continue interacting with one another even when there are risks involved that cannot be fully anticipated or controlled through pricing arrangements or coercive mechanisms.

Because virtually all social interaction involves some lapse of time between investment and payoff, Coleman's formulation underscores the centrality of trust to any understanding of social behavior. By focusing on the decision making of a rational individual, this formulation nevertheless leaves a number of important questions unanswered. For instance, rational actors presumably make decisions about whom to trust on the basis of some information about the people and circumstances under consideration. But how do they judge what information is relevant? A business manager deciding whether to trust a potential employee is likely to be oriented toward information different from that considered by a gang leader deciding whether to trust a potential gang member.

Coleman's approach implies that decision makers are influenced by the norms governing different situations, but his approach does not adequately take account of these norms. Consider the decisions someone implicitly makes in driving to work each morning. In Coleman's terms, the driver calculates the relationship between his or her investment of time and estimated costs (such as fuel and depreciation on one's automobile) and an expected payoff (getting to work safely and on time) by taking account of certain risks presented by other drivers (the possibility that one of them may cause an accident). The driver's calculations implicitly include a decision to trust the other drivers. But on what basis? Not because of being able to predict on any given morning that all other drivers will be trustworthy, but because of having observed certain patterns of behavior among drivers on previous mornings—most notably, the fact that accidents along one's route are relatively rare.

And further reflection suggests that accidents are rare for several reasons: drivers are conforming to certain norms of safety and courtesy that collectively maximize the chances of arriving at their destinations without incident, drivers can usually be trusted to exhibit at least minimal competence in their roles because they have passed an examination designed to certify their competence, and the trust one places in other drivers is to a degree enforceable because of police officers and traffic laws (specifying which side of the road to drive on, when to yield to other traffic, and how fast to drive). Coleman's rational actor, therefore, turns out to be embedded in a social system from which he or she derives information about how warranted or unwarranted it may be to embark on a routine automobile journey.

Coleman's rational actor is influenced in even subtler ways by the social system in which he or she is embedded. For instance, Coleman asserts that trust pertains to those risks associated with the behavior of other actors and not to risks that come about in other ways. But this distinction between kinds of risk depends on the social situation. If a tree is hit by lightning and smashes the automobile of our rational actor, Coleman's definition would appear to suggest that trust or lack of trust is not a relevant consideration. But suppose it were shown that the tree toppled because it had been weakened by previous storms or by insects, and that the highway maintenance crew was negligent in not noticing the potential danger and removing the tree. In that instance it would be appropriate to say that drivers were implicitly registering trust in maintenance crews as part of their assessment of the risks involved in traveling to work.

In addition, Coleman's view of trust takes for granted that actors have already identified the goals they wish to pursue. But where do these goals come from? And are they entirely independent of actors' calculations about trust? In the present case, someone commuting to work may decide that taking early retirement makes more sense than subjecting oneself to the hazards of the daily commute. Moreover, Coleman's view assumes that the rational actor is not only capable of behaving rationally but also regards himself or herself as a rational person. But this assumption suggests that trust expressed toward others is not completely independent of trust expressed toward oneself. For instance, a commuter with a bad hangover may realize that he or she is untrustworthy but assume that everyone else will behave in a trustworthy manner.

An equally ambitious effort to conceptualize trust came a few years after Coleman's work, in Francis Fukuyama's 1995 comparative study of the social factors encouraging or discouraging national economic prosperity. For Fukuyama, trust appears to be a shorthand way of describing the general level of sociability or communitarian orientation in a society. He contrasts low-trust societies, such as Taiwan and France, with high-trust societies, such as Japan and Germany, placing the United States historically with the latter but arguing that diminishing trust is likely to turn the United States into a low-trust society in the future if some corrective action is not taken. Fukuyama's argument draws on and is not unlike Coleman's, but Fukuyama clearly perceives trust to be a broad feature of societies that somehow becomes institutionalized, rather than the result of individual actors' calculations about specific transactions.

Fukuyama's understanding of trust, therefore, moves closer to a normative view of social structure than Coleman's does, particularly in emphasizing that rational actors do not make calculations about trust in isolation from the larger societal milieu in which they function. Implicitly, Fukuyama's association of trust with strong communal loyalties suggests that these loyalties are likely to facilitate trust. For instance, a business manager may be more willing to risk an entrepreneurial venture by virtue of knowing more about a potential partner as a result of being acquainted with that partner's family or being a member of a club or neighborhood association. But Fukuyama's concern about the supposed breakdown of trust in less communally oriented societies suggests a weakness in his formulation. This weakness becomes evident once it is granted that such societies also have a normative structure. Rather than trust disappearing, it may be warranted in terms of these alternative norms. For example, a business manager who cannot rely on personal networks to supply the information on which trust is based may instead rely on the fact that potential partners can be trusted because of legal restrictions on their activities, because of educational and certification requirements, or because information technology makes it easier to conduct background checks on their credit ratings.

The concept of trust also figured importantly in Robert Putnam's 1993 study of the associational bases of democratic government. Also drawing on Coleman, Putnam argues that social capital in the form of extensive involvement in voluntary associations is conducive to good democratic government. Putnam includes both networks and norms that encourage cooperation in his definition of social capital, conceptualizing these norms largely as a generalized sentiment that others can be trusted. Taking regions in Italy as his unit of analysis, he purports to show that over a twenty-year period those regions with higher levels of trust also enjoyed more effective democratic governmental structures.

Putnam's study operationalizes trust by aggregating survey responses at the regional level to a question asking individuals whether they believe most people can be trusted or whether one must be careful in one's dealings with people. The argument for measuring trust in this way is that such aggregated responses point to a kind of subculture or shared feeling about the extent to which people can be trusted. When trust is high, Putnam finds, regional government officials are more likely to benefit from citizens taking an active role in their communities and thus sharing in some of the responsibilities of democratic government. But relying on a single survey question to assess the normative climate of a region is clearly limiting. At minimum, one would want to know what the basis of greater trust in one region than in another is, whether it largely reflects more affluent economic conditions, and why it changes or remains stable.

Adam Seligman's 1997 book-length treatment of trust, which stands as one of the most historically informed studies of the theoretical underpinnings of the concept, draws on Coleman's lineage only to a small extent, and, similar to Fukuyama and Putnam, Seligman seeks to situate trust in a framework compatible with concerns about an apparent decline in the social bases of civil society. He argues that in tribal societies trust can be based largely on familiarity and intimate contact, whereas in modern societies trust comes to depend on something else. In brief, Seligman suggests that trust can be conceived of only as a solution to the problem of risk (as Coleman does) by making additional assumptions about the division of labor in modern societies and about modern conceptions of the self.

Of these works, Seligman's goes farthest toward situating trust within a broader understanding of social structure. For instance, he points out that Coleman's rational actor is itself contingent on certain notions of rationality that may be present in some contexts and not in others, and that cultural distinctions between public behavior and private behavior establish different frameworks for thinking about trust. Still, Seligman's approach suggests that more clarity is needed about what exactly trust is and about how people explain their reasons for trusting other people in some situations and not in others.

While these various studies have opened up rich avenues of theoretical and empirical investigation, all of them point toward a need to consider trust in relation to the larger structure in which social action takes place, rather than viewing it only in terms of dyadic social exchange. Trust does not depend only on judgments one person makes about another, but also on assumptions that emerge from the context in which relationships take place, on expectations derived from previous relationships, and on criteria for making judgments that are deemed legitimate by the actors involved.

A theoretical framework for thinking about trust as an element of social structure has yet to be worked out. The perspective presented by Coleman makes it possible to think about trust as the aggregate of many individual actors' calculations but leaves unspecified how those aggregated calculations become embedded in social institutions. Fukuyama's work leaves open the question of whether trust in itself is an important dimension of social life or is merely subsumed within larger considerations of sociability. Of the other contributions, Seligman's work is the most suggestive, but it raises the question of whether Coleman's individualistic perspective is largely correct in modern societies or whether there may be other ways to think about trust.

The tension in much of the literature on trust can perhaps be summarized as follows: Is trust best conceived of as a kind of attitude or perception that one individual has concerning another? Or can trust usefully be understood as a feature of the social structure in which individuals are embedded? If the former view is correct, then trust is largely a matter of information, and the best that can be done to improve social relationships is to give individuals more accurate information about whom they can and cannot trust. But if the latter view is correct, trust ceases to be an attribute only of individuals and becomes a part of the world that must be understood sociologically, just as social institutions, social stratification, and social change must be. If trust is truly an element of social structure, it must be situated in terms of what we know about social norms and how they shape human behavior.

A THEORETICAL PERSPECTIVE

Smelser's work is my starting point for thinking about trust as an element of social structure. This view contrasts sharply with ideas that emphasize only the exchange of goods and services among individuals or that regard social structure exclusively in terms of power relations or the distribution of wealth. It takes seriously Weber's insistence that social action is above all behavior that has come to be regarded as legitimate or meaningful by those who engage in it, and that structures of legitimacy are among the primary constraints that lead people to behave in certain ways. It also adopts Durkheim's idea of social facts as those regularities of behavior that exist apart from the decisions of particular individuals.

The normative perspective on social structure rests largely on the assumption that social actors are constrained by internalized rules and expectations. Many of these rules and expectations are bundled together in the definitions of roles to which we are socialized. Thus, an important aspect of social structure is composed by the norms that make up such primary roles as son, daughter, sibling, mother, father, and spouse. Other aspects of social structure are defined by such roles as citizen, neighbor, friend, and breadwinner. The rules and expectations governing these roles constitute the institutionalized regularities of social life. People who occupy the role of scientist, for example, behave in similar ways, and these patterns come to be taken for granted by scientists so much so that it may seem strange to them when one of their number starts to think or act in new ways. While such norms often generate voluntary compliance, they are usually reinforced by a system of rewards (prizes, salaries, or patents, in the case of scientists). Norms and social resources therefore interact in complex ways: power and wealth are used to reinforce norms, and norms may maintain differential distributions of wealth and power. Normative structure is also embedded in systems of legitimation, such as values and belief systems that provide reasons why it is good, right, or inevitable to behave in specified ways. These systems of legitimation give stability to social structure over time. But social structure is also subject to inherent tensions and contradictions that may cause it to change.

These ideas have several important implications for understanding trust, perhaps the most significant of which is simply that trust is a relevant consideration in any attempt to describe and explain social relationships. That is, social structure consists of norms and expectations, among which is the norm that people should be trustworthy and the expectation that they either are or are not trustworthy. Put differently, people behave the way they do not only because of the power they have, the wealth they own, or the income they desire to obtain but also because they have come to expect other people to behave in certain ways.

But if trust is relevant, its social basis must be specified. Trust is neither all of the normative order of a society or only a calculation of how likely or unlikely a person is to live up to his or her word. Trust pertains particularly to those instances in which, as Coleman suggests, people enter into or maintain social relationships on the assumption that they can count on or rely on other people. A further implication is that trust does not pertain only to dyadic relationships between individuals but also becomes institutionalized. Thus, an individual scientist may calculate whether or not another scientist is trustworthy, but citizens, government officials, private patrons, and consumers make judgments about the trustworthiness of science as an institution. They do so not because of the behavior of any particular individual but because of laws, training, and reward systems that encourage trustworthy behavior (Merton 1973: 267–80; Storer 1966).

ELABORATING THE PERSPECTIVE

Thus far I have suggested that an understanding of social structure in which norms are emphasized provides a starting point for bringing the study of trust into one of the mainstream traditions of sociological theory. But this understanding of social structure has also been evolving in recent years. Internalized norms and values have become a subject of particular scrutiny. Rather than inferring their existence from larger patterns of social behavior, observers argue that greater attention should be paid to how these norms and values are articulated and communicated. Cultural sociology has emerged as the subdiscipline in which much of this work is located.

In the work of contemporary cultural sociologists, culture is viewed less as a set of internalized predispositions and more as a repertoire of scripts, frames, and warrants that people deploy strategically to make sense of their behavior and the behavior of others. For instance, one formulation likens culture to a tool kit that actors can employ in order to make sense of their worlds and in other ways achieve their goals (Swidler 1986). One advantage of this formulation is that it acknowledges that actors select from a variety of cultural scripts, rather than their behavior being determined by one set of norms and values. But this view can leave the selection process too much up for grabs unless actors are situated squarely in their social contexts. In other words, people do not choose just any idea to make sense of their behavior: they choose ideas that seem legitimate in relation to the *norms* present in their social context.

For purposes of understanding trust, it is helpful to recognize that people actually think and talk about trust. They do so because trust itself is something that must make sense. We ask ourselves, implicitly at least, is it *warranted* to trust someone in a particular situation. And for this reason, *warrants* must be supplied that explain (to ourselves or anyone who may ask) why we have decided to trust someone. For instance, our commuter may not think much about trust most mornings, but were there to be rumors of exceptional danger, he or she might feel compelled to come up with some warrants, such as "I trust the highway department to get the bridge fixed before I arrive," or "I trust the police to be out in full force today."

One of the main conclusions that comes from thinking about trust this way is that there are a number of different ways in which trust can be warranted. And these alternative warrants, while seemingly arbitrary, are likely to reflect the norms of which social structure is composed in different contexts. A partial catalog of warrants for trust would likely include the following:

· Sincerity: A is persuaded that B's actions are an accurate reflection of who B is, that B's motives or intentions and behavior are consistent with one another, and that B is truthful or authentic.
· Empathy: A perceives that B cares about A in a way that extends beyond the instrumental roles one plays; this perception is likely to be based on some display of emotion.
· Affinity: A senses that A and B have a shared identity, common values, or mutual understanding, as in being of the same religion, ethnic group, or race; affinity affords legitimacy to the relationship by associating the roles that A and B play with a larger set of values.
· Altruism: A expects B to exercise restraint over B's self-interest and to behave in a way that takes account of A's interests and needs.
· Accessibility: A anticipates that B will be available when interaction is desired and believes that A has a valid claim to B's time and resources.
· Effectiveness: A regards B as efficacious, as able to get the job done or to achieve desired results; this implies that A believes B to have certain resources and to be able to mobilize those resources.
· Competence: A perceives B as having appropriate training, information, skills, and talents for performing the role in question (differs from believing that B will actually be able to produce results).
· Congeniality: A regards B as capable of engaging in such extrarole behavior as making small talk, being polite and friendly, and being easygoing, at ease, all of which help to align and sustain role behavior.
· Fairness: A expects B to follow prescribed procedures and abide by formal rules pertaining to B's role, thus treating A similarly to people who are in similar situations and not rendering arbitrary judgments.
· Reliability: A regards B as being dependable or stable by virtue of expecting B to behave in similar ways under similar circumstances over time.

These warrants are not mutually exclusive: A may trust B for several of these reasons or for only one reason. The point is that people do give reasons for trusting someone. These reasons help us understand what trust is. They also serve as verbal manifestations of the norms prevailing in different contexts. Thus, a person entering a courtroom as a plaintiff in a trial may trust the judge not because of congeniality or affinity but because the judge is expected to be fair. In a business setting, the primary warrant for trust is likely to be effectiveness or competence; and yet, since judgments about those may be made with imperfect knowledge, sincerity or accessibility may be important as well.

A related contribution of cultural sociology is that the cultural work in which people engage is likely to be different in unsettled times than in settled times. In settled times, people may not think much about whom they can or cannot trust. If pressed to give warrants for their trust, they may well emphasize the very settledness of relationships by talking about reliability. In less settled times, greater uncertainty is likely to prevail and thus people may feel compelled to give a wider variety of warrants to explain their trust. For instance, someone forming a new business may try to collect as much information as possible to determine whether potential partners are effective, competent, and reliable, but is also likely to insist on meetings that will generate information about affinity, sincerity, and congeniality.

During unsettled times or, indeed, whenever people's expectations are shattered, a common response is to develop explanations of what went wrong. These secondary warrants, as they might be called, help to realign and maintain social relationships (Wuthnow 1998, 1999). One strategy is to acknowledge that one's warrants were either wrong or wrongly prioritized; for instance, one might say that the person seemed trustworthy because of his or her congeniality, but that it would have been better to learn more about the person's competence. Another strategy is simply to acknowledge that social relationships are always risky and that some mistakes are likely. Yet another strategy is to focus more squarely on social structure itself—for example, by identifying norms leading to conflicting evaluations and then holding special meetings to resolve these conflicts.

A related insight that may be drawn from cultural sociology is that culture does not just happen but is produced. In more traditional formulations, social structure is sometimes regarded too passively as deep-seated norms that people mostly conform to without questioning them. In that view, trust is present, absent, or somewhere in between by virtue of the social context. But trust may be actively produced or manipulated as well. Individuals may intentionally display emotion in order to signal that they can be trusted because they have empathy. Or they may consciously engage in small talk to show that they are congenial. Organizations signal their trustworthiness in similar ways; for example, they may give employees special leaves or bonuses

on holidays to convey their empathy or congeniality, advertise that their leaders include people of a particular racial or ethnic background to suggest
affinity to a certain constituency, or develop a bureaucratic structure that
resembles that of other organizations in order to signal that they are competent and reliable (Meyer and Rowan 1977; DiMaggio and Powell 1983).

This point about trust being produced is important for two reasons. It suggests that the distribution of resources is an important part of any social
structural understanding of trust. Those who have wealth and power are better able to manipulate the messages that people use to legitimate trust;
people without wealth and power may be skeptical of these messages because
they understand this capacity to manipulate. It also suggests that trust may
be produced cynically, as when deception is deliberately used to generate an
image of trustworthiness. Under such circumstances, revelations of deception are likely to be particularly damaging. They undermine several of the
warrants for trust, especially affinity, empathy, and sincerity.

TRUST IN PROFESSIONAL-CLIENT RELATIONSHIPS

The relationships between professionals and clients provide one specific
context in which to consider the ways in which trust becomes institutionalized. These relationships usually involve a high level of trust on the part of
clients. Consider someone who visits a doctor seeking treatment for a serious illness. The client may have relatively little understanding of his or her
condition, let alone of the doctor's background or experience, yet the client
is willing to entrust the doctor with decisions that may literally have life-or-
death consequences. Furthermore, hundreds of thousands of clients establish such relationships with doctors (or other professionals) every day. In
each particular case, the client may weigh his or her options, but on the
whole there seems to be a general predisposition to trust doctors. At least if
public opinion polls are believed, the vast majority of the public registers
confidence in doctors and credits them with being trustworthy.

On what basis are such judgments made? In a small village, the client may
have grown up with the doctor, be acquainted with the doctor's kin, know
stories from neighbors and friends about how well the doctor has performed
in treating difficult cases, and see the doctor casually at the post office. To say
that a client of this kind trusts the doctor might mean any number of things:
that the doctor may feel a special obligation to take care of the client, that
the doctor is a person of good character, that the doctor has a good track
record, or that the doctor is an amiable person. But more than likely, the
client and doctor in contemporary settings do not know each other in these
ways. In the urban and suburban settings in which most people live, the
client's trust is likely to depend more on the fact that the doctor is listed as
an approved physician by a reputable health insurance provider that has

been selected by a knowledgeable committee in the human resources department at one's place of employment, on the fact that no doctor would appear on such a list without having attended medical school and passed certain residency requirements, and on the fact that the doctor had been personally recommended by another doctor with similar credentials. The client's willingness to trust the doctor to perform a specific procedure may further depend on securing and comparing opinions from several physicians, on reading articles about clients having undergone similar procedures, and perhaps on checking with one's lawyer about the nature of one's rights to make claims if anything goes wrong.

This example shows that clients' willingness to trust professionals is highly contingent on the way in which the role of professionals is structured in our society. This role, it might be said, is structured in such a way as to ensure a reasonably high level of trust on the part of most clients. Respect for the role causes clients to define certain bases of judging someone to be trustworthy as being relevant and others as being irrelevant. The doctor under consideration, for example, is judged trustworthy on the basis of having acquired certifiable training and experience, not because he or she owes a special debt to the particular client and not necessarily because he or she is a good parent or church member. In other words, certain arguments can reasonably be made about the doctor's trustworthiness, while others cannot.

Because roles are specific, the way in which trust is articulated must be equally specific. Thus, when a person explains that he or she trusts a doctor, what is probably meant is that the doctor is perceived to be dependable as far as treating a particular condition is concerned, not that the doctor is trustworthy in all other respects (such as making it to dinner on time or being a good source of advice about real estate). Of course, roles are not insulated from these broader judgments, either. Because becoming a doctor requires an extended period of higher education, clients may credit doctors with being trustworthy to the same extent that they expect other educated or middle-class people to be (such as paying their bills, caring for their children, and maintaining their homes). Insofar as illness and death are involved, patients may also judge doctors' trustworthiness in terms of empathy, sincerity, congeniality, and affinity (Lupton 1996).

But what happens when expectations of trustworthiness are violated? The comment of a prospective client of several social service agencies is instructive. Having spoken with social workers at several agencies and having been turned down for financial assistance, the man reported that he still trusted the agencies because the social workers appeared to be "sincere." His remark effectively excused the social workers from having to perform the desired service in order to be considered trustworthy by shifting to a secondary argument, namely, that they were truly trying to do what was in his best interest. In this case, the legal restrictions he assumed were in place to govern the social workers' behavior permitted him to regard them as trustworthy even if they could not be helpful.

The same prospective client illustrates another aspect of trust. The social worker he trusts most is a woman who phones him every month or so to see how his family is doing. Although she has also performed her role faithfully, it is this extra behavior ("going beyond the call of duty") that he appreciates most. His willingness to trust her is thus influenced by the connection he perceives between the role she plays and who she is as a person outside of this role. This connection makes him feel that she is authentic and truly believes in the caring values that her role embodies.

The relationships between professionals and clients are institutionalized in ways that encourage reasonably high levels of trust. But, as this example suggests, the occupants of these roles actively signal that they are trustworthy by engaging in activities that associate themselves with shared standards by which trustworthiness is judged. Organizations do this as well. For instance, carefully staged media coverage of corporate employees doing a community service project suggests to the wider public that the organization adheres to values higher than simply making a profit.

TRUST IN LOCAL COMMUNITIES

Whereas professional-client relationships are often highly formalized, those occurring in local communities are more likely to consist of informal networks. The bases of trust may therefore seem to depend more on individual characteristics and less on aspects of social structure. However, the same general considerations apply to trust in neighborhoods as to trust between clients and professionals. Behavior in both instances must conform to the norms governing recognized roles. But these norms in communities are of course different from those among professionals and clients.

The social interaction that takes place in local communities is subject to a great deal of uncertainty. One's neighbors may burglarize one's house or sell drugs to one's children; they may let their property become a fire hazard or deteriorate to the point that one's own property loses value; they may intrude on one's privacy by playing loud music or paying unexpected visits; they may be sources of help in emergency situations, but may also happen to be away when emergencies occur. To say that one's neighbors are trustworthy, therefore, can mean many different things.

Different norms for judging trustworthiness emerge in different kinds of neighborhoods. Two extreme cases will illustrate these differences. In one community, most of the families are from the same ethnic background, most of the men work at the same factory, and most of the women are housewives. In this community, the school is local, as is the church, and a lack of automobiles means that most of the shopping occurs locally as well. In the other community, the families are from many different backgrounds and ethnic identities are weak; most of the men and women are in the labor force, and they work at different locations and occupations; they also shop, attend religious services, and send their children to schools outside the neighborhood. In the first neighborhood, being a trustworthy neighbor probably means fitting in, being like others in the neighborhood, and showing up at expected events, such as church picnics and town meetings. In the second neighborhood, being a trustworthy neighbor is more likely to mean keeping one's property looking respectable, paying one's taxes, and not intruding on the privacy of one's neighbors.

These examples point to differences in the norms governing neighborhoods in the past and those governing a growing number of neighborhoods at present. The one kind of trust has been replaced by another. But does the one have worrisome consequences, as some observers suggest? Not if the consequences are considered in terms of the sociability and emergency services that tight-knit neighborhoods used to provide. Those are easily replaced by long-distance telephone calls or more frequent visits to distant friends and relatives and by rescue squads and better insurance programs. The costs are more likely to come from the loss of informal relationships that lead to other benefits for the local community. For instance, mobilizing people to attend school board meetings may be harder in the absence of ties among neighbors, and interest in local elections and zoning board initiatives may be weakened as well. Yet these local losses may be compensated for by the fact that people interact more at work or see a wider variety of people at professional meetings.

The other consequence of changing community norms may be in perceptions of generalized trust. In a relatively homogeneous setting, residents may be inclined to assume that most people can be trusted—if only because most of the people they know seem to be trustworthy. In a more diffuse setting, people may be more inclined to say that people vary in the extent to which they can be trusted, and this may be an accurate reflection of the fact that their social contacts are more diverse.

In local communities, then, trust is influenced by the patterns of interaction that have become familiar as a result of proximity, work schedules, and family life. Tightly bounded and more loosely connected neighborhoods each have a distinct kind of trust. The fact that trust is present in both settings also suggests that a bias in favor of believing in the trustworthiness of one's neighbors may be a feature of how neighborhoods are structured. Leaving aside communities divided by racial strife or ridden with crime, most neighborhoods develop tacit norms to which people conform. Some of these norms are reinforced by laws (such as laws against loud noise or leaving trash unattended), but many are habits that develop over time because they help people to believe that their neighbors can be trusted. In one neighborhood, the habits may include mowing lawns on Saturdays; in another, taking casseroles to the sick; and in another, keeping one's blinds pulled down.

TRUST AS AN ASPECT OF RELIGIOUS BEHAVIOR

Religious behavior provides an interesting contrast to the cases considered thus far. Although religious organizations resemble professional-client relationships insofar as the roles of clergy and congregants are concerned, and local communities insofar as people engage in informal interaction in their congregations, religious behavior is also a matter of expressing trust in a deity who embodies the highest values of the community. For this reason, religious behavior provides an occasion for considering how transcendent values may become part of the trusting relationships around which social structure is organized.

Religion is often conceptualized as a system of beliefs—beliefs about the existence of God, the divinity of Jesus, whether or not miracles happen, what a person must do to achieve salvation, and so on. But it is interesting to think about how our understanding of religion might be different if it were viewed as a system of trust—trust in God, trust that one's prayers will be answered, trust that one's choices are good, and so on. These ways of talking about religion are certainly common at the popular level, if not in all religions, then at least in contemporary expressions of Christianity. For instance, people sing praise choruses that emphasize their willingness to surrender themselves to Jesus, preachers call on congregants to trust God to supply all their needs, spiritual seekers describe how they have come to trust their feelings about God, and the nation's currency includes the phrase "in God we trust."

But if trust is central to some understandings of religion, then much of what we have considered about trust in other situations applies here as well. Religion ceases to be as much about doctrines and creeds (as when it is regarded as a system of beliefs) and becomes more about social relationships, which, in turn, are governed by roles and norms. One of the clearest examples of such roles and norms comes from research on rapidly growing nondenominational evangelical churches in which congregants' trust in God is modeled by their relationship with their pastor. In many such churches the pastor's authority is virtually unchecked because he or she is not subject to denominational rules and does not share power with an independently elected committee of lay leaders. The pastor's authority is further expressed through long expository sermons that feature the pastor's interpretation of the Bible and how it should be applied in the daily lives of congregants. In addition, rhythmic and repetitive music with lyrics expressing sentiments of dependence on God often plays a large role in the worship services at such churches. The combined effect is to cast the pastor and God in a close relationship with each other. To the extent that the congregant trusts God, he or she also trusts the pastor, and vice versa.

Although this kind of worship may reinforce pastoral authority, it also casts God in a certain role and legitimates trust in God with certain warrants. For instance, God is depicted as an intimate friend (so intimate in fact that the word *you* often replaces more explicit references to the deity) who is emotionally close and therefore trustworthy because this friend listens, cares, and empathizes with one's feelings. The same friend may become a sounding board, providing guidance when the congregant faces difficult decisions, but doing so in the way that a supportive friend might, rather than as an austere or righteous figure. God is trustworthy, then, less because of theological arguments about how the universe was created or about the metaphysics of sin and redemption and more because of being cast in a role similar to that of an imaginary friend.

Warm, intimate friendships in religious congregations may provide the tangible models that reinforce such images of God. For instance, many congregants join support groups in which sharing of feelings and developing close personal bonds are encouraged. But the rituals of prayer, speaking in tongues (in some instances), singing praise choruses, and listening to sermons also provide models for behavior in the wider world. At least congregants report that their relationships with family members and employers have improved, and those who participate in support groups frequently claim to have experienced forgiveness or to have consciously worked at repairing broken relationships (Lawson 1997).

What research on religious behavior suggests, then, is that trust extends beyond social relationships to include the pursuit of presumably abstract values, such as transcendence and salvation. Trust does so by being embedded in social relationships that dramatize these values, giving them more concrete expression and modeling them on norms and expectations experienced in everyday life. While it may be appropriate to say that people rationally calculate how to attain these higher-order values, it is probably more accurate to understand that people feel they can trust the deities, pastors, or friends who most clearly embody these values. Thus, it should not be surprising that some research has shown that one of the best ways to persuade people that others can be trusted to be caring and helpful is to tell stories about, and provide role models of, specific people who embody these values (Wuthnow 1991, 1995).

SOME EVIDENCE

Surveys generally provide sparse evidence about trust, especially because questions usually focus on generalized measures of trust or on levels of trust in specific people, such as presidential candidates, or groups, such as community leaders or the police. A national survey conducted by the author among a representative sample of 1,528 adults included several questions specifically concerned with probing the more nuanced ways in which trust may be understood (Wuthnow 1997).

Some of the results are shown in table 8.1. The first two items—"Most people can be trusted" and "You can't be too careful in your dealings with people"—have been asked as mutually exclusive options in previous surveys, and in those surveys a majority of the American public usually chooses the second option, leading observers to conclude that generalized trust is weak in the United States (Smith 1996). However, when people are given the opportunity to respond to each item separately, a different picture emerges. About two-thirds of the public (71 percent) agree that one cannot be too careful in dealings with people, but nearly as many (62 percent) also agree that most people can be trusted. It appears, then, that trust is conditional, or at least that people recognize the importance of somehow combining trust with watchfulness in their relationships.

The remaining items in table 8.1 suggest some of the ways in which people understand trust and how they create warrants for trusting others. A majority of the public believe that trust is a good thing (warranted) because people will rise to the occasion. In other words, trust is not simply a passive assessment of how others will behave but a positive attitude that is expected to elicit desirable responses from others. Yet an equally large majority recognize that some people will take advantage of the trust that is placed in them. This is a kind of secondary warrant or explanation which says, in effect, that trust is worth it even though one has to anticipate some proportion of the time when trust will fail. The final item shows that only about a third of the public think a person who lets you down should not be trusted. For most people, trust apparently means more than just being dependable, then, although that is certainly part of what it means.

Another way of examining trust is shown in table 8.2. When asked how likely or unlikely they would be to trust various kinds of people, 89 percent of the public say they would be very likely or somewhat likely to trust somebody who lives in their neighborhood. The high proportion who give this response suggests that a perception of affinity, congeniality, or reliability such as one would expect among neighbors is probably a strong warrant for trust. This interpretation seems compatible with the finding that a considerably smaller proportion (56 percent) say they would be likely to trust somebody in their neighborhood who keeps to himself or herself (i.e., who fails to signal his or her congeniality or affinity).

The responses to the item about somebody in a poor neighborhood who does not have a job are mixed (with 51 percent saying they would be likely to trust this kind of person and only 9 percent saying they would be very likely

TABLE 8.1 Attitudes about Trust (in Percentages)

	Mostly Agree	Mostly Disagree	Don't Know
Most people can be trusted	62	35	3
You can't be too careful in your dealings with people	71	26	3
If you trust people, they will usually rise to the occasion	71	22	7
Some people will always try to take advantage of you	69	27	4
If someone lets you down, you shouldn't trust them	37	55	8

TABLE 8.2 Likelihood of Trusting Different Kinds of People
(in Percentages)

	Very Likely	Somewhat Likely	Somewhat Unlikely	Very Unlikely
Somebody who lives in your neighborhood	37	52	6	2
Somebody who lives in your neighborhood who always keeps to themselves	12	44	29	9
Somebody in a poor neighborhood who doesn't have a job	9	42	28	13
Somebody who shares their personal feelings with you	38	50	6	2
Somebody who misses appointments	3	20	48	22
Somebody who does volunteer work in the community	37	51	5	2
Somebody who is running for political office	5	44	29	14

NOTE: "Don't know" responses not shown.

to trust this kind of person). One implication of this finding is that trust is closely linked with norms of middle-class respectability; thus, someone who violates these norms by living in a poor neighborhood and not having a job is viewed by a large number of people as being untrustworthy. But physical location and respectability are by no means the only warrants for trust. A large majority (88 percent) say they would be likely to trust somebody who shares his or her personal feelings, suggesting that empathy or congeniality can be a basis for trust, especially when signaled by displayed emotions.

The item about somebody who misses appointments provides further evidence about the role of reliability as a warrant for trust. While about a quarter of the public would be likely to trust such a person, 70 percent say they would not. That altruism or empathy may be important warrants for trust is indicated by the fact that nearly all respondents (88 percent) say they would be likely to trust somebody who does volunteer work in the community. In comparison, fewer than half (49 percent) say they would trust somebody running for political office.

While these data do not go far toward providing an interpretation of trust, they do suggest some of the broader social norms with which trust is associated. The data also make it possible to tease out some of the ways in which trust is related to specific norms. For instance, respondents who know most of their neighbors are significantly more likely to say they would trust somebody in their neighborhood than are respondents who know few of their neighbors. In other words, this kind of trust appears to be related to a sense of affinity or familiarity. But knowing one's neighbors does not influence the likelihood that people will say that most people in general can be trusted, or that they would trust somebody running for political office—a finding that casts some doubt on the idea that close social ties in one setting necessarily translate into more generalized forms of trust. Another finding from these data is that the claim that one would trust a jobless person living in a poor neighborhood is neither more likely nor less likely to occur among people who themselves live in poor neighborhoods than among people who live in more affluent neighborhoods. Here, the possibility of affinity generating trust seems to be outweighed by more general norms (perhaps communicated by the mass media) about the untrustworthiness of the poor and jobless. The limits of affinity as a basis for trust are also evident in the fact that people who say they are personally prone to miss appointments are still overwhelmingly unlikely to say they would trust someone else who misses appointments. In other words, they may sense some affinity for those who are unreliable but still prefer to put their trust in people who are dependable.

CONCLUSION

The main conclusion to be drawn from this discussion is that trust is not simply a matter of how an individual happens to feel toward another person; instead, trust is an aspect of the normative system that makes up the social structure in which we live. Or, put differently, the norms and expectations that govern social relationships also go a long way toward determining how much people feel they can trust others in those situations and what they can be trusted to do. This means that trust cannot be understood by imagining an isolated individual engaged in rational calculations of how to get what he or she wants. It means instead that trust can be understood only by paying attention to the ways in which roles are defined and to the norms that tell people whether (and on what basis) trust is warranted.

This way of thinking about trust has important implications for understanding the relatively low levels of trust expressed by the public toward politicians. The norms governing expectations about politicians are relatively diffuse compared to those concerning many other occupations. Unlike a physician, who is certified to perform certain medical procedures, politicians typically present a wide range of claims about themselves during electoral campaigns, ranging from credentials earned in other careers to previous accomplishments in public office to being amiable, jovial, hard working, a good parent, and a loyal spouse. Whereas the trust expressed by a prospective patient toward a physician may be restricted to the specific task the physician is expected to play (and therefore be high), the public's attitude toward a political candidate will be influenced by a much wider range of considerations. In addition, few physicians are openly criticized by their fellow physicians, whereas the party system in politics ensures that every political candidate will be subjected to such criticism. Over the past half century or so, the certification requirements governing most occupations have become more stringent, raising expectations about training and competence at the same time that roles have become more specific. In the political sphere, however, it remains possible for wealthy individuals, actors, widows, and other relative newcomers to the political process to seek and attain high offices. Thus it is not surprising that generalized levels of trust in politicians have declined.

A related implication is that greater attention must be paid to the situations in which trust is not warranted. In politics, the very foundations of democratic systems assume that officeholders often cannot be trusted and therefore must be subjected to constitutional checks and balances in order to prevent totalitarianism from arising. In business, such common expressions as "let the buyer beware" and "arms-length transactions" signal that prudence requires formalized contracts rather than unwarranted levels of trust. The more general point is that the norms that provide warrants for trust in specific relationships also reveal the limits of such warrants. Thus, during a recent episode of foundation fraud, investors who explained that they trusted the foundation leader because he was "a good Christian" were dubbed gullible because this warrant clearly should not have taken the place of other warrants more appropriate to the situation.

As this example suggests, the most important questions to be raised about trust are probably those pertaining to individuals in whom trust seems warranted and yet proves to be unwarranted: for instance, the doctor who turns out to be a fraud, the student who signs an honor code but cheats on exams, the minister who champions marital fidelity but sleeps with his secretary, and the suitor who proclaims lasting devotion but proves to be deceitful. Under most circumstances, these are the exceptions that prove the rule—the violations of norms that demonstrate how powerful the normative structure usually is. The expected response to such violations includes deploring the violations, ritualistically tightening or clarifying the norms (such as holding hearings about honor codes or stiffening penalties against fraud), and developing secondary warrants to account for and make sense of the violations (such as attributing the incident to improper upbringing, duress, or youthful indiscretion).

In the final analysis, trust is multifaceted because it reflects the highly diverse norms, roles, and warrants that govern social interaction. This is probably why trust has not been particularly emphasized as a compelling analytic concept in the social sciences (any more than love, virtue, or character). But trust does retain meaning in popular discourse. Although its meanings are often vague, the very vagueness of these meanings suggests that people are able to leave part of their understanding of it unspoken because its meanings are built into the taken-for-granted elements of their social interaction. Sorting out these meanings and understanding how they vary in different social contexts is one of the important tasks of social science.

REFERENCES

Coleman, James S. 1990. *Foundations of Social Theory.* Cambridge: Harvard University Press.

DiMaggio, Paul J., and Walter W. Powell. 1983. "The Iron Cage Revisited: Institutional Isomorphism and Collective Rationality in Organizational Fields." *American Sociological Review* 48: 147–60.

Fukuyama, Francis. 1995. *Trust: The Social Virtues and the Creation of Prosperity.* New York: Free Press.

Lawson, Matthew P. 1997. "Struggles for Mutual Reverence: Social Strategies and Religious Stories." In Penny Edgell Becker and Nancy L. Eiesland, eds., *Contemporary American Religion: An Ethnographic Reader,* pp. 51–78. Walnut Creek, Calif.: Alta Mira.

Lupton, Deborah. 1996. "Your Life in Their Hands: Trust in the Medical Encounter." In Veronica James and Jonathan Gabe, eds., *Health and the Sociology of Emotions,* pp. 157–72. Oxford: Blackwell.

Merton, Robert K. 1973. *The Sociology of Science: Theoretical and Empirical Investigations.* Chicago: University of Chicago Press.

Meyer, John W., and Brian Rowan. 1977. "Institutionalized Organizations: Formal Structure as Myth and Ceremony." *American Journal of Sociology* 83: 340–63.

Putnam, Robert D. 1993. *Making Democracy Work: Civic Traditions in Modern Italy.* Princeton, N.J.: Princeton University Press.

Seligman, Adam B. 1997. *The Problem of Trust.* Princeton, N.J.: Princeton University Press.

Smelser, Neil J. 1962. *Theory of Collective Behavior.* New York: Free Press.

———. 1988. "Social Structure." In Neil J. Smelser, ed., *Handbook of Sociology*, pp. 103–29. Beverly Hills, Calif.: Sage.

———. 1992. "The Rational Choice Perspective: A Theoretical Assessment." *Rationality and Society* 4: 381–410.

———. 1995. "Economic Rationality as a Religious System." In Robert Wuthnow, ed., *Rethinking Materialism: Perspectives on the Spiritual Dimension of Economic Behavior,* pp. 73–92. Grand Rapids, Mich.: W. E. Eerdmans Publishing.

Smelser, Neil J., and Richard Swedberg. 1994. "The Sociological Perspective on the Economy." In Neil J. Smelser and Richard Swedberg, eds., *The Handbook of Economic Sociology*, pp. 3–26. Princeton, N.J.: Princeton University Press.

Smith, Tom W. 1996. *Factors Relating to Misanthropy in Contemporary American Society.* GSS Topical Report no. 29. Chicago: National Opinion Research Center.

Storer, Norman W. 1966. *The Social System of Science.* New York: Holt, Rinehart, and Winston.

Swidler, Ann. 1986. "Culture in Action: Symbols and Strategies." *American Sociological Review* 51: 273–86.

Wuthnow, Robert. 1991. *Acts of Compassion: Caring for Others and Helping Ourselves.* Princeton, N.J.: Princeton University Press.

———. 1995. *Learning to Care: Elementary Kindness in an Age of Indifference.* New York: Oxford University Press.

———. 1997. *Civic Involvement Survey.* Princeton, N.J.: Princeton University. Machine readable data file.

———. 1998. *Loose Connections: Joining Together in America's Fragmented Communities.* Cambridge: Harvard University Press.

———. 1999. "The Role of Trust in Civic Renewal." In Robert K. Fullinwider, ed., *Civil Society, Democracy, and Civic Renewal,* pp. 209–30. New York: Rowman and Littlefield.

Chapter 9

The Organizational Foundations of University Capability

Differentiation and Competition in the Academic Sector of Society

Burton R. Clark

Three decades ago, in the early 1970s, Neil Smelser offered an illuminating analysis of the development of public higher education in California (1974). That essay, half a book in length, has remained virtually one of a kind in its blending of rich empirical material with a highly structured theoretical framework. The essay concentrated on both differentiation among types of universities and colleges—the tripartite structure set forth in the 1960 California master plan—and the internal elaboration of the University of California system. Smelser traced the effects of differentiation on interest-group formation and conflict among the major subsectors and then among old and new "academic estates" within the University of California, between, for example, core tenured faculty and growing ranks of full-time researchers and teaching assistants.

I use an international perspective to elaborate the sociological conception of academic differentiation in two directions: first, by asserting basic pathways of differentiation beyond the forms on which Neil concentrated, particularly emphasizing the fundamental role played by a growing diversity of subjects and disciplines and their supporting groups; and, second, by stressing the element of competition first powerfully brought forward by Joseph Ben-David in his comparisons of leading national academic systems (1972; Ben-David with Zloczower 1962). I want to point to the role of institutional and departmental competition in furthering differentiation and enhancing system flexibility. At the beginning of the twenty-first century, it is fair to say that national systems that are extensively differentiated and competitive fare better than those that are relatively undifferentiated and noncompetitive: they can do more things, and they are more alert. There are powerful structural reasons why even the time-honored systems of Europe look toward the American model. Facing the growing turbulence of the twenty-first century, we may stipulate that system disorder ought to be prized more than order, that flexibility is more valuable than constancy, and that "nonsystem" dynamics triumph over the system-making of planners and governments in determining university capability.

The frame I offer pursues differentiation deep within academic systems. Beyond the sectoral hegemony of the university world at large, noted in the sociological literature in passing comments by Ralf Dahrendorf (1979) and Niklas Luhmann (1982), we can specify not only institutional but also disciplinary species of differentiated hegemony within the system. Since universities base themselves on fields of knowledge, their base becomes more complex and variable as it is reshaped by the proliferation and specialization of their substantive territories. And, like politics, action in higher education can fruitfully be seen as highly localized—in individual universities and colleges and then deep down in their departments and interdisciplinary organized efforts. Macrostructures may constrain or enable. But it is the microstructures that enact, that do the system's work, as they serve as the operational platforms for research, teaching, and student learning.

THE PRIMACY OF SUBJECT

The university is uniquely bottom-heavy as an organizational type, particularly in contrast to the business firm and the government bureau. This defining feature is rooted in the curious way that dissimilar fields of knowledge—whether disciplinary, interdisciplinary, or transdisciplinary—slash across university boundaries to take up residence in departments and other basic units (Clark 1983). The positioning of departments in their own larger fields is a wondrous phenomenon to behold. To understand, for example, the contemporary status and orientation of the Department of Sociology at the University of Chicago, we must first study its own intellectual heritage and its evolving place in the discipline of sociology (Abbott 1999). There is simply no escaping this primordial feature. Across the "factory floor" of the university—from classics and history, to economics and political science, to physics, chemistry, and the fast-evolving array of biological sciences, to medicine, law, engineering, business, and education—the operating units are oriented not toward their local university alone but also toward their respective disciplines or subjects, and in a very fundamental way. Members of these bottom-located "tribes" that sit astride academic work and determine university productivity may or may not strongly identify with the university where job hunting and career movement have placed them, but they are dependably and strongly embedded in the cognitive "territories" on which they base their professional identity, competence, and status (Becher 1989; Clark 1987).

Since specialisms are anchoring points and matter a great deal, the department-discipline linkage becomes *the* source of strength and stability, and even steerage, in leading universities and would-be leading universities. Universities become strong on the backs of strong departments; they become great as they build great departments. This linkage is also *the* source of strain and discord when certain activities—preeminently research and advanced study in the American case—are emphasized to the seeming neglect of other efforts, such as the general education of undergraduates. Using the old distinction between locals and cosmopolitans, the latter grow ever stronger as specialization extends its grasp in the city of intellect. It is no less true now than in the past that, as Sheldon Rothblatt puts it, "the history of disciplines is an integral part—the central story really—of the internal history of universities" (1999: 292). Disciplinary departments develop a sense of individual nationhood, a phenomenon reflected to the extreme in physics at Berkeley, economics at Chicago, and history at Yale—the latter department even referring to itself as the Yale "flagship department." Although that intense self-identification on the part of the primary "production" units continues to be overlooked and underestimated in top-down perceptions, especially those based on business models, it culturally underpins the structural bottom-heaviness that characterizes universities.

An internalist perspective that portrays the university as an organization of subjects, then, highlights the deeply established ways in which the discipline rather than the institution becomes the dominant force in the working lives of so many academics. As we stress the primacy of the subject, we see the university as a collection—even a loosely coupled collection (Weick 1976)—of local chapters of organized disciplines, local representatives who import and implant the orientations toward knowledge, the norms, and the customs of the far-flung fields. Work becomes controlled by the internal norms and procedures of the various disciplines. As put cogently by Norton E. Long, a noted analyst of public policy and administration, such disciplines as physics and chemistry "are not organized to carry out the will of legitimate superiors. They are *going concerns* with problems and procedures that have taken form through generations of effort and have emerged into highly conscious goal-oriented activities" (1962: 83, emphasis added). And so it goes throughout the thirty or more major disciplines that compose the letters-and-science part of a modern university, along with all the specialized divisions now found in medical schools, engineering faculties, and business schools.

We may speak of new subjects that seek to become established in universities as subjects in search of discipline, in both senses of the word. They are trying to become "going concerns" that will powerfully orient their "own" departments by means of a respected body of theory and method. As they become established as a discipline, or even as a major interdisciplinary specialty, the members of the new field go not to regional and national meetings of universities—the central administrators do that—but to meetings of their "own" professional association, to meet up with others who speak their language (it may indeed be a strange one) and who otherwise have a similar professional interest and identity. As they do so, they substitute coordination by voluntary association for coordination by formal state machinery. Somewhat like a fraternal order, say, of Odd Fellows, academic associations satisfy individual and group self-interest while joining people in common causes. Such groups exist as an important part of the civic society of the university world that mediates between state and market. Who lobbies the "state" in Washington, D.C., on behalf of higher education? A fistful of associations of universities do, with various cadres of administrators (presidents, finance officers, admission personnel) carrying institutional banners. And a widening array of disciplinary associations do, ranging from the American Chemical Society to the Modern Language Association. And who responds to the "market demands" of the day? Disciplinary departments and their encompassing associations do, as well as institutional administrators, as they confront, for example, the rise and fall of demand for entry into various fields and the demand for particular, specialized graduates.

Academic systems can be seen as grand cases of matrix organization structured around two crosscutting bases of grouping, as all or nearly all the primary production "workers" have a double assignment to discipline and institution. Higher education must be centered in academized subjects, following the flows of knowledge, but it must simultaneously be pulled together in university-type enterprises, particularly for purposes of teaching and local service. And in a highly segmented academic labor market, institutions hire faculty by subject, competence in that subject, and command of a particular cognitive territory. In the crucial processes of hiring and promoting, as Smelser and Content have noted, the disciplines vary greatly in exactitude and consensus, with the "hard" sciences on the firm end of the continuum and certain subjects in the humanities—equipped with little or no agreement on core theory and methodology—near the opposite pole (1980: 11).

As old fields subdivide and recombine, and as new subjects seek discipline, the permanent structures of academic systems, and of individual universities, are arguably changed more by "spontaneous" incremental evolution in disciplines and departments than by top-down planning in systems and in the university at large. Since such basic discipline-driven change is not under anyone's control, it is "in the nature of things." Who on the worldwide stage controls the development of the field of history, let alone the life sciences? A few universities may set the pace in certain fields in their own country, but most universities must follow along as best they can in maintaining competence in one discipline after another, with bottom-up change, which is knowledge led and increasingly accelerated by rapid communication across national boundaries.

The disciplinarity argument can be summarized in three points: The core membership unit in universities is discipline- or subject-centered. Each disciplinary unit within the enterprise has self-evident and acclaimed primacy in a frontline task—for example, the training of physicists or economists or historians—and can claim to be authoritative within the university in its own field (Moodie and Eustace 1974: 61). Last, the disciplinary characteristics of core groups affect everything else important in the organization. Making the university highly pluralistic—a place of factions—these groups lead to interest-group tension and struggle. But professionalized disciplines also stimulate forms of collegial control, demanding, at the least, "shared governance" with the administration. To point to the organizational realities of academic life, analysts who pay close attention find themselves doomed by disciplinarity to adopt an unusual vocabulary of crafts and guilds, confederations and conglomerates, and a mixed bag of collegial, bureaucratic, political, and even anarchic forms of governance.

So we are on firm conceptual ground when we base our analytical perspective first on "subject": this highlights the disciplinarity that makes the university bottom-heavy in the location of authority and the operating springs of action. The commandment that follows is to ask not "whither the university" but whither the humanities, whither the social sciences, whither the biological sciences, whither the physical sciences and engineering, and whither medicine, law, and the other major and minor professional fields. We then move to solid ground inside what is otherwise a "black box" for differentiating the impact of such major forces of the day as new information technology (IT), new applications-generated knowledge, and new types of students—and even of the concrete influences that lie buried in "economic forces" and "globalization." The new information technology, for example, is not only accelerating change but is also disaggregating system responses in a very complicated fashion. Studying the likely impact of IT on instruction, Martin Trow has pointed to a probable diversification of new forms that "reflects the enormous diversity of students and subjects." To begin to grasp what is going on, "we must disaggregate the patterns of use of IT very finely along at least four crucial dimensions: by the nature of the subject taught; by the location of the student; by the purpose of the instruction—whether to transmit skills and knowledge or to cultivate mind and sensibilities—and by the academic talents and motivations of the learner." Disaggregation occurs "almost course by course" (1999: 322–23).

If we do not base our understanding on the differentiated reactions and tides of change in diverse parts of the academy, we simply plow on with the homilies found in commencement speeches. No one really believes that the medical school and the history department in a given university have the same springs of action and are on the same trajectory—the one caught up in the high costs and rough negotiations of health care and big-time medical research, and the other situated in the conceptual disarray of the humanities and affected negatively by the long-term university tilt toward science and technology. Why do we go on pretending they are one and the same?

In cultivating realistic understanding, the inductive approach of starting from the many academic parts of the university—going concerns in their own right—has many advantages. We thereby avoid the airborne leaps of all-embracing theory, the soggy expression of yet another totalizing "idea of the university," and yet another murky formulation of "the soul of the university." We are led to pursue the "is" before turning to the "ought," to get the internal dynamics straight as a foundation for what can be. Probing the complexities of operational settings, a bottom-up, inside-out approach undermines the belief that planners can be smart enough to figure out centrally the comprehensive future of an entire system and of entire universities. Remaining close to practice, the inductive approach is also a natural antidote to the increasing traffic of management fads that come and go and fade away to early deaths because they do not fit the way universities are put together and must essentially operate (Birnbaum 2000).

THE DIFFERENTIATION PHENOMENON

Clark Kerr, in a collection of his astute essays, highlighted the power of three sets of values and allegiances in modern university systems and appropriately portrayed them as "heritage versus equality versus merit." The accumulated heritage of universities in each modern country has increasingly faced the twin—generally contradictory—imperatives of equality and merit. While other observers commonly leave this clash of major values to arguments about the compelling veracity of different ideas—an endless debate—Kerr immediately cuts to the chase, asking, "Are there reasonable, if not perfect, solutions to the contradictions of heritage versus equality versus merit?" And further, "How can equality and merit best live together in the longer run?" His primary answer is to look to "a differentiation of functions among institutions rather than homogenization" (1994: 81). After reviewing the changing structures of higher education systems in many countries, paying special attention to the one established by the California master plan, Kerr concluded that "the evidence generally supports the development [internationally] of a convergence model of differentiated, not homogenized, institutions of higher education, reflecting differentiated students, differentiated faculty, differentiated curricula, and differentiated occupations in the labor market—each too differentiated to be placed effectively in one kind of homogenized institution" (98).

We should note in passing the difference between nominal integration and operational differentiation. In recent years various nations and political authorities have allowed polytechnics, teachers colleges, and other nonuniversity institutions to adopt the title of university, thereby offering up a nominal integration. Britain is the most important recent case, with fifty universities becoming one hundred, in effect, at the stroke of a pen in the early 1990s. The result has been to increase the range of enterprises that use the same general title; the institutions range along a much extended dimension that stretches from extremely research-driven to almost completely teaching-led. Britain does not simply fund one hundred universities to a high and equal level of resource. The government has been saying and doing just the opposite since 1980. With competitive allocation of research funds, and with the capacity of high-repute universities to raise additional monies, the Matthew Effect is strengthened—"To them that has, more will be given." Groups of somewhat similar institutions have increasingly banded together to fight for resource allocation that favors their self-interests; the Russell Group, composed of the top twenty universities that garner the bulk of research funds, is an example. The differentiation phenomenon marches on. Kerr reasonably concludes that, since the name *university* proves so attractive, "it is much better to share the title than to homogenize the functions. Differentiation of functions is the important point" (86).

How that differentiation is accomplished matters immensely. When all or nearly all the places called universities are lumped together in one formal system, coercive comparisons (what you have I should get) and the dominance of high-prestige activities (basic research, for example) stimulate academic drift. The drift typically does not bring full convergence onto the dominant model ("isomorphism"), but rather places the imitators in various uncomfortable positions partway between the old and the new. The former nonuniversity institutions also leave behind a vacuum in their previous activities: perhaps in their former curriculum, generally somewhat vocational, and in their student catchments, generally students of poorer backgrounds. To fill that vacuum—"nature" has it right—a new set of institutions soon emerges and settles in. Thus, in Britain, just seven years after the polytechnics became known as universities, a group of "further education" colleges are trying quite openly to "reinvent the polytechnics." The Brits call this "back to the future" (*The Times Higher Education Supplement* [November 5, 1999]: 1, 3.) This emerging adjustment is a nigh-perfect example of how poor system planning can cause higher education to proceed in dysfunctional circles; unanticipated and undesired consequences abound. For good reason Kerr, Smelser, and others frequently point to the efficacy of the California formal tripartite structure of three subsystems of higher education. That structure is broad enough in its definitions of types of institutions in the 1960 master plan to allow for some institutional autonomy and some space for local evolution; as an example, San Diego State University, full of ambition and with a research-competent faculty, has moved vigorously toward a research posture, overlapping several University of California campuses in this regard. But the structure has been firm enough to keep apart two kinds of universities—essentially research-led and teaching-led—and to hold community colleges in place as two-year institutions (Douglas 2000).

At this gross level of differentiation, system organization at state and national levels matters a great deal. The nearly perfect way to make all institutions unhappy is to throw them all together in one huge system and fund them out of a common set of pots. They are then forced into nasty zero-sum competition. To make system differentiation of institutional types and functions work, diversification of income sources and channels becomes the royal road to wisdom.

As higher education became more complex during the last half of the twentieth century, differentiation within national systems also increasingly took place by level of study and degree attainment. The largest single distinction has been between completion of the first major degree and the pursuit of advanced study. The undergraduate/graduate distinction has loomed especially large in the American system because of the early formal separation of "the graduate school" from the undergraduate realm (Clark 1993, 1995), with such basic operating differences as selection of students by the campus or "college" on the lower level and selection by individual departments on the higher. But differentiation by degree level goes far beyond this dichotomy. We can readily identify five levels in the American system (similar levels are emerging elsewhere). The majority of American students enter higher education via the community college, and a majority of these students go no further that the two-year associate in arts degree. These students are marginal to, if not completely outside of, the "city of intellect," unless we give an extremely open-ended definition to that conception. The second level is the well-known and deeply established four-year bachelor's degree; the third is the fast-growing and newly valued one- or two-year master's degree—a recent "secret success story" (Conrad, Haworth, and Millar 1993). The fourth is the doctoral degree and other such advanced degrees, such as the M.D., that require eight years or more of higher education. And now a fifth level has clearly been put in place, in the form of one-, two-, and three-year postdoctoral appointments that have become the rule rather than the exception in many scientific disciplines. These five levels have different links to the general labor market, as well as the academic labor market, and each level has a growing number of subject-based links between university training and postuniversity placement.

More as an unplanned than a planned phenomenon, such differentiation marches on, extending the range of completion levels in higher education and especially the number of subtypes within each. The master's in business, for example, is very different from the master's in education, and both are unlike the master's in physics or history. In the first case, the master's is a valuable terminal degree leading directly to employment; in the second, it is a job-oriented degree still quite subordinate to the doctorate; and in the third, it is but a way station in progress to a much more valuable doctoral degree—and as such is used frequently as a consolation award for doctoral candidates who are not going to make it. Now on the horizon are many types of short-term completion certificates in the emerging for-profit sector; its enterprises work close to the immediate needs of a rapidly changing labor market, particularly the huge demand for specific professional upgrading. Certificates of completion are like money in the pocket; they help to buy job placement and advancement.

Traditional universities have always been somewhat differentiated from one another by accumulated heritage and public reputation as well as by geographic location. Such differentiation is particularly stimulated by competition that encourages public claims of attractive individual identity. In the intensively competitive American system, virtually all small liberal arts colleges—as the advertising copy goes—claim they sit atop a high hill overlooking a lovely valley and combine urban convenience with rural charm. But each college also somehow presents a different heritage—in effect, a particular hill and a special valley, an uncommon location between city and farm. Established major universities in this competitive setting powerfully accumulate a heritage and a public image repeatedly and richly depicted in their alumni magazines and in the public press. The University of Michigan, referring to the delights of its geographic location, goes so far as to tell us in a brochure that the university is fortunately located in Ann Arbor, a city of about 110,000 residents, which "provides a small town appeal with big city excitement." Even in formally noncompetitive systems that claim homogeneity among universities, heritage differentiates students, faculty, and resources: in the lingering past, for example, we find the towering attractiveness and advantage of the Sorbonne in France, Cambridge and Oxford in Britain, Uppsala in Sweden, the ancient universities of Leiden and Utrecht in the Netherlands, the deeply rooted elite standing of the University of Tokyo in Japan, and the centrality of Universidad Nacional Autónoma de México, the sprawling monster university in Mexico. Heritage mattered in the past; it still matters tremendously in university distinction in the twenty-first century.

Beyond all the gross differentiation just noted among types of universities and colleges in research-teaching balance, level of study and degree attainment, and accumulated heritage and public recognition, there lies the subtle but powerful *substantive differentiation* that has flowed with increasing vigor from the disciplinarity phenomenon. As departments seek the effective capacity to be competent carriers of different bodies of knowledge, they segment universities from the bottom up.

The modern takeoff of disciplinary differentiation dates from the birth of the academic research group in German universities during the early and mid–nineteenth century. Historians have shown with increasing clarity how emerging disciplinarians in the German setting, using Humboldtian ideas as covering ideology, elaborated new fields and won resources as, by trial and error, they worked out such specific local forms as the research-centered laboratory and the research-oriented seminar that allowed them to reap the competitive advantages of specialization (McClelland 1980; Holmes 1989; Morrell 1990; Olesko 1991; Clark 1995). In a prodigious essay written in the late 1980s, Walter Metzger, the American historian, provided an overview of how new disciplines emerged in American higher education during the course of the nineteenth and early twentieth centuries—a rich story that he conceptualized as "substantive growth," in contrast to "reactive growth" in which expansion of faculty and curricula stems more from an increased student body and extended labor force demands (1987). Metzger showed how growth often stemmed from the faculty pursuit of both individual and group advantage and the altruistic "advancement of knowledge." He identified four processes that led to this form of growth: In *subject parturition,* new fields are born from older ones. In *program affiliation* and *subject dignification,* formerly excluded fields are admitted to the family of legitimate subjects, as exemplified in the American system by the affiliation of professional fields of medicine and law and by the full dignification of such previously low-rated fields as modern languages and technology. In *subject dispersion* (or *subject imperialism,* we might also call it), the field of history, for example, constantly expands its scope to cover more societal sectors, more time periods, and more geographic locales, producing such three-way specialties as the history of science in Japan during the nineteenth century.

The processes of substantive growth sped up remarkably during the twentieth century: the gestation period for new subjects became shorter and shorter—witness the rapid emergence and growth of computer science; subject dignification ran amok—you name it, we will teach it; and subject dispersion increasingly became virtually a genetic form of discipline aggrandizement. Economics, for example, is willing to attempt to explain any and all societal sectors and social practices: an economics of the family, an economics of love, and, of course, a very chancy economics of hedge funds.

Other examples of the current magnitude of substantive growth at the discipline level may be readily noted. A set of large "medical sciences" has grown up as a separate group of academic fields (pharmacology, epidemiology, and immunology are among them) alongside of, rather than subsumed under, the biological sciences. A fast-growing set of "engineering sciences" (examples are aeronautical, chemical, and materials) has taken up residence outside the physical sciences. If we look at internal features of specific disciplines, we find that, as of the early 1990s, in the vast field of mathematics over two hundred thousand new theorems were published each year; journals exceeded one thousand; and review journals classified over forty-five hundred subtopics arranged under sixty-two major topics (Madison 1992). Psychology had become huge and extensively fragmented; the American Psychological Association exhibited a structure of over forty major specialties, one of which, social psychology, claimed seventeen subfields (Leary 1992; Hewstone 1992).

We know how to count students in higher education and analyze trends in student growth and decline, and we know how to count universities and colleges and analyze their developmental tendencies. But due to the tunnel vision of routinized approaches, we have let substantive growth largely escape us. Fortunately, the basic information with which to pursue this primary form of university and system development is never far away. Subject differentiation in the twenty-first century can be found in successive university catalogs viewed over decades. It can be found in the readily available data of such counting houses as the Institute for Scientific Information (ISI), which monitors the production and citation of scientific literature. The ISI reported at the end of the 1980s that it was able to track more than "8,200 currently active specialty areas in science" (ISI newsletter *Science Watch*). Knowledge growth can be traced in the changing range and depth of encyclopedias. A new encyclopedia of the social sciences (coedited by Smelser) required fifty section editors to pull together materials in twenty-six volumes on twenty major fields and on a number of interdisciplinary subjects, rather than on the half dozen or so seen as basic four decades ago. Now such major fields as economics and psychology insist on two hundred articles or more with which to explain what they are about (*International Encyclopedia of the Social and Behavioral Sciences* 2001). A new encyclopedia devoted to the field of philosophy has attempted to cover the waterfront and sort out the complexity of this ambiguous subject, now in serious conceptual disarray, in ten volumes containing over fifteen hundred articles assembled by over thirty section editors (*Routledge Encyclopedia of Philosophy* 1998). The current extreme of knowledge fragmentation is apparently revealed in a new seven-hundred-page *Encyclopedia of Semiotics* (the study of "signs"!), which renders chaos chaotically: it has an entry on "text" but not on "context"; "space" but not "time"; "apartheid" but not "fascism"; "Buddhism" but not "Christianity"; "baseball" but not "cricket" or "rugby" or even "chess" (*Encyclopedia of Semiotics* 2000; Harris 2000).

The differentiation of academic specialisms within the knowledge foundation of higher education has gotten well ahead of our imagination, let alone our empirical grasp. Subject fragmentation has arguably become *the* source of ever-growing system complexity. It is a source more powerful and extensive in its effects than the expanded inputs of students and the more varied outputs to the general labor force on which analysts commonly concentrate when they observe the scale and scope of modern universities and national systems of higher education. Many universities are able to cap their size and to limit their training lines, but they cannot control the national and international growth in knowledge. Research production and related specialization drive the cognitive fragmentation and turn it into extremely complicated *institutional* differentiation.

Two further examples illustrate. Peter Syverson, in a penetrating analysis of graduate training in U.S. higher education, has revealed that the 125 "research-intensive" universities listed in the Research I and Research II categories of the Carnegie classification actually enrolled in 1998 just 44 percent of all graduate students and 59 percent of students in science and engineering. Another 800 institutions spread throughout seven other Carnegie categories are also involved in the graduate education enterprise; they account for the converse figures of 56 percent of all graduate students and 41 percent in science and engineering. These other institutions include doctoral-granting universities that are more teaching-led than research-led, master's level universities, bachelor's level colleges that have some graduate programs, and a miscellany of "specialized institutions"—detached medical schools, business schools, engineering schools, all accredited, which do not fit readily into any of the other categories. This extended assortment of an additional 800 institutions, operating beyond the 125 positioned "at the top of the academic food chain," granted in 1997 more than 230,000 master's degrees and 9,000 doctoral degrees (Syverson 1999). In short, even the graduate level of the American system is extremely diversified in its institutional locations, and it steadily becomes more so. The many locations differ enormously in resources, faculty, student peers, and programs (Gumport 1993). Everybody is doing it, by means of a thousand and one niches in combining subjects and institutional settings.

My second example comes from the decade-long research on the rapid changes taking place in the life sciences at universities undertaken by Walter Powell and colleagues. They have highlighted the rise of new, complicated organizational forms: research collaboration now "spans the academy, private industry, nonprofit research institutes and hospitals, and government laboratories." Here, "coevolution" occurs, with a sustained blurring of the old distinction between basic and applied research (Powell and Owen-Smith 1998: 272). In this dynamic set of disciplines, the university is part of a diffusely located shift in the nature of knowledge, a shift that adds transdisciplinary or "applications-generated" knowledge to disciplinary and interdisciplinary knowledge, and does so through the elaboration of new interorganizational networks.

The differentiated subterritories of a university, then, are first of all subject territories. Following the contours of unplanned change in and among disciplines, and of simple imitation among institutions, the addition and recasting of these basic components is considerably subject to disciplinary and institutional drift. Such drift has long served well, keeping inquiry open and adapting organizational structures. It will continue to be necessary. But its costs in financial and human resources have been rising sharply, heightening the need for tough choices and deepening the importance of who decides and how they go about doing it. From department to faculty or school to university as a whole, what perspectives, topics, specialties, and disciplines must be included, and which excluded? Or, on a more practical continuum, which are to be highlighted, which are to be maintained well above the line of acceptable competence, which are to be maintained even below that line, which should suffer death by a thousand cuts during the next decade, and which should be and can be eliminated tomorrow?

Whatever the particular proactive steps that departments and universities now take to maintain and enhance their competence, knowledge differentiation will continue to fracture the subject foundation in a thousand interacting pieces. A major American research university mounts over four thousand courses. Even a small liberal arts college in the United States, determined to keep up with the new while maintaining the old, will offer five hundred or more. Variegated enterprises indeed, adding up operationally, even in formal systems, to a nonplanned national composite of virtually unlimited scope. And if we think universities are now internally chaotic, just wait. As Clifford Geertz has noted, "We are witnessing an increasingly rapid proliferation, an onslaught, actually, of what Thomas Kuhn called disciplinary matrices—loose assemblages of techniques, vocabularies, assumptions, instruments, and exemplary achievements that, despite their specificities and originalities, or even their grand incommensurabilities, bear with intensifying force and evolving precision upon the speed, the direction, and the fine detail of one another's development" (2000: 206).

THE ELEMENT OF COMPETITION

Competition—among research groups, departments, universities, and entire national systems of higher education—plays an increasingly prominent part in determining academic capability. Since the American system became internationally dominant during the last half of the twentieth century, and has now lodged itself as an eight-hundred-pound gorilla, we must grasp the part played by competition in its development and contemporary composition. In cross-national comparison, the American system stands as very large, radically decentralized, extremely diverse, intensely competitive, and full of institutional initiative. Colossal size is evident in the over thirty-five hundred accredited universities and colleges, and in a student body, well over 13 to 14 million (the national countings are very gross), much larger than the population of Sweden or Norway or Finland. According to various indicators, the U.S. system is ten, twenty, or fifty times larger than the national systems, large and small, found on the European continent.

More imposing in its effects is the radical decentralization of control that comes from simultaneous private and public dispersion. Privateness has great historical depth, richly embellished traditions, and much contemporary prestige, as exemplified by such leading universities as Harvard and Stanford and such leading bachelor-level colleges as Swarthmore and Oberlin. The quality of some eighteen hundred private institutions ranges from these peaks down to the bottom of the barrel. But all proceed largely on their own initiative in finding niches in the ecology of the system. Competition is in their bones, from competition for sheer survival to competition to be anointed as the best university in the world. In turn, public higher education, numerically dominant from the 1960s onward, has taken the shape of a bottom-heavy federalism in which the support and authority of the individual state dominates that of the national government, producing fifty public systems rather than one formal national one. Who owns the public universities located in Mississippi, or in New York, or in Wisconsin, or in California? Who sustains their football teams?

Extreme institutional diversity has followed like night the day from this extreme decentralization of control in a very large system. A classification of institutions that has a sufficiently fine mesh to turn up women's colleges, historically black colleges, and Catholic universities and colleges needs thirty to forty categories, to go beyond the simple public-private distinction and such broad distinctions as found in the three public sectors named in California. When we fine-tune the categories in which nationally we lump two hundred or even five or six hundred demonstrably different institutions, we get lost among the trees and cannot see the forest. But when we work with, say, four categories, as when we speak of the three public sectors and a private sector in California, we radically understate the vast differences among individual institutions and groups thereof that have developed through the decades in a largely unplanned fashion. In this particular academic forest, the trees come in many sizes and shapes and numerous species, and they are thoroughly intermingled.

That confusing mix was well in place by 1900. By that early date the United States had a census of institutions, more private than public, that already approached one thousand, an astonishing number. By the standards of the major European universities, the hundreds of small U.S. colleges—as put by an American scientist in the late nineteenth century—were more like a swarm of mosquitoes than a few soaring eagles. Eagles, first mainly private and then public, began to soar as "the age of the university" replaced "the age of the college." But at the same time, the previous forms did not disappear. Nonuniversity institutions of all sizes and shapes continued to exist and to diversify. The decentralization and diversity then in place insured a twentieth-century system characterized by sharp competition for faculty, students, and institutional status. Privates compete with privates; state institutions with one another; and private and public with one another. The U.S. system has become a distinctively open one in which competitive disorder and a market-based status hierarchy heavily condition the ways that institutions define themselves, seek resources, and arrange the conditions for research, teaching, and student learning.

The competition has forced many institutions to exercise alert initiative. Whoa! Princeton has just taken away our most promising young political scientist. Whoa! A state-college-turned-university just down the way has aggressively promoted a research profile, despite state government restraints, while the rest of us in the sector have not. Whoa! Other adjacent communities colleges are walking away with our students by offering more attractive campus conditions, courses, and schedules. To stand still is to fall behind. Other institutions continuously move ahead to amass financial resources, fashion attractive packages for recruiting and retaining faculty, increase the stipends for graduate students, improve the quality of undergraduate life, and paint an evermore glorious public image. Within this localization of initiative, especially in this day and age of rapid change, trustees, administrators, faculty, students, alumni, and assorted well-wishers can join hands. Who other than such institutional loyalists would plaster their cars with stickers pointing with pride to "their" particular university or college?

It is clearly not only the leading research universities that have to stay awake and take competitive action. The hundreds of private four-year colleges are in a very competitive situation in which finance, student body, and faculty are largely determined by local institutional characteristics and initiatives. The comprehensive universities and colleges—formally nondoctoral granting but heavily invested in graduate and professional education— are no strangers to the competitive mode of interaction. They are restless; they are also active. And public community colleges take part in the general free-for-all for undergraduate student clientele in their local area.

Competition, then, is arguably the central process of the American system of higher education, the overall process that most drives the system. Its effects in localizing initiative and stimulating an active autonomy go a long way in explaining the great international success of American (and Californian in particular) higher education in the last half of the twentieth century. That success has notably included the turning of a number of universities and colleges into intellectual magnets that attract talent—streams of talent—from around the world. At the same time, the competitive process is central to major system weaknesses, all the way from great variability in standards across the nation to underfunding of beginning undergraduate programs to magnified sins of pride in claims of local virtue.

In nations where higher education has come under strong state control, particularly that of national government, there is a bias for aggregation. Things must be added up, integrated, and vouched for. In Britain, for example, "British standards" are a nationalized responsibility. Someone is supposed to be in charge; at the top, everybody is supposed to be embarrassed when a particular institution mounts programs seen as below the threshold of acceptability. Planning is supposed to decide how equity and merit will be reconciled. But a deeply rooted decentralized system, like the United States, tends to remain decentralized, despite extensive state-level planning: too many features are beyond anyone's control. The structure of incentives encourages key institutional actors to initiate autonomous actions. The individual states even join the general free-for-all, as they back their own universities and colleges in competition for financial plums from "the Feds" and for enhanced esteem in the eyes of the general population.

THE INTERACTION OF DIFFERENTIATION AND COMPETITION

The more that systems of higher education are internally differentiated along the many lines established earlier, the more they escape the integration of central control. They slide toward competitive processes in which indirect coordination takes place through marketlike interaction and local professional determination. Differentiation promotes competition; in turn, competition is a differentiating force. As universities and their departments search for niches in which they can exercise particular competencies and thereby prosper, institutional specificities grow. Prestige maximization, as economists point out, is the name of the game. And gains in prestige can no longer be made by simple imitation of one's "betters." The academic sphere—a place of small worlds, different worlds—increasingly calls for selective investment of human and financial resources.

To compete most effectively, an institution must be selectively different. The clearest and most important examples at the moment in the United States of this growing need are the responses of leading public universities to the leap in institutional strength of leading private universities that successfully invested their endowments in the last two decades. Salary differentials between the private and public institutions—on the average—have become so great in such categories as Research University I and Research University II in the Carnegie classification that central administrators in the state institutions have openly worried about a "brain drain" emigration from their establishments. But averages conceal diversity, in this case critical differences in how the public universities have responded. Some have worked harder and have been more successful in diversifying their sources of income, including endowment and fund-raising drives of their own. Some have been able to increase revenue from state government and from higher student tuition. Notably, "many top public institutions have prioritized specific academic disciplines, schools, and/or colleges to receive additional salary-based resources for faculty recruitment and retention. . . . This process allows some selected academic disciplines to remain competitive," according to F. King Alexander. Special "star" programs devised to hire and retain high-quality faculty are also more extensively used. To fund such efforts, resources often have to be channeled away from other fields on the same campus. Fighting back effectively against the lures of financially blessed private universities, then, has entailed more vigorous external efforts to raise money from a multiplicity of sources and also greater internal differentiation among fields of study and individual academics, regarding salary and departmental conditions of work (Alexander 2001).

As Alexander has shown, such major public universities as the University of Michigan, the University of Virginia—both at the cutting edge of income diversification—and numerous campuses of the University of California system (e.g., Berkeley, UCLA, Riverside, Santa Cruz) have done well in holding down the salary gap. In contrast, the average salary at a large number of state flagship institutions slipped, to twenty thousand to thirty thousand dollars less (for full professors), in 1997–1999 figures, than the private universities paid. Washington and Oregon, in the Pacific Northwest, are examples of this slip, as are Kansas and Wisconsin in the Midwest and Florida and Louisiana in the South. In short, in the top four major categories in the Carnegie classification within which universities are grouped, state-by-state and institution-by-institution differences in level of resource and in assembled capacity to compete effectively with counterpart private universities are increasing. And although the data are not at hand, we can be sure that the variation around the average has also increased among the private universities. Those that embarked upon the striking investment possibilities of the 1980s and 1990s with initial major endowments will have benefited handsomely. But the many private universities and colleges that have lived off student tuition, with little endowment, will have a different story to tell.

CONCLUSION

The phenomenon of academic differentiation on which Neil Smelser concentrated a yearlong effort in the early 1970s—mobilizing formal categories of differentiation and segmentation—has become central in understanding basic differences among national and provincial systems of higher education. Neil focused on California alone, in all its grand complexity of major sectors, basic fault lines, and resulting interest-group formation and conflict. California was a fortunate choice: three decades later, the entire world still wants to know what is basic in that state's master plan. But in the years since Neil wrote, research in higher education has become importantly comparative. Crucial findings have centered on the topic of academic competition, a subject Joseph Ben-David early on effectively pursued as he integrated the sociology of science with a sociology of higher education and university life.

The analysis and highlighting of the role of competition has extended greatly the contemporary understanding of the sociological-organizational foundations of system and institutional capability.

Differentiation and competition in their interaction propel system development. Lack of differentiation becomes a major constraint: one type of institution, one set of disciplines, cannot offer the multiple competencies that are needed. One-kind-, one-size-fits-all has proven to be a major blunder in government planning. Having little or no competition leads at best to passive autonomy in which collegiality is biased toward the status quo and even the status quo ante. Institutions go on conforming to historical blueprints and engrained mythologies; they have little reason to break the mold. American primary and secondary education show us vividly that a combination of highly decentralized authority and lack of competition can be disastrous. It is competition that turns passivity into active autonomy, into a search for distinctive institutional and departmental niches and other platforms of comparative competence.

A combination of perspectives established by Smelser and Ben-David three and four decades ago now more than ever leads toward fundamental sociological explanations of why some universities prosper while others do not; why some national systems of higher education are more appropriately structured than others to handle contradictory values; why some universities and systems are better able to reconcile the new and the old in adaptable capabilities. Universities will continue to be organizations very difficult to understand; systems of "postsecondary" education will become more confusing, not less. To better understand these unusual organizations and these tangled systems, conceptions that offer analytical power, drawn from the various social sciences, are much needed. In sociology, the ideas of differentiation and competition now head the list.

REFERENCES

Abbott, Andrew. 1999. *Department and Discipline: Chicago Sociology at One Hundred.* Chicago: University of Chicago Press.

Alexander, F. King. 2001. "The Silent Crisis: The Relative Fiscal Capacity of Public Universities to Compete for Faculty." *Review of Higher Education* 24 (2): 113–29.

Becher, Tony. 1989. *Academic Tribes and Territories: Intellectual Enquiry and the Cultures of Disciplines.* Milton Keynes, U.K.: Society for Research into Higher Education and Open University Press.

Ben-David, Joseph. 1972. *American Higher Education: Directions Old and New.* New York: McGraw-Hill.

Ben-David, Joseph, with Awraham Zloczower. 1962. "Universities and Academic Systems in Modern Societies." *European Journal of Sociology* 3: 45–84.

Birnbaum, Robert. 2000. *Management Fads in Higher Education: Where They Come From, What They Do, and Why They Fail.* San Francisco: Jossey-Bass.

Clark, Burton R. 1983. *The Higher Education System: Academic Organization in Cross-National Perspective.* Berkeley and Los Angeles: University of California Press.

———. 1987. *The Academic Life: Small Worlds, Different Worlds.* Princeton, N.J.: Carnegie Foundation for the Advancement of Teaching.

———. 1995. *Places of Inquiry: Research and Advanced Education in Modern Universities.* Berkeley and Los Angeles: University of California Press.

———. 2002. "University Transformation: Primary Pathways to University Autonomy and Achievement." In Steven Brint, ed., *The Future of the City of Intellect: The Changing American University,* pp. 322–42. Stanford: Stanford University Press.

———, ed. 1993. *The Research Foundations of Graduate Education: Germany, Britain, France, United States, Japan.* Berkeley and Los Angeles: University of California Press.

Conrad, Clifton F., Jennifer Grant Haworth, and Susan Bolyard Millar. 1993. *A Silent Success: Master's Education in the United States.* Baltimore: Johns Hopkins University Press.

Dahrendorf, Ralf. 1979. *Life Chances: Approaches to Social and Political Theory.* Chicago: University of Chicago Press.

Douglas, John Aubrey. 2000. *The California Idea and American Higher Education: 1850 to the 1960 Master Plan.* Stanford: Stanford University Press.

Encyclopedia of Semiotics. 2000. Ed. Paul Bouissac. Oxford: Oxford University Press.

Geertz, Clifford. 2000. *Available Light: Anthropological Reflections on Philosophical Topics.* Princeton, N.J.: Princeton University Press.

Gumport, Patricia J. 1993. "Graduate Education and Research Imperatives." In Burton R. Clark, ed., *The Research Foundations of Graduate Education: Germany, Britain, France, United States, Japan,* pp. 261–93. Berkeley and Los Angeles: University of California Press.

Harris, Roy. 2000. Review of *Encyclopedia of Semiotics,* ed. Paul Bouissac. *Times Higher Education Supplement* (February 11, 2000): 28.

Hewstone, M. 1992. "Social Psychology." In Burton R. Clark and Guy Neave, eds., *The Encyclopedia of Higher Education,* pp. 2150–63. Oxford: Pergamon Press.

Holmes, Frederic L. 1989. "The Complementarity of Teaching and Research in Liebig's Laboratory." In Kathryn M. Olesko, ed., *Science in Germany: The Intersection of Institutional and Intellectual Issues,* pp. 121–64. *Osiris,* 2d ser., vol. 5.

International Encyclopedia of the Social and Behavioral Sciences. 2001. Ed. Neil J. Smelser and Paul B. Baltes. Amsterdam: Elsevier Science.

Kerr, Clark. 1994. *Higher Education Cannot Escape History: Issues for the Twenty-First Century.* Albany: State University of New York Press.

Leary, D. E. 1992. "Psychology." In Burton R. Clark and Guy Neave, eds., *The Encyclopedia of Higher Education,* pp. 2136–50. Oxford: Pergamon Press.

Long, Norton E. 1962. *The Polity.* Chicago: Rand McNally.

Luhmann, Niklas. 1982. *The Differentiation of Society.* Trans. Stephen Holmes and Charles Larmore. New York: Columbia University Press.

Madison, B. L. 1992. "Mathematics and Statistics." In Burton R. Clark and Guy Neave, eds., *The Encyclopedia of Higher Education,* pp. 2372–88. Oxford: Pergamon Press.

McClelland, Charles E. 1980. *State, Society, and University in Germany, 1700–1914.* Cambridge: Cambridge University Press.

Metzger, Walter. 1987. "The Academic Profession in the United States." In Burton R.

Clark, ed., *The Academic Profession: National, Disciplinary, and Institutional Settings,* pp. 123–208. Berkeley and Los Angeles: University of California Press.

Moodie, Graeme C., and Rowland Eustace. 1974. *Power and Authority in British Universities.* Montreal: McGill-Queen's University Press.

Morrell, J. B. 1990. "Science in the Universities: Some Reconsiderations." In Tore Frangsmyr, ed., *Solomon's House Revisited: The Organization and Institutionalization of Science,* pp. 51–64. Canton, Mass.: Watson Publishing International.

Olesko, Kathryn M. 1991. *Physics as a Calling: Discipline and Practice in the Konigsberg Seminar for Physics.* Ithaca, N.Y.: Cornell University Press.

Powell, Walter W., and Jason Owen-Smith. 1998. "Universities and the Market for Intellectual Property in the Life Sciences." *Journal of Policy Analysis and Management* 17 (2): 253–77.

Rothblatt, Sheldon. 1999. "Historical Methods of Reshaping the Map of Learning." *Minerva* 27 (3): 281–93.

The Routledge Encyclopedia of Philosophy. 1998. Ed. Edward Craig. 10 vols. London: Routledge.

Smelser, Neil J. 1974. "Growth, Structural Change, and Conflict in California Public Higher Education, 1950–1970." In Neil J. Smelser and Gabriel Almond, eds., *Public Higher Education in California,* pp. 9–142. Berkeley and Los Angeles: University of California Press.

Smelser, Neil J., and Robin Content. 1980. *The Changing Academic Market: General Trends and a Berkeley Case Study.* Berkeley and Los Angeles: University of California Press.

Syverson, Peter D. 1999. "Forty Percent of the System: The Contribution of DMOS [Doctorate, Master's, and Other Specialized] Institutions to Diversity in Science and Engineering Graduate Education." *Council of Graduate Schools Communicator* 32 (6): 8–10.

Trow, Martin. 1999. "From Mass Higher Education to Universal Access: The American Advantage." *Minerva* 37 (4): 303–28.

Weick, Karl. 1976. "Educational Organizations as Loosely Coupled Systems." *Administrative Science Quarterly* 21: 1–19.

PART III

Beliefs

Introduction

Jeffrey C. Alexander

As my coeditors and I suggest in the introduction to this volume, Neil Smelser was one of the few powerful voices in late-twentieth-century sociology to emphasize the autonomy and interrelation of the three fundamental levels of social organization: emotions, social structures, and beliefs. While the chapters in this section cover wide ground, their most important connection to Smelser's oeuvre is their relevance to his studies of beliefs.

Smelser's approach is distinguished foremost by his insistence that beliefs matter. While deeply related to emotional hopes and social structural strains, beliefs are continuously generalized and thus attain a life of their own. Smelser studied such generalized beliefs carefully, teasing out the internal meaning references of the symbolic that are embedded in economic, political, and emotional forms. When he examined the industrial revolution—and, more generally, the economic division of labor—as a social movement, he emphasized the important stimulus provided by the utopian narrations of technology and efficiency, on the one hand, and of social tranquility and social justice, on the other. In his second major book, he argued that similar sorts of generalized beliefs were central to every form of collective behavior, from fads and fashions to revolutionary and reform movements. Later, he showed how British and American educational reforms were forcefully affected by traditional beliefs, whose cultural integrity often created difficulties for political reform.

Smelser's approach to how beliefs work in society was guided by "state-of-the-art" theory during the years of his intellectual formation. This was a period before philosophy had taken the linguistic turn, or at least before this turn had become a matter of self-conscious intellectual reflection. This was also several decades before the cultural turn in the social sciences, when the insights of literary, hermeneutic, and linguistic methods and theories transformed sociology's theoretical terrain. Smelser applied "value analysis" to his study of beliefs, drawing on the approaches to religion, literature, myth, cultural history, and popular culture that were cutting-edge in that day.

To this broad synthesis of extant culture analysis, Smelser added three particular and important twists:

- He brought psychoanalytic thinking into play, with its attention to such emotionally inspired ideational figures as wish fulfillment, splitting, neutralization, projection, repression, and displacement.
- He continually applied to these reconstructions of beliefs two important distinctions: primordial/modern and general/specific. As a modern liberal thinker, Smelser was concerned with the manner in which primordial beliefs often prevented the kind of rational reorganization that would allow stubborn social problems to be solved. He was a bit less critical about the generalized nature of beliefs. While criticizing them for their antirealistic utopianism, he recognized their social significance for stimulating social movements and social change; he appreciated them, in other words, as a source of social energy.
- He paid careful attention to culture as a social process. Actions, whether individual or collective, always involve some reference to generalized belief, but these cultural patterns never become more than part of the story. Their effects are mediated by several layers of other kinds of social structure, from norms to organizations to adaptive resources. As a result, beliefs never play themselves out as such; their effects depend on how they are funneled and institutionalized by less symbolic and less generalized parts of society.

Christian Joppke's chapter takes its reference points from Smelser's interest in the continuing role of primordial beliefs and his insistence on looking at the role of beliefs in terms of context and social process. In Britain's postcolonial immigration policy, Joppke finds, politicians of every ideological stripe wanted to give preference to "patrials"—that is, to noncitizens who had some prior attachment, by birth or kinship, to the British homeland. This preference emerged from shared generalized beliefs among Britain's elites and masses, beliefs about race, culture, and religion. Joppke shows, however, that the only publicly acknowledged legitimate primordial belief was kinship, and that the patrial preference was articulated in precisely that way. He suggests that such "aesthetic," cultural concerns with exemplary validity increasingly countered "liberal norms of neutrality." Eventually, Joppke believes, continuing pressure for critical universalism undermined the patrial policy and forced Britain to find more evenhanded and pluralist policies. In this manner, the modern state became differentiated not only from economy and religion but also from ethnicity. Following the other, noncultural parts of Smelser's argument, in other words, Joppke finds that the reality of social complexity can often undermine the exemplary validity of generalized belief.

Lyn Spillman's contribution elaborates on this contingent, multidimensional approach to beliefs. She suggests that Smelser's insistence on flow and process—on the value-added, multiple quality of causality—might well be viewed as introducing a new, nonstructural approach to cause and effect. Covering-law models aim at creating generalizations that can subsume every similar historical case. Drawing on recent philosophical developments of historical method, Spillman demonstrates that Smelser's value-added emphasis on contingency aims not at static covering law but at colligation, which refers to an ambition to locate an event in social process by specifying what led up to it and what it led to. This series of processual events is then named by reference to an existing concept; for example, it is called a revolution or a goal-oriented or norm-oriented social movement. Such contributions, Spillman points out, are less causal in the positivist sense than they are conceptual. They are built into explanations by way of the "parametric knowledge" that, according to Smelser, is one of the most persistently ignored elements of social scientific thought.

James Jasper argues that the early critics of Smelser's concept of generalized beliefs erred by ignoring not only its colligatory connotations but also the continuing significance of their causal effect. In light of recent developments in the sociology of culture and emotions, Jasper writes, Smelser's emphasis on generalized belief in collective behavior "has begun to look as if it were ahead of its time rather than behind the times." What Jasper faults in Smelser's approach is what he views as its emphasis on the irrationality of such generalized beliefs. He links such a putative emphasis to the influence on Smelser of the psychoanalytic approaches to ideation. The Freudian-inspired method emphasizes the failure of reality testing and the presence of fantasy, rather than the connection between such nonempirical tropes and the symbolic resources made available by culture structure. While Jasper makes a strong argument that contemporary conceptual tools provide a superior method—"there is plenty of room for unconscious processes in cultural approaches"—he possibly overemphasizes the exclusivity of the Freudian as compared to the other theoretical inputs in Smelser's early approach to generalized belief. While the notion of "short-circuiting" does indeed seem to suggest illogic, fantasy, or neurosis, Smelser actually seems to most often mean by it something else: the tendency for utopian thinking about the possibilities of social change to ignore the complex, intermediating levels of economics, politics, and social structure. Yet, if Jasper does not agree with all of Smelser's answers, he emphatically concludes that "we must return to some of Smelser's questions, long buried" but still of the utmost importance.

Piotr Sztompka makes a similar argument in regard to Smelser's method of doing sociology more generally. Inspired by Smelser's lifelong commitment to theorizing as sociological vocation, Sztompka embraces the notion that theory provides the sociological apprentice with the "language" and "vision" required to engage in any kind of empirical work. To educate the sociological imagination, it is vital to be trained in theory, for only such generalized empirical beliefs can supply a map allowing sociologists to orient themselves to the social world. Sztompka goes on to crystallize the different modes of theorizing in which Smelser has so fruitfully engaged. In addition to historical approaches to the legacy of earlier sociological theory, which should teach theoretical pluralism and tolerance, theorizing breaks down into explanatory, heuristic, and analytic types. Over the course of his career—indeed, in every one of his empirical and theoretical monographs— Smelser engaged in each of these different kinds of theoretical activities. As my colleagues and I point out in the introduction to this volume, Smelser explained widely studied social events and processes in new ways, and in the course of doing so established a series of new analytic concepts. It is surely by reason of such conceptual plurivocality that he was able not only to establish himself as a wunderkind but also to remain an innovative and influential sociological theorist until this very day.

Chapter 10

Primordial Beliefs and Immigration Policy

The Case of Britain's Patrials

Christian Joppke

Though perhaps more closely and more enduringly associated with Parsonian sociology than any other in the impressive gallery of scholars who took it as their point of departure, Neil Smelser traveled as far away from Talcott Parsons as did Harold Garfinkel, Clifford Geertz, and Robert Bellah, to name just a few. In his fascinating notes on "collaborating with Talcott Parsons," Smelser summarized their different intellectual styles this way: "First, Parsons would as though instinctively think in terms of general categories, and I would tend to convert these categories into outcomes of some process, and begin to think in terms of causes or conditions producing these outcomes. Second, Parsons would move continuously toward the more abstract representation of a concept whereas I would struggle to produce illustrative empirical instances of it" (1981: 149). At first acting as the "change man" within Parsons's cathedral, where history was a tool subordinate to the construction and perfection of sociological theory (1959), Smelser subtly and almost unnoticeably came to reverse this priority. In his magisterial 1991 study of working-class education in nineteenth-century Britain, the line dividing sociology and history is invisible, and what may still pass as "sociological theory" is now put to the service of understanding the "complex patterning of the historical process" (355), and is itself couched in the historical "process" terms *critical moments, truce points,* and so on.

At one level, Smelser's intellectual journey entails the self-effacement of sociology, and thus perhaps epitomizes the sense of crisis in which the discipline is caught today. However, Smelser's subordination of theory to history also adroitly displays the habitus of cutting-edge sociology today: intellectual modesty confronting a complex reality, and a resistance to singling out a "most important factor" as commanded by the warring churches of sociology—ideas, interests, conflict, consensus, and so on (Smelser 1991: 355).

Smelser's diction has always been synthesis—between theoretical perspectives that individually offer a one-sided picture of the social world, but that, in combination, allow us to see the totality of one of this world's multiple constellations.[1] This "totalizing" thrust may remotely echo Parsons, but it has the decisive difference of subordinating theories (always in the plural) to the (always empirical) task at hand and refusing to identify with any one theory or perspective in a creedal, churchlike way.[2] In Smelser's historically minded synthetic agnosticism, sociology as a discipline dissolves, and good sociological practice becomes possible.

Within the sociological church of modernization theory, one of Smelser's heresies was to point to the stubborn persistence of "primordialism," which he broadly defined as "fundamental cultural values and beliefs that are the first premises for organizing and legitimizing institutions, roles, and behavior" (1991: 39). In his history of primary-school education in Britain, this meant taking seriously the givens of class, religion, and region as "fram[ing] all thought and debate about education, and [being] direct determinants of many of its institutional characteristics" (39).[3] However, while paying tribute to the autonomy of primordial beliefs and allegiances (particularly religion), the next, and characteristically Smelserian, move was to pin down the "mechanisms" by which the forces of secularization were chipping away at them "despite the avowed commitment of the society to religion"—examples being the antiauthoritarian and thus rationalizing logic of Protestantism itself or the needs of political compromise-finding and administrative standardization (362–66). In the case at hand, the result was the institutionalization of nonreligious—that is, "universal, free, compulsory, and unsectarian"—primary school education in a society that was not less, but differently, religious.

The persistence or demise of primordial beliefs in another sector of society, the state's immigration policies, is the subject of this chapter. I tackle it in a Smelserian manner, with respect for the complexity of the historical case and a stress on process and mechanisms that does not prejudice beforehand the relative role of ideational, structural, or contingent factors. On the most general plane, immigration policy permits a political community to distribute the precious good of membership and thus decide its own internal composition. One might thus expect this policy to be driven by the primordial beliefs that constitute this community as bounded and particular. Michael Walzer canonized this view from a communitarian perspective, arguing that the distribution of the elementary good of membership (in contrast to that of all other goods) cannot itself be subject to considerations of justice, its function being the reproduction of historical "communities of character" (1983: ch. 3). But even from a liberal perspective, it has been argued that individuals need some primordial givens as "context of choice" (Kymlicka 1995), and one could deduce from this that the state's membership policies (i.e., immigration and citizenship policies) should serve the reproduction of these primordial givens (labeled "societal culture" by Kymlicka).

However, in reality one can observe that the space for primordial immigration policies, which select newcomers according to ethnicity, race, or national origins, is tightly restricted in contemporary liberal states. A prime example for this is the United States, which shifted from a primordial policy of selecting immigrants according to their national origins, and of excluding them on the basis of race, to a universalist policy of selecting on the basis of skills and individual family ties. As shown by the opposition to reintroducing primordialism under the guise of "diversity quota" in the Legal Immigration Act of 1990 (see Legomsky 1993), anything else would smack of discrimination or—to use the language of the opponents of the diversity quota—affirmative action for whites. One could argue that the American shift from a primordial to a universalistic immigration policy simply reflects its particular self-definition as a nonethnically, politically constituted "nation of immigrants." Conversely, one could argue that in the ethnic nation-states of Europe, immigration policies (to the limited degree that they exist there at all) are in the service of reproducing these states' ethnic self-definitions, selecting immigrants on the basis of primordial criteria (for this view, see Coleman and Harding 1995).

This view, which construes a symmetry, or direct causal link, between a political community's self-definition and its membership policies, is flawed. First, it cannot explain why, before 1965, the United States held to a primordial, racially exclusive immigration policy. Second, and this leads to the topic of this chapter, it cannot explain why, in the ethnic nation-states of Europe also, primordial—that is, ethnically selective—immigration policies have everywhere come under pressure and are at the point of disappearing, though with a characteristic delay. This suggests a different root image: instead of a symmetry between self-definitions of a political community and membership policy (which also suffers from a reification of such "communities" as personalities writ large), there is an inbuilt tension between universalist and particularist elements in all liberal nation-states (the limited pool of states subject to this discussion). The liberal component commands nonascriptive, universalist criteria and equity in the selection of immigrants; the national component sometimes commands the opposite, in the service of reproducing the primordial beliefs that constitute a political community.[4] As we shall see in the British case, in the very moment that a primordial policy produces a "loser," and a fundamental equity concern is raised, it will come under pressure: then the "liberal" component of the state will be played out against its "national" one.

To contextualize the British case, it is at first necessary to ferret out the different ways in which primordial beliefs have historically come to shape immigration policies. A first fundamental difference is between policies that select positively or negatively. The most infamous example of negative primordial selection is Chinese and Asian exclusion, which was explicitly or implicitly practiced in all new settler states (Canada, Australia, the United States) well into the mid-1960s. Far more interesting than negative selection—which is universally outlawed today and, if practiced at all, can at best be practiced implicitly—is positive primordial selection. It operates on a floor of equality, and it accords privileged treatment to certain ethnic or national-origins groups. Prominent examples are the German and Israeli Laws of Return, which provide automatic access to territory and citizenship to ethnic Germans residing under communist regimes and to Jews, without any geographic restriction, respectively (see Joppke and Rosenhek 2002). Less-known examples are privileged immigration and nationality rules for citizens of Ibero-American states in Spain, and citizens of Lusophone states in Portugal. Finally, there is patriality in Britain, the subject of this chapter.

The interesting recent development is that even positive primordial selection policies have come under pressure everywhere. The reason for this is simple. All Western states, including the traditionally emigrant-sending states of Spain or Portugal, have since the 1980s become immigrant-receiving states, with a large number of these immigrants arriving or residing under illegal precepts or as asylum seekers. In the context of greatly diversified immigrant populations, positive selection is ipso facto negative selection. Preferential access to territory or nationality granted to some ethnic or national-origin groups is the denial of such privileges to other such groups, who may already have established themselves in the territory and who may claim to be discriminated against in light of the better treatment accorded to some other groups. This is precisely the mechanism that brought down the national-origin system in place in the United States until 1965. On its face, this was a system of positive discrimination for immigrants from countries to which the majority of the U.S. population according to the 1890 census could trace its origins (that is, northwestern Europeans). However, the system in fact entailed negative discrimination for immigrants from countries that came to predominate slightly later—mostly southern and eastern Europeans, who would constitute the main lobby for the new system of source-country universalism established in 1965 (see Joppke 1999: 26). This negative discrimination was not incidental but fully intentional.

A second relevant dimension along which primordial immigration policies differ is their justification. Some such policies are justified as being in the interest of the receiving society because culturally and ethnically close immigrants are deemed better assimilable than those who are not. This was the main justification of the national-origin system in place in the United States between 1924 and 1965. On the opposite side, some primordial immigration policies are couched in the language of individual rights. These include the German and Israeli Laws of Return, which invest some immigrants with constitutional (Germany) or natural law entitlements (Israel). Underlying these different, assimilationist versus rights-based justifications is a different phenomenology of immigrants in both cases: in the assimilationist discourse, immigrants are conceived of as culturally or ethnically "similar to" but essentially different from the state-bearing nation; in the rights-based discourse, immigrants are conceived of in terms of "sameness" and a priori membership in the state-bearing nation. It is not surprising that both justifications have sharply different survival chances in liberal states: assimilationist justifications and the immigration policies that flow from them violate multicultural sensibilities and have mostly succumbed to the verdict of discrimination or racism. By contrast, rights-based justifications and related immigration policies are fully compatible with the proliferating rights talk in liberal states and thus have proved more resistant to attack.

In between the assimilationist and rights-based justifications is a third type of justifying primordial immigration policies, one that evokes a state-transcending historical-cultural community. This "communitarian" justification can be found in the historical context of some versions of European colonialism, in which the settlement of Europeans in presumably uncharted lands overseas has led to a transfer of language and culture and to the creation of genealogical ties, which call for expression even after the formal independence of the new settlements. The notion of a state-transcending community can be most explicitly found in the Spanish and Portuguese justifications of their primordial immigration policies that give preference to Latin Americans and Lusophones, respectively.

The British case also has to be understood within the context of colonialism, but with a twist. The purpose of its so-called patriality provision in immigration law, which granted all Commonwealth citizens with at least a grandparental connection with the United Kingdom the right of entry, was to filter out within the class of postcolonial immigrants a privileged subclass with primordial ties to the United Kingdom. This required an ad hominem inquiry into the veracity of individual descent claims. By contrast, the Spanish and Portuguese recognition of primordial ties operated on the basis of treaty-based, interstate reciprocity, according to which all citizens of contracting countries were granted privileged entry to Spain or Portugal, provided that Spanish or Portuguese citizens enjoyed reciprocal rights in the other state. Interestingly, the reciprocity alternative to patriality was briefly considered in Britain but discarded. As we shall see, there are contingent reasons for this. However, the discarding of reciprocity, which would have implied the inclusion of aboriginal people, among others, without any British origins or family ties also expresses a desire for limiting immigration privileges to the proved descendants of former settlers. The patriality scheme thus echoes, however remotely, the distinctly British style of colonialism, which, much in contrast to Luso-Hispanic colonialism, has always shunned miscegenation and racial mixing, and which caused colonials and natives to live in sharply divided parallel societies (see Hartz 1964).

Three parameters shaped British postcolonial immigration policy: the absence of a perceived economic or demographic need for immigrants; the nonexistence of a metropolitan citizenship that would permit a clear-cut distinction between citizens and aliens; and the existence of British settlements overseas (the so-called Old Commonwealth or Dominions: Australia, New Zealand, and Canada) whose primordial closeness to Britain called for statutory expression. All three parameters converged in an immigration policy that sought to make the cuts where the pressure was: among immigrants from the New Commonwealth—that is, Britain's former possessions in East Africa, the Caribbean West Indies, and the Indian subcontinent. That most of them happened to be nonwhite has spurred the accusation, raised by legions of mostly British scholars, that this policy was racist or racialist (e.g., Dummett and Nicol 1990; Paul 1997). This not only simplifies a complex problematic but also is forgetful of the fact that imperialism alone had conditioned the earlier open-door policy. Since, for the critics of British immigration policy, it was out of the question to retain imperialism in a postimperial age, the case for maintaining an open-door approach rested on a theory of compensation or reparation never truly articulated, whose normative and empirical bases are dubious.

An often-raised, though somewhat weaker, claim in this context is that postcolonial immigrants were officially invited when there was an economic need for them, so that later they could not be disposed of at will. While this had been a major justification for dealing humanely with continental European "guest workers" (see Joppke 1999: ch. 3), a deliberate recruitment had never existed for British postcolonial immigrants. There was punctuated recruitment in the early 1950s, such as that of West Indian nurses under the health minister Enoch Powell, in order to put down acute demands for higher wages by domestic nurses, and some private schemes of recruiting West Indians by London Transport and the British Hotel and Restaurants' Association. But these measures do not add up to a concerted state policy of proactively recruiting postcolonial immigrants. On the contrary, during a brief moment, in the late 1940s, when there was a perceived economic and demographic need for immigrants, the British government turned toward European rather than postcolonial sources (Paul 1997: ch. 3).

Having turned its back on labor migration early on, Britain faced the problem of containing postcolonial immigration, put on the map by alarming societal disapproval since the late 1950s.[5] Containment of this mostly unwanted immigration was made difficult by the lack of an exclusive citizenship scheme, which also might have allowed the trickle of wanted post-colonial immigration from the Old Commonwealth to filter in. Between 1948, when the British Nationality Act was passed, and 1981, Britain only disposed of an overinclusive, quasi-imperial "United Kingdom and colonies citizenship," which did not distinguish the natives and residents of the metropole from those of Britain's vast possessions around the globe. It was complemented by a second status, held by "citizens of independent Commonwealth countries," which afforded broadly identical rights, including free entry to the United Kingdom. This 1948 British Nationality Act, the first explicit citizenship scheme in British history, had a backward-looking purpose: to retain the uniform status of British subject throughout the empire, which had become threatened by Canada's introduction of a local citizenship in 1946. It was certainly not meant to allow immigration from the New Commonwealth. The only free movement intended at the time was the movement of Old Dominion citizens; that of colonial subjects was at best tolerated if occurring only temporarily and among limited numbers (see Hansen 2000: ch. 2).

One has to realize the anachronism as well as the immense self-confidence expressed in the 1948 citizenship scheme. At a time when all other Commonwealth states, most notably Canada and Australia, busily controlled the immigration of British subjects, especially those who, for racial reasons, were not wanted, Britain was deliberately abstaining from all such controls, including the racially mischievous ones, in its noble quest to "maintain our great metropolitan tradition of hospitality to everyone from every part of our Empire" (Sir David Maxwell Fyfe, quoted in Hansen 2000: 50). The result was free entry rights for some 600 million British subjects around the globe, which proved most difficult to correct because of the path-dependent inertia of the underlying citizenship scheme.

If more than one decade of unsolicited and socially contested New Commonwealth immigration passed by without the introduction of controls, this is because the wish not to erect a "colour bar," shared by Labour and Conservative Party elites alike, put before the government the uncomfortable alternative of either controlling all immigration from the Commonwealth, including the Old, or not having any controls at all. This alternative was dramatically placed before the cabinet by Colonial Secretary Alan Lennox-Boyd in 1955 (Hansen 2000: 71–73), and a Tory-led government opted for "no controls" at the time. To the degree that there was elite division, it was institutional, with the Labour Ministry and Home Office opting for controls, and the Colonial and Commonwealth Offices opting against.[6] Seven years later, against the backdrop of rising numbers, increasing social tensions, and a Colonial Office losing clout within the Cabinet, a likewise Tory-led government opted "for controls," in its passing of the first Commonwealth Immigrants Act.

The 1962 Commonwealth Immigrants Act pioneered the peculiar approach of "legislating by exception," which was necessitated by the absence of a metropolitan citizenship (the quote is from Enoch Powell, in *Parliamentary Debates,* House of Commons, 8 March 1971, c.77). In this approach, all "Commonwealth citizens" (another word for "British subjects" after 1948), except a privileged subclass of primordial "belongers," were made subject to controls.[7] In 1962, these "belongers" were defined as people either born in the United Kingdom or possessing passports issued by the U.K. government. This mechanism was meant to distinguish—within the overinclusive "United Kingdom and colonies citizenship" category— between the natives and residents of the metropole and the colonial rest. Interestingly, this narrow definition of *belonging* did not permit distinction between Old and New Commonwealth immigrants, thus accepting control of the former as a price for controlling the latter, under the overarching imperative of avoiding a "colour bar."[8]

The distinction between privileged Old and nonprivileged New Commonwealth immigrants became possible only with the "patrial" category introduced in the 1971 Immigration Act. Technically, this act completed the gradual move toward a uniform immigration regime, in which most Commonwealth immigrants were equated with "normal" immigrant aliens; politically, the act was forced on a reluctant Tory government by "Powellism," that is, Enoch Powell's immensely popular anti-immigrant crusade at the time. At one level, the notion of patriality is the functional equivalent of citizenship for an immigration policy that could not be based on citizenship—"a quasi-nationality for immigration purposes" (Dummett and Nicol 1990: 217).

Who were the patrials? In the words of Home Secretary Reginald Maudling, *patrial* was a word for "people who have a right of abode" (*Parliamentary Debates,* House of Commons, 8 March 1971, c.45). The definition of *patrial* included citizens of the United Kingdom and its colonies who either were residents or had a parent or grandparent who had been born in the United Kingdom. Controversy arose over the original bill brought to Parliament in March 1971 because its patrial notion also included "any Commonwealth citizen who had a father or mother or grandparent born in the UK" (Home Secretary Maudling, in *Parliamentary Debates,* House of Commons, 8 March 1971, c.45). Though formally neutral concerning the race or geographic origins of the respective (Old or New) Commonwealth immigrant, this provision in fact favored the descendants of white Old Dominion settlers, in recognition of "special ties of blood and kinship" (Home Secretary Maudling, quoted in Macdonald 1972: 16), while excluding many of the British-passport holding Asians stranded in the nationalizing states of West Africa. This "racial contrast" immediately incensed the liberal conscience (the quote is from David Steel [Liberal Party], in *Parliamentary Debates,* House of Commons, 8 March 1971, c.113).

Interestingly, the storm unleashed over the patrials took the Tory government completely by surprise. While the word was new, the underlying concept "has been evolved *[sic]* in principle by succeeding Governments," as Home Secretary Maudling put it at the second reading of the Immigration Bill (*Parliamentary Debates*, House of Commons, 8 March 1971, c.46). Every independence act since the 1950s had included a special citizenship provision for former colonials with at least a grandparental connection with the United Kingdom. When passing the second Commonwealth Immigrants Act of 1968, the Labour government, intent on excluding Asian British passport-holders in Kenya (see Hansen 1999), had widened the original circle of "belongers" to include citizens of the United Kingdom and its colonies who had a grandparental connection. Considering these precedents, the patrial category was indeed more a syllogism derived from past practice than the fundamental conceptual innovation that it was later perceived to be and attacked for being.

There were two ways of defending patriality. The official government version was that patriality was not a racial category, but one that simply recognized a "family connection" (Home Secretary Maudling, in *Parliamentary Debates*, House of Commons, 8 March 1971, c.46). Indeed, the line between patriality as an individual right recognizing family ties and an ethnic-group or national-origin concept is exceedingly thin. Every state grants citizenship rights to first-generation descendants born abroad, and extending this to second-generation descendants makes for a difference that is one "of degree rather than kind" (Hansen 2000: 195). However, there was a second, more dubious defense of patriality, advanced only by some Tory backbenchers but picked up by the liberal critics as revealing the "true" government intention. According to this version, the intention of the Immigration Act was to cut "coloured" immigration because this was the source of all troubles, and there was no point, in an act of "bogus uniformity," according to Tory Member of Parliament Kenneth Clarke, in also excluding white immigrants from the Old Commonwealth. They, after all, faced no problem of acceptance in society:

> It is intellectually dishonest for liberal opinion . . . to pretend that the debate about immigration control . . . centres on anything other than the racial problems which the country faces. . . . It is desirable to restrict the number of coloured immigrants into this country. . . . Why should a system which faces up to that regrettable necessity impose hardship on groups of people, in particular those who are the descendants of fairly recent emigrants from this country to Australia, New Zealand and British South Africa?[9]

Liberal critics of patriality focused on the fact that it included citizens of other (Commonwealth) countries while excluding some whose only citizenship was that of the United Kingdom and colonies. David Steel of the Liberal Party put it this way:

> One gets into a situation where a one-year-old female child who emigrated with its parents . . . 150 years ago, could be the grandmother of somebody today claiming entry under the patrial clause. . . . If we contrast that . . . with somebody who . . . holds a United Kingdom passport but who lives with no other citizenship, say, in East Africa, we realize the racial contrast which exists under this legislation. (*Parliamentary Debates,* House of Commons, 8 March 1971, c.113)

Only this second, exclusionary aspect made patriality suspicious, which in its inclusive dimension was homologous to the "law of return" provisions found in all emigrant-sending states.[10]

However, there was in addition a nonliberal, restrictionist critique of grandparental patriality.[11] It was formulated above all by the flamboyant Tory outsider Enoch Powell. Powell branded grandparental patriality a reversed "Grossmutter nicht in Ordnung" rule, by means of which the Nazis had expelled Jews from the German nation: "We, conversely, are saying that such is the magic of birth within this country that one quarter of such descent is sufficient to mark a man out from the rest of humanity and to make him one of us" (*Parliamentary Debates,* House of Commons, 8 March 1971, c.80). He went on to say that "hundreds of thousands" of "Anglo-Indian" people—that is, people of mixed race—would qualify for entry under grandparental patriality. Later he would add to this the open-ended scenario of (nonwhite) New Commonwealth immigrants with children born in the United Kingdom returning to their home countries: these children, he pointed out, would be "patrials" for two generations of New Commonwealth immigrants in the future (*Parliamentary Debates,* House of Commons, 21 February 1973, c.627).

The synergetic confluence of liberal and restrictionist critiques of grandparental patriality forced the government into a retreat. In committee stage, a small majority supported a motion by Enoch Powell to limit patriality for Commonwealth citizens to people with a parental (rather than grandparental) connection with the United Kingdom. Powell was joined by liberal Tories and Labour and Liberal Party critics, most notably David Steel, many of whom opposed patriality as such and for altogether different reasons.[12] Interestingly, when trimmed to include only the parental connection, Commonwealth patriality suddenly appeared to be a measure of sex equality. Already according to existing law, any Commonwealth citizen (as was true for any other alien, for that matter) whose *father* was born in the United Kingdom enjoyed automatic entry and residence rights in the United Kingdom. Commonwealth patriality only extended this right to any Commonwealth citizen whose *mother* was born in the United Kingdom, thus removing an obvious case of sex discrimination.[13] The "racism" charge, even if dubious from the start, now lost every basis: "It has always been the law that someone born in this country or the child of a father born in this country had a special position. We are now extending it to mothers."[14] Thus converted into a "progressive" equality measure, patriality was obviously a bird whose feathers could take on many a color.

Had that been the end of the matter, patriality could hardly have been the ethnically, or even racially, flavored concept that it came to be known as. When the Immigration Rules implementing the 1971 Immigration Act were put before Parliament in late October 1972, they also included the free movement provisions for European Community (EC) nationals to frame Britain's pending entry into the European Economic Community in January 1973. Now an altogether different contrast opened up: that between privileged EC nationals and nonprivileged, nonpatrial Commonwealth citizens, downgraded to "aliens" by the new Immigration Act. This was the historic moment when Britain finally "turned away from the open seas" (Enoch Powell, in *Parliamentary Debates*, House of Commons, 22 November 1972, c.1396), toward a Europe seen more as economic necessity than an object of emotional allegiance. And it was a historic moment in which even for liberal Labourites the "open seas" was above all the Old Commonwealth. Labour frontbencher Peter Shore pointed out that "no other country in Europe or in the world has had this experience of its people forming separate yet linked states in other continents as we have done in Australia, New Zealand and Canada." He even compared the links between them to the links between "people . . . divided by war between countries or civil war"—such as the two Germanies, Koreas, and Vietnams. To be downgraded to "third countries" had to be a "deep and unforgivable offence" to the Old Commonwealth states, "which share with us the same Head of State, operate a substantially open door for our own citizens, and are peopled predominantly with British people" (*Parliamentary Debates*, House of Commons, 22 November 1972, c.1442). Old-Commonwealth ties came alive in Parliament when an Australian Labour member of Parliament exchanged "the cap I normally wear as the Member of Feltham" for his "Australian cap," reminding his peers that Australia not only had always provided "good and cheap food" to Britain but also had fought at its side during World War II against a European enemy: "My first experience of this country was . . . flying Lancasters over Germany with, be it noted, a mixed Commonwealth aircrew" (Russell Kerr, *Parliamentary Debates*, House of Commons, 22 November 1972, c.1396–7).

However, the tempestuous debate over the Immigration Rules was above all a field day for a heady backbench alliance of Old Commonwealth loyalists and Euro-skeptics within the ruling Conservative Party, which eventually would bring about "the most important Government defeat in post-war Parliamentary history" (Norton 1976: 413). Much like the liberal critics of patriality during the debate over the Immigrant Act, the conservative advocates of nonpatrial Commonwealthers used invidious contrasts to bring out apparent injustice. One Tory cited his relatives, who "went from Connecticut to New Brunswick in 1776 . . . because they . . . want[ed] to be subjects of her Majesty the Queen." Their offspring were now downgraded to aliens, whereas the people living just off the coast on a small island still constituting a department of metropolitan France "will be perfectly entitled to enter Britain with no conditions," even though they "have done nothing for us" (*Parliamentary Debates*, House of Commons, 22 November 1972, c.1436).

Home Secretary Robert Carr sought to assure the Old Commonwealth loyalists that, with the new Immigration Rules, "patrial Commonwealth citizens will be more favourably treated than EEC citizens, and nonpatrial Commonwealth citizens will be more favourably treated than non-EEC aliens" (*Parliamentary Debates*, House of Commons, 22 November 1972, c.1374). However, this fourfold hierarchy of citizens and aliens precisely dodged the main point of contention: that nonpatrial Commonwealth citizens were accorded status below that of EC citizens. Even when assuring, now more to the point, that nonpatrial Commonwealthers, once admitted, enjoyed all the rights of British subjects, which EC nationals did not enjoy (such as the rights to vote and to stand for Parliament),[15] the government passed over the fact that these rights were without value if not accompanied by the right of entry and residence. The oddity of EC citizens and nonpatrial Commonwealthers being reversely privileged before and after entry was aptly captured by Enoch Powell: "We have said to one set of people[,] 'You cannot come in except under certain pretty stringent controls. But, once you are in, you belong to us. . . . To another set of people we have said[,] 'You can all come in for work.' . . . However, once you are in, you are an alien. . . . That is an absurdity" (*Parliamentary Debates*, House of Commons, 22 November 1972, c.1395).

After its defeat on the Immigration Rules, the government had to win back the Old Commonwealth loyalists within its own Conservative Party. This is how the old concept of grandparental patriality for Commonwealth citizens, a concept that had been dead for two years, was resurrected within redrafted Immigration Rules presented to Parliament in January 1973. Interestingly, the leaders of the Tory rebels had long been in favor of an alternative solution to affirm the special ties with Old Commonwealth countries, and one advocate of finding an alternative solution, the moderate Tory G. Sinclair, had actually taken part in knocking down grandparental Commonwealth patriality in 1971. This alternative to patriality was "reciprocity." It would have meant that all citizens (and not just the patrial subclass of them) of contracting countries would enjoy free entry and residence privileges in Britain, provided these countries granted the same privileges to Britons. As even Home Secretary Carr had to admit, patriality was not at all liked by the Old Commonwealth governments (*Parliamentary Debates,* House of Commons, 21 February 1973, c.598). It divided their citizenries, between French origin and British origin in Canada, European origin and British origin in Australia, and Maori origin and British origin in New Zealand; of course, patriality also divided British-origin citizens themselves along the random generational marker—and all this divisiveness in a moment when these states were desperately struggling for post-British national unity. However, according to the Home Secretary, initial negotiations with these governments over reciprocal immigration rights had been unsuccessful, which is why reinstating grandparental patriality for Commonwealth citizens returned to the agenda.[16]

The larger irony of this final outcome of the struggle over the patrials should not be overlooked: an Immigration Act notionally committed to bringing down overseas immigration to the "inescapable minimum" opened Britain's doors to an estimated 8 million Old Commonwealth patrials (the quote is from Home Secretary Carr, *Parliamentary Debates,* House of Commons, 21 February 1973, c.598). And patriality was not all. To win back the rebellious Old Commonwealth loyalists, the eventual Immigration Rules of February 1973 also extended from three years to a five-year maximum the "working holiday-maker" scheme, which was formally open to all Commonwealth citizens but in fact used mostly by young people from the Old Commonwealth. This meant that these "visitors" could make their stay permanent by registering as citizens with a right of abode after four years. When the Labour frontbencher Shirley Williams made Home Secretary Carr aware of this "very wide loophole," he responded that, under the new Immigration Rules, this citizenship acquisition was no longer as-of-right but discretionary on the part of the state—not mentioning that such discretion was only in the rarest of cases used against Old Commonwealth citizens.[17]

Moreover, the "racial contrast" that had provoked the first row over patriality in 1971 came full circle. When announcing the revised Immigration Rules, whose purpose was to "give the freest possible access to Commonwealth citizens whose close family ties are with this country," Home Secretary Carr also pointed out, in the same breath, that there would be no further "generosity" for the seventy thousand to eighty thousand Asian holders of British passports still stranded in East Africa, who were thus left effectively stateless.[18] "The door opens to the whites, but closes on the Asians"[19]—this remained the quintessence of patriality.

After its contested birth, patriality for (Old) Commonwealth citizens remained alive for only ten years, succumbing to an almost unnoticed death in the British Nationality Act of 1981. This act "redeployed" patriality as "British citizenship" (Fransman 1983), thus finally living up to the mantra, recited by all parties since the first controls of Commonwealth immigration were introduced in the early 1960s, that what Britain really needed was an exclusive concept of citizenship to put its immigration policies on a rational basis. All living Commonwealth patrials before the enactment of the new law on 1 January 1983 retained their privileged status. This was partly (that is, for those Commonwealth patrials already residing in the United Kingdom) a realization of the earlier promise that the immigration status of no one in the United Kingdom would be negatively affected by the act (see Fransman 1989: 147). However, the crucial novelty was that no Commonwealth citizen born after the new act could claim patrial status; Commonwealth patriality was thus made to disappear after one generation. While the informal dynamics leading to the death in principle of Commonwealth patriality is not known, there is a formal, architectonic reason for this restriction. If the whole point of the new nationality law was to make the right of abode the privilege of British citizens (with some derogations allowed solely for a transitional period), this purpose would have been destroyed by making the right of abode available, on an open-ended basis, for some other (Commonwealth) nationalities also. Interestingly, the 1981 act, while habitually criticized for epitomizing "the larger postwar discourse of blood, family, and kith and kin" (Paul 1997: 183), had the exact opposite effect, at least with respect to the reviled concept of Commonwealth patriality.[20]

Was Britain's Commonwealth immigration policy racist? In line with much British scholarship, Kathleen Paul finds at the origins of this policy the "policy-making elite's racialized understanding of the world's population," the latter trickling down through an "educational campaign" to a previously "liberal" mass public (1997: 132, 133). This turns reality on its head. Public hostility to New Commonwealth immigration has caused hesitant and overall liberal elites to give up the old ideal of free movement within the empire (Hansen 2000). It also dodges the question of why this "racialized understanding," if not solicited by public hostility, could suddenly pop up in the late 1950s (a moment of serious race unrest), in complete contradiction to the inclusive "great hospitality" stance that had still guided the Nationality Act of 1948.

In retrospect, the most striking feature of Britain's Commonwealth immigration policy is the discrepancy between its obvious origins—public hostility to nonwhite New Commonwealth immigration—and the complete absence of any formal ethnic, racial, or national-origins distinctions in this policy. Patriality is no exception to this, because it is at heart a kinship category, though one with intended ethnic and racial consequences. Its scandal was not so much its inclusion of the descendants of former settlers (which, on its own, would have hardly lifted an eyebrow) as its prevention of some present "United Kingdom and colonies" citizens from entering and residing in Britain—or, more precisely, its scandal has been the coincidence that it did both, which raised concern about fundamental equality. In this limited and indirect way, Britain's Commonwealth immigration policy had a (covert) racial component. However, equating the latter with the overt racial exclusivity prevailing in the new settler states until the mid-1960s is little more than polemic, because it ignores the real dilemma of selecting immigrants without a firm basis of citizenship.[21]

THE DEMISE OF PRIMORDIAL IMMIGRATION POLICIES IN THE LIBERAL STATE

A striking feature of the British patriality story is the contingency of its primordial dimension. This suggests that primordial beliefs do not ipso facto shape immigration policies. While throughout the period considered here there seems to have been a shared sense of special ties with the "kith and kin" in the Old Dominion (as noted, even among the Labour Party), these ties found no expression in immigration policy between 1962 and 1971; and they found their way into the 1971 Immigration Act only because of the situational concatenation of accession to the European Community and putting Commonwealth citizens on a par with ordinary foreigners. One can formulate this as a counterfactual: if the Tory government had not made the unnecessary move (and thus tactical error) of tabling the new rules resulting from EC accession together with the new Immigration Rules, which suddenly opened up the invidious contrast of privileged European Union foreigners and nonprivileged Commonwealth citizens, the Tory rebellion against its own government would not have occurred, and there would have been no need for the latter to acquiesce to the former by upgrading parental to grandparental patriality. The earlier provision of parental patriality, not contested by any party for two years, hardly went beyond the recognition of elementary (i.e., one-generational) kinship ties, known in the nationality laws of all states, and was certainly not an ethnic (or racist) provision, a claim that was central to the attack on grandparental patriality. While something akin to the patriality notion was structurally required within the context of Britain's overinclusive, pre-1981 citizenship regime, grandparental patriality for Commonwealth citizens, and thus a primordial immigration policy, was only the result of highly contingent circumstances.

A second interesting aspect of the patriality story is the reticence of the British government to acknowledge the ethnic dimension of patriality. The official line of the government was that patriality only recognized family ties and was not an ethnic or even racial category. In fact, the urge to be neutral or impartial was so strong that, until 1962, there were no controls on New or Old Commonwealth immigration at all, and, from 1962 to 1971, Commonwealth immigration controls were the same for all, independently of the special ties later recognized by means of the patriality concept. When the ethnically or racially flavored notion of grandparental patriality created a stir in the parliamentary debates leading to the 1971 Immigration Act, the government immediately ducked and, in effect, reduced patriality to a sex-equality measure. Finally, without much debate, the same Tory government simply buried the privileged immigration of Old Commonwealth "kith and kin" in the 1981 Nationality Act. This shows the difficulty for a liberal state, which is structurally committed to public neutrality and equality, to select immigrants along the primordial markers of ethnicity, race, or national origins. The admission of new members, which is nominally at the discretion of the sovereign state, or of the political community constituting it, is in reality tightly constricted by liberal norms of neutrality and equality—in the ethnic nation-states of Europe evidently as much as in the nonethnic immigrant states overseas.

The demise of patriality in Britain, whose purpose was to filter out among postcolonial immigrants the "kith and kin" in the Old Dominions, is part of a general demise of primordial immigration policies across liberal states. The only primordial ties still respected in these states' immigration policies are family ties, and this is because the integrity of family life is a fundamental human right protected by the constitution of all states and a plethora of supranational conventions. Interestingly, the family continues to be the universally recognized primordial unit in contemporary nation-states, while the ethnic group does not (except in the limiting case of protected "minority" groups; see Kymlicka 1995). This points to a differentiation of the modern state not just from religion but also from ethnicity. This latter differentiation is epitomized by the demise of primordial immigration policies. Though they are definitionally bounded units, states have lost the capacity to reproduce the "communities of character" from which they derive their legitimacy as "nation-states" by means of an ethnically or culturally selective immigration policy (quote from Walzer 1983: 62). The obvious watershed event that brought about this loss of capacity is Nazism, which delegitimized a too-close association between state and ethnic group and launched a trend toward the de-ethnicization of contemporary states. Interestingly, the one exception to this is Israel, founded by Nazism's main victims, which is the only state today to reproduce its ethnic (Jewish) character by means of an openly propagated, ethnically selective immigration policy.

Immigration policy is a good indicator of the trend toward the de-ethnicization of liberal states. It came in two rounds, the first outlawing negative selections (à la Chinese exclusion in the United States), the second incriminating positive selections as well. The reason for the latter is that, in a world of porous borders and intensified and diversified migrations, positive discriminations are bound to produce losers, similarly situated migrant groups that do not partake in the privileges bestowed on the preferred group or groups. This is the moment in which positively selective primordial immigration policies come under fire: Why are Latin Americans formally privileged, but not Moroccans, as in the case of Spain? Why are third-generation

Turks still excluded from the citizenry, while "ethnic Germans" from eastern Europe and the former Soviet Union are automatically included, as in the case of Germany? And in the case of Britain, why are certain citizens of Australia or New Zealand "in," whereas certain nominal U.K. citizenship holders are "out" (a distinction that acquired its vitriolic quality because it overlapped with race)? Scholars have had much to say about the top-down pressure of global human rights regimes on the particularistic immigration and citizenship policies of nation-states (e.g., Soysal 1994; Sassen 1998). The impact of these external regimes is undeniable; however, too little attention has been paid to the bottom-up pressure emanating from domestic society that has pushed these states toward de-ethnicized and liberalized membership policies.

The withering of primordialism in immigrant selection is mirrored by the withering of primordialism on the side of immigrant integration, which rounds off the loss of capacity of contemporary liberal nation-states to reproduce their particular contours and identities through immigration. A quick survey shows the same thinning of integration and naturalization requirements across Western states (e.g., Hansen and Weil 2001; Joppke and Morawska 2003): while the old idea of assimilating immigrants into a thickly conceived majority culture is rejected everywhere, even in France, the two residual integration requirements imposed on immigrants are to respect the formal rules and procedures of liberal democracies and to learn the official language or languages of the state. The language requirement, much stressed also in the recent "Americanization" campaign in the United States (see Pickus 1998), is certainly ambiguous, because it is a functional exigency of any state qua state to agree on a (minimum of) shared language or languages, but the requirement may also take on identitarian and primordial contours.[22] However, the main trend in liberal states is to reject the existence of a "dominant culture" to be adopted by immigrants in obligatory terms.[23] The thinning of integration requirements in liberal states completes the paradox: while in principle the foremost expression of a state's sovereignty, the admission and integration of new members is now decoupled from the primordial beliefs that constitute the state-bearing nation.

In his story of the differentiation of public education from primordial (class and religious) attachments in nineteenth-century Britain, Smelser hinted at the possibility that "primordialism may reassert itself with equal strength in more new, less familiar, and possibly less manageable, arenas" (1991: 366). If primordialism becomes removed from the policies and institutions of the liberal state, in public education as much as in the regulation of immigration, this does not mean that it has disappeared. On the contrary, the underlying impulse of "exclusiveness" (40) now becomes available to maverick entrepreneurs outside established institutions, and in this respect indeed "less manageable," to reiterate Smelser. The rise of xenophobic and anti-immigrant movements and parties in contemporary Europe (and beyond) may be seen as the flip side of liberal states that have radically purged themselves of primordial imagery. The triumph of a liberalizing polity thus bears new risks for society at large.

NOTES

1. Smelser's penchant for synthesis is perhaps most impressively displayed in his *Theory of Collective Behavior* (1962). It married elegantly what has come apart since in the study of collective behavior and social movements, offering a single model to cover everything from crowds to political movements, with a synthetic stress on structural conditions, resource mobilization, and ideational framing ("generalized beliefs").

Incidentally, and with a rather more modest scope, I took a similarly synthesizing stance with respect to social movement theories when I wrote my dissertation under Smelser (Joppke 1993).

2. Once, commenting on a seminar paper of mine, which was on Bourdieu's class theory and betrayed a good deal of enthusiasm for it, Smelser remained skeptical. For him, "it [Bourdieu] is always the same"—that is, the self-same theory illustrated by exchangeable empirical references, instead of exchangeable theories put to the service of a better understanding of social reality.

3. In including "class" in the list of primordial "givens," Smelser differs from Geertz's classic account, which conceives of the former as a "functional" group attachment different from the "primordial attachments" based on "congruities of blood, speech, custom" (Geertz 1973: 259).

4. Following Smelser (1991), and differing from Geertz (1973), this notion of primordialism comprises functional and civic attachments, to the degree that they take on the quality of unquestioned and unalterable "givens" of thought and practice. The notion of primordialism is thus indifferent to the distinction between civic or ethnic nationhood. The attachment to a civic nation, even though it contains an element of contract and voluntarism, is also primordial in the sense that it is attachment to a particular nation with a particular history, disattachment from which is as exceptional and unlikely as the exit from an ethnic nation (for good critiques of the civic-ethnic distinction in the nations and nationalism literature, see Yack 1996 and Brubaker 1999). In a nutshell, membership in or attachment to a nation is primordial by definition, irrespective of the specific (ethnic or civic) quality of the nation. This still leaves the possibility of better or worse fits between (always) primordial nationhood and the exigencies of liberal stateness: civic nationhood is easier to reconcile with liberal stateness than ethnic nationhood, which helps explain the earlier and unambiguous turn toward a nonprimordial, universalist immigration policy in the United States.

5. Britain's rejection of labor migration, exceptional in postwar western Europe, was certainly made possible by the free availability of Irish labor migrants, the single biggest (yet strangely invisible) group to emigrate to Britain after World War II (see Paul 1997).

6. See the curious career of Ian Macleod, a staunch defender of an open-door pol-

icy when at the helm of the Colonial Office (1959–1961), and an equally staunch opponent of such a policy when in charge of the Labour Ministry (1957–1959). Hansen (2000) gives a detailed account of intraelite divisions over New Commonwealth immigration, which is difficult to reconcile with the blanket charge of "elite racism" (e.g., Paul 1997).

7. The notion of belonging was introduced in Home Secretary R. A. Butler's presentation of the Commonwealth Immigrants Act to Parliament: "Except from control [are] . . . persons who in common parlance belong to the United Kingdom" (*Parliamentary Debates*, House of Commons, 16 November 1961, c.695).

8. The Commonwealth Immigrants Act's actual impact on Old Commonwealth entries was minuscule, as the numbers were low already before its passing and subsequently were absorbed mostly by Category B of the Act's employment voucher system, which was for skilled immigrants. In addition, there were positive discriminations in the implementation of the act. Shorthand typists, for example, were put into Category B because the majority were women from the Old Commonwealth. In addition, many Old Commonwealth immigrants entered as "working holiday-makers" who, though admitted as visitors, took up employment (see Paul 1997: 173).

9. Kenneth Clarke, in *Parliamentary Debates*, House of Commons, 8 March 1971, c.126f. Identical reasoning can be found in a variety of *Times* editorials, for instance, "The Price We Pay for Hypocrisy" (22 November 1972).

10. When the Immigration Rules implementing the 1971 Immigration Act were finally approved in February 1973, the Labour Party openly endorsed the positive inclusion aspect of patriality: "We recognize the need for a special link with citizens of [New Zealand, Australia, and Canada]" (Peter Shore, *Parliamentary Debates*, House of Commons, 21 February 1973, c.580).

11. For the distinction between "liberal" and "restrictionist" challenges to primordial immigration policies, see Joppke and Rosenhek (2002).

12. The liberal part of this strange coalition was heavily lobbied by the National Council for Civil Liberties, which opposed patriality in toto ("Liberty Powell," *Times*, 8 April 1971).

13. The next logical step was to remove this sex discrimination for non-Commonwealth aliens as well, as brought forward in a motion by Liberal David Steel (*Parliamentary Debates*, House of Commons, 16 June 1971, c.459–60). State Secretary Sharples in the Home Office retorted, "[Mr. David Steel] asked whether it was intentional that there should be discrimination in favour of Commonwealth citizens. The answer is a clear 'Yes'" (c.464).

14. Home Secretary Maudling, during the third reading of the Immigration Bill (*Parliamentary Debates*, House of Commons, 17 June 1971, c.770).

15. As stressed in the closing statement by Foreign Secretary Alec Douglas-Home, in *Parliamentary Debates*, House of Commons, 22 November 1972, c.1447.

16. Ibid., c.592–3. Technically, it was not within government's authority to undo by means of an administrative rule change the legislative ban on grandparental Commonwealth patriality. What it reinstated was a weaker form of grandparental patriality for Commonwealth citizens, who (unlike other patrials) remained subject to deportation, whose entry clearance could be refused, and—most important—whose privilege could be withdrawn by means of another (nonlegislative) rule change. The most precise (though mocking) definition of this "new privileged elite" would be

"non-patrial Commonwealth citizens with a United Kingdom grandparent" (Arthur Davidson, *Parliamentary Debates,* House of Commons, 21 February 1973, c.622).

17. See the exchange between Williams and Carr in *Parliamentary Debates,* House of Commons, 25 January 1973, cc.657 and 659. In the early 1970s, only one in two hundred requests for a permanent residence permit by Old Commonwealth citizens was rejected (figure provided by Foreign Secretary Douglas-Home, in *Parliamentary Debates,* House of Commons, 22 November 1972, c.1448). One may reasonably assume that applicants' treatment at citizenship registration would be equally generous.

18. In late summer 1972, a Tory government admitted some twenty-eight thousand Asian British passport holders threatened by ethnic cleansing in Uganda—in marked contrast to a Labour government that had rejected Kenyan Asians four years earlier.

19. This is how the *Economist* (27 January 1973) titled its report on Home Secretary Carr's double-edged statement on immigration before Parliament.

20. The main food for this critique was the abolishment, in the 1981 Nationality Act, of the unconditional *jus soli,* and its replacement by a mixed *jus sanguinis* and *jus soli* regime. With this reform, Britain only abandoned an anomaly, stemming from its feudal past and prolonged by the experience of empire, and moved to the continental European norm of citizenship that mixes elements of *jus sanguinis* and *jus soli* (a good overview of the present scene is Hansen and Weil 2001).

21. This polemical equation is made by Dummett and Nicol: "While the United Kingdom had been strengthening racial discrimination in its immigration controls, the countries which had imposed racial restrictions in the early years of the century were getting rid of them" (1990: 231).

22. An example of the primordial use of the language requirement is Quebec, which defines itself as a separate "nation" within Canada through its *francophonie,* and which also prioritizes French-speaking immigrants while imposing on all others French-language schooling.

23. This is confirmed by the outcome of the recent German debate on a "dominant German culture" *(deutsche Leitkultur)* that, according to the conservative opposition party (Christlich-Demokratische Union/Christlich-Soziale Union [CDU/ CSU]), immigrants would have to adopt as the price of being admitted (see Joppke 2001: 445 ff). After a storm of protest, even from within their own party, the CDU/ CSU had to withdraw this notion.

REFERENCES

Brubaker, Rogers. 1999. "The Manichean Myth: Rethinking the Distinction between 'Civic' and 'Ethnic' Nationalism." In Hanspeter Kriesi et al., eds., *Nation and National Identity.* Chur, Switzerland: Ruegger.

Coleman, Jules, and Sarah Harding. 1995. "Citizenship, the Demands of Justice, and the Moral Relevance of Political Borders." In Warren Schwartz, ed., *Justice in Immigration.* New York: Cambridge University Press.

Dummett, Ann, and Andrew Nicol. 1990. *Subjects, Citizens, Aliens, and Others.* London: Weidenfeld and Nicolson.

Fransman, Laurie. 1983. "Patriality: Its Redeployment as British Citizenship under the British Nationality Act, 1981—I." *New Law Journal* (5 August): 691–92, 707.
———. 1989. *Fransman's British Nationality Law.* London: Fourmat Publishing.
Geertz, Clifford. 1973. "The Integrative Revolution: Primordial Sentiments in the New States." *The Interpretation of Cultures,* pp. 255–310. New York: Basic Books.
Hansen, Randall. 1999. "The Kenyan Asians, British Politics, and the Commonwealth Immigrants Act, 1968." *Historical Journal* 42 (3): 809–34.
———. 2000. *Citizenship and Immigration in Post-War Britain.* New York: Oxford University Press.
Hansen, Randall, and Patrick Weil, eds. 2001. *Towards a European Nationality.* New York: Palgrave.
Hartz, Louis. 1964. *The Founding of New Societies.* New York: Harcourt, Brace, and World.
Joppke, Christian. 1993. *Mobilizing against Nuclear Energy.* Berkeley and Los Angeles: University of California Press.
———. 1999. *Immigration and the Nation-State: The United States, Germany, and Great Britain.* New York: Oxford University Press.
———. 2001. "Multicultural Citizenship: A Critique." *Archives européennes de sociologie* 42 (2): 431–47.
Joppke, Christian, and Ewa Morawska, eds. 2003. *Toward Assimilation and Citizenship: Immigrants in Liberal Nation-States.* New York: Palgrave Macmillan.
Joppke, Christian, and Zeev Rosenhek. 2002. "Contesting Ethnic Immigration: Germany and Israel Compared." *Archives européennes de sociologie* 43 (3): 301–35.
Kymlicka, Will. 1995. *Multicultural Citizenship.* Oxford: Clarendon Press.
Legomsky, Stephen. 1993. "Immigration, Equality and Diversity." *Columbia Journal of Transnational Law* 31: 319–35.
Macdonald, Ian. 1972. *The New Immigration Law.* London: Butterworths.
Norton, Philip. 1976. "Intra-Party Dissent in the House of Commons." *Parliamentary Affairs* 29 (4): 404–20.
Paul, Kathleen. 1997. *Whitewashing Britain.* Ithaca, N.Y.: Cornell University Press.
Pickus, Noah, ed. 1998. *Immigration and Citizenship in the Twenty-First Century.* Lanham: Rowman and Littlefield.
Sassen, Saskia. 1998. "The De Facto Transnationalizing of Immigration Policy." In C. Joppke, ed., *Challenge to the Nation-State: Immigration in Western Europe and the United States,* pp. 49–85. New York: Oxford University Press.
Smelser, Neil. 1959. *Social Change in the Industrial Revolution: An Application of Theory to the British Cotton Industry.* Chicago: University of Chicago Press.
———. 1962. *Theory of Collective Behaviour.* London: Routledge and Kegan Paul.
———. 1981. "Notes on Collaborating with Talcott Parsons." *Sociological Inquiry* 51: 134–54.
———. 1991. *Social Paralysis and Social Change: British Working-Class Education in the Nineteenth Century.* Berkeley and Los Angeles: University of California Press.
Soysal, Yasemin. 1994. *Limits of Citizenship.* Chicago: University of Chicago Press.
Walzer, Michael. 1983. *Spheres of Justice.* New York: Basic Books.
Yack, Bernard. 1996. "The Myth of the Civic Nation." *Critical Review* 10 (2): 193–211.

Chapter 11

Causal Reasoning, Historical Logic, and Sociological Explanation

Lyn Spillman

As Neil Smelser has pointed out, sociology is constituted under the influence of three distinct intellectual orientations—the scientific, the humanistic, and the artistic—that generate and regenerate inevitable tensions in the discipline. Among these tensions are familiar methodological oppositions between positivism and phenomenology, quantitative and qualitative analysis, formal statistical analysis and ethnography, and aggregative-causal and case analysis. As a result, any claim about explanatory logics in sociological inquiry necessarily invites counterclaims and counterexamples. Nevertheless, I suggest here an encompassing framework within which to understand differing logics of inquiry that could soften, if it does not resolve, these disputes. I like to think that this argument is made in the spirit of Smelser's integrative understanding of sociological methodology and, more specifically, that it elaborates his claim that the opposition between ideographic and nomothetic approaches is "not quite so diametric as is often supposed" (1976: 204; 1997).

One of the big stakes in methodological debates is the possibility and significance of general causal explanation. At one extreme, the ideal of developing generalizable causal explanation by discovering and refining universally applicable "covering laws" that account for a variety of different phenomena is still implicit in many standard accounts of sociological inquiry. Against this, general causal explanation is rejected as inappropriate because social phenomena involve meaning-making on the part of their subjects and analysts, because they are inevitably situated in unique historical circumstances, and because they are the outcomes of such complex patterns of causal antecedents that no causal law alone can provide useful explanation.

Of course, most adherents of both views recognize some value in opposing modes of inquiry, if only exploratory or superficial. Further, methodological developments from both starting points bring the extreme positions closer together—on the one hand by refining strategies for careful causal inference in aggregate, multivariate studies, and on the other, by articulating and refining causal logic in small-N studies. Nevertheless, contrary presuppositions about the significance of causal logic to sociology continue to underpin most methodological discussion (Steinmetz 1998).

I argue here that these differences arise not so much because of the limits of each position but because of an unnecessarily restricted view of causality they share. I begin by examining standard causal logic in sociology, and go on to outline some alternative views of causal explanation in the philosophy of history. In the third part of this chapter, I articulate a more comprehensive understanding of causal explanation that could encompass nomothetic and ideographic inquiry in the same explanatory logic. This is not an argument for an entirely new approach to explanation, but rather a case for better understanding and integrating existing sociological work.[1]

Although issues of causal explanation are significant in all areas of sociology, they are especially salient to comparative-historical methodologists, who address them frequently and explicitly. To focus my argument, I examine reflections on causal explanation in historical and comparative sociology, beginning with Smelser's *Comparative Methods in the Social Sciences* (1976), which remains one of the most lucid and comprehensive treatments of the subject. I suggest that Smelser's work, and later developments, tests the limits of the standard language of causality in ways that implicitly demonstrate the value of a more comprehensive logic of inquiry.

SOCIOLOGY AND THE LOGIC OF STANDARD CAUSAL EXPLANATION

While it might seem like a back-roads detour to comparative historical methodologists, it is important to begin here by recalling that many standard methodological discussions of causal explanation seek to impose limits on the empiricist "constant conjunction" formula "If C then (and only then) E" associated with David Hume. Extensive methodological literatures in sociology elaborate practical strategies for making claims about correlation more plausible as claims about causality—for example, by addressing issues of spurious correlation and suppressor effects. As Howard Becker points out, "Sociologists have typically solved the problem of cause by embodying it in procedures which we agree will serve as the way we know that A caused B, philosophically sound or not" (1992: 205). Logically, though, the constant conjunction formula cannot be sufficient for causal inference because, in Hume's view, no one could ever "show a material or 'ontological' relationship between a cause and an effect"—"the conclusion of the unamended Humean view is that there is no difference between statements of cause and effect and all other statements of association" (Simon 1969: 436, 438).

Under what logical conditions, then, might a correlation be accepted as causal?

For much of the twentieth century, the textbook answer to this question came from logical positivism and appealed to theory or scientific law. In Carl Hempel's influential formulation, scientific explanation (by contrast with "pseudo-explanations" like fate) "amounts to the statement that, according to certain general laws, a set of events . . . is regularly accompanied by an event of kind E." General laws are crucial in connecting causes with effects under stipulated conditions. They are often hypothetical, and they may be statistical rather than absolute. But they are always general statements of regularities, and indeed, "the object of description and explanation in every branch of empirical science is always the occurrence of an event of a certain *kind*"—that is, classes or properties of individual events (1949: 459–60). Causal explanation always implies a more general statement of the relation between all events of type C and all events of type E under given conditions, assuming C and E are independently characterized. Causal attributions in singular cases, without some implicit general claim, are meaningless.

If "covering-law" versions of causal explanation seem dated, more honored in the breach than the observance, it is important to emphasize how much they have influenced sociology, even when flouted. In a methodological text widely read for some years, Walter Wallace writes of "the paramount goal of all science: to identify Necessity in nature," which, "in full recognition of the impossibility of success, we irresistibly pursue . . . chiefly through the past-future, explanatory-predictive references of theory" (1971: 60, 61). More recently, Andrew Abbott has suggested that the logical positivist view that causal statements should really be understood as shorthand for statements about logical, theoretical relations—not the world—is the "philosophical foundation of standard methodology," "taught in the best sociological methods courses today" (1992: 432, 431). And though they distinguish their argument from positions like Hempel's in a number of ways, Edgar Kiser and Michael Hechter follow the path from Hempel to the claim that "causal explanation works by subsuming events under causal laws . . . [that] derive from general theories" (1991: 6).

Sophisticated methodological reflection focuses effort on saving the standard causal model. Hubert Blalock's influential classic on *Causal Inferences in Nonexperimental Research,* for instance, provides detailed specifications of the conditions for causal inference. But in the end, "no matter how elaborate the research design, certain simplifying assumptions must be made." In the complex causal models most appropriate to sociology, these assumptions are by no means trivial. Paradoxically, this leads Blalock to agnosticism about cause: "One admits that causal thinking belongs completely on the theoretical level and that causal laws can never be demonstrated empirically. But this does not mean that it is not helpful to *think* causally and to develop causal models that have implications that are indirectly testable" (1964: 26, 6).[2] Like Blalock, generations of sociological researchers adopted a combination of somewhat contradictory strategies in the face of logical and empirical difficulties in making causal claims—on one hand, refining methodological tools to address potential flaws in causal logic, and on the other hand, ignoring those logical difficulties with epistemological agnosticism. As Abbott suggests, "In practice, sociologists never took the separation of statement and reality [implied by logical positivism] all that seriously" (1992: 432).

This pattern—pragmatic patching and something close to epistemological agnosticism—has also characterized comparative and historical methodology. Smelser's *Comparative Methods in the Social Sciences* is notable for the way he identifies *shared* problems underlying all methodologies while, at the same time, elaborating on the particular form these issues take in comparative research. For Smelser, efforts at social explanation involve problems of causal inference, whatever the methodology:

> For any phenomenon that a social scientist might wish to explain, the number of causal conditions that affect it is, at first sight, discouragingly great. . . . The initial picture, then, is one of a *multiplicity* of conditions, a *confounding* of their influences on what is to be explained (the dependent variable) and an *indeterminacy* regarding the effect of any one condition or several conditions in combination. The corresponding problems facing the investigator are to *reduce* the number of conditions, to *isolate* one condition from another, and thereby to *make precise* the role of each condition, both singly and in combination with other conditions. (1976: 152–53)

Smelser's evenhanded treatment identifies numerous familiar problems of causal logic in all types of research design. Case studies cannot establish causal claims, and any causal implications they do have rest on "implicit comparisons[,] . . . 'other knowledge' and the imaginary experiment," which do not "permit rigorous empirical control" because possible causes and effects do not vary (199). Expanding the number of cases is "an effort to establish parametric control over potentially operative variables, and, as such, approximate the logic of Mill's method of difference" (201–202). But "the number of potentially operative variables still far exceeds the number of cases studied," and asserted similarities "may obscure important differences along the very dimensions on which the cases are claimed to be similar" (202). Increasing the number of cases further in order to make parametric statistical tests of correlation possible enables both tests of "strength of association between variables (Mill's method of concomitant variation)" and the possibility of ruling out "extraneous independent variables by holding constant or otherwise controlling sources of variation, thus creating a presumption in favor of other independent variables (Mill's method of difference)" (205).

However, even when the number of cases is large enough to allow statistical controls, correlations are not, of course, causes. Spurious correlation is especially problematic when "variables are defined at global levels" but inferences are drawn at lower levels of generality (Smelser 1976: 207). Some causes, too, may not be expressed in correlations. Suppressed causes may be especially dangerous to causal inference in macrocomparison, because "in different social units parametric differences may obscure, overwhelm, reverse, or otherwise change the pattern of correlation and causation in different units" (210). Increasing the sophistication of sampling, standardization, and multivariate analysis "like all methods of control . . . does not succeed in establishing causal relations; it only increases confidence in the plausibility of such relations by ruling out the effect of other possible causes" (222–23).

For Smelser, all these problems point to the crucial importance of the theoretical and conceptual context of causal claims: "Causal knowledge hinges, then, not only on establishing relations and ruling out alternatives, but also on a network of parametric assumptions resting on 'other knowledge' that varies in adequacy" (1976: 232). For this reason, explicitness and structure in theoretical context is important for causal assessment. Theoretical reflexivity is key in every element of research design—in choice and classification of units, in concepts, variables, and indicators, as well as in the structuring of variables in a causal claim. This is not the epistemological agnosticism about cause that is evident in more empiricist methodological reflections like Blalock's, but it comes to something very similar—causal claims in sociology are properties of theoretical statements more than of the world.

Smelser seems to take standard views of causality for granted throughout *Comparative Methods* and does not address them at length. Yet characterizing his work simply in these terms does not capture its full force, precisely because of the sustained and detailed treatment he gives to conceptualization in discussing all methodological issues in social explanation. Even classification, description, and measurement—which are treated at the same length as issues of association and causation—display, for him, an "essential parallel [with] . . . the operation known as explanation." Indeed, "classification, selecting variables, and selecting indicators—often seen as preceding and differing from explanation—are various forms of explanation as I have defined the term" (1976: 194). Further, claims about association and cause inherently depend on assumptions about invariant conditions, intervening mechanisms, modes of causality, and the role of the observer, so it is important to examine

> not only causes and effects but the network of assumptions that inform their relations. . . . It is especially important to identify what is "frozen" into parametric givens, not only because of the importance of these for the structure of explanation, but because these often constitute repositories of the kinds of

weaknesses of theory that are often most difficult to discern—weaknesses involving unverified generalizations, questionable assumptions, and unmeasured variables. (237)

Overall, the analysis seems to push the limits of the standard epistemology of causal claims, in part by emphasizing questions of classification and questions about the conditions and mechanisms of causal relations (174, 185). I argue below that implicit in this work is a form of generalizable explanatory logic that encompasses but transcends standard causal epistemology—a logic for which philosophers of history have provided a better language of inquiry.

Theda Skocpol's subsequent promotion of Mill's logic downplayed larger epistemological problems with causal claims in favor of a pragmatic, problem-solving approach to justifying causal explanation. She is not agnostic about causes, noting that "the investigator assumes that causal regularities—at least regularities of limited scope—may be found in history," but dismisses "the dogma of universality" appeal to universal laws. And unlike Smelser (or Blalock), she does not favor appeals to theory to justify causal statements, arguing instead for "theoretical skepticism" as "a practical strategy of immense value" in "formulating valid causal arguments about [historical] regularities" (1984: 374, 376, 385). As some critics have pointed out, this position does not seem to fulfill the standard requirements for grounding general causal claims (e.g., Lieberson 1991, 1994; Kiser and Hechter 1991; Nichols 1986). Critics converge in identifying problems about the independence of units of analysis (McMichael 1990; Goldthorpe 1997) and in making time-independent generalizations about historical phenomena (Burawoy 1989; Griffin 1992). Nevertheless, Skocpol's arguments encouraged the adoption of Mill's logic as a methodological standard in subsequent comparative historical research and encouraged numerous innovations (e.g., Ragin 1987; Amenta 1991; Mahoney 1999).

Beyond that, a range of developments in the logic of inquiry has been proposed within and beyond comparative historical sociology that, for some, has shifted the grounds of methodological debate. One set of alternatives focuses on generalizable causal mechanisms (rather than causal "laws"). Such alternatives range from pragmatic arguments that finding general causal mechanisms is more feasible than pursuing the impossible ideal of covering-law explanations (Elster 1998), to arguments that understanding mechanisms can improve general theories (Hedstrom and Swedberg 1998; Kiser and Hechter 1991; Stinchcombe 1991), to arguments that all valid explanations *necessarily involve* mechanisms because covering laws do not or cannot explain (Tilly 1999; Bunge 1997).

Another set of innovations includes a range of different arguments for greater attention to narrative logic. Some methodologists argue for the reflective integration of narrative logics into causal explanation (Bates et al. 1998; Griffin 1993; Stryker 1996); others see formalized narrative logics as an alternative to existing methodologies (Abbott 1992, 1995; Griffin 1992). Narrative analysis is also viewed as important grounding for interpretive, hermeneutic research in sociology (Hall 1999; Somers and Gibson 1994).

This range of innovations greatly enriches methodological possibilities available in sociology and especially in comparative historical inquiry. So far, though, there has been little discussion between innovators and little reflection on whether their projects are related. Moreover, different suggestions about mechanisms or narrative logic still tend to distribute themselves on an ideographic/nomothetic continuum, the same oppositions often reemerging in somewhat new language. The methodological innovation has yet to be integrated in a more broadly based reformulation of logics of inquiry in sociology, a synthesis providing a common language that transcends the standard methodological dichotomies in ways meaningful to those with strong commitments to either side. There is certainly no synthesis yet that can provide an alternative foundation to the picture of inquiry, which remains a staple of methodology classes—a picture assuming lawlike generalization about cause-effect relations but also tolerating idiosyncratic, undertheorized residues of ideographic insight.

HISTORIANS' LOGICS: CONDITIONS, MECHANISMS, AND COLLIGATION

For obvious reasons, historians responded to the challenges of the covering-law model more directly and more radically than sociologists, arguing either that it was inapplicable or that it was inadequate for historical reasoning. Most of their arguments share the preliminary observation that historical laws are empty, even if they are possible. Arthur Danto, for example, sees the historian's interest and questions as different from those of scientific explanation. The historian, he says, is concerned with what is " 'unique,' relative to a certain cast of experience," and general laws seem, from this point of view, to explain both "too much and too little" (1956: 29; Porter 1975). Nevertheless, philosophers of history still argued that explanation, even causal explanation, was possible.

Several alternative conceptualizations of historical reasoning developed in the philosophy of history in response to Hempel are particularly relevant to sociological inquiry. First, strong arguments were made for the possibility of singular causal explanation, against the generality of causal claims necessitated by logical positivism. Second, these arguments relied on a broad Aristotelian view of causality, not the more restricted post-Humean view. Third, some argued that historical explanation involved colligation rather than causal reasoning.

For instance, Alasdair MacIntyre suggested that causal explanation is *pri-*

marily particular rather than general: "We often in *both* the natural and social world identify and understand particular causal relationships without invoking law-like generalizations" (1976: 144). Particular causal relationships exhibit "that which makes *this* happen rather than *that* which would otherwise have happened" (149). Such relationships may be near-universal—as in the relationships between pressure, temperature, and volume specified by gas law equations—but are more often contingent, when the relationship is crucially dependent upon antecedent conditions. (Even gas law equations specify relationships that could vary under certain conditions beyond earth.) Because of the importance of antecedent conditions and mechanisms, "that hallowed formula 'Whenever an event of type A occurs, then an event or state of affairs of type B occurs' *never* by itself specifies any possible causal relationship" (152). The more complex and historically dependent a phenomenon is, the more important are preexisting states of affairs in explaining a particular causal relationship—and this is true of physical as well as social phenomena. In this view, singular causal claims are possible but require a different sort of rationale from that required in views of causality emphasizing lawlike generalization—attention to initial conditions and mechanisms of (potentially singular, not general) causal relations. Arguably, attention to initial conditions and mechanisms of causal relations is especially important in history (and sociology) because social phenomena are extremely variable in these ways.

Second, emphasizing conditions and mechanisms of causal claims involved a return to a broader Aristotelian analysis of causation, an analysis that distinguished between material, formal, efficient, and final causes: "The material cause . . . provided the passive receptacle on which the remaining causes act. The formal cause . . . contributed the essence, idea, or quality of the thing concerned; the efficient cause . . . [was] . . . the external compulsion that bodies had to obey; and the final cause was the goal which everything served" (Bunge 1968: 32). Post-Humean ideas of causality emphasized "efficient" causality—the external compulsion in the causal relation—to the exclusion of other dimensions of a causal claim. By contrast, philosophers of history have built arguments for justifying causal statements around "material" causes—initial conditions—and "formal" causes, or mechanisms internal to the causal relation.

So, for instance, Maurice Mandelbaum argues that the covering-law model overlooks the fact that "the establishment of the precise nature of . . . initial and boundary conditions is a complicated task, *and is itself the task of the historian*" (1974: 60, emphasis in original). Moreover, causal attribution is not made on the basis of "constant conjunction" and general law, but on the basis of productive efficacy: "We seem to see a direct connection or transfer of power between events. . . . What is seen is not two successive events, but a continuous process" (Mink 1978: 216). Causal attributions can and should be made in singular cases, but this demands special attention to conditions and mechanisms of causal relations.

An important literature in the philosophy of history, deserving more attention from qualitative sociologists, discusses the methodological principles for assessing singular causal arguments. At issue is how to distinguish causes from conditions in particular cases, without appeal to general laws. Causes may be distinguished from conditions because they are seen as disrupting "a settled state of affairs," as restricting "ongoing processes or movements," or as the "active" or "forcing" conditions. Causal attributions in particular arguments depend on explicit statements of conditions and on identifying the mechanism by which the outcome is produced. Therefore, historical debates often focus on conceptualization rather than on justifying general statements of causal relations. As Elazar Weinryb argues after examining causal claims in three important historical debates, "A redescription of the cause-phenomenon or the effect phenomenon either negates or substantiates the supposed causal connection" (1975: 49; Dray 1978). To justify singular causal theses, historians look to the proper conceptual analysis of the phenomenon (as well as the consistency of this analysis with the empirical evidence). Criticizing a historical explanation involves claiming, on factual or theoretical grounds, that "normal" historical conditions have been improperly distinguished from active causes, or that the mechanism involved in the active cause does not operate as claimed, or that the effect itself has been improperly described. In all such arguments it is conceptual analysis of the phenomena, and not the general applicability of the causal relation itself, that is at stake (Martin 1982; Stinchcombe 1978).

Some philosophers of history responded to covering-law models, then, by arguing that singular causal claims were justifiable, emphasizing the importance of conditions and mechanisms to any causal claim, and specifying how causal claims in history were grounded and assessed. Another alternative that emerged in response to covering-law models elaborates on the idea that historians explain by locating events in a context of "the continuing process to which they belong or bear witness." For W. H. Walsh, the proper grouping of events in an identifiable process—colligation—is one of the major explanatory strategies in history. Originally, Walsh derived the unity in colligatory concepts from purposes and policies linking the events: but he later retracted this argument from agency to argue that "the ideas of process, movement, and development rather than that of realized policy should be taken as primary" (1974: 127, 134).

Colligatory concepts group sequences of different events in naming a particular process, and so they do not classify events as similar, or provide explanations of classes of events, in the way required by the covering-law model of explanation. But some, like Walsh, claim that they do provide a form of explanation: "A regular way in which historians answer the question 'Why did that happen?' is to show the place the event in question had in a continuous development, by specifying what led up to it and what it led on to, and by colligating the various happenings concerned under a single appropriate conception" (1974: 134; cf. Bunge 1968: 300–10; McCullagh 1978). This explanation is not causal in the way most sociologists think of causality, but it explains a part in terms of its place in a whole: the determining relationships are "internal" to the phenomenon studied, rather than "external" as they would be in causal explanation. This form of explanation has its own methods of empirical grounding, focusing on the conditions of truth of "narrative networks," as opposed to isolated statements, and the methodological principles for identifying "central subjects" (Hull 1975).[3]

Can explanation by colligation be general explanation? Walsh's original formulation of the idea of colligation involved the grouping of different events in a colligatory concept referring to something unique. As McCullagh notes, "What Walsh has insisted upon throughout is that the processes of historical change, by means of which historical events are colligated, are unique. . . . The terms referring to or naming these processes, therefore, are always singular, not general" (1978: 268; Griffin 1992). But others have suggested that some colligatory concepts, like "revolution," "renaissance," or "feudalism," refer to general phenomena. McCullagh illustrates the use of general colligatory terms in numerous historical studies, pointing out that they "normally draw attention to the similarities between that movement and others which have been similarly named," despite the fact that "historians are generally wary of forming general laws of historical change" (1978: 277; Abbott 1984). It is important to note, though, that classifying a set of events by means of a general colligatory term is not generalizing in the usual sense of the word, because the classificatory statement has a singular subject. The generality occurs in "naming" a phenomenon with a concept that is applied to more than one instance, not in asserting a determining relation that is true of more than one instance. However, as the discussion above of the importance of conceptualization of causal conditions and mechanisms suggests, colligation is more important than is often recognized in social explanation.

So philosophers of history responded to the challenge of the "covering-law" model more directly than many sociologists, by explicitly rejecting it earlier and theorizing alternative forms of explanation. These alternatives included providing rationales for singular causal claims, emphasizing conditions and mechanisms in causal explanation, and theorizing colligation, or the proper grouping of events in a process, as a form of explanation. They all involve stressing conceptualization, and in this sense they echo the calls of many sociological methodologists, especially in historical comparative inquiry. But they differ in two important ways. First, they are seen not as preliminary to explanation but as integral to it. Second, they involve more explicit reflection on methodological principles for assessing explanatory claims not grounded in covering-law epistemology.

HISTORICAL LOGIC AND SOCIOLOGICAL EXPLANATION

What would happen if sociologists were to take this alternative set of responses to covering-law epistemology seriously? With these tools, we could construct a language of sociological inquiry that clarifies how nomothetic and ideographic approaches to research fit together in a larger epistemological picture, that provides a framework for integrating the great variety of recent methodological innovations, that reflects much better what sociologists actually do, and that makes a simpler and less tendentious basis for surveying and introducing real sociological methodology than the standard models of causal logic do. Contributions to methodological debates need neither constantly attempt to remedy the weakness of (standard) causal logic in existing research, nor completely dismiss the appropriateness of causal explanation.

Important elements of such a framework would include:

1. An explicit return to Aristotelian views of causality. Post-Humean views about C-E relations, constant conjunction, and the associated need for generalized "covering laws" to rescue causal claims have been inappropriate for a long time, and many different reflections on sociological methodology challenge them without providing a sufficiently encompassing alternative.

2. Explicit recognition that it is appropriate to make well-grounded claims about "efficient" causality with different degrees of generalization. Singular causal claims are possible: philosophers of history provide a logic for better justification of such claims, and some arguments for narrative methodologies in sociology are also heading in this direction. At the same time, very broad causal claims—close to "causal laws"—are also possible, depending on the nature of the conditions necessary for the "efficient" cause to operate. The plausibility of a broad generalization about a causal relation would depend on whether the conditions necessary for that causal relation to operate are near-universal (Zelditch 1979; Martin and Sell 1979; Molm 1997: 272–79). In sociology, neither singular causal claims nor causal laws are likely to be as useful as generalizations about causal relations whose scope is precisely specified in terms of conditions and mechanisms. The methodological sensibilities of economists and psychologists provide a contrast here: sociologists typically respond to generalized economic or psychological "laws" with questions about scope conditions or mechanisms.

3. More recognition that any causal claim should give as much attention to *conditions* under which "efficient" causes will operate, and to *mechanisms* of the causal relation, as to the causal relation itself. Some important sociological contributions, which would be very weak causal arguments according to standard models, are better understood as providing a new view of conditions or mechanisms.

4. Greater emphasis on the fact that an important part of sociological generalization and explanation—often more important than strictly causal claims—is generalization about social conditions and mechanisms. Even if a causal claim is made about a specific outcome or singular event, it need not be only "exploratory," requiring generalized support from other cases. It may be that the importance of the work involved lies in the conceptualization (and empirical support) of a generalized claim about conditions, or mechanisms, of some (strictly) causal relation.

5. Recognition that sociologists, like historians, colligate, often explaining some phenomenon by placing it in terms of some larger conceptualization. Colligations are generalizable, and indeed are important and frequently debated generalizations in sociology (though some historians limit colligation to particulars). Sociological innovation often involves new colligations, rather than new causal claims. In terms of broader Aristotelian causal logic, colligation is crucial in debates about the nature of causal conditions and mechanisms.

6. Continued and increased redirection of methodological efforts away from the search for ways to buttress the validity of generalized claims about "efficient" causality to efforts to improve methodological principles and procedures for understanding conditions, mechanisms, and colligatory generalization in causal claims.

This approach synthesizes many common elements of implicit methodological wisdom in sociology, points that have been made in debates across standard methodological divides and points that have been made in passing about standard causal logic, although often with little epistemological support. What I want to emphasize here, though, is that the synthesis offers a language and logic of inquiry that can bring a wide variety of methodological strictures and innovations into focus in a new way.

So, for instance, the importance of Smelser's emphasis on the influence of theoretical context on studies of empirical variation is further reinforced and explained. Indeed, as he points out, operations like classification "are not operations distinct from scientific explanation, but are in many respects identical to it" (1976: 174). This is because generalization about conditions and mechanisms of causal relations is an important part of social explanation. Such generalization may include colligation—classifying different sorts of phenomena together as part of the same process—as well as generalization, classifying similar phenomena together. Moreover, Smelser's call for reflectiveness about invariant conditions, intervening mechanisms, modes of causality, and the role of the observer gains new weight (237)—these are important dimensions of causal explanation, not simply preliminaries to good causal claims.

More inductive approaches can also be justified better. For instance, Skocpol's focus on "regularities of limited scope" and "concrete causal configurations" (1984: 374, 375), which makes little sense in terms of standard causal epistemology, is better grounded in the explicit recognition that claims about ("efficient") causality may be made with different degrees of generalization, from singular to near-universal, depending on the scope conditions of the problem. And the force of her argument about "causes" of revolution, despite the extensive doubts that have been raised about her use of Mill's logic, might be seen as deriving from the conceptualization, colligation, and narrative grounding of new "conditions" for a causal relation that is better understood as singular. Some important criticisms of her causal claim make sense in this framework, too. For instance, Sewell's 1985 argument that she is wrong to dismiss ideology as an important factor in revolution is an argument that she is ignoring important mechanisms that underpin her causal argument. Another significant criticism, that she is wrongly ignoring the influence of historical period (McMichael 1990; Burawoy 1989), in effect "controlling for time," is a debate about whether the causal conditions she has identified have been wrongly characterized.

The recent methodological interest in causal mechanisms represents a shift to neo-Aristotelian from post-Humean epistemological rationales for causal claims. As I note above, though, arguments in favor of examining causal mechanisms vary: are mechanisms elements of general causal laws, or substitutes for them? In the language of inquiry I suggest here, neither characterization is adequate. On the one hand, generalizable claims about "efficient" causal relations are not the only valid form of causal explanation (however well-grounded with attention to the mechanisms underpinning the relation) and probably not the most important one. On the other hand, knowledge about social mechanisms will still leave many important sorts of questions in social inquiry unexplored. For example, scope conditions for the operation of postulated mechanisms seem to be more important than has yet been recognized in this literature, as Smelser has argued about the institutional conditions under which rational choice mechanisms operate (1998, 1992).

Recent methodological arguments emphasizing narrative logic are still too disparate to characterize quickly in terms of this broader view of causal explanation. However, a more extended treatment would likely suggest that some who seek to integrate narrative into causal arguments want to use narrative techniques to identify mechanisms, to "account for outcomes by identifying and exploring the mechanisms that generate them" (Bates et al. 1998: 12; Hall 1999: 102). Others aim to recognize temporal *conditions* on causal claims—and the path dependence such conditions might generate (Mahoney 1999: 1164). Narrative arguments also imply a greater tolerance than standard causal logic for singular causal claims, although they may also allow colligatory generalization about processes (Abbott 1992: 447).

This analysis suggests, then, that the more encompassing causal logic I articulate here can integrate a wide range of approaches in comparative and historical sociology within one framework. What about the broader set of epistemological issues summarized in the opposition between ideographic and nomothetic inquiry? These issues are key to logics of inquiry in other types of sociology besides comparative historical work. In the framework suggested here, firmer epistemological grounding is provided for the claim that nomothetic and ideographic inquiry are not opposed, but rather contribute differently to sociological understanding.

Nomothetic logic—emphasizing numerous cases, probabilistic lawlike generalization, causal models, and parametric control of extraneous variables—helps one understand Humean "efficient" causality, when that is appropriate to the problem. Arguments based on this logic can be improved with attention to conditions and mechanisms of proposed causal relations (rather than by the theoretically grounded transmutation of correlation into cause).

Ideographic logic is characterized by detailed attention to one or a few concrete configurations, the examination of how parts fit a whole, deterministic rather than probabilistic claims, and implicit rather than explicit comparison and control. It contributes to causal explanation by generalizing and colligating to make arguments about important social conditions and mechanisms. Arguments grounded in this logic can be improved by resisting the tendency to dismiss their causal implications and by articulating better methodological criteria for assessing ideographic claims (rather than applying the wrong criteria or relying on intuition). Two sorts of causal implications should be addressed. First, how do ideographic arguments affect relevant "efficient" causal claims? (Do they reconceptualize scope conditions or underlying causal mechanisms in consequential ways?) Second, what are the rationales for claims that explain a part by its place in the whole, and are they fulfilled?

CONCLUSION

I argue here for a view of causality and a language of inquiry that might integrate forms of social research often considered disparate, if not opposed. From nomothetic positions on sociological inquiry, I retain the focus on causal logic but argue that many previous understandings of this logic have been inadequate, and that ideographic challenges to standard causal logic may be understood as emphasizing (sometimes colligatory) generalizations about conditions or mechanisms of singular causal relations, rather than simple (if ideally universal) cause-effect claims.

This argument is epistemologically modest compared to a number of important methodological suggestions now current, which imply that causal reasoning is frequently inappropriate to social explanation. Such suggestions are being made not only by hermeneutically oriented narrative theorists but also by methodologists within nomothetic traditions of inquiry. For instance, Richard Berk concludes his overview of causal inference by suggesting that it is not appropriate to many sociological questions. One option, he notes, is to proceed "despite serious epistemological, conceptual, and practical difficulties. Presumably, researchers taking this path have to assume that their activities are in fact sensible, and that eventually, philosophers and statisticians will figure out why." Other options are to "be satisfied with non-causal statements about the empirical world" or to "develop different conceptions of cause . . . that correspond to the questions being asked" (1988: 168). Michael Sobel argues that standard regression analysis and related techniques do not sustain standard causal inference, even when causal ordering is correctly specified and a theoretical framework guides the inference; like Berk, he suggests that "many sociological questions neither require nor benefit from the introduction of causal considerations, and the tendency to treat such questions as if they are causal only leads to confusion" (Sobel 1996: 376; cf. McKim and Turner 1997).

The development of a new ontological and epistemological basis for social investigation is certainly worth pursuing, and indeed the prospects for such a project seem good (Steinmetz 1998; Archer et al. 1998). But the wide impact and diffusion of alternative logics of inquiry seem unlikely, considering the strong institutionalization of standard causal logic, and nomothetic inquiry more broadly, in the discipline. Indeed, some alternatives would entail dismissing the sociological work of several generations. So it seems worthwhile to explore the option of reconceptualizing causal logic, rather than denying the relevance of that logic to many forms of investigation. The inevitable tensions in the discipline could then be more productively focused away from methodological orientations—like the distinction between ideographic and nomothetic inquiry—and toward substantive differences about the purpose of sociological inquiry itself.

NOTES

Thanks to Joe Rumbo for research assistance, and to Al Bergesen, Ron Breiger, Mark Chaves, Russell Faeges, Andrew Gould, Miller McPherson, Linda Molm, Joel Stillerman, and Art Stinchcombe for stimulating responses to the argument. I would also like to record here a larger debt. Among Neil Smelser's many accomplishments must be included his capacity as an ideal advisor: interested and supportive, generous and prompt with his comments, yet never unduly directive.

1. I assume here that "ideographic" accounts often involve causal claims, although such causal claims are cramped by a misunderstanding of causal logic or by the necessity of using a restricted language of inquiry. Of course, they also involve *verstehen*, understanding, and I do not mean to suggest that understanding is simply a matter of causal logic, however broadly understood.

2. This pragmatic agnosticism can make sense in sociological practice, and because the following discussion draws mostly from considerations of causality in historical-comparative sociology, that goal is slighted. Nevertheless, my conclusions about singular causal inference, conditions, mechanisms, and colligation seem to offer useful conceptual frameworks for sociological practice too—and moderate Flyvbjerg's dismissal of standard social science logic (2001).

3. On narrative and colligation, see Walsh 1974: 139–41; Hull 1975: 266–68. On truth in narrative, see Hurst 1981; Topolski 1981. See also Kane 2000; Hall 2000; Lorenz 1998, 2000.

REFERENCES

Abbott, A. 1984. "Event Sequence and Event Duration: Colligation and Measurement." *Historical Methods* 17: 192–204.

———. 1992. "From Causes to Events: Notes on Narrative Positivism." *Sociological Methods and Research* 20: 428–55.

———. 1995. "Sequence Analysis: New Methods for Old Ideas." *Annual Review of Sociology* 21: 93–113.

Amenta, E. 1991. "Making the Most of a Case Study: Theories of the Welfare State and the American Experience." *International Journal of Comparative Sociology* 32: 172–94.

Archer, M., R. Bhaskar, A. Collier, T. Lawson, and A. Norrie, eds. 1998. *Critical Realism: Essential Readings*. New York: Routledge.

Bates, R., A. Greif, M. Levi, J. Rosenthal, and B. Weingast. 1998. *Analytic Narratives*. Princeton: Princeton University Press.

Becker, H. 1992. "Cases, Cause, Conjunctures, Stories, and Imagery." In C. Ragin and H. Becker, eds., *What Is a Case?*, pp. 205–16. New York: Cambridge University Press.

Berk, R. 1988. "Causal Inference for Sociological Data." In N. J. Smelser, ed., *Handbook of Sociology*, pp. 155–72. Newbury Park, Calif.: Sage.

Blalock, H. 1964. *Causal Inferences in Nonexperimental Research*. Chapel Hill: University of North Carolina Press.

Bunge, M. 1968. *Causality*. Cambridge: Harvard University Press.

———. 1997. "Mechanism and Explanation." *Philosophy of the Social Sciences* 27: 410–65.

Burawoy, M. 1989. "Two Methods in Search of Science: Skocpol versus Trotsky." *Theory and Society* 18: 759–805.

Danto, A. 1956. "On Explanation in History." *Philosophy of Science* 23: 15–30.

Dray, W. 1978. "Concepts of Causation in A. J. P. Taylor's Account of the Origins of the Second World War." *History and Theory* 18: 149–74.

Elster, J. 1998. "A Plea for Mechanisms." In P. Hedstrom and R. Swedberg, eds., *Social*

Mechanisms: An Analytical Approach to Social Theory, pp. 45–73. New York: Cambridge University Press.

Flyvbjerg, B. 2001. *Making Social Science Matter.* New York: Cambridge University Press.

Goldthorpe, J. 1997. "Current Issues in Comparative Macrosociology." *Comparative Social Research* 16: 1–26.

Griffin, L. 1992. "Temporality, Events, and Explanation in Historical Sociology." *Sociological Methods and Research* 20: 403–27.

———. 1993. "Narrative, Event-Structure Analysis, and Causal Interpretation in Historical Sociology." *American Journal of Sociology* 98: 1094–1133.

Hall, J. 1999. *Cultures of Inquiry.* New York: Cambridge University Press.

———. 2000. "Cultural Meaning and Cultural Structures in Historical Explanation." *History and Theory* 39: 331–47.

Hedstrom, P., and R. Swedberg. 1998. "Social Mechanisms." In P. Hedstrom and R. Swedberg, eds., *Social Mechanisms,* pp. 1–31. New York: Cambridge University Press.

Hempel, C. 1949. "The Function of General Laws in History." In H. Feigl and W. Sellars, eds., *Readings in Philosophical Analysis,* pp. 459–71. New York: Appleton-Century-Crofts.

Hull, D. 1975. "Central Subjects and Historical Narratives." *History and Theory* 14: 253–74.

Hurst, B. 1981. "The Myth of Historical Evidence." *History and Theory* 20: 278–90.

Kane, A. 2000. "Reconstructing Culture in Historical Explanation: Narratives as Cultural Structure and Practice." *History and Theory* 39: 311–30.

Kiser, E., and M. Hechter. 1991. "The Role of General Theory in Comparative-Historical Sociology." *American Journal of Sociology* 97: 1–30.

Lieberson, S. 1991. "Small N's and Big Conclusions." *Social Forces* 70: 307–20.

———. 1994. "More on the Uneasy Case for Using Mill-Type Methods in Small-*N* Comparative Studies." *Social Forces* 72: 1225–37.

Lorenz, C. 1998. "Can Histories Be True? Narrativism, Positivism, and the 'Metaphorical Turn.'" *History and Theory* 37: 309–29.

———. 2000. "Some Afterthoughts on Culture and Explanation in Historical Inquiry." *History and Theory* 39: 348–63.

MacIntyre, A. 1976. "Causality and History." In J. Manninen and R. Tuomela, eds., *Essays on Explanation and Understanding,* pp. 137–58. Dordrecht: D. Reidel Publishing.

Mahoney, J. 1999. "Nominal, Ordinal, and Narrative Appraisal in Macrocausal Analysis." *American Journal of Sociology* 104: 1154–96.

Mandelbaum, M. 1974. "The Problem of Covering Laws." In P. Gardiner, ed., *The Philosophy of History,* pp. 51–65. London: Oxford University Press.

Martin, M., and J. Sell. 1979. "The Role of the Experiment in the Social Sciences." *Sociological Quarterly* 20: 581–90.

Martin, R. 1982. "Causes, Conditions, and Causal Importance." *History and Theory* 21: 53–74.

McCullagh, C. B. 1978. "Colligation and Classification in History." *History and Theory* 17: 267–84.

McKim, V., and S. Turner, eds. 1997. *Causality in Crisis? Statistical Methods and the Search for Causal Knowledge in the Social Sciences.* Notre Dame, Ind.: University of Notre Dame Press.

McMichael, P. 1990. "Incorporating Comparison within a World-Historical Perspective." *American Sociological Review* 55: 385–97.

Mink, L. 1978. "Review of Mandelbaum's *Anatomy of Historical Knowledge*." *History and Theory* 17: 211–23.

Molm, L. 1997. *Coercive Power in Social Exchange*. New York: Cambridge University Press.

Nichols, E. 1986. "Skocpol on Revolution." *Comparative Social Research* 9: 163–86.

Porter, D. 1975. "History as Process." *History and Theory* 14: 297–313.

Ragin, C. 1987. *The Comparative Method*. Berkeley and Los Angeles: University of California Press.

Sewell, W., Jr. 1985. "Ideologies and Social Revolutions: Reflections on the French Case" [review essay]. *Journal of Modern History* 57: 57–96.

Simon, J. 1969. *Basic Research Methods in Social Science*. New York: Random House.

Skocpol, T. 1984. "Emerging Agendas and Recurrent Strategies in Historical Sociology." In T. Skocpol, ed., *Vision and Method in Historical Sociology*, pp. 356–91. New York: Cambridge University Press.

Smelser, N. 1976. *Comparative Methods in the Social Sciences*. Englewood Cliffs, N.J.: Prentice-Hall.

————. 1992. "The Rational Choice Perspective: A Theoretical Assessment." *Rationality and Society* 4: 381–410.

————. 1997. *Problematics of Sociology: The Georg Simmel Lectures, 1995*. Berkeley and Los Angeles: University of California Press.

————. 1998. "The Rational and the Ambivalent in the Social Sciences." *American Sociological Review* 63: 1–15.

Sobel, M. 1996. "An Introduction to Causal Inference." *Sociological Methods and Research* 24: 353–79.

Somers, M., and G. Gibson. 1994. "Reclaiming the Epistemological 'Other': Narrative and the Social Constitution of Identity." In C. Calhoun, ed., *Social Theory and the Politics of Identity*, pp. 37–99. Cambridge, Mass.: Blackwell.

Steinmetz, G. 1998. "Critical Realism and Historical Sociology: A Review Article." *Comparative Studies in Society and History* 40: 170–86.

Stinchcombe, A. 1978. *Theoretical Methods in Social History*. New York: Academic Press.

————. 1991. "The Conditions and Fruitfulness of Theorizing about Mechanisms in Social Science." *Philosophy of the Social Sciences* 21: 367–88.

Stryker, R. 1996. "Beyond History versus Theory: Strategic Narrative and Sociological Explanation." *Sociological Methods and Research* 24: 304–52.

Tilly, C. 1999. "Wise Quacks." *Sociological Forum* 14: 55–61.

Topolski, J. 1981. "Conditions of Truth in Historical Narratives." *History and Theory* 20: 47–60.

Wallace, W. 1971. *The Logic of Science in Sociology*. Chicago: Aldine-Atherton.

Walsh, W. 1974. "Colligatory Concepts in History." In P. Gardiner, ed., *The Philosophy of History*, pp. 127–44. London: Oxford University Press.

Weinryb, E. 1975. "The Justification of a Causal Thesis: An Analysis of the Controversies over the Theses of Pirenne, Turner, and Weber." *History and Theory* 14: 32–56.

Zelditch, M. 1979. "Can You Really Study an Army in a Laboratory?" In A. Etzioni and E. W. Lehman, eds., *A Sociological Reader on Complex Organizations*, pp. 528–39. 3d ed. New York: Holt, Rinehart, and Winston.

Chapter 12

Intellectual Cycles of Social Movement Research

From Psychoanalysis to Culture?

James M. Jasper

Neil Smelser's *Theory of Collective Behavior* (1962) is a classic, meaning—alas—that it is cited more often than actually read. When it is cited today in books on social movements (around page 10, in those I examined), the recognition is usually brief but inevitably favorable (for example, Klandermans 1997; della Porta and Diani 1999). Most often, it is cited to show that ideas have long been taken seriously by sociological observers of social movements. Interestingly (we shall see why later), in my brief survey it is cited most extensively and taken most seriously in Alberto Melucci's *Challenging Codes* (1996), a book that concentrates on cultural meanings.

The continuing citations are impressive, given that Smelser's book is not only forty years old but also concerns a field—collective behavior—that today barely exists. As a distinct area of study, collective behavior grouped social movements with less organized activities, such as fads and panics, an association that caused movements to be viewed pejoratively, as—at their heart—irrational crowd phenomena. Soon after Smelser's book appeared, intellectual boundaries were redrawn so that social movements were studied alongside more institutionalized political action, such as interest groups and class conflict. Rereading *Theory of Collective Behavior* today offers a fascinating picture of not only how the study of social movements has changed but also how social science more generally has gained a number of conceptual tools that it lacked forty years ago, primarily having to do with culture.

By reexamining *Collective Behavior,* we can engage in the sociology of knowledge. In some views, social science progresses in an orderly way, accumulating knowledge just as the natural sciences (supposedly) do. Others see the social sciences as moving through cycles, in which one aspect of the world is exaggerated because the previous intellectual generation tended to ignore it. The pendulum swings back in the following generation. A brief examination of Smelser's book and a later, psychoanalytically oriented article in light of subsequent developments shows that research on social movements, at least, combines the two motions. Smelser raised questions that the next generation of scholars rejected; only today, as that generation's own paradigm wanes, are we again asking many of those same questions, especially having to do with ideas and the mind. But with new tools for cultural analysis at our disposal, we can, and do, give very different answers. The pendulum has not swung back to exactly the same place.

Research on social movements has undergone two important shifts since Smelser published his book in 1962 and article in 1968. In the first, beginning around 1970, a structural and organizational paradigm, almost behaviorist in its denial of meanings and minds, displaced the collective-behavior tradition of Smelser and others (such as Ted Gurr, Ralph Turner, and Lewis Killian). Known first as "resource mobilization" and in a later guise as "political process," this vision highlighted financing, interactions with the state, competition among protest groups, and the logic of conflict (Oberschall 1973; Gamson 1975; McCarthy and Zald 1977; Tilly 1978; McAdam 1982). The classic works of this generation almost entirely avoided any mention of Smelser's book, except for McAdam's caricature of the "classical model" (1982). The new paradigm seemed to rely, usually surreptitiously, on rational-choice images of human nature, in which people (or in some cases organizations) were calculatingly rational, and in which political structures and economic interests were "objective" rather than culturally constructed. This latter bias set the stage for the next paradigm shift, because the structural vision that eclipsed Smelser's book in the 1970s is itself currently on the ropes.

In the late 1980s, researchers began to realize that all political action is shaped by cultural meanings and so must—to some degree—be interpreted. The first breakthrough was the concept of frame alignment, in which movement organizers try to find the right frames to appeal to potential supporters (Snow et al. 1986). In the 1990s, the concept of collective identity was used to show how groups form, how people develop a sense of what their interests are (for a summary, see Polletta and Jasper 2001; Snow 2002). Frames and identities are emotional as much as cognitive, so the most recent extension of the cultural approach has been to incorporate emotions into the study of social movements (Kleinman 1996; Groves 1997; Jasper 1997; Goodwin, Jasper, and Polletta 2001). Inevitably, increased attention is once again being paid to psychology (Scheff 1994) and social psychology (Gamson 1992; Klandermans 1997). Newer books that reflect this cultural turn seem more likely than earlier works to cite *Theory of Collective Behavior* (for example, it was missing from the 1994 edition of Sidney Tarrow's *Power in Action* but made it into the more culturally oriented 1998 one).

These two swings of the pendulum have led us back to study many aspects of social movements prominent in Smelser's *Collective Behavior,* which in these respects has begun to look as if it were ahead of its time rather than behind the times. The structural paradigm that intervened now looks like something of a detour. Not only ideas but emotions—in some ways the heart of collective-behavior and psychoanalytic approaches—have returned to the foreground.

GENERALIZED BELIEFS

As I noted, Smelser shared with most scholars in 1962 (and earlier) the assumption that there was something wrong with political action outside normal institutional channels. Smelser was not as condemning as, say, Eric Hoffer (1951), who thought protest was nothing more than the working out of personality flaws, without any real external grievances. Smelser saw it as deviant activity, but it reflected the failure of the social system to send consistent and unambiguous signals about proper behavior (he never uses the word *irrational*). Smelser went as far as one could with the root metaphor of a "system" under which he had been trained. Indeed, his book so thoroughly and powerfully related collective behavior to Talcott Parsons and Edward Shils's basic components of social action that there seemed little more to say about collective behavior at a theoretical level. (Smelser's book is a model of how to build typologies, now a neglected art in the field of social movements.) Only empirical investigation could yield an alternative picture.

Theory of Collective Behavior is most often cited for the central role it gives to "generalized beliefs" in the development of collective behavior. I think the concept also shows why the vision of social movements has been so different in the two intellectual generations to follow. In Smelser's book such beliefs represent a "short-circuited" form of thought, because leaps are made from one level of reality to another without attention to the institutional steps in between. Ideas ignore the levels of social reality logically needed to support them. An economic crisis can be blamed on Jews, for instance, without a shred of solid evidence linking the two. The most basic generalized belief is hysteria, which exaggerates the urgency of the problem; wish fulfillment, the idea that we can solve the problem, is built on hysteria; upon both is constructed hostility, in which a perpetrator is singled out for blame. Such beliefs are allowed to form because of uncertainties in our understanding of the world—or "ambiguities," as Smelser calls them, apparently implying that a properly functioning social system would leave no question unanswered, no meaning up for grabs. Ralph Turner commented on this in reviewing the book: "Collective behavior seems to be contrasted to a highly rational model of behavior in which there is no short-circuiting from the general to the specific levels of the components: we wonder where such behavior is to be found in society" (1963: 827). (Nonetheless, the idea that social systems are rife with ambiguities and dilemmas is a promising path that systems theory could have taken.)

What strikes me in Smelser's discussion of generalized beliefs is that most of it is a straightforward description of how humans use meanings, combined with an extraneous insistence that there is something wrong with such operations. These two components have little to do with one another, and if the pejorative material on short-circuiting were eliminated, the text would read just fine. Smelser was describing culture without the conceptual tools that we have at our disposal today. So instead, like more than one anthropologist of the period dealing with puzzling and apparently irrational natives, he treated ideological statements as though they were scientific or truth claims, and had to conclude that they lacked adequate evidence.

Many of the "short circuits" simply reflect the way the human mind works. Culture and cognition operate partly through poetic and symbolic leaps. Some are instances of synecdoche or metonymy, in which leaps are made from whole to part, from incorporeal to corporeal, effect to cause, agent to attribute, or (as Kenneth Burke used the terms) from quantity to quality (synecdoche) or the reverse (metonymy). Metaphor more generally makes a wide range of leaps, transferring meanings and giving new meanings to objects, people, and actions—a process crucial to learning. As scholars across a range of disciplines have shown (drawing on thinkers like Ernst Cassirer and Susanne Langer), we make sense of the world through representation and metaphor, which help lend coherence to our ideologies (e.g., White 1973; Goodman 1976, 1978; Lakoff and Johnson 1980).

Other leaps are based on emotional connections that remain invisible if we treat beliefs and statements only as truth propositions. Like the symbolic connections, the emotional ones may be more or less accurate in reality, but that is simply the way the human mind works. Webs of meaning and of feeling can resonate as strongly with people whether or not there is good scientific evidence for them. Yes, blaming Jews for Germany's woes was a leap without evidence, but one rooted deeply in German culture: it had its own logic even if it was untrue. A cultural approach today would be less eager to distinguish true and false beliefs: the two can have the same impact on action.

Ideology is a similar case. Although Smelser does not discuss it much, he seems to follow a long tradition in treating it as though it were composed of false beliefs to be contrasted with the true beliefs available through science (a position that only a few Marxists, I suppose, still hold today). Daniel Bell published *The End of Ideology* (1960) while Smelser was working on his own book—brought out by the same press. It would have been hard at the time not to see ideology as immature distortion. (This is one reason that later cultural theorists would mostly avoid the term.)

People make intuitive mental leaps all the time, and cultural specialists have gradually, often painfully, learned not to assume they are irrational as a result. When antinuclear movements appeared in the 1970s, for example, experts in risk analysis busily demonstrated the irrationality of participants, who misunderstood the technology, misapplied principles of probability, concentrated on easily remembered cases, and so on. It eventually became clear to risk analysts, however, that people's opposition was related to basic values concerning democracy, corporate accountability, and community safety, just as pronuclear views were related to concern for economic growth and jobs and technological progress (Jasper 1988). People themselves had made intuitive (reasonable although not reasoned) leaps that were at first beyond the limited logics of the experts, who ultimately appeared to be the irrational ones by concentrating on expected fatality rates as the only standard.

Through the cultural lens of today, we are more likely to view beliefs such as hysteria, wish fulfillment, and hostility as standard rhetorical strategies to, respectively, establish the urgent need for action, reassure participants that their own action can help, and identify human agents to be stopped or transformed. Emotions must be aroused in order to motivate action (Gamson, Fireman, and Rytina 1982; Gamson 1992). The paired tendency to exaggerate the power of the protestors and the evil of the perpetrators is interesting (103), because in his 1968 article Smelser attributed the same phenomenon to oedipal urges, choosing a psychoanalytic concept to explain a straightforward cultural dynamic. (He later found yet another cause for it: ambivalence [Smelser, 1998:184].) At the time, psychoanalysis seemed a promising means for grappling with the interior world of the individual, especially in the absence of other conceptual tools (of cultural analysis) or an academic psychology that took the mind seriously (as cognitive psychology would). It was one of the richest methods then available for interpreting meanings.

EMOTIONS

In his 1968 article "Social and Psychological Dimensions of Collective Behavior," Smelser directly incorporated a theory of the human mind into the study of collective behavior, recognizing that individuals respond differently to the same social conditions. The psychology Smelser chose for doing this was Freudian, indeed the oedipal complex, which many consider to be the core of classical psychoanalysis.[1] Smelser exploited what is perhaps the greatest power of psychoanalysis, its ability to explain emotions strong enough to propel people into action—something that cognitive beliefs alone can seldom do. In one of the rare efforts to integrate sociological and psychological models of collective behavior, Smelser recognized what few others have, that "the deepest and most powerful human emotions—idealistic fervor, love, and violent rage, for example—are bared in episodes of collective behavior" (1968: 92). It was the emotional dimension of social movements that would be most thoroughly hidden in the structural paradigm that would soon dominate the field (Goodwin, Jasper, and Polletta 2000).

The one assumption that Smelser shared with the structuralists who displaced his paradigm (and for whom nothing of interest went on inside people's heads) was that the presence of strong emotions made protestors unreasonable—but he emphasized the emotions and potential irrationality, whereas the structuralists denied them. According to Smelser, protestors were working out oedipal impulses: "On the one hand there is the unqualified love, worship, and submission to the leader of the movement, who articulates and symbolizes 'the cause.' On the other hand there is the unqualified suspicion, denigration, and desire to destroy the agent felt responsible for the moral decay of social life and standing in the way of reform, whether he be a vested interest or a political authority" (1968: 119–20).[2] This may have seemed a plausible interpretation of the student rebellion of the 1960s, which especially on college campuses took an intergenerational form (although, ironically, the establishment news media may have glorified the leaders more than their supposed followers did [Gitlin 1980]). But this model did not sit well with those studying, and sympathetic to, the labor or civil rights movements.

As with the cognitive dimensions of culture, we now have additional ways of thinking about the emotions of protest. Smelser was absolutely right that emotions permeate social movements. They are filled with both strong and weak emotions, although his predispositions again led him to concentrate on the strongest, most polarizing of them. Here, too, the pejorative addition seems unnecessary, as complex emotions are found in all social life, not just collective action. There is no reason to conclude, let alone assume, that strong emotions render action irrational, in the sense that individuals are motivated by a need to manage their internal psychological conflicts rather than by a desire to respond to or change the external world. This becomes clearer when we view emotions as part of culture (Jasper 1998).

NEW TOOLS

The new conceptual tools for the study of culture that have emerged since the 1960s amount to what many have dubbed the "cultural turn" of the social sciences. Thomas Kuhn published *The Structure of Scientific Revolutions* the same year that Smelser's book appeared, igniting debates among historians and philosophers of science over the cultural and social background of scientific facts. Anthropologists had always addressed culture, but scholars such as Mary Douglas, Clifford Geertz, and Victor Turner developed concepts that were especially amenable to exportation to neighboring disciplines. Historians like E. P. Thompson, Hayden White, and Lynn Hunt also crafted tools picked up by other disciplines. Literary critics like Raymond Williams and

Fredric Jameson reached out to the social sciences. Even a few economists, such as George Akerlof and Tibor Scitovsky, grudgingly admitted that humans had minds, and researchers like Amos Tversky and Daniel Kahneman began to work the intersection of economics and psychology. If there was anyone who had not noticed it, the Foucault fervor of the early 1980s certainly brought culture to their attention. (On cultural approaches to politics, see Jasper 2004.)

Cognitive psychology had roots in the 1950s (indeed, Jerome Bruner and George Miller were doing their initial work at Harvard when Smelser was a graduate student there), but it would have taken an acute observer indeed to anticipate the rich harvest it would yield. Even in the 1960s it was, to borrow Marxist terms, a movement in itself but not yet for itself. Behaviorism's hegemony in the academy was only beginning to crumble, and psychological tools for understanding the human mind remained sparse. That changed in the 1970s with an explosion of work on schemas, scripts, decision-making heuristics, narratives, and other "mental models" (e.g., Bransford and Franks 1971; Kahneman, Slovic, and Tversky 1982; Johnson-Laird 1983). There eventually emerged a self-proclaimed "cultural psychology" (Shweder 1991).

New tools for the study of emotions were also being crafted in smaller numbers and with a slight lag behind the cultural and cognitive revolutions. Sociologists of emotions emerged in the late 1970s (Kemper 1978; Hochschild 1979, 1983) and flourished in the 1980s (sections of the American Sociological Association devoted to culture and to emotions were both founded in the mid-1980s), but emotion research mostly remained a field of psychology until the late 1990s. At that time, emotions seemed to be everywhere. Anthropologists (Lutz 1988), psychologists (Ekman and Davidson 1994), philosophers (Griffiths 1997; Nussbaum 2001), and even rational-choice theorists (Elster 1999a,b) were grappling with them.[3]

American psychoanalysis, still notoriously orthodox in the 1960s, soon reflected the cultural turn. Ego psychology continued to flourish, with an emphasis on the cognitive strengths and adaptive responses of the ego that encouraged a more rational, less pejorative model of protest, in which the ego was adapting realistically to external circumstances, not simply projecting internal conflicts (Greenstein 1987). Erik Erikson's culturally and historically grounded approach reached broader audiences, and in the 1970s Heinz Kohut publicized an image of humans as (potentially) coherent, creative selves with considerable agency—a more positive image than that of traditional psychoanalysis. Roy Schafer's similar efforts to portray individuals as coherent selves rather than as simply the locus for conflicting drives (which themselves, he claimed, were too often portrayed as autonomous agents) began in 1968 with *Aspects of Internalization;* he criticized traditional hydraulic imagery in which drives were seen as being "dammed up," "pressing for discharge," and potentially growing "toxic" if not finding an "outlet."

Finally, English translations began to appear of Jacques Lacan's efforts to recast psychoanalysis in terms of language, symbol, and the imaginary (Turkle 1978). Developments like these might have allowed a psychoanalytic portrait of those engaged in collective behavior more as cultural agents, less as victims of their own drives.

As I mentioned earlier, culture eventually came to the study of social movements, first in the form of frames (Snow et al. 1986), then as collective identity (Taylor and Whittier 1992; Gamson 1995), eventually as discourse (Steinberg 1998, 1999) and narrativity (Polletta 1998). The mid-1990s saw efforts to define broad cultural approaches (Morris and Mueller 1992; Melucci 1996; Jasper 1997). Even most of these efforts remained highly cognitive, with little attention paid to the emotions—a gap just now being filled (Goodwin 1997; Jasper 1998; Goodwin, Jasper, and Polletta 2000, 2001, 2004).

The proliferation of new tools for studying cognition and emotion raises an obvious question: how does cultural analysis, perhaps supplemented with cognitive psychology, compare with psychoanalysis (whether it is implicit as in Smelser's book or explicit as in his article)? What are the strengths and weaknesses of each of these interpretive methods? This is an awfully broad issue (about which my ignorance is nearly complete), but by concentrating on one empirical area—social movements—I hope to give a preliminary assessment. The new cultural analysis can do much of what psychoanalysis was once called upon to do, I think, but the latter may still have an edge when it comes to grappling with individual meanings rather than public, shared ones. What we see most of all is a tendency toward convergence.

PSYCHOANALYSIS AND CULTURE

Psychoanalytic and cultural analyses are both methods for interpreting meanings, and both have been applied to the meanings involved in politics and conflict. Cultural concepts such as frames and schemas are used to understand social conflicts, narratives to place them in historical context, exaggerations and dichotomies to arouse strong mobilizing emotions, and so on. Demonization of enemies and adulation of fellows are common activities in political conflict of all sorts, generating an emotional energy important for retaining recruits to a movement. This kind of polarization seems a natural cognitive and emotional process (which Claude Lévi-Strauss traced to structures of the brain) of the kind that cognitive psychology is good at grasping. All social conflict operates through such cognitive dynamics.[4]

Social conflict may also entail dynamics of a more psychodynamic sort—using shame that derives from childhood, for instance—but these seem less universal than the cultural and cognitive processes. Psychoanalysis concentrates on conflicts located within individuals, and social conflict is often interpreted as somehow derived from these. Psychodynamics are seen as root causes of participation (such as the need to join something larger than oneself), whereas cultural approaches more often portray dynamics that can be found in any sort of conflict no matter what the cause. Cultural meanings and feelings are not usually presented as prime movers in the way the instinctual drives posited by psychoanalysis traditionally have been. Traditional psychoanalysis combined interpretive tools with a detailed model of what meanings we should look for, whereas cultural approaches have been more open to any kind of content. I am not sure we can know the content in advance.

Recent psychoanalysis has relaxed its developmental model while retaining its interpretive tools. The object-relations school, introduced to sociology largely by Nancy Chodorow (1978), posits little more than a need for attachment to others but leaves the content of that attachment relatively open. Ego psychology's core concept of apparatuses (such as memory and perception) pointed the way to cognitive psychology, which went even further in portraying people as active processors of information but also as planners of projects and makers of moral judgments. This is similar to the narrative vision of Roy Schafer and others, who have downplayed biology in favor of symbol and meaning. Traditional psychoanalysis had a very specific theory of drives, combined with more general concepts such as repression, ambivalence, symbolic association, and splitting. To the extent that psychoanalysis moves toward general symbolic processes, it converges with cognitive psychology.

What about emotions? Cultural analysts have largely ignored emotions, it is true, but as I have argued elsewhere, most emotions can be understood with the same cultural tools that are regularly applied to cognitions (Jasper 1997, 1998). This is especially true of more complex emotions such as compassion, as opposed to simpler ones like surprise or anger (gut reflexes connected more closely to the body). The emotions that drive politics are generally complex cultural constructions, internalized more or less properly by individuals, who then apply them in appropriate (or sometimes inappropriate) ways—just as they do cognitions. Our social context tells us which feelings are correct and which are deviant in a given situation (Thoits 1990). Traditional psychoanalysis, in contrast, presents emotions as primarily efforts to resolve inner conflicts, placing them largely outside ongoing cultural shaping. A cultural approach seems to recast emotions as social and normal, rather than neurotic interferences with rationality. This is a debate that has yet to be settled (e.g., Kemper 2001), but it will probably be resolved by distinguishing different categories of emotions.[5] Psychoanalysis may have an edge in insisting on the importance of one's early years for learning emotions: this may be what gives emotions the feeling of being automatic and out of our control. A thorough cultural constructionism seems to ignore the commonsense view of emotions as impulses that seize hold of us. Psycho-analysis might mediate between overly biological and overly constructionist extremes.

The psychological processes featured by psychoanalysis and those amenable to cognitive and cultural analysis may exist side by side. The trend in psychology today seems to be to recognize more than one system for pro-cessing information and making decisions, located in different parts of the brain and having different evolutionary origins. At one extreme are elabo-rate systems that take years of training to master, such as cost-benefit analy-sis or medical decisions based on expensive equipment. At the other are the gut decisions made with little conscious thought, such as that of the police officer who returns fire. Howard Leventhal (1984), for example, distin-guishes three levels: a hardwired system of gut reactions; an intuitive, affect-laden form of processing; and an abstract, cognitive and explicit system. Oth-ers, such as Seymour Epstein (1994), recognize only two. More intuitive or symbolic decision-making could incorporate a number of unconscious psy-chodynamic processes. It is a mistake to distinguish these systems too rigidly, however, as they thoroughly interpenetrate one another; it is less that humans switch from one to another so much as they use a variety of tools to approach an issue, depending on how much time, training, information, and emotional attachment they have to it.

Neither cognitions nor emotions are entirely determined by social expec-tations, of course. We do not all respond in exactly the same way in every sit-uation (although we come close to that in many situations—the insight that originally inspired the field of collective behavior). Normally, we think of personality as the primary source of these differences. Smelser turned to psy-chology precisely to explain why different individuals respond differently in the same situations, with some joining a movement and others not. (This issue disappeared entirely once structural social-movement scholars could assure themselves that different responses were due to placement in social networks.)

Psychoanalysis, with a history much longer than that of other theories, has considerable explanatory power when it comes to personality differences. Some of the alternative theories come closer to being cultural perspectives, emphasizing past experience, the absorption of selected cultural meanings, a history of interactions with others, and so on. Trait theory, for instance, focuses on current personality characteristics more than on their origins—and in fact may be compatible with a psychoanalytic account of those origins (Matthews and Deary 1998). Self-concepts, schemas, and similar tools have been used to develop an explicitly cognitive approach to personality (Kelly 1955; Nisbett and Ross 1980; Turk and Salovey 1985; Pervin 1984). (Phe-nomenological approaches like those of Rogers [1951] or Maslow [1970] seem too ideographic to be of much use in studying organized activities like those of social movements, but many would make the same charge against psychoanalysis.) Few if any of these approaches can exclude psychodynamic factors altogether. What is more, object-relations traditions recognize a range of experiences as shaping personality, again moving toward trait theories and cognition theories.

In the end, though, students of politics do not need an explanation of the origins of personality, only a recognition of its importance (something entirely absent in the structural paradigm, in which it is an untested truism that personality does not matter). More important is a good working typology and predictions. In this case, the two approaches may be complementary: culture provides general meanings and feeling rules, but psychoanalysis may help us account for individual variations within them. We need a typology of personalities that is attuned to how individuals might act and interact in social movements. Qualities such as self-esteem or a sense of mastery might be especially relevant.

A common dilemma of all personality research is whether to paint a portrait meant to be universal or to craft a theory that deals well with individual variations. Psychoanalysts have often painted rich portraits of individuals but then radically jumped to make claims about entire societies or complex social phenomena like protest movements. This feels like some kind of short-circuited leap (to adapt Smelser's phrase), because in psychoanalysis personality is not linked closely enough to culture. Psychoanalysts such as Erik Erikson have tried to remedy this but have not fully succeeded. Can psychoanalysis recognize the public, shared nature of most cognitions and even emotions? If not, it may fall under the rubric of what Charles Tilly censures as phenomenological individualism, the "reduction of all social processes to individual awareness" (1999: 409). Cultural approaches to personality may suffer from the opposite problem, inadequate attention to individual variations, but in sociological explanation this seems to be the preferable error. Again, some synthesis may be the solution (e.g., Chodorow 1999).

What about the unconscious? This was possibly Freud's greatest discovery, around which most psychoanalytic tools were crafted. There is plenty of room for unconscious processes in cultural approaches. All the scripts, narratives, and heuristics of cognitive psychology were designed to show that our thought is shaped at a level beneath full consciousness. Nor do we need to be aware of our emotions and affective allegiances. But the unconscious of cognitive approaches is largely shared in a culture and is relatively easily unearthed (rather like Freud's preconscious), whereas the psychoanalytic unconscious is idiosyncratic to individuals, as it derives from repressed childhood materials. It is "the" unconscious: persistent, structured, and resistant to discovery. One is a shared, cross-sectional entity, while the other reaches back in time. One seems to have the edge for grappling with social phenomena, the other for treating individuals' problems. And yet one of the most powerful tool kits for cultural interpretation, deconstruction, similarly seeks the repressed, the unsaid, the absent center of texts. (Power hides its tracks.)

At the heart of the concept of the unconscious is the claim that there are actually multiple selves (or other forces or urges) within a person, with the conflicts between them worked out beneath consciousness. This is certainly true, and there are nonpsychoanalytic efforts to recognize the same truth. In a cultural twist drawing on symbolic interactionism, Norbert Wiley (1994) sees three selves—of the past, the present, and future—carrying on something like a conversation. Like the ego, id, and superego, no single one of the selves should come to dominate the others: healthy individuals achieve a kind of solidarity among them. Like Freud, Wiley sees a "decentered self" rather than the unitary one that Freud demolished, but the intrapsychic processes Wiley envisions have a decidedly cultural cast. In many cases when we seem to be observing multiple selves, we are simply observing a dilemma and tradeoff between long- and short-run interests, or between actions designed for different audiences (Elster 1986). The specific tripartite model of psychoanalysis may be less useful than its general recognition of the dynamics of conflict.

In psychoanalytic and cultural traditions, the unconscious seems to differ in the degree to which it derails us from effective action. Psychoanalysis, even or especially in Lacan's linguistic form, seems committed to the distinction between the real and the illusionary. Certainly, if we generate our own illusions that have little to do with any external reality to be negotiated, then illusions are irrational and should, if possible, be transformed. But if illusions are simply part of our cultural repertory, something like Kuhn's paradigms or other necessary mental baggage through which we grapple with the world, then there is less urgency in attacking them.

The concept of ambivalence, the subject of Smelser's 1997 presidential speech to the American Sociological Association, also demonstrates some differences between cultural and psychoanalytic approaches to meaning (Smelser 1998: ch. 9). He introduces the concept to show some limits of rational-choice theory, limitations already familiar to cultural theorists (e.g., Adams 1999). Love and hate may simultaneously be present in the same person for the same object. Smelser's first political example is a society's feelings about its political leaders, especially in the period of mourning after the death of one of them, when both love and hate are displayed. But in most cases, those who love the character are not the same as those who hate him or her, suggesting to me disagreement rather than ambivalence. Once again, social conflict is assumed to originate inside individuals. Worse, an unmeasured degree of repression of ambivalence is posited, making problems of evidence rather tricky. According to Smelser, when protestors express indignation against authority, or authorities engage in nasty repression of protestors, the other side of the ambivalence that each feels has simply been repressed. Protestors also love the authorities, who in turn also love protestors. To me, this stretches credibility—or at any rate would require many hours of evidence from analytic sessions to demonstrate (also see Hagan 2001).[6]

With a richer, more cultural view of the emotions, ambivalence fades in interest. We expect diverse emotions to be present in any complex situation or relationship (and politics is always complex). Some reinforce one another, others contradict one another. Some are simply mixed. Our thoughts may well tend toward the binary, but our feelings are numerous and complexly related. Much of social life consists of sorting through them, displaying some and hiding others, building on some and suppressing others. This is a central source of uncertainty and creativity in social life. Ambivalence is only one possibility.

We come next to the question of evidence. The structuralists of the 1970s criticized their predecessors for, above all, "armchair theorizing" as a substitute for empirical research into collective action. From afar, it was easier to view crowds and other forms of protest as irrational, disorganized, even a form of madness. For his book, Smelser relied on previously published materials. Although they were the best research then available, they had some limitations.

But if sociology has high standards for evidence, psychoanalysis has even higher (albeit quite different) ones. At its core, it depends on lengthy clinical contact with a patient before diagnoses can be made. Perhaps not the daily visits specified by Freud and his immediate followers, but at least weekly visits over many years. Indeed, it is hard if not impossible to demonstrate the presence or absence of many of the causal mechanisms posited by psychoanalysis without this kind of clinical evidence—and perhaps even with it (Grünbaum 1984). The notorious difficulty of falsifying its claims has been one of the main charges against psychoanalysis. On what grounds can the leap be made to interpreting a range of people engaged in a complex activity—especially when they are participating for many different reasons and in many different ways (some come to a single event, others devote their lives to political activity)? On what basis does a psychoanalyst generalize beyond her own patients? It may be possible to psychoanalyze someone in the absence of clinical contact. Psychobiographers such as Erik Erikson, Robert Tucker, and John Mack have written impressive books about historical figures by delving into all possible evidence about their subjects. But they did so by concentrating exhaustively on single individuals, not groups.

Cultural and psychoanalytic approaches share a belief in interpretation. One must get inside people's heads, something the structuralists are loath to do. All interpretive approaches run up against issues of evidence; it is harder to adjudicate between competing interpretations than between competing statistical predictions. Yet because of its deep interiority, psychoanalytic interpretation seems riskier to me when it comes to the study of social phenomena. In cultural approaches, the interpreter is dealing with meanings already there, usually in public form, and pushing a little beyond them, linking them in certain ways, asking interviewees to elaborate on them. She may talk to subjects to get them to elaborate or even undercut the usual meanings. But the meanings exist in written documents, public speeches, and collective actions. The psychoanalytic interpreter primarily or exclusively uses the materials of subjects' memories, often of things that occurred long ago, as well as of the subjects' feelings about these memories. Psychoanalysis commits one to the idea that the truth, the causal mechanisms that generate action, are deeply buried. Plus, subjects resist their discovery. Like Marxist notions of false consciousness, this resistance allows (perhaps even encourages) the interpreter to dismiss many of the statements of her subjects, or to take them as evidence of a deeper and different "truth." It seems rarer for cultural interpreters to dismiss what they are told, as opposed to simply probing the surface meanings a little more. This may be a strength of psychoanalysis in dealing with an individual, but a weakness in interpreting social phenomena.

Unfortunately Freudian approaches have been applied primarily to people and activities the analyst dislikes. In the collective-behavior tradition, scholars set out to explain what to them were obvious pathologies, so the clinical approach of psychoanalysis fit well. William McGuire gets at this, along with the considerable malleability of the approach, in a review of political psychology, speaking of the uses to which it was put during World War II: "Psychoanalytically-oriented theorists demonstrated that the Japanese national character was oral . . . , and anal . . . , and phallic . . . , illustrating the protean quality, at once admirable and worrisome, of psychoanalytic theory. Contemporaneous analyses of American national character tended to be less Freudian" (1993: 18). Even today there is a propensity for students of social movements to develop quite different theories to explain those movements they like and those they dislike (e.g., Stein 2001)—a failing I would hate to see encouraged. Psychoanalytic interpretation must prove itself on more admired movements.

Undertaking hundreds of hours of analysis respects the rich complexity of human beings like few other techniques could do. But to take one weapon from that arsenal, such as the oedipal complex, and apply it to complex social phenomena in which hundreds or thousands of individuals participate seems contrary to the psychoanalytic spirit. To the extent that psychoanalysis reaches beyond individual cases, based on depth analysis of individuals, it abandons its strength and becomes just another cultural interpretation. It is one thing to discover an oedipal complex in an individual through empirical investigation, another to assume that it is shared widely enough to explain social phenomena. But this is another potential source of convergence between culture and psychoanalysis. (Indeed, those who use psychoanalysis most cogently in political research either deal with individuals, combine psychoanalytic with cultural evidence, or—like Lynn Hunt [1992]—use psychoanalytic ideas primarily as organizing principles rather than explanatory mechanisms.)

What kinds of interpretive tools does psychoanalysis offer to cultural-political researchers? Peter Loewenberg suggests looking in the following places for unconscious meanings: affect, imagery, behavior, sexuality and gender, money, character, repetition, fantasy, humor, internal conflict, absence of material, action or inhibition, frustration, tolerance, aggression and hostility, rationalization, splitting, symbolic politics and anxiety, trauma, narcissism, crises, and life space (2000: 109–11). Such a sweeping list seems to include everything, and only a couple of items seem to me to be particularly psychoanalytic. A good interpretive sociologist might use any of them without referring to psychoanalysis. Perhaps psychoanalysis, at least judging from Loewenberg's list, has so permeated contemporary culture that it has little left to distinguish it.

As psychoanalysis has been reshaped by the cognitive revolution, it has come to look like other forms of cultural analysis. Sure, you can get the explanatory job done this way, but to an outsider it appears cumbersome. As Voltaire said, you can kill a sheep with magic, as long as you give it some arsenic at the same time. Why stick to a psychoanalytic approach if a cognitive approach can do all that psychoanalysis can and more—and more simply? If psychoanalysis had not traditionally presented itself as a complete system—often with sharply enforced boundaries—it would be easier to select parts to synthesize with more cognitive elements. Perhaps the day is here when a broad interpretive approach can offer psychoanalytic tools on the rack alongside various other sorts, so that we can choose between them on the basis of practicality more than ideology.

Psychoanalysis nonetheless offers a challenge to today's cultural sociologists. They have easily incorporated many cognitive insights from psychology and elsewhere, but they have yet to find a place for emotions in their models. Psychoanalysis reminds us of the power and universality of emotions, whatever their sources. Until we understand human longing, fantasy, nostalgia, demonization, shame, and other passions, we will never really understand cultural meanings.

CONCLUSIONS

Smelser wrote his book and article in a period when the dominant view of protestors was still pejorative. He avoided the most dismissive attitudes of the time, but the very definition of the subfield he addressed linked social movements and collective behavior. Instead of viewing protestors as being like interest groups and "normal" politicians, he saw them as being somehow like hula-hoop faddists or crowds fleeing a theater. For most of the last thirty years, a different sensibility has reigned, as biased in seeing protestors as rational, normal people instrumentally adapting means to ends as the old view was in viewing them as the opposite. In the structural vision, personality cannot matter, as this would seem to be an intrusion from a non- or even irrational world.

Today the pendulum has swung back, but not quite to the same place. There is emerging something like a synthesis, in which we can recognize a wealth of cognitive and emotional processes without casting doubt on the rationality of participants. What if our gut impulse were to see protestors as people generally optimistic about the future, with more self-esteem and self-confidence than average, with a sense of mastery over their environments? This differs from the pathological images of collective behavior but also from the rational automatons of the structuralists. Must we replace psychoanalysis, developed to deal with psychopathologies, if we are to understand people who show no great need for therapy beyond the kind of minor neuroses that affect most of us? Or can we incorporate psychoanalysis into a wide-ranging and psychologically astute cultural vision?

We must return to some of Smelser's questions, long buried. What kinds of people join protests, for what kinds of reasons? Which personalities are represented, and which are not? Who devotes a lifetime to this kind of work, and how do they differ from casual participants? What are protestors thinking, and what do they want? What do they feel at different moments and stages of a social movement? How do they craft their goals and set out to pursue them? These are the kinds of questions that make social life worth studying—and living. That Smelser gave interesting answers to them forty years ago shows what it takes to make a book a classic.

NOTES

Thanks to Jeff Alexander, Sarah Rosenfield, Neil J. Smelser, and Christine Williams for comments on earlier drafts.

1. The psychoanalytic tradition had appeared only briefly in the 1962 book, in the form of Freud's (and other psychoanalysts') approval of Gustave Le Bon's theory of crowds as irrational herds, in which, in Freud's words, "individual inhibitions fall away and all the cruel, brutal and destructive instincts, which lie dormant in individuals as relics of a primitive epoch, are stirred up to find free gratification" (1959: 11). A form of regression that undoes the work of civilization—hardly a positive image.

2. Smelser's brief formulation necessarily leaves a number of questions unanswered. Do women join movements for different reasons than men do? Does it matter if movement leaders are men or women? Do individuals who have successfully resolved their oedipal complexes avoid social movements? And how are oedipal motives related to other possible motives?

3. Smelser's sweeping *Handbook of Sociology* (1988) contained chapters on religion and science but not culture or emotions.

4. Cultural sociology could learn a lot more from cognitive psychology. The former's suspicion arises from the latter's links to the natural sciences (artificial intelligence, neurology, and evolutionary biology), with their universalist aspirations.

5. For a start, I distinguish affective ties like love and hate; immediate reflexes such as fear and disgust; moods like resignation and cynicism; personality-based traits such as anxiety; joy and other pleasures attendant upon some activity; and emotions such as compassion that are complex moral and cultural accomplishments. These are quite distinct categories (Griffiths 1997).

6. Smelser's interesting discussion of ambivalence also seems to suggest that a society has "a culture" viewed as a relatively coherent whole. If it contains conflicting expressions of love and hate for the same object, then there must be ambivalence. In contrast, the new cultural tools tend to avoid images of "a" culture, preferring to look at specific schemas, meanings, emotions, and so on. In this view, culture is more like building blocks that can be put together in many ways than like a completed edifice.

REFERENCES

Adams, Julia. 1999. "Culture in Rational-Choice Theories of State-Formation." In George Steinmetz, ed., *State/Culture: State Formation after the Cultural Turn*. Ithaca, N.Y.: Cornell University Press.

Bransford, John D., and Jeffrey J. Franks. 1971. "The Abstraction of Linguistic Ideas." *Cognitive Psychology* 2: 331–50.

Chodorow, Nancy. 1978. *The Reproduction of Mothering*. Berkeley and Los Angeles: University of California Press.

———. 1999. *The Power of Feelings*. New Haven, Conn.: Yale University Press.

della Porta, Donatella, and Mario Diani. 1999. *Social Movements*. London: Blackwell.

Ekman, Paul, and Richard J. Davidson, eds. 1994. *The Nature of Emotion*. New York: Oxford University Press.

Elster, Jon. 1986. Introduction to Jon Elster, ed., *The Multiple Self*. Cambridge: Cambridge University Press.

———. 1999a. *Alchemies of the Mind: Rationality and the Emotions*. Cambridge: Cambridge University Press.

———. 1999b. *Strong Feelings: Emotion, Addiction, and Human Relations*. Cambridge: MIT Press.

Epstein, Seymour. 1994. "Integration of the Cognitive and the Psychodynamic Unconscious." *American Psychologist* 49: 709–24.

Freud, Sigmund. 1959. *Group Psychology and the Analysis of the Ego*. Trans. James Stachey. 1922. New York: W. W. Norton.

Gamson, Joshua. 1995. "Must Identity Movements Self-Destruct? A Queer Dilemma." *Social Problems* 36: 351–67.

Gamson, William A. 1975. *The Strategy of Social Protest*. Homewood, Ill.: Dorsey Press.

———. 1992. *Talking Politics*. Cambridge: Cambridge University Press.

Gamson, William A., Bruce Fireman, and Steven Rytina. 1982. *Encounters with Unjust Authority*. Homewood, Ill.: Dorsey Press.

Gitlin, Todd. 1980. *The Whole World Is Watching.* Berkeley and Los Angeles: University of California Press.

Goodman, Nelson. 1976. *Languages of Art.* Indianapolis: Hackett Publishing.

———. 1978. *Ways of Worldmaking.* Indianapolis: Hackett Publishing.

Goodwin, Jeff. 1997. "The Libidinal Constitution of a High-Risk Social Movement: Affectual Ties and Solidarity in the Huk Rebellion." *American Sociological Review* 62: 53–69.

Goodwin, Jeff, and James M. Jasper. 1999. "Caught in a Winding, Snarling Vine: The Structural Bias of Political Process Theory." *Sociological Forum* 14: 27–54.

Goodwin, Jeff, James M. Jasper, and Francesca Polletta. 2000. "The Return of the Repressed: The Fall and Rise of Emotions in Social Movement Theory." *Mobilization* 5: 65–84.

———. 2004. "Emotional Dimensions." In David Snow et al., eds., *Handbook of Social Movements.* London: Blackwell.

———, eds. 2001. *Passionate Politics: Emotions and Social Movements.* Chicago: University of Chicago Press.

Greenstein, Fred I. 1987. *Personality and Politics.* Princeton, N.J.: Princeton University Press.

Griffiths, Paul E. 1997. *What Emotions Really Are.* Chicago: University of Chicago Press.

Groves, Julian McAllister. 1997. *Hearts and Minds.* Philadelphia: Temple University Press.

Grünbaum, Adolph. 1984. *The Foundations of Psychoanalysis: A Philosophical Critique.* Berkeley and Los Angeles: University of California Press.

Hagan, John. 2001. "Cause and Country: The Politics of Ambivalence and the American Vietnam War Resistance in Canada." *Social Problems* 48: 168–84.

Hochschild, Arlie. 1979. "Emotion Work, Feeling Rules, and Social Structure." *American Journal of Sociology* 85: 551–75.

———. 1983. *The Managed Heart.* Berkeley and Los Angeles: University of California Press.

Hoffer, Eric. 1951. *The True Believer.* New York: Harper and Row.

Hunt, Lynn. 1992. *The Family Romance of the French Revolution.* Berkeley: University of California Press.

Jasper, James M. 1988. "The Political Life Cycle of Technological Controversies." *Social Forces* 67: 357–77.

———. 1997. *The Art of Moral Protest: Culture, Biography, and Creativity in Social Movements.* Chicago: University of Chicago Press.

———. 1998. "The Emotions of Protest: Affective and Reactive Emotions in and around Social Movements." *Sociological Forum* 13: 397–424.

———. 2004. "Culture, Knowledge, Politics." In Thomas Janoski, Robert Alford, Alexander M. Hicks, and Mildred A. Schwartz, eds., *A Handbook of Political Sociology.* Cambridge: Cambridge University Press.

Johnson-Laird, P. N. 1983. *Mental Models: Towards a Cognitive Science of Language, Inference, and Consciousness.* Cambridge: Harvard University Press.

Kahneman, Daniel, Paul Slovic, and Amos Tversky, eds. 1982. *Judgment under Uncertainty: Heuristics and Biases.* New York: Cambridge University Press.

Kelly, George A. 1955. *A Theory of Personality: The Psychology of Personal Constructs.* New York: W. W. Norton.

Kemper, Theodore. 1978. *A Social Interactional Theory of Emotions*. New York: Wiley.
———. 2001. "A Structural Approach to Social Movement Emotions." In Jeff Goodwin, James M. Jasper, and Francesca Polletta, eds., *Passionate Politics*. Chicago: University of Chicago Press.

Klandermans, Bert. 1997. *The Social Psychology of Protest*. London: Blackwell.

Kleinman, Sherryl. 1996. *Opposing Ambitions*. Chicago: University of Chicago Press.

Lakoff, George, and Mark Johnson. 1980. *Metaphors We Live By*. Chicago: University of Chicago Press.

Leventhal, Howard. 1984. "A Perceptual-Motor Theory of Emotion." *Advances in Experimental Social Psychology* 17: 117–82.

Loewenberg, Peter. 2000. "Psychoanalysis as a Hermeneutic Science." In Peter Brooks and Alex Woloch, eds., *Whose Freud? The Place of Psychoanalysis in Contemporary Culture*. New Haven, Conn.: Yale University Press.

Lutz, Catherine A. 1988. *Unnatural Emotions*. Chicago: University of Chicago Press.

Maslow, Abraham H. 1970. *Motivation and Personality*. New York: Harper and Row.

Matthews, Gerald, and Ian J. Deary. 1998. *Personality Traits*. Cambridge: Cambridge University Press.

McAdam, Doug. 1982. *Political Process and the Development of Black Insurgency, 1930–1970*. Chicago: University of Chicago Press.

McCarthy, John D., and Mayer N. Zald. 1977. "Resource Mobilization and Social Movements: A Partial Theory." *American Journal of Sociology* 82: 1212–41.

McGuire, William J. 1993. "The Poly-Psy Relationship: Three Phases of a Long Affair." In Shanto Iyengar and William J. McGuire, eds., *Explorations in Political Psychology*. Durham, N.C.: Duke University Press.

Melucci, Alberto. 1996. *Challenging Codes*. Cambridge: Cambridge University Press.

Morris, Aldon D., and Carol McClurg Mueller, eds. 1992. *Frontiers in Social Movement Theory*. New Haven, Conn.: Yale University Press.

Nisbett, Richard E., and Lee Ross. 1980. *Human Inference: Strategies and Shortcomings of Social Judgment*. Englewood Cliffs, N.J.: Prentice-Hall.

Nussbaum, Martha C. 2001. *Upheavals of Thought: The Intelligence of Emotions*. Cambridge: Cambridge University Press.

Oberschall, Anthony. 1973. *Social Conflict and Social Movements*. Englewood Cliffs, N.J.: Prentice-Hall.

Pervin, Lawrence A. 1984. *Current Controversies and Issues in Personality*. 2d ed. New York: Wiley.

Polletta, Francesca. 1998. "Contending Stories: Narrative in Social Movements." *Qualitative Sociology* 21: 419–46.

Polletta, Francesca, and James M. Jasper. 2001. "Collective Identity and Social Movements." *Annual Review of Sociology* 27: 283–305.

Rogers, Carl R. 1951. *Client-Centered Therapy: Its Current Practice, Implications, and Theory*. Boston: Houghton Mifflin.

Scheff, Thomas J. 1994. *Bloody Revenge*. Boulder, Colo.: Westview.

Shweder, Richard A. 1991. *Thinking through Cultures: Expeditions in Cultural Psychology*. Cambridge: Harvard University Press.

Smelser, Neil J. 1962. *Theory of Collective Behavior*. New York: Free Press.

———. 1968. "Social and Psychological Dimensions of Collective Behavior." In Smelser, *Essays in Sociological Explanation*. Englewood Cliffs, N.J.: Prentice-Hall.

————. 1998. "The Rational and the Ambivalent in the Social Sciences." In Smelser, *The Social Edges of Psychoanalysis*. Berkeley and Los Angeles: University of California Press.

————, ed. 1988. *Handbook of Sociology*. Beverly Hills: Sage.

Smith, Christian. 1996. *Resisting Reagan: The U.S. Central America Peace Movement*. Chicago: University of Chicago Press.

Snow, David A. 2002. "Collective Identity and Expressive Forms." *International Encyclopedia of the Social and Behavioral Sciences*. London: Elsevier.

Snow, David A., E. Burke Rochford Jr., Steven K. Worden, and Robert D. Benford. 1986. "Frame Alignment Processes, Micromobilization, and Movement Participation." *American Sociological Review* 45: 464–81.

Stein, Arlene. 2001. "Revenge of the Shamed: The Christian Right's Emotional Culture War." In Jeff Goodwin, James M. Jasper, and Francesca Polletta, eds., *Passionate Politics: Emotions and Social Movements*. Chicago: University of Chicago Press.

Steinberg, Marc W. 1998. "Tilting the Frame: Considerations on Collective Action from a Discursive Turn." *Theory and Society* 27: 845–72.

————. 1999. "The Talk and Back Talk of Collective Action: A Dialogic Analysis of Repertoires of Discourse among Nineteenth-Century English Cotton Spinners." *American Journal of Sociology* 105: 736–80.

Tarrow, Sidney. 1998. *Power in Movement: Social Movements and Contentious Politics*. 2d ed. Cambridge: Cambridge University Press.

Taylor, Verta, and Nancy E. Whittier. 1992. "Collective Identity in Social Movement Communities: Lesbian Feminist Mobilization." In Aldon D. Morris and Carol McClurg Mueller, eds., *Frontiers in Social Movement Theory*. New Haven, Conn.: Yale University Press.

Thoits, Peggy A. 1990. "Emotional Deviance: Research Agendas." In Theodore D. Kemper, ed., *Research Agendas in the Sociology of Emotions*. Albany: State University of New York Press.

Tilly, Charles. 1978. *From Mobilization to Revolution*. Reading, Mass.: Addison-Wesley.

————. 1999. "Epilogue: Now Where?" In George Steinmetz, ed., *State/Culture*. Ithaca, N.Y.: Cornell University Press.

Turk, Dennis C., and Peter Salovey. 1985. "Cognitive Structures, Cognitive Processes, and Cognitive-Behavior Modification, Parts I and II." *Cognitive Therapy and Research* 9: 1–17, 19–33.

Turkle, Sherry. 1978. *Psychoanalytic Politics*. New York: Basic Books.

Turner, Ralph. 1963. Review of *Theory of Collective Behavior*, by Neil Smelser. *American Sociological Review* 28: 827.

White, Hayden. 1973. *Metahistory*. Baltimore: Johns Hopkins University Press.

Wiley, Norbert. 1994. *The Semiotic Self*. Chicago: University of Chicago Press.

Chapter 13

Shaping Sociological Imagination

The Importance of Theory

Piotr Sztompka

I had my first taste of sociological theory in Neil J. Smelser's graduate class at Berkeley in 1972–1973. Following on the themes already developed in his *Essays in Sociological Explanation* (1968), he discussed the works of the great classical scholars: Karl Marx, Max Weber, Emile Durkheim, and Alexis de Tocqueville. It struck me immediately that he was not just contemplating, commenting on, or analytically dissecting them. Instead he was using them, trying to unravel the structure and logic of their theoretical explanation of concrete issues: social inequality in the case of Marx, power in the case of Weber, cultural cohesiveness in the case of Durkheim, and the functioning of democracy in the case of Tocqueville. It was the ability to explain such crucial social issues that made them great sociologists, because theory, in their view, and clearly in the view of Smelser, was empirically and historically rooted general explanation. It was, as Smelser was defining it, "an enterprise of accounting for regularities, variations, and interdependencies among the phenomena identified within the sociological frameworks" (1968: 55).

I looked up Smelser's own major theoretical contribution, *Theory of Collective Behavior* (1963), and found the same focus on explanation, but not just any explanation. He put forward a dynamic explanatory model incorporating a temporal dimension in the "value-added sequence." According to his model, the necessary preconditions for episodes of collective behavior or social movements cumulatively emerge in stages: from structural conduciveness; to structural strain, initiating events, spread of generalized beliefs, and attempts at social control; to the emergence of the explained social phenomenon. This account, "logical patterning of social determinants, each contributing its 'value' to the explanation of the episode" (1968: 99), was obviously the realization of Smelser's creed that "sociological explanation consists in bringing constructions such as hypotheses, models and theories to bear on factual statements" (58). This theory was causal, empirical, genetic, and operational and demonstrated forcefully that social facts do not exist statically but are in a state of continual emergence, "social becoming," as I later called it (Sztompka 1991). To this day Smelser's model is an exemplar of what sociological explanation (that is, sociological theory) should look like.

Soon after my Berkeley class, I had the opportunity to study under two other American theorists who, in spite of basic differences in the orientation and substance of their theories, seemed to share with Smelser the focus on explanation. One was Robert K. Merton, who put forward his influential program of middle-range theory to resolve the dilemma between abstract "grand theory," seen in Talcott Parsons's style, and the narrow-empirical data gathering, which dominated some subdisciplines of sociology. The other theorist was George Homans, with his critique of Parsonian functionalism in the name of the covering-law model of explanation, borrowed from Carl Hempel's classic logical work. Both Merton and Homans were trying to show what sociological explanation—that is, sociological theory—should look like.

I have become more and more convinced that explanatory theory is the most important, illuminating, and useful aspect of that vast and multifaceted enterprise that runs today under the label of theory. In my sociological education, and later my own academic work, it was explanatory theory that turned out to be crucial. In this chapter, I argue why explanatory theory should remain in the forefront of sociological teaching and not be put aside by some other, trendy modes of theorizing.

THE EDUCATIONAL FOCUS: SOCIOLOGICAL IMAGINATION

The education of sociologists has four aims: (1) to teach the language of the discipline, a set of concepts with which social reality is understood, (2) to develop a particular vision, a perspective from which social reality is approached, (3) to train in the methods, procedures, and techniques of empirical inquiry, and (4) to provide information about main facts and data concerning contemporary social life. Let us put the points 1 and 2—language and perspective—under one label, "sociological imagination," borrowed from the classic book *Sociological Imagination* by C. Wright Mills. He explains the notion as follows: "The sociological imagination enables us to grasp history and biography and the relation between the two within society" (1959: 3). Let us elaborate the full meaning of this statement and extend the concept beyond Mills's insight.

I consider sociological imagination to be a complex skill or ability made up of five components, including the abilities to (1) see all social phenomena as produced by some social agents, individual or collective, and to identify those agents, (2) understand deep, hidden, structural, and cultural resources and constraints that influence social life, including the chances for agential efforts (as Mirra Komarovsky puts it, "It takes patient training of the sociological sight to enable the students to perceive the invisible social structure" [1951]), (3) recognize the cumulative burden of tradition, the persisting legacies of the past, and their continuing influence on the present, (4) perceive social life in its incessant, dynamic, fluid process of "social becoming" (Sztompka 1991), and (5) recognize the tremendous variety and diversity of the forms in which social life may appear. Everett Hughes defines one of the main goals of sociological education: "The emancipation through expansion of one's world by penetration into and comparison with the world of other people and other cultures is not the only aspect of sociological imagination. . . . But it is one great part of it, as it is of human life itself" (1970: 16).

To put it another way: Sociological imagination is the ability to relate anything that happens in a society to a structural, cultural, and historical context and to the individual and collective actions of societal members, recognizing the resulting variety and diversity of social arrangements. Mills gives us an example:

> One result of reading sociology ought to be to learn how to read a newspaper. To make a sense of a newspaper—which is a very complicated thing—one must learn how to connect reported events, how to understand them by relating them to more general conceptions of the societies of which they are tokens, and the trends of which they are a part. . . . My point is sociology is a way of going beyond what we read in the newspaper. It provides a set of conceptions and questions that help us to do this. If it does not, then it has failed as part of liberal education. (1960: 16–17)

Teaching sociology cannot be limited to sociology in books. It must go beyond that toward sociology in life, allowing deeper interpretation, better understanding of everything that surrounds us. As another classical author, Robert Park, emphasizes, "When there is no attempt to integrate the things learned in the schoolroom with the experience and problems of actual life, learning tends to become mere pedantry—pedantry which exhibits itself in a lack of sound judgement and in a lack of that kind of practical understanding we call common sense" (1937: 25). Mirra Komarovsky makes the same point: "There is no greater educational danger than this: that the students learn the sociological concepts on a purely formal verbal level without the richness and fullness of meaning; that this body of words remains a sterile segment of mentality, relatively unrelated to the confused stream of life which it sought to interpret" (1945).

I consider the training of the sociological imagination, and the skill to apply it to concrete problems of social life, to be absolutely crucial for the education of sociologists, both those who think about academic careers and those who go on to practice-oriented professions.

SOCIOLOGICAL IMAGINATION AND THEORETICAL RESOURCES

To a great extent, training the sociological imagination is synonymous with training in sociological theory. However, this is not in the sense of memorizing names, schools, definitions, and arguments, but rather in the sense of using theory—that is, referring to concrete experience, looking at the current problems in the surrounding society, its dilemmas and opportunities. It also applies to our personal biographies and life chances. Sociological imagination should provide a map to ensure a better orientation in the chaos of events, change, and transformation. It should give us a deeper understanding, more thorough enlightenment, and, in this way, provide more opportunities for informed, rational life and sound practice. In this chapter I review the resources for such indispensable theoretical training that we possess in the sociological tradition, as well as in recent social theory.

One huge pool of theoretical ideas is found in the history of the discipline, from the early nineteenth century onward. Teaching the history of sociology is not an antiquarian pastime. The tradition of our discipline is still extremely vital. Most of the concepts, models, issues, and queries that we study today have been inherited from the nineteenth-century masters. They put solid foundations under the sociological enterprise, and their work is still very much alive. They should be studied, not in a historical or biographical way, but in the context of our time, as their seminal ideas throw light on our present realities. Of course they must be studied critically and selectively, because not all have left an equally relevant heritage. My personal selection includes, of course, the "big three": Weber, Durkheim, and Marx—the true undisputed giants of sociology—as well as Auguste Comte, Herbert Spencer, Georg Simmel, Ferdinand Toennies, Vilfredo Pareto, Alexis de Tocqueville, Charles Cooley, William Sumner, and George H. Mead. Reading and rereading them are crucially important to discovering new insights and questions and formulating sociological problems by entering into a sort of dialogue with them to assess our own ideas. Perhaps most important, they can show us the best models for intellectual work. As Robert Merton puts it, "Exposure to such penetrating sociological minds as those of Durkheim and Weber helps us to form standards of taste and judgement in identifying a good sociological problem—one that has significant implications for theory—and to learn what constitutes an apt theoretical solution to the problem. The classics are what Salvemini liked to call 'libri fecondatori'—books that sharpen the faculties of exacting readers who give them their undivided attention" (in Sztompka 1996a: 31–32). There is one additional benefit: the student learns that the social world is multidimensional and extremely complex, and that it therefore requires many approaches to understand it. Studying the history of sociological theories is a great lesson in theoretical pluralism, tolerance for variety, and diversity of perspectives, and the best medicine against narrow-minded dogmatism and orthodoxy.

But let us leave sociological tradition, as my main focus here is current sociological theory and its relevance for teaching. I argue that we have four types of theory and theorizing in contemporary sociology, and that they are of unequal importance for educational purposes in training the sociological imagination. In order of diminishing importance, I discuss explanatory theory, heuristic theory, analytic theory, and exegetic theory. This classification partly overlaps with the triple distinction of "theories of," presuppositional studies, and hermeneutical theory as proposed by Jeffrey Alexander (1998b). But his preferential order is different from mine, and he does not recognize my third category: analytic theory.

THEORETICAL BOOM

In general, the last decade of the twentieth century was a good time for sociological theory. Only half a century ago, in the middle of the twentieth century, there was a lot of talk about the crisis of sociological theory (e.g., Gouldner 1971). Even quite recently, a rather pessimistic appraisal was given by Alexander, who perceived diminishing influence of sociological theory in the recent period, both within the discipline and without, accompanied by the growing importance of theoretical work in economics, philosophy, and literary studies (1988a). But now the situation seems to have changed. I share the opinion of a British sociologist, Gerard Delanty: "Social theory is in a position of great strength at the moment" (1998: 1).

To support this claim, I offer some institutional or organizational facts. The Research Committee on Theory (RC 16), which I founded together with Jeffrey Alexander in 1986, has grown to become one of the biggest of more than fifty committees of the International Sociological Association. In the American Sociological Association (ASA), the theory section is one of the largest groups. During the last decades of the century, the circulation of theoretical journals dramatically increased, and many new titles appeared: *Theory, Culture, and Society; European Journal of Social Theory; Sociological Theory* (published by the ASA); and *Theory and Society*. A new publication, *Journal of Classical Sociology*, has been launched by Sage under the editorship of Bryan Turner. A number of major compendia of theoretical knowledge have come out: *Polity Reader in Social Theory* (1994), *Blackwell Companion to Social Theory* (1996), *Major Social Theorists* (2000), and *Handbook of Social Theory* (2000). New monographs are taking stock of current theory: for example, Patrick Baert's *Social Theory in the Twentieth Century* (1998) and John Scott's *Sociological Theory: Contemporary Debates* (1995). Major publishers, including

Polity Press, Cambridge University Press, and Sage, put out rich lists of theoretical work, both classical and recent, including important book series: for example, Cambridge Cultural Social Studies (edited by Jeffrey Alexander and Steven Seidman). All around the world, there are theoretical conferences focusing on theoretical issues, including for example, "Reappraising Theories of Social Change" at Montreal (2000) and "New Sources of Critical Theory" at Cambridge (2000).

It is notable that theory has returned to its cradle, to Europe, after a long detour to North America (Nedelman and Sztompka 1993). Of course, apart from the continuing influence and presence of the "old guard"—Robert K. Merton, Neil Smelser, Seymour M. Lipset, Lewis Coser, Peter Blau, and others—a number of influential theorists from the younger generation work and publish in the United States, including Jeffrey Alexander, Randall Collins, Craig Calhoun, and Jonathan Turner, to mention just a few. But Britain, France, and Germany currently provide the most fertile grounds for original theoretical work. As Neil Smelser admits, "In fact, in the past 50 years, the center of gravity of general theoretical thinking has shifted from the United States to Europe, and this shift is represented in the works of scholars like Alain Tourine, Pierre Bourdieu, Jurgen Habermas, Niklas Luhmann, and Anthony Giddens. Much of current theoretical thinking in the US stems from the influence of these figures on faculty and graduate students" (1990: 47–48). From the European side, this is echoed by Bryan Turner, who predicts, "European social theory may once more emerge to evolve to a new form of domination in the world development of social theory" (1996b: 16).

EXPLANATORY THEORY

How can the above-mentioned facts and tendencies be interpreted? Sticking to the old, traditional opposition of "theory versus research" or "theoretical versus empirical sociology" (as exemplified by the Parsons-Merton debate in 1947 at the annual ASA convention; see Merton 1948) could lead one to conclude that the ascent of theory indicates a shift from research to scholasticism and the realm of pure ideas. In other words, empirical research is abandoned and real social problems and concrete social facts are ignored. In fact, nothing could be farther from the truth. The impressive reputation of theory is due to the fact that it won its way into all domains of empirical sociology, found a place in all specialist areas of sociology, and has finally become accepted as a valid and necessary component of sociological research. The separation of theory and research is no longer feasible. Instead we witness a proliferation of theories dealing with various substantive social problems and issues.

Theorists and researchers now meet halfway. Most theorists no longer pursue purely abstract ideas, but are looking at real problems: globalization, identity, risk, trust, civil society, democracy, new forms of labor, social exclusion, cultural traumas, and so on. At the same time, empirical researchers no longer confine themselves to fact-finding and data-gathering but propose models, generalizations of their domains informed by accumulated research: theories of deviance, collective behavior, social movements, ethnicity, mass media, social capital, postmaterialist values, and so on. For example, the *Handbook of Sociology*, by Stella Quah and Arnaud Sales (2000), which sums up the state of the art in various sociological subdisciplines, in fact includes a considerable amount of theory in each chapter. The book illustrates that theory is coming closer to addressing real social problems, as opposed to esoteric sociological problems—that is, the problems experienced by common people as opposed to the professional concerns of sociologists. Theory can provide explanations of pressing social issues by generating more or less directly testable hypotheses and can thus influence more people in society by providing them with guidelines for thinking and mental maps of specific domains of their social life-world.

This first theoretical approach can be labeled "explanatory theory." It represents what Bryan Turner calls a "strong program" for theory (1996b: 6). First, we must ask three questions about a theory: It is a theory of what, for what, and for whom? A theory of what? Of real social problems: why more crime, why new social movements, why poverty, why ethnic revival? According Merton, Smelser, Bourdieu, and Bryan Turner, theory should grow out of research and be directed toward research. "For theoretical contributions to be worthwhile, they need to be question-driven" (Baert 1998: 202). "Social theory thrives and survives best when it is engaged with empirical research and public issues" (Turner 1996b: 12). A theory for what? For providing explanations, or at least models allowing better organization of dispersed facts and phenomena, and interpretation of multiple and varied events and phenomena. A theory for whom? Not only for fellow theorists but also for common people, to provide them with an orientation, enlightenment, and understanding of their condition. An important role of theories is to "inform democratic public discourse" (Calhoun 1996: 429). This role will become even more pronounced as more societies become democratic, and even more in a "knowledge society" of the future, composed of informed, educated citizens who care about public issues, and where democracy takes a form of "discursive democracy" (Dryzek 1990).

One can formulate a hypothesis in the framework of the "sociology of knowledge": the driving force behind the developments in explanatory theory are found in rapid, radical, and overwhelming social change. We are experiencing the next "great transition" (to paraphrase Karl Polanyi). Theories are especially in demand in times of change. There is pressure on sociologists from both the common people and politicians to provide explanations of the chaos. Everyone wants to know where we have come from, where we are, and where we are going. Facts and data alone cannot answer such questions. Only generalized explanatory models can provide an overall view. "Nothing presses this theoretical venture on us more firmly than the experience of historical change and cross-cultural diversity" (Calhoun 1996: 431).

Teaching explanatory theories is, in my opinion, the most important goal of sociological education, and particularly so in periods of overwhelming social change. This kind of theory provides the strongest stimulus in developing the sociological imagination, as it links theorizing with concrete experience.

HEURISTIC THEORY

Let us move on to a second kind of theoretical approach: theoretical orientation, or what I call a heuristic theory (not directly testable but useful in generating relevant concepts, images, and models). It is closest to social philosophy, and particularly the ontology or metaphysics of the social world, as it attempts to answer three perennial ontological questions about the constitution of social reality: What are the bases of social order? What is the nature of human action? And what is the mechanism and course of social change? Such questions have been addressed by all classical founders of sociology. Good examples of the classical orientations dominating in the middle of the last century, which attempted to deal with such issues, were structural functionalism, symbolic interactionism, exchange theory, and Marxism. Since then, several new trends have emerged, which I discuss later.

What are the characteristics of this kind of theory? Again, let us ask our three questions. Theory of what? Of the foundations of social reality. It poses questions not of "why" but of "how": How is social order possible (how do social wholes exist; how do people live together, cooperate, cohabit)? How is social action carried out? How does social change proceed? Theory for what? For the conceptual framework for more concrete explanatory theoretical work, for sensitizing us to specific types of variables, for suggesting strong categories to help us grasp the varied and dispersed facts. Theory for whom? Mostly for researchers building explanatory models of specific domains of reality and answering concrete problems.

The formidable growth of such heuristic theories by the end of the century cannot be explained by reference to social facts, but rather by intellectual developments. Heuristic theory should be seen in terms of the history of ideas rather than the sociology of knowledge. It seems to be related to new, contingent intellectual developments—that is to say, new trends and attractive, innovative, original perspectives. There is the excitement of a "paradigmatic shift" (Kuhn 1970); in fact we have witnessed three parallel paradigmatic shifts in recent theory. The first shift, from "first" to "second" sociology (Dawe 1978), moves from a view of fixed organic systems to fluid fields of social forces. Social order is seen to be a constantly emerging and constructed achievement of agents, produced and reproduced by human action. Examples of such perspectives are found in the work of Berger, Thomas Luckmann, Elias, Giddens, and Bourdieu. The second shift is from evolution or social development to social becoming. There is an emphasis on open-ended historical scenarios, determined by decisions and choices but also by contingent, random occurrences. Examples of this perspective are found in historical sociology—represented by authors like Tilly, Archer, Theda Skocpol, and myself (Sztompka 1991, 1996b). The third shift is from images of *homo economicus*, the calculating, rational, purposeful actor (still at the heart of rational choice theory, e.g., James Coleman and Jon Elster), and *homo sociologicus*, the normatively directed role player (still found in neo-functionalism, e.g., Alexander, Luhmann, and Richard Munch), to *homo cogitans*, the knowledgeable and meaningful actor informed and constrained by collective symbolic systems of knowledge and belief. This shift is also seen as an interpretative turn, cultural turn, or linguistic turn. "Contemporary social theory has done an about-face in analytical terms by giving prominence and priority to cultural phenomena and cultural relations," according to Bryan Turner (1998). It has many varieties. In one, which is sometimes called mentalism, there is a stress on the invariant components of the human mind. Examples include the structuralism of Claude Lévi-Strauss or Ferdinand De Saussure and the phenomenology of Alfred Schutz. The second kind, what some authors call textualism, is represented by poststructuralism, or theory of discourses by Foucault, where social reality appears as a form of text with specific semantic meaning and its own rules of grammar. The third is sometimes also labeled intersubjectivism, to which Habermas made a great contribution in his theory of communicative action. Finally, there is the reaction against the "overintellectualized image of man." The emphasis shifts to practical knowledge (Giddens) and ethno-methods (Harold Garfinkel) but also to seeing the body as an instrument of action (Bryan Turner) and emotions as accompanying actions, things one uses, objects encountered, environment providing context for action. Individuals are seen as the carriers of routine but complex, characteristic sets of practices (Bourdieu).

Thus we presently have a rich and varied menu of heuristic orientations. Teaching should sensitize students to the necessity of using many of these orientations to look at society from various perspectives and different sides in order to attain a fuller understanding of social life.

ANALYTIC THEORY

The third theoretical approach can be called analytic theory. What it does is generalize and clarify concepts, providing typologies, classifications, explications, and definitions applicable in explanatory theory. It has an important but subsidiary role to play. However, there is a danger that it can become merely a method to sharpen conceptual tools without ever resulting in a specific orientation or producing a binding system of concepts. The attempts to construct closed conceptual systems and special languages to cover the whole domain of sociology seem to have ended with Niklas Luhmann's huge effort (earlier only Talcott Parsons had similar ambitions). But on a more limited level, this variety of theorizing is useful and necessary, coming close to what Merton labeled "middle range theory" (in Sztompka 1996a: 41–50). These are empirically informed conceptual schemes, applicable to concrete empirical problems (e.g., his theories of roles and role sets, reference groups, stratification, mobility, anomie, deviance, etc.).

What is the nature of such a theory? Again we must ask our three questions. Theory of what? Of rich concepts useful for grasping phenomena. Theory for what? For identifying, unraveling, explicating phenomena or important dimensions of phenomena. Theory for whom? For sociologists, providing them with a canonical vocabulary, the technical language to deal with their subject matter. Teaching analytic theory is crucial to developing students' ability to think and talk sociologically. It provides them with the basic tools of the trade. The focus in introductory courses of sociology should be on precisely this kind of theory.

EXEGETIC THEORY

Finally, there is the fourth kind of theory, which can be called exegetic theory. It comes down to analysis, exegesis, systematization, reconstruction, and critique of existing theories. It is, of course, a valid preparation for theoretical work. It should be seen as a stage of a scientific career, a period of apprenticeship. Most major theorists have gone through such a stage: Parsons with *The Structure of Social Action* (1937), Giddens with *Capitalism and Modern Social Theory* (1971), Alexander with his four-volume *Theoretical Logic in Sociology* (1982), and Smelser with *Essays in Sociological Explanation* (1968). I also include my *Sociological Dilemmas* (1979) in this category. However, we can lose sight of what is truly important if we let dissecting and analyzing the work of fashionable authors become the main concerns: what certain scholars said; how they could supposedly say it better; what they could have said but did not; are they consistent; what do they, or do they not, really mean? The more esoteric, incomprehensible, and muddled a theory, the greater opportunity it provides for exegetic debate. It inspires the frantic search "in a dark room, for a dark dog, which is not there." This is the secret of some current theories (e.g., the whole school of postmodernism and deconstructionism) and explains their popularity among interpreters. If a theory is straightforward, problem-oriented, precise, and clear, there is not much to interpret and criticize.

Our three questions are especially revealing in the case of the fourth kind of theory. Theory of what? Of other theories, certain books, texts, and phantoms of sociological imagination, resulting in self-referential exercises. Theory for what? For apologies or destructions of proposed theories—which easily implies factionalism, dogmatism, orthodoxy of schools, sects, and fans, and which degenerates from the free market of ideas into a vicious battlefield of ideas. Theory for whom? For other theorists who play intellectual games within the sects of the initiated. Such theories are the least consequential and often futile and irrelevant. They often deteriorate into epigonism. This opinion is shared by several theorists: "Social theory is at once the most futile and the most vital of intellectual enterprises. It is futile when it turns inward, closes into itself, degenerates into a desiccated war of concepts or an invidious celebration of the cognitive exploits of this author, that school, my tradition, your orthodoxy" (Wacquant 1998: 132). "It is necessary to let fresh air into the often closed compounds of indoor theorizing. Social theory is not only conceptualizations and discourse on other theoretician's concepts" (Therborn 1998: 132). "Without these political and public commitments, social theory is in danger of becoming an esoteric, elitist, and eccentric interest of marginal academics" (Turner 1996b: 13). "Quite a number of scholars seem to assume that theoretical progress depends solely on close scrutiny and recycling of preceding social theories. . . . This strategy is unlikely to provide innovative and penetrating social knowledge" (Baert 1998: 203).

Needless to say, I would not recommend exegetic theories for sociology students. If included at all, their place in the curriculum should be only marginal, perhaps limited to graduate or postgraduate levels as a kind of mental exercise in reading and debunking of esoteric texts.

CONCLUSION

It has been argued that the most important, fruitful, and promising types of theory, crucial for sociological imagination, are the explanatory and heuristic theories. Analytic theories have a subsidiary role in sharpening conceptual tools and providing the language for sociological thinking. Exegetic theories are useful only in preparing a background for theorizing and the development of critical skills, but they do not contribute to theory proper, and they should not replace other forms of theorizing.

Explanatory and heuristic theories make up a pluralistic mosaic of theoretical explanations and theoretical orientations. How should we deal with this fragmentation of the theoretical field? The attitude of "disciplined eclecticism" is a good way to address explanatory, practical theory, which is useful for the people, not only for the theorists (the quote is from Merton

1976: 169). This should be imparted to sociology students. Being disciplined means having a critical approach, appraising theories on their internal merits, coherence, persuasiveness, and ability to generate hypotheses. Being eclectic means having an open, inclusive, tolerant attitude, free from one-sided dogmatism. The spirit of Neil Smelser's work is clearly congruent with this strategy. He explicitly suggests "an attitude of permissiveness for a variety of theoretical and empirical activities, combined with an obligation to relate these to the core of sociology" (1968: 61). More recently, some other authors have argued in the same, ecumenical direction: "It is generally not possible to ask all the interesting questions about any really significant phenomenon within the same theory or even within a set of commensurable, logically integratable, theories" (Calhoun 1996: 435). "It is possible to gain cumulative knowledge about the world from within different and competing points of view" (Alexander 1988a: 79).

Disciplined eclecticism allows us to cross not only intertheoretical borders but also interdisciplinary borders, to go back toward social theory as practiced by the classics rather than engage only narrowly defined sociological theory. Already in the 1960s, Neil Smelser opted for this kind of true theoretical integration, which is not to be confused with creating interdisciplinary institutes: "A major requirement of integration is that some common language be developed so that the elements of the different social sciences can be systematically compared and contrasted with one another" (1968: 43). Twenty years later, Immanuel Wallerstein argued that, by intellectual necessity, sociology should link with psychology, economics, anthropology, cognitive sciences, and political science, and that it is important to abandon some pernicious interdisciplinary divisions which emerged in the nineteenth century and have proved resilient (1988). The same message was forcefully articulated a decade later by Mattei Dogan: "The networks of cross-disciplinary influences are such that they are obliterating the old classification of the social sciences. The trend that we perceive today is from the old formal disciplines to new hybrid social sciences" (1997: 442). The persistent emphasis on the same need for integration over several decades proves in itself that the promise is not yet fulfilled. It remains as perhaps the biggest challenge facing sociological theory and sociological education today.

REFERENCES

Alexander, Jeffrey C. 1982. *Theoretical Logic in Sociology*. 4 vols. London: Routledge and Kegan Paul.

———. 1988a. "New Theoretical Movement." In Neil J. Smelser, ed., *The Handbook of Sociology*, pp. 77–102. Newbury Park: Sage.

———. 1988b. "Sociology, Theories of." In E. Craig, ed., *Routledge Encyclopedia of Philosophy*. London: Routledge.

Baert, Patrick. 1998. *Social Theory in the Twentieth Century.* Cambridge, U.K.: Polity Press.

Calhoun, Craig. 1996. "Social Theory and the Public Sphere." In Bryan S. Turner, *The Blackwell Companion to Social Theory,* pp. 429–70. Oxford: Blackwell.

Dawe, Allan. 1978. "Theories of Social Action." In T. B. Bottomore and R. Nisbet, eds., *The History of Sociological Analysis,* pp. 362–417. New York: Basic Books.

Delanty, Gerard. 1998. "Introduction to *International Journal of Theoretical Sociology.*" *European Journal of Sociology Theory* 1, no. 1 (July 1998): 5–6.

Dogan, Mattei. 1997. "The New Social Sciences: Cracks in the Disciplinary Walls." *International Social Science Journal* 153: 429–43.

Dryzek, John S. 1990. *Discursive Democracy.* Cambridge: Cambridge University Press.

Giddens, Anthony. 1971. *Capitalism and Modern Social Theory.* Cambridge: Cambridge University Press.

Gouldner, Alvin. 1971. *The Coming Crisis of Western Sociology.* New York: Basic Books.

Hughes, Everett C. 1970. "Teaching as Fieldwork." *American Sociologist* 5 (1): 13–18.

Komarovsky, Mirra. 1945. "A Note on a New Field Course." *American Sociological Review* 9: 194–96.

———. 1951. "Teaching College Sociology." *Social Forces* 30: 252–56.

Kuhn, Thomas. 1970. *The Structure of Scientific Revolution.* 2d ed. Chicago: University of Chicago Press.

Merton, Robert K. 1948. "The Position of Sociological Theory." *American Sociological Review* 13: 164–68.

———. 1976. *Sociological Ambivalence.* New York: Free Press.

Mills, C. Wright. 1959. *Sociological Imagination.* New York: Oxford University Press.

———. 1960. "Introduction." In *Images of Man: The Classic Tradition in Sociological Thinking,* pp. 16–17. New York: George Braziller.

Nedelman, Birgitta, and Piotr Sztompka. 1993. *Sociology in Europe.* Berlin: De Gruyter.

Park, Robert E. 1937. "A Memorandum on Rote Learning." *American Journal of Sociology* 43 (July): 23–36.

Parsons, Talcott. 1937. *The Structure of Social Action.* Glencoe: Free Press.

Polity Reader in Social Theory. 1994. Cambridge, U.K.: Polity Press.

Quah, Stella, and Arnaud Sales. 2000. *International Handbook of Sociology.* London: Sage.

Ritzer, George. 2000. *The Blackwell Companion to Major Social Theorists.* Oxford: Blackwell.

Scott, John. 1995. *Sociological Theory: Contemporary Debates.* Cheltenham: Edward Elgar.

Smelser, Neil J. 1963. *Theory of Collective Behavior.* New York: Free Press.

———. 1968. *Essays in Sociological Explanation.* Englewood Cliffs, N.J.: Prentice-Hall.

———. 1990. "Sociology's Next Decades: Centrifugality, Conflict, Accommodation." *Cahiers de recherche sociologique* 14: 35–49.

Sztompka, Piotr. 1979. *Sociological Dilemmas: Toward a Dialectic Paradigm.* New York: Academic Press.

———. 1991. *Society in Action: A Theory of Social Becoming.* Cambridge, U.K.: Polity Press.

———. 1996a. *Robert K. Merton on Social Structure and Science.* Chicago: University of Chicago Press.

———. 1996b. *The Sociology of Social Change.* Oxford: Blackwell.

Therborn, Goran. 1998. "The Tasks of Social Theory." *European Journal of Social Theory* 1 (1): 127–35.

Turner, Bryan S. 1996a. *The Blackwell Companion to Social Theory.* Oxford: Blackwell.

———. 1996b. Introduction to *The Blackwell Companion to Social Theory*, pp. 1–19. Oxford: Blackwell.

———. 1998. "The Tasks of Social Theory." *European Journal of Social Theory* 1 (1): 127–35.

Wacquant, Loic. 1998. "The Tasks of Social Theory." *European Journal of Social Theory* 1 (1): 132–33.

Wallerstein, Immanuel. 1988. "Should We Unthink the Nineteenth Century?" In Francisco O. Ramirez, ed., *Rethinking the Nineteenth Century*, pp. 185–91. Westport, Conn.: Greenwood Press.

CONTRIBUTORS

Jeffrey C. Alexander is Professor and Chair of the Sociology Department at Yale University and codirector of the Yale Center for Cultural Sociology. His most recent books are *The Meanings of Social Life: A Cultural Sociology* (Oxford, 2003) and *Cultural Trauma and Collective Identity* (coauthored with R. Eyerman, B. Giesen, N. Smelser, and P. Sztompka; University of California Press, 2004).

Nancy J. Chodorow is Professor of Sociology and Clinical Faculty in Psychology at the University of California, Berkeley, and a psychoanalyst in private practice. She is the author of *The Reproduction of Mothering* (which won the Jessie Bernard Award; University of California Press, 1978), *Feminism and Psychoanalytic Theory* (Yale University Press, 1989), *Femininities, Masculinities, Sexualities* (University Press of Kentucky, 1994), and *The Power of Feelings* (which won the L. Bryce Boyer Prize; Yale University Press, 1999). She is recipient of the Distinguished Contribution to Women and Psychoanalysis Award of the American Psychological Association and of numerous fellowships, including those from the Radcliffe Institute for Advanced Study, Guggenheim Foundation, American Council of Learned Societies, National Endowment for the Humanities, and the Center for Advanced Study in the Behavioral Sciences.

Burton R. Clark is Allan M. Cartter Professor Emeritus of Higher Education, Graduate School of Education and Information Studies, University of California, Los Angeles. His significant published work includes *The Open Door College* (1960), *The Distinctive College* (1970), *The Higher Education System* (1983), *Places of Inquiry* (1995), and *Creating Entrepreneurial Universities* (1998). He has won book and achievement awards from the Association for the Study of Higher Education, the American Educational Research Association, the European Consortium of Higher Education Researchers, and the

European Association for Institutional Research; the Comenius Medal from UNESCO; and honorary degrees from the University of Strathclyde, Scotland, and the University of Turku, Finland.

Yiannis Gabriel is Professor of Organizational Theory at the Business School, Imperial College, London. His main research interests are in organizational and psychoanalytic theories, consumer studies, storytelling, folklore, and culture. He has written extensively on organizational narratives and stories. He has been editor of the journal *Management Learning* and is currently associate editor of *Human Relations*.

Arlie Russell Hochschild is the author of *The Second Shift* (Viking, 1989), *The Time Bind* (Metropolitan Books, 1997), *The Managed Heart* (University of California Press, 1983), and, most recently, *The Commercialization of Intimate Life* (University of California Press, 2003) and *Global Woman* (coedited with Barbara Ehrenreich; Metropolitan Books, 2003). She has won the Charles Cooley and Wilhelm Aubert Awards, as well as Guggenheim and Fulbright fellowships. She teaches sociology at the University of California, Berkeley.

James M. Jasper has written about states and policies (*Nuclear Politics* [Princeton University Press, 1990]), social movements (*The Animal Rights Crusade* [Free Press, 1992] and *The Art of Moral Protest* [Chicago, 1997]), and culture (*Restless Nation* [Chicago, 2000]), among other topics. He recently donated his fifth gallon of O-positive blood.

Christian Joppke is Professor of Sociology at the International University, Bremen. His most recent book is *Ethnic Migration in the Liberal State* (Harvard University Press, 2004).

Alberto Martinelli is Professor of Political Science and Sociology and former Dean of the Faculty of Political and Social Sciences at the University of Milan. His recent works in English include *Overviews in Economic Sociology* (with N. J. Smelser [Sage, 1990]), *International Markets and Global Firms* (Sage, 1991), *Recent Social Trends in Italy* (McGill-Queens University Press, 1999), and *Modernization and Modernity* (Sage, forthcoming). He was section editor for "Organization and Management Studies" of the *International Encyclopedia of the Social and Behavioral Sciences* (Elsevier, 2001). Between 1998 and 2002 he was President of the International Sociological Association.

Gary T. Marx is Professor Emeritus at MIT. He also taught at the University of California, Berkeley, Harvard, and the University of Colorado. He is the author of *Protest and Prejudice* (Harper and Row, 1967), *Undercover: Police Surveillance in America* (University of California Press, 1988), *Windows into the Soul: Surveillance and Society in an Age of High Technology* (University of Chicago Press, forthcoming), and articles in academic and popular media, available at www.garymarx.net.

Lyn Spillman is Associate Professor of Sociology at the University of Notre Dame. She is the author of *Nation and Commemoration: Creating National Identities in the United States and Australia* (Cambridge University Press, 1997), editor of *Cultural Sociology* (Blackwell, 2002), and recipient of a Guggenheim Fellowship in 2001.

Piotr Sztompka is Professor of Theoretical Sociology at the Jagiellonian University of Krakow, Poland. He is recognized internationally as the member of numerous academies, including the American Academy of Arts and Sciences, and is currently President of the International Sociological Association. His best-known books are *Robert K. Merton: An Intellectual Profile* (St. Martin's Press, 1986), *Society in Action: A Theory of Social Becoming* (Polity Press, 1991), *The Sociology of Social Change* (Blackwell, 1993), and *Trust: A Sociological Theory* (Cambridge University Press, 1999).

R. Stephen Warner received his Ph.D. from the University of California, Berkeley, in 1972. He currently is Professor of Sociology at the University of Illinois at Chicago. A past president of the Association for the Sociology of Religion and the Religion Section of the American Sociological Association, he has held Guggenheim and National Endowment for the Humanities fellowships, and his research has been supported by the Lilly Endowment and the Pew Charitable Trusts. Recent publications include *Gatherings in Diaspora: Religious Communities and the New Immigration* (Temple University Press, 1998) and *Korean Americans and Their Religions: Pilgrims and Missionaries from a Different Shore* (Pennsylvania State University Press, 2001).

Christine L. Williams is Professor of Sociology at the University of Texas, Austin. Her research interests include gender, sexuality, and psychoanalytic theory. She is the author of *Gender Differences at Work* (University of California Press, 1989) and *Still a Man's World* (University of California Press, 1995). She currently edits the journal *Gender & Society*.

Robert Wuthnow is the Gerhard R. Andlinger Professor of Sociology and Director of the Center for the Study of Religion at Princeton University. He is the author of more than twenty books on American culture and religion, including *The Restructuring of American Religion: Society and Faith since World War II* (Princeton University Press, 1988) and *Loose Connections: Joining Together in America's Fragmented Communities* (Harvard University Press, 1998).

Viviana A. Zelizer (Lloyd Cotsen 1950 Professor of Sociology at Princeton University) studies economic processes, American social history, and childhood. She has published books on the development of life insurance, the changing economic and sentimental value of children in the United States, and the place of money in social life. Recently she has been examining the interplay between monetary transfers and different sorts of social relations.

INDEX

Page numbers in italics indicate tables.

Abbott, Andrew, 218, 219
academic differentiation, 81, 168–85; competition interacting with, 183–85; as university phenomenon, 173–80
adolescence, ambivalence and, 95
affect. *See* emotion
agency. *See* structure-agency problem
AGIL theory, 2–3, 11n1
Akerlof, George, 240
Akin, David, 126
Alexander, F. King, 184
Alexander, Jeffrey C., 11, 22, 262; on Coleman, 92; on Smelser, 1–11, 191–94; *Theoretical Logic in Sociology*, 263; and theory, 258, 259, 263
ambiguities, 7, 236–37
ambivalence, 93–96, 118; consumption and, 19–20, 49–50, 52, 95; dependency and, 17, 64, 71, 94–95, 113–17; expressions of, 115; family, 52, 94–95; fleeing, 49–50; generation of, 114–15; intrapsychic, 113; about religion, 79, 112–18; splitting, 5, 115–16; in workplace, 63–66. *See also* Smelser's theme of ambivalence
American Psychological Association, 178
American Sociological Association (ASA), 2, 240; Parsons-Merton debate (1947 convention), 259; Smelser's presidential address (1997), 4–5, 22, 78, 82–83, 93, 103, 245–46; theory section of, 258

Ammerman, Nancy, 103, 105
anarchism, local currencies and, 136
anthropology, and individuality, 23, 25, 27
apparatuses, in ego psychology, 242
Aristotelian view of causality, 222, 223, 226, 227, 228
Arrow, Kenneth, 86
Asian American college students, and parents' religion, 110, 113–14
Asians: immigration policy toward, 198, 202, 203, 207, 214n18. *See also* Japanese
Aspects of Internalization (Schafer), 240
assimilation, and immigration policy, 199, 211
Australia, 200, 201, 205
authority: in organizations, 86; pastoral, 160–61. *See also* legitimacy, structures of

baby boomers, 31–32, 115–16
Bak, Sangmee, 71
Bales, Kevin, 53n13
barter, 130
Bauman, Zygmunt, 62–63, 68, 70
Bayon, Denis, 131
Becker, Gary, 85, 87, 99
Becker, Howard, 217
beliefs, 189–267; generalized, 191, 192–93, 236–38; general/specific, 192; primordial/modern, 192; religion as system of, 160; Smelser's perspective on, 7, 191–93, 236–37. *See also* primordial beliefs
Bell, Daniel, 237

drives, psychoanalysis and, 240–41, 242
Durkheim, Emile, 25, 90, 145; and rational utilitarianism, 84, 85, 92; and sacred, 42;
Smelser's reading of, 146, 254; on social
facts, 85, 152; in sociological education, 257

eclecticism, disciplined, 264–65
economic rationality, 82–86, 88, 93, 96,
97–98, 124. *See also* rational choice
"Economic Rationality as a Religious System"
(Smelser), 93
economic sociology, 3, 6, 94
economy: capitalism as destabilizing, 47,
54n19; family activity in, 123–24; and
immigration policy, 200; market equilibrium and, 84, 85, 87–88, 97–98; new, 60;
price theory, 7; religious imagery and,
105–7; secular individualism and, 47; of
university system, 171, 183–84. *See also*
commodification; economic rationality;
economic sociology; labor force
Economy and Society (Parsons and Smelser), 3,
78, 82
education: and beliefs, 191; British working-
class, 5, 195, 196, 211; differentiation in,
81, 168–85; of sociologists, 255–58, 261,
263, 264–65. *See also* teaching; university
system
efficient causality, 223, 226, 227, 228, 229
efficient symbols, 48
ego defense, 43, 53n5
egoists, rational, 87, 88
Ehrenreich, Barbara, 53n3
either/or thinking, ambivalence and, 115
elective parochials, 104
Elster, Jon, 83, 91, 98, 262
emotion, 57–58, 242–43; and ambivalence, 5,
17, 66, 95; cultural-affective identity,
31–32; cultural and cognitive psychologies, 240–44, 248; family, 42, 47, 50, 95;
generalized beliefs and, 237, 238; intimacy defined by, 138; labor of, 66–67;
odyssey situations, 114; rational choice
and, 87, 94–95, 113, 240; reconfiguration
of, 63; religious, 110; Smelser's perspective on, 5, 6, 7, 17, 66, 95, 191; social
movements and, 235, 236, 238–39, 242,
245–46; sociology of, 27, 193, 240. *See also*
enchantment; personalization
empirical studies, 10, 20, 259; of causality,
218–19, 224, 225, 227, 230; by Chodorow,

18; of circuits of commerce, 126, 136; of
higher education, 168, 178; of immigration policy, 200; of rationality, 82, 85, 90,
91, 96, 97, 99, 100; Smelser and, 4, 5, 7, 9,
18, 78, 105, 195, 227, 254–55, 265; of
social movements, 236, 241, 246, 247–48;
and theory, 194, 196, 212n2, 227, 254–55,
259–60, 263, 265; of trust, 147, 151.
See also research
empowerment, in religion, 107–8
Enchanting a Disenchanted World (Ritzer),
61–63
enchantment: of consumption, 62; crisis of,
39, 42–43, 48, 50, 57–58, 60, 61–62, 70;
reenchantment, 57, 62–63, 64, 70; of
wife-mother, 39, 42, 48. *See also* emotion
The End of Ideology (Bell), 237
Engels, Friedrich, 6
England. *See* Britain
entrepreneur, notion of (Schumpeter), 93
Epstein, Seymour, 243
equality: immigration policy and, 204–5,
208–10; positive primordial selection
and, 198; in university system, 173.
See also discrimination; rights
equilibrium, market, 84, 85, 87–88, 97–98
Erikson, Erik, 28, 32, 240, 244, 246
Essays in Sociological Explanation (Smelser), 4,
254, 263
Essays in Sociological Theory (Parsons), 4
ethnicity: family ties vs., 210; immigration
policy and, 197, 198, 209–10. *See also*
minorities; racial exclusion
European American college students, and
parents' religion, 110, 113–14
European Community (EC) nationals,
British immigration policy on, 205–6, 209
European Economic Community, 205
evangelism, 110, 114
exchange circuit/exchange spheres, 125
exit option, 64, 65, 95
explanandum (dependent variable), 118
explanans (independent variable), 109
explanation, 4, 254–55; causal, 216–31;
explanatory theory, 258, 259–61, 264; historical logic and, 226–29; rational choice
and, 96. *See also* covering laws; theory

family, 39–53; ambivalence and, 17, 52,
94–95, 113–17; commodifying, 39,
40–53, 99; dependency and, 17, 94–95,

parents: ambivalence and, 94–95; children's
religion and, 110, 113–16, 118; dependency on, 17, 118n5; differentiation and,
43, 46–47; immigration policy and,
204–5; single, 46; state aid to, 46; of
World War II generation, 34–35. *See also*
mothers
Pareto, Vilfredo, 84, 85, 86, 89, 90, 257
Park, Robert, 256
Parsonian thinking, 4, 22
Parsons, Talcott, 145, 195; and AGIL, 2–3,
11n1; collaborations with Smelser by, 3,
6, 78, 82, 145–46, 195; debate with Merton (1947 ASA convention), 259; *Economy and Society* (with Smelser), 3, 78, 82;
Essays in Sociological Theory, 4; and
rationality, 85, 89, 96; Smelser's diver-
gences from, 4, 195, 196; and social
action, 3, 6, 11n1, 85, 96, 107, 236, 263;
and socialization, 22, 46, 92; *The Structure of Social Action,* 263; and theory, 4,
196, 255, 263
pastoral authority, trust in, 160–61
patrials, 192–93, 195–214; defined, 202
Paul, Kathleen, 208
payment modes: for care, 139; corporate circuits and, 127–28
pegged currencies, 130–32, 135
Perrot, Etienne, 132
personality differences, 243–44
personalization: secular individualism, 47.
See also depersonalization; emotion; individuality
phenomenology, 243–44, 262
Pizzorno, Alessandro, 91
plausibility theory, 117
pluralism: Smelser and, 7, 77–78, 194; in
sociological education, 257–58
Polanyi, Karl, 260
political sociology, 104
politics: and beliefs, 191; and collective
action, 99–100, 234–50, 254; and trust,
150, 165. *See also* democratic politics;
social movements
"The Politics of Ambivalence" (Smelser), 24
Portugal, immigration policy of, 198, 199
positive primordial selection, immigration
policy and, 198, 210–11, 213n8
positivism, logical, 218, 219
postmodernism, 25, 263
postmodernity, 58–72

poststructuralism, 25, 262
postulates, 117–18
Powell, Enoch, 200, 202, 204, 206
Powell, Walter, 179
Power in Action (Tarrow), 235
The Power of Feelings (Chodorow), 23, 26
predictability, rational choice and, 93–94
preferences: absolute, 95; stable, 86–87,
88–89
Presbyterian church, 104, 118n8
"The Presence of the Self" (Krieger), 24
primordial beliefs, 192, 212n4; British
"belongers," 202, 203; as context of
choice, 196–97; demise of immigration
policy based on, 209–12; and family, 210;
and immigration policy, 195–214; positive primordial selection, 198, 210–11,
213n8. *See also* religion
Problematics of Sociology (Smelser), 7
process. *See* social process
professional-client relationships, trust in,
156–58, 160
proselytization, 110
Protestant ethic, 57, 61, 64, 68, 70
Protestants: antiauthoritarian/rationalizing
logic of, 196; fundamentalist, 110; individuals switching churches, 109–10; Mexican American converts, 115, 118n6;
Presbyterian church, 104, 118n8;
Reformed tradition, 116
Pryor, Frederick, 125
psychoanalysis: and beliefs, 192, 193, 238;
Chodorow on, 18, 21–35; and collective
behavior, 238, 239; cultural analysis and,
241–48, 249; cultural turn and, 240–41;
and myth of California, 67; Smelser and,
3–4, 6, 17–18, 21–23, 192, 193, 238, 239,
241, 243; tripartite model of, 245. *See also*
Freudianism; individuality; self
"The Psychoanalytic Mode of Inquiry"
(Smelser), 3–4
psychology: academic fragmentation of, 178;
cognitive, 238, 240–44, 248, 250n4; cultural, 240–41; depth, 18, 53n5; ego, 240,
242; and social movements, 235, 240–44,
247–48
public opinion surveys: democratic politics
and, 95; on trust in doctors, 156
public service, Smelser's, 11
purposive action, 84, 85–86. *See also* rational
choice

Text:	10/12 Baskerville
Display:	Baskerville
Compositor:	Binghamton Valley Composition, LLC
Printer and Binder:	Maple-Vail Manufacturing Group